Introduction to Research Methods in Psychology

Visit the *Introduction to Research Methods in Psychology, third edition* Companion Website at **www.pearsoned.co.uk/howitt** to find valuable **student** learning material including:

- Learning objectives for each chapter
- Multiple choice questions to help test your learning
- Internet resources
- Report writing guide

PEARSON
Education

We work with leading authors to develop the strongest
educational materials in psychology, bringing cutting-edge
thinking and best learning practice to a global market.

Under a range of well-known imprints, including Prentice
Hall, we craft high quality print and electronic publications
which help readers to understand and apply their content,
whether studying or at work.

To find out about the complete range of our publishing
please visit us on the World Wide Web at:
www.pearsoned.co.uk

Introduction to Research Methods in Psychology

Dennis Howitt

Duncan Cramer

Harlow, England • London • New York • Boston • San Francisco • Toronto
Sydney • Tokyo • Singapore • Hong Kong • Seoul • Taipei • New Delhi
Cape Town • Madrid • Mexico City • Amsterdam • Munich • Paris • Milan

Pearson Education Limited
Edinburgh Gate
Harlow
Essex CM20 2JE
England

and Associated Companies throughout the world

Visit us on the World Wide Web at:
www.pearsoned.co.uk

First published 2005

ISBN 0 131 39984-5

British Library Cataloguing-in-Publication Data
A catalogue record for this book is available from the British Library

Library of Congress Cataloging-in-Publication Data
A catalog record for this book is available from the Library of Congress

10 9 8 7 6 5 4 3 2 1
08 07 06 05

Typeset in 10/12pt Times by 35
Printed by Ashford Colour Press Ltd., Gosport

The publisher's policy is to use paper manufactured from sustainable forests.

Summary of contents

Companion Website resources
Visit **www.pearsoned.co.uk/howitt** to find valuable online resources

For student
- Learning objectives for each chapter
- Multiple choice questions to help test your learning
- Internet resources
- Report writing guide

Also: The Companion Website provides the following features:

- Search tool to help locate specific items of content
- E-mail results and profile tools to send results of quizzes to instructors
- Online help and support to assist with website usage and troubleshooting

For more information please contact your local Pearson Education sales representative or visit **www.pearsoned.co.uk/howitt**

Contents

Part 2 Quantitative research methods — 115

Preface

Introduction to Research Methods in Psychology is the final part of a trilogy which began with *Introduction to Statistics in Psychology* and *A Guide to Computing Statistics with SPSS for Windows*, now called *Introduction to SPSS12 in Psychology*. To mark the completion of the trilogy, new editions of the companion books have been produced. *Introduction to Statistics in Psychology* is now in its 3rd edition with extra features and coverage. These include new pedagogy and chapters on logistic regression. The text has thorough and extensive coverage, while remaining user friendly even when presenting the most advanced statistics. We are confident that it will continue to provide the best conceptual introduction to statistics in psychology for students at any stage. It is the only statistics text that most of us will need.

Introduction to SPSS12 in Psychology is not simply an updating to a new version of SPSS (Statistical Package for the Social Sciences). It has been revised throughout to present statistical analysis with SPSS in a step-by-step visual fashion, assuming minimal statistical knowledge. It tackles head-on the major problem with SPSS – the mass of irrelevant output. Using screenshots of data entry, data analysis and analysis output screens, the book highlights the key features of data input, analysis and output required to carry out a first rate statistical analysis on one's data. The new format continues the tradition of previous editions of providing detailed advice and examples on how to report one's findings. Each chapter provides an overview of the statistical and methodological basics that the user will need when planning their data analysis.

Turning to this volume, *Introduction to Research Methods in Psychology* is designed to complement the other two books. We do not believe that research methods and data analysis can be covered satisfactorily in a single volume, though you will find examples of successful textbooks based on this formula in almost any bookshop. The reason for this is that modern psychology is extremely varied in the styles of research employed and enjoys a level of statistical sophistication undreamed of even just a few years ago. So it does students a disservice to provide them with the basics, which once would have been sufficient but now are hopelessly inadequate. To our minds, the incredible progress of modern psychology means that teaching resources must struggle to keep up to date and to cope with the variety of different educational experiences provided by universities. At their heart, all volumes in our trilogy are modularly constructed. That is, we do not expect that all of their contents will be covered by lecturers and other instructors. Instead, there is a menu of largely self-contained chapters which can be chosen from.

This is illustrated by the coverage of *Introduction to Research Methods in Psychology*. At the broadest level it covers both quantitative and qualitative research. These are easily but wrongly seen as alternative and incompatible approaches. For some researchers, there may be an intellectual incompatibility between the two, but it is important that students understand the intellectual roots of the two traditions, how research is carried out in these traditions, and what each is capable of. We believe that the student who is so informed will be in a better position to make intelligent appropriate choices about the style of research appropriate for the research questions they wish to address. On its own, the qualitative material in this book would effectively support any qualitative research done by modern students. There is as much detailed practical advice and theory as is available anywhere. But this is on top of quantitative coverage, which easily outstrips any competition in terms of variety, depth and authority. We have tried to provide students with resources to help them in ways largely ignored by most other texts. For example, the chapter on literature searches is extremely comprehensive and practical. Similarly, the chapter on ethics meets the most recent standards and deals with them in depth. The chapter on writing research reports places report writing at the centre of the research process rather than as an add-on at the end. We would argue that a student requires an understanding of the nature of research in psychology to be able to write a satisfactory report.

As far as is possible, we have tried to provide students with practical skills as well as the necessary conceptual overview of research methods in modern psychology. Nevertheless, there is a limit to this. The bottom line is that anyone wishing to understand research needs to read research. Hence, almost from the first page we emphasise that reading is not merely unavoidable but crucial. Without reading, the point of the book is missed. It is not intended as a jumble of technical stuff too boring to be part of any module other than one on research methods. The material in the book is intended to fill out one's understanding of psychology by explaining just how researchers go about creating psychology. At times this can be quite exciting.

This is the fifth book the authors have written together. It is also the one that came close to spoiling a long friendship. What became very clear while writing this book is how emotive the topic of research methods can be. We found out probably for the first time how different two people's thinking can be, even when dealing with seemingly dry topics. As a consequence, rather than smooth over the cracks – make joins when none are possible – you will find that we have incorporated the differences of opinion. This is no different from the disparity of positions to be found within the discipline itself.

The main features of this book are:

- In-depth coverage of both quantitative and qualitative methods.
- A range of pedagogic features including summaries, exercises, boxes and step-by-step instructions where appropriate.
- Analysis strategies provided for the research designs discussed.
- Detailed information about the structure, purpose and contents of research reports.
- The use of databases and other resources.
- Suggestions about how to develop research ideas for projects and similar studies.
- Ethics as an integral feature of the work of all psychologists.

Education is a cooperative effort. So should you find errors then please let us know. These can be difficult to spot but easy to correct. Ideas and comments of any sort would be most welcome.

We wish to thank Morten Fugelvand of Pearson Education for encouraging us to write this book, and Emma Travis for making sure that we did and did so on time (well just about).

Dennis Howitt
Duncan Cramer
August 2004

Publisher's acknowledgements

We are grateful to the following to reproduce copyright material:

Thomson Scientific for Figures 5.1, 5.2, 5.3, 5.4, 5.5, 5.6, 5.7 and 5.8 Data owned and provided by Thomson Scientific, hosted by MIMAS; American Psychological Association for four screenshots, Figures 5.9, 5.10, 5.11 and 5.12, reprinted with permission of the American Psychological Association, publisher of the PsycINFO database, all rights reserved.

In some instances we have been unable to trace the owners of copyright material, and we would appreciate any information that would enable us to do so.

PART 1
The basics of research

1 The role of research in psychology

Overview

■ Research is central to all the activities of psychologists as it is to modern life in general. A key assumption of psychology is that the considered and careful collection of research data is an essential part of the development of the discipline.

■ The vast majority of psychology involves the integration of theoretical notions with the outcomes of research. Psychology characteristically emphasises causal explanations. Many psychologists adhere to the belief that a prime purpose of research is to test causal propositions.

■ A good psychologist – researcher or practitioner – needs to be familiar with the way in which good research is carried out. This enables them to determine the adequacy and value of the findings claimed from a particular study.

■ All psychologists need the resources to be able to read research reports in detail – for example, studies reported in journals of psychological research. This requires an understanding of the purposes, advantages and disadvantages of the different research methods used to investigate issues.

■ Research reports become much clearer and easy to understand once the basics of psychological research methods are known. Very often research reports are concisely written and so assume a degree of knowledge of the topic and research methods. The study of research methods will help prepare students for this.

■ Psychologists have traditionally distinguished between true experiments and non-experiments. True experiments are typical of laboratory studies in psychology whereas non-experiments are more typical of more naturalistic studies in the field (community or other real-life settings).

■ Many psychologists believe that true experiments (laboratory studies) in general provide a more convincing test of causal propositions. Others would dispute this on the grounds that such true experiments often achieve precision at the expense of realism.

■ Conducting one's own research is a fast method to understanding research methods. Increasingly, research is seen as an integral part of the training and work of all psychologists irrespective of whether they are practitioners or academics.

Research is exciting – it is the lifeblood of psychology. Without understanding research methods, one cannot fully appreciate psychology. Modern psychology simply would not exist in the absence of research. To be sure, the subject matter of psychology is fascinating, but this is not enough. Although initially psychology provides many intriguing ideas about the nature of people and society, eventually one begins to appreciate the challenges and complexities of the research processes that helped generate these ideas. Psychological issues are intriguing – for example, why are we attracted to some people and not to others? Why do we dream? What causes depression and what can we do to alleviate it? Can we improve our memory and, if so, how? What makes us aggressive and can we do anything to make us less aggressive? The diversity of psychology means that our individual interests are well catered for. It also means that research methods must be equally diverse if we are to address such a wide range of issues. Psychology comes in many forms and so does good psychological research.

Students often see research methods as a dull, dry and difficult topic. They much prefer their other lecture courses on exciting topics such as interpersonal attraction, mental illness, forensic investigation, brain structure and thought. What they overlook is that these exciting ideas are created by active and committed researchers. For these psychologists, psychology and research methods are intertwined – psychology and the means of developing psychological ideas through research cannot be differentiated. For instance, it is stimulating to learn that we are attracted to people who have the same or similar attitudes to us. It is also of some interest to be given examples of the kinds of research which support this idea. But is this all that there is to it? Are there not many more questions that spring to mind? For example, why should we be attracted to people who have similar attitudes to our own? Do opposites never attract? When does similarity lead to attraction and when does dissimilarity lead to attraction? The answer may have already been found to such questions. If not the need for research is obvious. Research makes us think hard – which is the purpose of any academic discipline.

Box 1.1 contains definitions of various concepts such as variable and correlation to which you may need to refer to if you are unfamiliar with these terms.

BOX 1.1   KEY CONCEPTS DEFINED

Cause   Something which results in an effect, action or condition.
Data   The information from which inferences are drawn and conclusions reached. Much data are collected in numerical form but it is equally viable to use data in the form of text for an analysis.
Randomised experiment   This refers to a type of research in which participants in research are allocated at random (by chance) to an experimental or control condition. The experimental and control conditions involve differences in procedure related to the hypothesis under examination.
Reference   In psychology this refers to the details of the book or article that is the source of the ideas or data being discussed. The reference includes information like the author, the title and the publisher of the book or the journal in which the article appears.
Variable   A variable is any concept that varies and can be measured or assessed in some way. Intelligence, height and social status are simple examples.

1.1 Reading

The best way of understanding psychological research methods is to read in detail about the studies which have been done and build on them. Few psychological textbooks give research in sufficient detail to substitute effectively for this. Developing a better understanding of how research is carried out in a particular area is greatly helped when one reads some of the research work that lecturers and textbook writers refer to. University students only spend a small part of a working week being taught – they are expected to spend much of their time on independent study, which includes reading a great deal as well as independently working on assignments. Glance through any textbook or lecture course reading list and you will see the work of researchers cited. For example, the lecturer or author may cite the work of Byrne (1961) on attraction and similarity of attitude. Normally a list of the 'references' cited is provided. This provides information on the kind of work it is (e.g. what the study is about) and where it has been presented or published. The details are presented in the following way:

Byrne, D. (1961). Interpersonal attraction and attitude similarity. *Journal of Abnormal and Social Psychology*, 62, 713–15.

The format is standard. The last name of the author is given first, followed by the year in which the reference was published. After this comes the title of the work. Like most research in psychology, this work was published in a journal. The title of the journal is given next together with the number of the volume in which the article appeared together with the numbers of the first and last pages of the article. These references are generally listed alphabetically according to the last name of the first author. Where there is more than one reference by the same author or authors, they will be listed according to the year the work was presented. This is known as the Harvard system or author–date system. This is described in much more detail in Chapter 4 which is about writing a research report. We will cite references in this way in this book. However, we will cite very few references compared to psychology texts on other subjects as many of the ideas we are presenting have been previously summarised by other authors (although usually not in the same way) and have been generally accepted for many years.

Many of the references cited in lectures or textbooks are to reports of research that has been carried out to examine a particular question or small set of questions. As already indicated, the prime location for the publication of research is journals. Journals consist of volumes which are usually published every year. Each volume typically comprises a number of issues or parts that come out say every three months but this is variable. The papers or articles that make up an issue are probably no more than 4000 or 5000 words in length. This necessitates them being written concisely. As a consequence, they are not always easy to read and often require careful study. An important aim of this book is to provide you with the basic knowledge which is required to read these papers – and even to write them. Often there appear to be obstacles in the way of doing the necessary reading. For example, there are many different psychology journals – too many for individual libraries to stock all, so they subscribe to a limited number of them. If the reference that you are interested in is important and is not available locally, then you may be able to obtain it from another library or it is worthwhile trying to obtain a copy (usually called offprints) from the author. Chapter 5 on searching the literature suggests how you can access publications which are not held in your own library.

You may have questions about a topic that have not been addressed in lectures or textbooks. For example, you may wonder whether attraction to someone depends on the nature of the attitudes that are shared. Are some attitudes more important than others and, if so, what are these? This is the sort of intellectual curiosity required to become a good researcher. Furthermore, you probably will want to know what the latest thinking and research are on the topic. If you are interested in a topic, then wanting to know what other people are thinking about it is only natural. There is a great deal to be learnt about finding out about what is happening in any academic discipline. Chapter 5 also discusses how we go about searching for the current publications on a topic.

1.2 Evaluating the evidence

Psychology is not simply about learning what conclusions have been reached on a particular topic. It is perhaps more important to find out and carefully evaluate the evidence which has led to these conclusions. Why? Well, what if you have always subscribed to the old adage 'opposites attract'? Would you suddenly change your mind simply because you read in a textbook that people with similar attitudes are attracted to each other? Most likely you would want to know a lot more about the evidence. For example, what if you checked and found that the research in support of this idea was obtained simply by asking a sample of 100 people whether they believed that opposites attract. In other words, all the researchers had really established was that people generally thought it was true that people are attracted to people with similar attitudes. After all, simply because people once believed the world was flat did not make the world flat. It may be interesting to know what people believe, but wouldn't one want different evidence in order to demonstrate that attraction is a consequence of similarity of attitudes? You might also wonder if it is really true that people once believed the world to be flat.

We probably would be more convinced of the importance of similarity in attraction if a researcher actually investigated how attracted to each other couples were and then showed that those with the most similar attitudes tended to be the most attracted to one another. Even then we might still harbour some doubts. For example, just what do we mean by attraction? If we mean wanting to have a drink with the other person at a pub then we might prefer the person with whom we might have a lively discussion – that is, someone who does not share our views. On the other hand, if willingness to share a flat with a person were the measure of attraction would a housemate with similar outlooks to our own be preferred? So we are beginning to see that the way in which we choose to measure a concept (or variable) such as attraction may be vital in terms of the answers we get to our research questions.

It is possibly even more difficult to get a satisfactory measure of attitudes. This is partly because there are many different topics that we can express attitudes about. So, for example, would we expect attraction to be affected in the same way if two people share the view that there is life on Mars compared to if two people share the same religious views? Would it matter that two people had different tastes in music compared to if they had different views about openness in relationships? That is, maybe some attitudes are more important than others in determining attraction. One could study this by asking about their attitudes to a variety of different topics and then how important each of these attitudes is. Alternatively, if we thought that some attitudes were likely to be more important than others, we could focus on those particular attitudes in some depth. So it should be clear that the process of evaluating the research in a particular field is not a narrow, nit-picking exercise. Instead it is a process by which new ideas are generated as well as stimulating research to test these new propositions.

These various propositions about the relationship between attraction and similarity are all examples of *hypotheses*. A hypothesis is merely a supposition or proposition which serves as the basis of further investigation – either through the collection of research data or through reasoning. The origin of the word hypothesis comes from the Greek word for foundation – perhaps confirming that hypotheses are the foundation on which psychology develops. Precision is an important characteristic of good hypotheses. So, our hypothesis that similarity of attitudes is related to attraction might benefit from refinement. It looks as if we might have to say something more about the attitudes that people have (and what we mean by attraction for that matter). If we think that the attitudes have to be important, then the hypothesis should be reformulated to read that people are more attracted to those with similar attitudes on personally important topics. If we thought attraction was based on having a similar attitude towards spending money, we should restate the hypothesis to say that people are more attracted to those with similar attitudes towards spending money.

The evaluation of research evidence involves examining the general assertion that the researcher is making about an issue and the information or data that are relevant to this assertion. We need to check whether the evidence or data support the assertion or whether the assertion goes beyond what could be confidently concluded. Sometimes, in extreme cases, researchers draw conclusions which seem not to be related to their data. Any statement that goes beyond the data is speculation or conjecture and needs to be recognised as such. There is nothing wrong with speculation as such since hypotheses, for example, are themselves speculative in nature. Speculation is necessary in order to go beyond what we already know. However, it needs to be distinguished from what can legitimately be inferred from the data.

1.3 Inferring causality

The concept of causality has been important throughout the history of psychology. Other disciplines might consider it almost an obsession of psychology. The meaning of the term is embodied in the phrase 'cause and effect'. The idea is that things that happen in the world may have an effect on other things. So if we speak of a causal relationship between attitude similarity and attraction we mean that attitude similarity is the cause of attraction to another person. Not all data allow one to infer causality with confidence. Sometimes researchers suggest that their research demonstrates a causal relationship when others would claim that it demonstrates no such thing. In strictly logical terms, some claims of a causal relationship can be regarded as an error since they are based on research methods which by their nature are incapable of establishing causality with certainty. Frequently the research findings are consistent with a causal relationship but are equally consistent with other explanations.

A great deal of psychology has as its focus causes of things even though the word 'cause' is not used. Questions such as why we are attracted to one person rather than another, why people become depressed and why some people commit violent crimes are typical examples of this. The sorts of explanations that are given might be, for example,

BOX 1.2 CAUSAL EXPLANATIONS – PSYCHOLOGY'S WEAKEST LINK?

It is well worth taking the time to study the history of psychology. This will help you to identify the characteristics of the discipline (e.g. Hergenhahn, 2001; Leahy, 2004). What is very obvious is that psychology has been much more concerned about causality than many of its closely related disciplines – sociology is a good example. There are a number of reasons why this should be the case:

- Psychology was much more influenced by the philosophy of logical positivism than these other disciplines. Logical positivism was a development of the basic philosophy of the natural sciences such as physics and chemistry. It basically holds that knowledge is obtained through observation. So the more focused and precise the empirical observation the better. Hence, a precisely defined cause and an equally precisely defined effect would be regarded as appropriate. Logical positivism is discussed in some detail in Chapter 15.

- Psychology has traditionally defined itself as much as a biological science as a social science. Consequently, methods employed in the natural sciences have found a substantial place in psychology. In the natural sciences, laboratory studies in which small numbers of variables are studied at a time are common, as they have been in psychology.

- By emulating the natural sciences approach, psychologists have tended to seek general principles of human behaviour just as natural scientists believe that their laws apply throughout the physical universe. Translated into psychological terms, the implication is that findings from the laboratory are applicable to situations outside of the psychological laboratory. Randomised laboratory experiments tend to provide the most convincing evidence of causality – that is what they are designed to do.

Modern psychology is much more varied in scope than this and the issue of causality is not as crucial as in the past. There is a great deal of research that makes a positive contribution to psychology which eschews issues of causality. For example, the forensic psychologist who wishes to predict suicide risk in prisoners does not have to know the causes of suicide amongst prisoners. So if research shows that being in prison for the first time is the strongest predictor of suicide then this is a possible predictor. It is irrelevant whether the predictor is in itself the direct cause of suicide.

Many modern psychologists regard the search for causal relationships as somewhat counterproductive. It may be a good ideal in theory, but in practice it may have a negative influence on the progress of psychology. One reason for this is that the procedures which can help establish causality actually result in highly artificial and contrived situations, with the researcher focusing on fine detail rather than obtaining a broad view, and the findings of such research are often not all that useful in practice.

some people commit violent crimes because they were physically abused as children. In other words, physical abuse as a child is a *cause* of adult violent crime. There may be a relationship between physical abuse and violent crime, but does this establish that physical abuse is a cause? To return to our main example, suppose a study found that people who were attracted to each other had similar attitudes. Pairs of friends were compared with pairs of strangers in terms of how similar their attitudes were. It emerged that the friends had more similar attitudes than pairs of strangers. Could we conclude from this finding that this study showed that similar attitudes cause people to be attracted towards one another? If we can conclude this, on what grounds can we do so? If not, then why not?

There are at least three main reasons why we cannot conclude definitively from this study that similar attitudes lead to people liking each other:

■ Attraction, measured in terms of friendship, and similarity of attitudes are assessed once and at the same moment in time. As a consequence we do not know which of these two came first. Did similarity of attitudes precede friendship as it would have to if similar attitudes led to people liking each other? Without knowing the temporal (time) sequence, definitive statements about cause and effect are not possible.

■ Friendship may have preceded similarity of attitudes. In other words, friends develop similar attitudes because they happen to like one another for other reasons. Once again the basic problem is that of the temporal sequence. Because this study measures both friendship and similarity of attitudes at the same time we cannot tell which came first. In other words we cannot determine which caused which.

■ The development of attraction and similarity may be the result of the influence of a third factor. For example, if one moves to university one begins to be attracted to new people and, because of the general influence of the general campus environment, attitudes begin to change. In these circumstances, the relationship between attraction and similarity is not causal (in either direction) but the result of a third factor which is the effect of the move to campus.

Care needs to be taken here. It is not being suggested that the research in question is worthless simply because it cannot definitively establish that there is a causal relationship. The findings of the research are clearly compatible with a causal hypothesis and one might be inclined to accept the possibility of a causal relationship. Nevertheless, one cannot be certain and may find it difficult to argue against someone who rejects the idea.

Some of the most characteristic research methods of psychology are geared towards addressing the issue of causality. Some of these will be outlined in due course. Most importantly, the contrast between randomised experiments so familiar to psychologists in the form of laboratory experiments and research outside the laboratory has this issue at its root.

The role of causality in psychology is a controversial topic. See Box 1.2 for a discussion of this.

1.4 Types of research and the assessment of causality

In this section we will describe a number of different types of study in order to achieve a broad overview of research methods in psychology. There is no intention to prioritise them in terms of importance or sophistication. They are:

■ correlational or cross-sectional studies
■ longitudinal studies
■ experiments – or studies with randomised assignment

As this section deals largely with causality, all of the types of research discussed below involve a minimum of two variables examined in relation to each other. Types of study which primarily aim to describe are dealt with elsewhere. Surveys, for example, are discussed in Chapter 11, and qualitative methods are covered in depth in Chapters 15 to 21.

Correlational or cross-sectional studies

Correlational (or cross-sectional) studies are a very common type of research. Basically what happens is that a number of different variables are measured more or less simultan-eously for a sample of individuals. Generally in psychology, the strategy is to examine the extent to which these variables measured at a single point in time are associated (that is correlated) with one another. Correlation is a statistical index or test which describes the degree and direction of the relationship between two characteristics or variables. To say that there is a correlation between two characteristics merely means that there is a relationship between them.

The correlation coefficient is not the only way of testing for a relationship. There are many other statistical techniques which can be used to describe and assess the relationship between two variables. For example, we could correlate the extent to which people are friends or strangers with how similar are their attitudes using the correlation coefficient. An equivalent way of doing this is to examine differences. This is what is normally done in this kind of study. One would look at whether there is a difference in the extent to which friends are similar in their attitudes compared to how similar random pairs of strangers are. If there is a difference between the two degrees of similarity, it means that there is a relationship between the variable friends/strangers and the variable similarity of attitudes. However a test of differences (e.g. the *t*-test) is applied rather than a correlation coefficient. A more accurate term for describing these studies is cross-sectional in that they measure variables at one point in time or across a slice or section of time. This alternative term leaves open how we analyse the data statistically. This general topic is discussed in depth in Chapter 3.

Correlational or cross-sectional studies are often carried out in psychology's sub-disciplines of social, personality, developmental, educational, and abnormal or clinical psychology. In these areas such designs have the advantage of enabling the researcher to measure a number of different variables at the same time. Any of these variables might possibly explain why something occurs. It is likely that anything that we are interested in explaining will have a number of different causes rather than a single cause. By measur-ing a number of different variables at the same time, it becomes possible to see which of the variables are most strongly related to what we are seeking to explain.

Confounding variables

A major reason why we cannot infer causality is the problem of the possible influence of unconsidered variables. Sometimes this is referred to as the third variable problem. For example, it could be that both friendship and similarity of attitudes are determined by the area, or kind of area, in which you live (such as a campus as mentioned earlier). You are more likely to make friends with people you meet – who are more likely to live in the same area as you. People living in the same area also may be more likely to have the same or similar attitudes. For example, they may be more likely to share the same religious attitudes or eat the same food. When you ask people to take part in a study they are likely to come from different areas. It could be that it is the area, or kind of area, that people come from that determines both who the friends are and their attitudes. Variables which either wholly or partially account for the relationship between two other variables are known as *confounding* variables. Area, or type of area, could be a confounding variable which we may need to check.

One could try to hold constant in several ways the area from which people come. For example, one could select people from the same area. If you did this, then there may still be other factors which account for the fact that people are attracted to others who have similar attitudes to them. It is not always obvious or easy to think what these other factors might be. Because we have to study a number of friendships, it is likely that the people making up these friendships will differ in various ways. It would be very difficult to hold all of these different factors constant. One such factor might be age. Pairs of friends are likely to differ in age. Some pairs of friends will be older than other pairs of friends. It could be that any association or relationship between being friends and having similar attitudes is due to age. People are more likely to be friends with people who are similar in age to them. People of a similar age may have similar attitudes, such as the kind of music they like or the kinds of clothes they wear. So age may determine both who becomes friends with whom and what their attitudes are. The easiest way to control for confounding variables is to try to measure them and to control for them statistically. There is another way which we will mention shortly.

Longitudinal studies

Suppose we measured both friendship and similarity of attitudes at two (or more) different points of time, could we then determine if friendship led to having similar attitudes? This kind of study is known as a longitudinal study as opposed to a cross-sectional one. It is more difficult to organise this kind of study, but it could and has been done. We would have to take a group of people who did not know each other initially but who would have sufficient opportunity subsequently to get to know each other. Some of these people would probably strike up friendships. One possible group of participants would be first-year psychology students who were meeting together for the first time at the start of their degree. It would probably be best if any participants who knew each other before going to university or came from the same area were dropped from the analysis. We would also need to measure their attitudes towards various issues. Then after a suitable period of time had elapsed, say three or more months, we would find out what friendships had developed and what their attitudes were.

Suppose it were found that students who subsequently became friends started off as having the same or similar attitudes and also had the same or similar attitudes subsequently, could we then conclude that similar attitudes lead to friendship? Well it is certainly stronger evidence that similarity of attitudes may result in friendship than we obtained from the cross-sectional study. Nevertheless, as it stands, it is still possible that there may be other confounding variables which explain both the friendships and the similarity in attitudes despite the longitudinal nature of our new study. It might be that this association between friendship and attitude similarity can be explained in terms of confounding variables. For example, people who come from similar kinds of areas may be the most likely to become friends as they find out they are familiar with the same customs or have shared similar experiences. They may also have similar attitudes because they come from similar areas. Thus similarity of area rather than similarity of attitudes could lead to friendships.

As with cross-sectional studies, there are statistical methods of controlling these confounding variables in longitudinal studies. Longitudinal studies provide more information than cross-sectional ones. In our example, they will tell us how stable attitudes are. If attitudes are found not to be very stable and if similarity of attitudes determined friendships, then we would not expect friendships to be very stable. Because these studies are more complex, the analyses of their results will be more complicated and will take more effort to understand. As with cross-sectional studies, the major problem is that we fail to take into account all of the confounding factors that may have brought about the results. If we could guarantee to deal with all the confounding variables in this sort of research, it could claim to be an ideal type of research method. Unfortunately, there can be no such guarantee.

Studies with randomised assignment – experiments

We have now identified a basic problem. Researchers simply do not and cannot know just what variables affect their key measures. Is there any way in which all confounding variables can be taken into account when we do not know what those variables are? For some psychologists, the answer to the major problems of research design lies in the process of randomisation. Basically we would form two groups of participants who are given the opportunity to interact in pairs and get to know each other better. In one condition, the pairs are formed by choosing one member of the pair at random and then the other member selected at random from the participants who had similar attitudes to the first member of the pair. In the other condition, participants are selected at random but paired with another person dissimilar in attitude to them, again selected at random. By allocating participants to similarity and dissimilarity conditions by chance, any differences between the conditions cannot be accounted for by these confounding variables. By randomising in this way, similarities and dissimilarities in the areas from which the participants come, for example, would be expected to be equalised between groups.

The simplest way of randomisation in this example is to allocate participants to the different conditions by tossing a coin. We would have to specify before we tossed the coin whether a coin landing heads facing upwards would mean that the person saw a person with the same attitude as them or with a different attitude from them. If we tossed a coin a fixed number of times, say 20 times, then it should come up heads 10 times and tails 10 times on average. If we had decided that a head means meeting someone with the same attitude, 10 people will have been chosen to meet someone with the same attitude as them and 10 with a different attitude from them. This kind of procedure is known as random assignment. People are randomly assigned to different situations which are usually called conditions, groups or treatments. (Actually we have not solved all of the difficulties as we will see later.)

If half the people in our study came from, say, Bristol and half from Birmingham, then about half of the people who were randomly assigned to meeting a person with the same attitude as them would be from Bristol and the remaining half would be from Birmingham. The same would be true of the people who were randomly assigned to meeting a person with a different attitude from them. About half would be from Bristol and the remaining half would be from Birmingham. In other words, random assignment should control for the area that people come from by ensuring that there are roughly equal numbers of people from those areas in the two groups. This will hold true for any factor such as the age of the person or their gender. In other words, random assignment ensures that all confounding factors are held constant – without the researcher needing to know what those confounding factors are.

Sampling error

The randomised study is not foolproof. Sampling error will always be a problem. Toss a coin any number of times, it will not always come up heads half the time and tails half the time. It will vary from one extreme of no heads to the other extreme of all heads with the most common number of heads being half or close to half. In other words, the number of heads will differ from the number expected by chance. This is known as sampling error and is a feature of any study. A sample is the number of people (or units) that are being studied. The smaller the sample is, the greater the sampling error will be. A sample of 10 people will have a greater sampling error than one of 20 people. Although you may find doing this a little tedious, you could check this for yourself in the following way. Toss a coin 10 times and count the number of heads. Do this, say, 20 times. Note the number of times heads comes up. Now do this again but toss the coin 20 times on each occasion rather than 10 times. You will find that the number of heads is closer to half when tossing the coin 20 times on each occasion rather than 10 times. Many studies will have as few as 20 people in each group or condition because it is thought that the sampling error for such numbers is acceptable. See our companion statistics text, *Introduction to Statistics in Psychology* (Howitt and Cramer, 2005*a*) for a more detailed discussion of sampling error.

The intervention or manipulation

So, in many ways, if the purpose of one's research is to establish whether two variables are causally related, it is attractive to consider controlling for confounding variables through random assignment of participants to conditions. To determine whether similar attitudes lead to friendship, we could randomly assign people to meet strangers with either similar or dissimilar attitudes to themselves as we have already described. But remember that we have also raised the possibility that that people's attitudes are related to other factors such as the area or kind of area they come from. Assuming that this is the case, participants meeting strangers with the same attitudes as themselves might actually be meeting people who come from the same area or kind of area as themselves. On the other hand, participants meeting strangers with different attitudes from them may well be meeting people who come from a different area or kind of area to themselves. In other words, we still cannot separate out the effects of having the attitude similarity from the possible confounding effects of area similarity. It is clear that we need to disentangle these two different but interrelated factors. It is not possible to do this using real strangers because we cannot separate the stranger from the place they come from.

Let's consider possible approaches to this difficulty. We need to ensure that the stranger expresses similar attitudes to the participant in the same attitudes condition. That is, if they did not share attitudes with a particular participant, they would nevertheless pretend that they did. In the different attitudes condition, then we could ensure that the stranger always expresses different attitudes from those of the participant. That is, the stranger pretends to have different attitudes from the participant if they so happen to have similar attitudes in

Table 1.1 Manipulating similarity of attitude

Condition	Participant	Stranger
Same attitude	same as stranger	no acting
	different from stranger	act as if the same
Different attitude	same as stranger	act as if different
	different from stranger	no acting

reality. See Table 1.1 for an overview of all of this. In effect, the stranger has become the accomplice, confederate, stooge or co-worker of the researcher.

The number of times the stranger does not have to act as if they have a different attitude from the one they have is likely to be the same or similar in the two conditions – that is, if participants have been randomly allocated to them. This will also be true for the number of times the stranger has to act as if their attitude is different from the one they have.

Unfortunately, all that has been achieved by this is an increase in complexity of the research design for no other gain. We simply have not solved the basic problem of separating similarity of attitude from area. This is because in the same attitude condition some of the strangers who share the same attitude as the participant may well be attractive to the participant actually because they come from the same area as the participant. Similarly, some of the participants in the different attitudes condition will not be attracted to the stranger because the stranger comes from a different area. Quite how this will affect the outcome of the research cannot be known. However, the fact that we don't know means that we cannot assess the causal influence of attitude similarity on attraction with certainty.

We need to try to remove any potential influence of place entirely or include it as a variable in the study. Probably the only way to remove the influence of place entirely is by not using real people as the stranger. One could present information about a stranger's attitude and ask the participant how likely they are to like someone like that. This kind of situation might appear rather contrived or artificial. We could try to make it less so by saying that we are interested in finding out how people make judgements or form impressions about other people. Obviously the participants would not be told the proposition that we are testing in case this affects their behaviour. For example, they may simply act in accordance with their beliefs about whether or not people are attracted to others with similar attitudes. Not telling them, however, does not mean that the participants do not guess what the idea behind the study is.

What we are interested in testing may not be apparent to the participants because they would only be required to take part in one of the two conditions. Consequently they would not realise what was happening in the other condition (unless they talked to other people who had already participated in the study). We could disguise the purpose of our study by providing further fictitious information about the stranger such as what they had done and what they wanted to do. This information would be the same for the stranger in both conditions. The only way in which the information would differ is in terms of the attitudes of the stranger. In one condition attitudes would be the same as those of the participant while in the other condition they would be different.

If (a) the only difference between the two conditions is whether the stranger's attitudes are similar or dissimilar to those of the participant and (b) we find that participants are more attracted to strangers with similar than dissimilar attitudes then this difference in attraction must be due to the only difference between the two conditions; i.e. the difference in attitudes. Even then there are problems in terms of how to interpret the evidence. One possibility is that the difference in attraction is not directly due to differences in attitudes but is due to factors which participants believe are associated with differences in attitudes. For example, participants may believe that people with the same attitudes as them may be more likely to come from the same kind of area or be of the same age. Thus these beliefs would be responsible for the difference in attraction. In other words when we manipulate a variable in a study we may in fact inadvertently manipulate other variables without realising it. We could try to hold these other factors constant by making sure that the stranger was similar to the participant in these respects, or we could test for the effects of these other factors by manipulating them as well as similarity of attitude.

This kind of study where:

■ the presumed cause of an effect is manipulated
■ participants are randomly assigned to conditions
■ all other factors are held constant

has been called a *true experiment* by Campbell and Stanley (1963). If any of the above three requirements do not hold then the study may be described as a *non-experiment* or *quasi-experiment*. In the latest revision of their book, the term 'true' has been replaced by 'randomised' (Shadish *et al.*, 2002, p. 12). These terms will be used in this book. True or randomised experiments are more common in the sub-disciplines of perception, learning, memory and biological psychology where it is easier to manipulate the variables of interest. The main attraction of true experiments is that they provide logically more convincing evidence of the causal impact of one variable on another. There are disadvantages which may be very apparent in some fields of psychology. For example, the manipulation of variables may result in very contrived and implausible situations. Furthermore, exactly what the nature of the manipulation of variables has achieved may not be clear. Studies are often conducted to try to rule out or to put forward plausible alternative interpretations or explanations of a particular finding. This is beneficial to the development of knowledge in a field of research. We will have more confidence in a finding if it has been confirmed or replicated a number of times, by different people and using different methods.

It should be clear that the legitimacy of assertions about causal effects depend on the design that has been used to study them. If we read that a causal effect has been established, we need to be certain that the study or studies which showed this effect were true experiments rather than quasi-experiments. Furthermore, how effectively the causal variable was manipulated needs to be considered. Is it possible that other variables were inadvertently varied at the same time? The nature of the design and of any manipulations that have been carried out are described in journal papers in the section entitled 'Method'.

These and other designs are discussed in more detail in subsequent chapters. There is no single dominant method in most areas of research. However, certain methods are more characteristic of particular fields of psychology. For example, consider the following survey of the types of study published in the prestigious journal called the *Journal of Personality and Social Psychology*. A survey of a random sample of studies published in this journal in 1996 (Sherman *et al.*, 1999) revealed that:

■ 55% of them employed what could be described as a true or randomised experimental design.
■ 23% employed a cross-sectional design.
■ 14% employed a longitudinal design.
■ 8% used other designs.

Studies investigating the content of psychology journals are not frequent and this is one of the more recent ones. Knowing about the strengths and weaknesses of research designs should help you to be in a better position to critically evaluate their findings. There is more on design considerations in later chapters.

1.5 Practice

Psychologists believe in the importance of the empirical testing of research ideas. Consequently, doing research is a requirement of most degrees in psychology. For example, to be recognised by the British Psychological Society as a practising psychologist you need to show that you have a basic understanding of research methodology and the skills to carry it out. This is the case even if you do not intend to carry out research in your profession. Training in research is an important part of the training of most practitioners such as educational and clinical psychologists. Practising psychologists simply cannot rely on academic psychologists to research all of the topics from which psychological practice might benefit. The concept of practitioner–researcher has developed in recent years. This is the idea that practitioners such as occupational psychologists and forensic psychologists have a responsibility to carry out research to advance practice in their field of work. To be brutally frank, a student who is not prepared to develop their research skills is doing themselves and the discipline of psychology no favours at all.

1.6 Conclusion

Most psychological ideas develop in relation to empirical data. Propositions are made, tested and emerge through the process of collecting and analysing data. The crucial activity of psychologists is the dissemination of ideas and findings which emerge largely through empirical work in the many fields of psychology. The prime location to find such developments and ideas is in the academic and practitioner journals which describe the outcomes of psychological research. Other important contexts for this are academic and practitioner conferences geared to the presentation of ongoing research developments in psychology and, to a lesser degree, academic books. These various forms of publication and presentation serve a dual purpose:

■ To keep psychologists abreast with the latest thinking and developments in their fields of activity.
■ To provide psychologists with detailed accounts of developing research ideas and theory so that they may question and evaluate their value.

Although the issue of causality has had less of a role in psychological research in recent years, it remains a defining concern of psychology – and is less typical of some related field. The basic question involved in causality is the question of whether a particular variable or set of variables causes or brings about a particular effect. Many would argue, though this is controversial, that the best and most appropriate way of testing causal propositions is by conducting 'true' experiment in which participants have been randomly assigned to conditions which reflect the manipulation of possible causal variables. The archetypal true experiment is the conventional laboratory experiment. Even then, there is considerable room for doubt as to what variable has been manipulated in a true experiment. It is important to check out the possibility that the experimental manipulation has not created effects quite different from the ones that were intended. Alternative interpretations of the findings should always be a concern of psychologists. However, the biggest problem is that there are many variables which simply cannot be manipulated by the researcher – for example, it is not possible to manipulate variables such as schizophrenia, gender, social economic status or intelligence for the convenience of testing ideas using true experiments. However, the variety and stimulation of using the more naturalistic or realistic research methods which are often the only rational choice in field settings is a challenge which many psychologists find rewarding.

Often these are described as non-experimental designs which, from some points of view, might be regarded as a somewhat pejorative term. It is a bit like describing women as non-men. It implies that the randomised experiment is the right and proper way of doing psychology. The truth is that there is no right and proper way of intellectual progress. The development of psychology is *not* dependent on any single study but the collective activity of a great many researchers and practitioners. Until there is widespread acceptance and adoption of an idea, it is not possible to judge its value.

Key points

- As a research-based discipline, psychology requires a high degree of sophistication about research and research methods, even as part of the training of psychologists. A vital link in this process is the research article or paper published in academic journals. All psychologists should be able to critically, but constructively, evaluate and benefit from reading such publications.

- Research articles take time to read as they will refer to other research as well as principles of research methodology with which one at first may not be familiar. As one becomes more familiar with the research in an area and with the principles of doing research, the importance of the contents of research papers becomes much quicker and easier to appreciate.

- One major feature of a research study is the design that it uses. There are various designs. A very basic distinction is between what has been called a true or randomised experiment and everything else which can be referred to as a non-experiment.

- True experiments involve the deliberate manipulation of what is presumed to be the causal variable, the random assignment of participants to the conditions reflecting that manipulation and the attempt to hold all other factors constant. Whether or not true experiments should hold a hallowed place in psychology is a matter of controversy. Many researchers and practitioners never have recourse to their use or even to the use of their findings.

- Even if their value is accepted, the use of true experiments is not straightforward. The manipulation of the presumed causal variable and holding all other factors constant is often very difficult. Consequently, a study is never definitive in itself since it requires further research to rule out alternative interpretations of the manipulation by allowing for particular factors which were not held constant in the original study.

■ Psychologists generally favour the true experiment because it appears to be the most appropriate way for determining causal effects. If you have only manipulated one variable, held all else constant and found an effect, then that effect is likely to be due to the manipulation. But at the same time, this is also a potential fatal flaw of true experiments. In real-life, variables do not operate independently and one at a time so why should research assume that they do?

■ Furthermore, it is not always possible to manipulate the variable presumed to be a cause or to manipulate it in a way which is not contrived. Anyway, not all psychologists are interested in testing causal propositions. Hence the trend for psychologists to increasingly use a wide variety of non-experimental research designs.

■ Because of the centrality of research to all aspects of psychology, psychology students are generally required and taught to carry out and write up research. This experience should help them understand what research involves. It also gives them an opportunity to make a contribution to a topic that interests them.

Activities

1. Choose a recent study that has been referred to either in a textbook you are reading or in a lecture that you have attended. Obtain the original publication. Were the study and its findings correctly reported in the textbook? Do you think that there were important aspects of the study that were not mentioned in the text or the lecture that should have been? If you do think there were important omissions, what are these? Why do you think they were not cited? Did the study test a causal proposition? If so, what was this proposition? If not, what was the main aim of this study? In terms of the designs outlined in this chapter what kind of design did the study use?

2. Either choose a chapter from a textbook or go to the library and obtain a copy of a single issue of a journal. Work through the material and for every study you find, classify it as one of the following.

   ■ correlational or cross-sectional study
   ■ longitudinal study
   ■ experiment – or study with randomised assignment

   What percentage of each did you find?

2 Aims and hypotheses in research

Overview

■ Different research methods are effective at doing different things. There are methods which are particularly good at describing a phenomenon in some detail, estimating how common a particular behaviour is, evaluating the effects of some intervention, testing a causal proposition or statistically summarising the results of a number of similar studies.

■ The aims and justification of the study are presented in the first section or introduction of the report or paper. All research should have clear objectives and need clear justification for the expenditure of time and effort as well as the procedures carried out in the research.

■ Hypotheses are a key component of research studies. In psychology, the hypotheses are usually formally stated in a clear and accurate form. They also need to be justified. It should be made apparent why it is important to test the hypotheses and what the basis or rationale is for them.

■ Alternatively, the general aims and objectives of the research can be summarised if the research in question is not particularly conducive to presentation as hypotheses about relationships between small numbers of variables.

■ Hypotheses are the basic building blocks of psychology. Some research attempts to test hypotheses, other research attempts to explore hypotheses, and yet other research seeks to generate hypotheses.

■ In their simplest form, hypotheses propose that a relationship exists between a minimum of two variables.

■ There is an important distinction between research hypotheses (which guide research) and statistical hypotheses (which guide statistical analyses). Research hypotheses are evaluated by a whole range of different means, including statistics. Statistical hypothesis testing employs a very restricted concept of hypothesis.

■ Of course, frequently the researcher has an idea of what the relationship is between two variables. That is, the variables are expected or predicted to be related in a particular way or direction. So wherever possible, the nature (or direction) of the relationship should be clearly stated together with the reasons for this expectation.

- The variable that is manipulated or thought to be the cause of an effect on another variable is known as the independent variable. The variable that is measured or thought to be the effect of the influence of another variable is known as the dependent variable.

- The terms 'independent' and 'dependent' are sometimes restricted to true experiments where the direction of the causal effect being investigated is clearer. However, they are frequently used in a variety of contexts and are terms which can cause confusion.

By now, it should be clear that research is an immensely varied activity with many different objectives and purposes. In psychology, these range as widely, perhaps more so, as in any other discipline. In this chapter we will look in some detail at the keystones of research in psychology – the aims and hypotheses underlying a study. Research is a thoughtful, rational process. It does not proceed simply by measuring variables and finding out what the relationship is between them. Instead, research is built on a sense of purpose on the part of the researcher who sees their work as fitting in with, and building on, established psychological knowledge in their chosen field. This sense of direction in research is not simply something that happens, it has to be worked at and worked towards. The idea of research is not simply to create new information or facts but to build on, expand, clarify and illuminate what is already known. To collect data without a sense of direction or purpose might be referred to, cruelly, as mindless or rampant empiricism. Simply collecting data does not constitute research.

The sense of purpose in research has to be learnt. Most of us develop it slowly as part of learning to appreciate the nature of psychology itself. That is, until one has begun to appreciate that psychology is more than just a few facts to learn then good research ideas are unlikely. There are a number of aspects to this:

- It is vital to understand how real psychologists (not just textbook authors) go about psychology. The only way to achieve this is to read and study in depth the writings of psychologists – especially those interested in the sorts of things that you are interested in.

- The way in which real psychologists think about their discipline, their work, and the work of their intellectual colleagues has to be studied. Throughout the writings of psychologists, one will find a positive but sceptical attitude to theory and research. There is a sense in which good psychologists regard all knowledge as tentative and even temporary – the feeling that, collectively, psychologists could always do better.

2.1 Types of studies

One useful way of beginning to understand the possible aims of psychological research is to examine some broad research objectives in psychology and decide what each of them contributes. We will look at the following in turn:

- descriptive or exploratory studies
- evaluation or outcome studies
- meta-analytic studies.

Descriptive or exploratory studies

An obvious first approach to research in any field is simply to describe in detail the characteristics and features of the thing in question. Without such descriptive material, it is difficult for research to progress effectively. For example, it is difficult to imagine research into, say, the causes of schizophrenia without a substantial body of knowledge which describes the major features and types of schizophrenia. Descriptions require that we categorise in some way the observations we make. Curiously, perhaps perversely, psychology is not replete with famous examples of purely descriptive studies. In Part 4 of this book we discuss in detail qualitative research methods. Typical of this type of research is the use of textual material which is rich in detail – this may include descriptive textual material.

Case studies are reports that describe a particular case in detail. They are common in psychiatry though, once again, relatively uncommon in modern psychology. An early and often cited instance of a case study is that of 'Albert' in which an attempt was made to demonstrate that an 11-month-old boy could be taught or conditioned to become frightened of a rat when he previously wasn't (Watson and Rayner, 1920). Whether or not this is a purely descriptive study could probably be argued either way. Certainly the study goes beyond a mere description of the situation – for example, it could also be conceived as investigating the factors that can create fear.

In some disciplines (such as sociology and media studies), one sort of descriptive study, known as *content analysis*, is common. The main objective of this is to describe the contents of the media. So, it is common to find content analyses which report the features of television's output. For example, the types of violence contained in television programmes could be recorded, classified and counted. That is to say, the main interest of these studies lies in determining how common certain features are. Actually we have already seen a good example of content analysis. One aim of the study by Sherman and his colleagues (1999) mentioned in Chapter 1 was to find out whether or not there had been any changes in the characteristics of studies published between 1968 and 1996 in the *Journal of Personality and Social Psychology*. The type of research design employed was one of the categories used by the researchers to classify the contents of the journal.

Evaluation or outcome studies

Other research has as its aim to test the effectiveness of a particular feature or intervention. Generally speaking, such studies simply concentrate on the consequences of certain activities without attempting to test theoretical propositions or ideas – that is to say, they tend to have purely empirical objectives. They often do not seek to develop theory. Good examples of an intervention into a situation are studies of the effectiveness of psychotherapeutic treatments. Ideally in such studies participants are randomly assigned to the different treatments or conditions and, usually, one or more non-treated or control conditions. These studies are sometimes referred to as evaluation or outcome studies. When used to evaluate the effectiveness of a clinical treatment such as psychotherapy, evaluation studies are known as randomised controlled trials. Usually the purpose of the evaluation study is to assess whether the intervention taken as a whole is effective. Rarely is it possible to assess which aspects of the intervention are producing the observed changes. Nevertheless, one knows that the intervention as a whole has (or has not) achieved its desired ends. Since interventions usually take place over an extended period of time, it is much more difficult to hold other factors constant than it would in many laboratory studies that last just a few minutes.

So evaluation studies frequently seek to examine whether an intervention has had its intended effect. That is, did the intervention cause the expected change. However, explanations about why the intervention was successful are secondary or disregarded as the primary objective is not theory development.

Meta-analytic studies

A meta-analysis has the aim of statistically summarising and analysing the results of the range of studies which have investigated a particular topic. Of course, any review of studies tries to integrate the findings of the studies. Meta-analysis does this in a systematic and structured way using statistical techniques. Because it provides statistical methods for combining and differentiating between the findings of a number of data analyses, it forms a powerful integrative tool. For example, we may be interested in finding out whether cognitive behaviour therapy is more effective in treating phobias or intense fears than no treatment. If we obtain reports of studies which have investigated this question, they will contain information about the statistical trends in the findings of each of these studies. These trends may be used to calculate what is known as an *effect size*. This is merely the size of the trend in the data adjusted for the variability in the data.

There are several different measures of effect size. For example, in Chapter 32 of the companion volume *Introduction to Statistics in Psychology* (Howitt and Cramer, 2005*a*), we describe the procedures using the correlation coefficient as a measure of effect size. As the correlation coefficient is a common statistical measure, it is familiar to most researchers. There are other measures of effect size. For example, we can calculate the difference between the two conditions of the study and then standardise this by dividing by a measure of the variability in the individual scores. Variability can either be the standard deviation of one of the conditions (Glass's Δ) or the combined standard deviation of both conditions of the study (Cohen's *d*) (see Rosenthal, 1991). We can calculate the average effect size from any of these measures. Because this difference or effect size is based on a number of studies, it is more likely to give us a more complete assessment of the effects found.

We can also see whether the effect size differs for the ways in which the studies themselves might differ. For example, some of the studies may have been carried out on student volunteers for a study of the treatment of phobia. Because these participants have not sought professional treatment for their phobias these studies are sometimes referred to as analogue studies. Other studies may have been conducted on patients who sought professional help for their phobias. These studies are sometimes called clinical studies. We may be interested in seeing whether the effect size differs for these two types of study. It may be easier to treat phobias in students because they may be less severe. If there are differences in the effect size for the two kinds of study, we should be more cautious in generalising from analogue studies to clinical ones. Actually, any feature of the studies reviewed in the meta-analysis may be considered in relation to effect size such as the year in which it was published. The results of earlier research may be compared with later research.

When reading the results of a meta-analysis, it is important to check the reports of at least a few of the studies on which the meta-analysis was based. This will help you to familiarise yourself with specifics of the designs of these studies. Some social scientists have argued against the use of meta-analyses because they combine the results of well designed studies with poorly designed ones. The results of different types of studies might also be combined. For example, they may use studies in which participants were randomly assigned to conditions together with ones in which this has not been done (Shadish and Ragsdale, 1996). Differences in the quality of design is more likely to occur in evaluation studies which are more difficult to conduct without adequate resources. However, one can compare the effect size of these two kinds of studies to see whether the effect size differs. If the effect size does not differ (as has been found in some studies), then the effect size is unlikely to be biased by the more poorly designed studies. Sometimes, meta-analytic studies have used ratings by researchers of the overall quality of each of the studies in the meta-analysis. In this way, it is possible to investigate the relationship between quality of the study and the size of the effects found. None of this amounts to a justification for researchers conducting poorly designed studies.

While few students contemplate carrying out a meta-analysis (though it is difficult to understand this reluctance), meta-analytic studies are increasingly carried out in psychology.

2.2 Aims of research

Already it should be abundantly clear that psychological research is an intellectually highly organised and coherent activity. Research, as a whole, does not proceed willy-nilly at the whim of a privileged group of dilettante researchers. The research activities of psychologists are primarily directed at other psychologists. In this way, individual researchers and groups of researchers are contributing to a wider, collective activity. Research which fails to meet certain basic requirements is effectively excluded. Research which has no point, which has a bad design, or is faulty in some other way has little chance of being published, heard about and read. The dissemination of research in psychology is subject to certain quality controls which are largely carried out by a peer review process in which experts in the field recommend whether a research report should be published or not.

Researchers have to account for the research they do by justifying key aspects of their work. Central to this is the requirement that researchers have a good, sound purpose for doing the research that they do. In other words, researchers have to specify *the aims* of their research. This is two-fold:

■ The researcher needs to have a coherent understanding of what purposes the research will serve and how likely it is to serve these purposes. A researcher who cannot see the point of what they are doing is likely to be a dispirited, bad researcher. Obviously, this is most likely to be the case with student researchers doing research under time pressure to meet course requirements. So clarity about the aims of research is, in the first instance, an obligation of the researcher to themselves.

■ The researcher needs to be able to present the aims of their studies with enough clarity to justify the research to interested, but critical, others. This is always done in research reports, but it is also necessary, for example, in applications for research funds to outside bodies.

Clearly stated aims are essential means of indicating what the research can contribute. They also help clarify just why the research was done in the way in which it was done. By clarity, we mean a number of things. Of course it means that the aims are presented as well written, grammatical sentences. More importantly, the aims of the research need to be clearly justified by providing their rationale. The introduction of any research report is where the case for the aims of the research is made. Justifying the aims of research can involve:

■ Explaining the relevance of the research to what is already known about the topic. The explanation of and justification for the aims of a piece of research may include both previous theoretical and empirical advancements in the field. For many topics in psychology there may well be a great deal of previous research literature. This can be daunting to newcomers. (Chapter 5 on searching the literature describes how one can efficiently and effectively become familiar with the relevant research literature on a topic.) Examples of some of reasons for doing research on a particular topic are discussed in Chapter 22.

■ Reference to the wider social context for research. Psychological research is often a response to the concerns of broader society as exemplified by government, social institutions such as the legal and educational system, business and so forth. Of course, there is substantial published material which emanates from these sources – government publications, statistical information, discussion documents and professional publications. These are largely not the work of psychologists but are relevant to their activities.

2.3 Research hypotheses

The use of hypotheses is far more common in psychological research than in disciplines such as sociology, economics and other related disciplines. It is a concept which derives from natural sciences such as physics, chemistry and biology which have influenced psychology more than other social and human sciences. The aims of a great deal of research in psychology (but by no means all) may be more precisely formulated in terms of one or more working suppositions about the possible research findings. These are known as hypotheses. A hypothesis does not have to be true since the point of research is to examine the empirical support or otherwise for the hypotheses. So hypotheses are working assumptions or propositions expressing expectations linked to the aims of the study.

In practice, it is not a difficult task to write hypotheses once we have clarified just what our expectations are. Since a hypothesis is merely a statement which describes the relationship expected to hold between two (or more) variables, at a minimum we need to identify what two variables we are interested in and propose that there is a relationship between the two. We could go one step further and specify the nature of that relationship. Taking the idea that we introduced in Chapter 1 that people are attracted to other people on the basis of having similar attitudes to each other, what would the hypothesis be? The two variables which derive from this might be 'attitude similarity' and 'attraction'. The hypothesised relationship between the two is that the greater the attitude similarity then the greater the attraction to the other person. Expressed as an hypothesis this could read something like: 'Higher levels of attitude similarity lead to higher levels of attraction.' However, there are many ways of writing the same thing as the following list of alternatives demonstrates:

■ People with more similar attitudes will be more attracted to each other than people with less similar attitudes.
■ Greater attitude similarity will be associated with greater interpersonal attraction.
■ Attitude similarity is *positively* linked with interpersonal attraction.

The terms positive and negative relationship or association are fundamental concepts in research. It is important to understand their meaning as they are very commonly used phrases:

■ A positive or direct association is one in which *more* of one quality (attitude similarity) goes together with *more* of another quality (interpersonal attraction).
■ A negative or inverse association is one in which more of one quality (attitude similarity) goes together with less of another quality (interpersonal attraction).

An example of a negative or inverse association would be that greater attitude similarity is associated with *less* attraction. This is *not* the hypothesis we are testing though some might consider it a reasonable hypothesis – after all there is an old saying which suggests that opposites attract. Both past research and theory have led us to the expectation that similarity leads to attraction. If that did not exist, then we would have little justification for our choice.

The precise phrasing of a hypothesis is guided by considerations of clarity and precision. Inevitably, different researchers will use different ways of saying more or less the same thing.

Hypotheses can be somewhat more complex than this example. For example, a third variable could be incorporated into our hypothesis. One such example would be the importance of the attitudes to the individual. So it might be suggested that the more important the attitude is to the person the more they will be attracted to someone with a similar attitude. So this hypothesis actually contains three variables:

■ 'attitude importance'
■ 'attitude similarity'
■ 'interpersonal attraction'.

In this case, the hypothesis might be expressed something like this: 'The relationship between attitude similarity and attraction will be greater when the attitudes are important.' This is quite a technically complex hypothesis to test. It requires a degree of sophistication about aspects of research design and statistical analysis. So, at this stage, we will try to confine ourselves to the simpler hypotheses that involve just two variables.

Few researchers do research which has a single aim. Usually studies involve several interrelated aims. This helps the researcher to take advantage of economies of time and other resources. A study which tests several hypotheses at the same time also potentially has more information on which to base conclusions. Of course, studies carried out as part of training in psychological research methods may be more effective for teaching purposes if a single hypothesis is addressed.

2.4 Four types of hypotheses

The distinction between relationships and causal relationships is important. Hypotheses should be carefully phrased in order to indicate the causal nature or otherwise of the relationships being investigated.

The statement that attitude similarity is associated with attraction is an example of a non-causal hypothesis. It indicates that we believe that the two variables are interrelated but we are *not* indicating that one variable is causing the other. An association between two variables is all that we can infer with confidence when we measure two variables at the same time. Many psychologists would argue that, strictly speaking, hypotheses should be presented in a non-causal form when a non-experimental design is used. When a true experimental design is used, then the use of terms which refer directly or indirectly to a causal relationship is appropriate. True experimental designs involve the manipulation of the causal variable, participants are randomly assigned to conditions and all else is held constant. Expressing the hypothesis of a true experiment in a non-causal form does not give credit to the main virtue of this design.

There is a range of terms which psychologists use which indicate that a causal relationship is being described or assumed. Such phrases would be that, say, attitude similarity:

'. . . leads to . . .'	'. . . affects . . .'
'. . . causes . . .'	'. . . has an effect on . . .'
'. . . brings about . . .'	'. . . results in . . .'

interpersonal attraction. These phrases are so associated with questions of causality that they are best reserved for when causality is assumed.

The direction of the expected relationship should be incorporated into the wording of the hypothesis if at all possible. Hypotheses which indicate direction could be:

■ Greater attitude similarity will lead to greater attraction.
■ Greater attitude similarity will be associated with greater interpersonal attraction.

Since such hypotheses indicate the direction of the relationship expected they are referred to as *directional hypotheses*. There are circumstances in which we may not be able to make predictions as to the direction of the relationship with any confidence. For example, there may be two different, but equally pertinent, theories which lead us to expect contradictory results from our study. For example, social learning theory predicts that watching aggression should lead to greater aggression whereas the idea of catharsis predicts that it should lead to less aggression.

Of course, it is not always possible to pin a direction to a relationship. Sometimes hypotheses have to be stated without specifying a direction simply because there are reasonable arguments to expect either outcome and there is no strong reason to predict a particular direction of outcome. There are important issues connected with the statistical analyses of such hypotheses. These are discussed in Box 2.1.

Table 2.1 summarises the four possible types of hypothesis which can be generated by considering the causality versus non-causality and directional versus non-directional hypotheses. The letters A and B refer to the two variables. So A could be attitude similarity and B interpersonal attraction.

It should be stressed that without a rationale for a hypothesis based on theory or previous research, the case for examining the relationship between two variables is weakened. Consequently, consideration should be given to other reasons for justifying researching the relationship between two variables. Given the billions of potential variables that could be available to psychologists, why choose variable 2 743 322 and variable 99 634 187 for study? Research is *not* about data collection and analysis for its own sake. Research is part of a systematic and coordinated attempt to understand its subject matter. Until one understands the relationship between research and advancement of understanding, research methods will probably remain a mass of buzzing confusion.

The aims and hypotheses of a study are its driving force. Once the aims and hypotheses are clarified, other aspects of the research fall into place much more easily. They help focus the reading of the published literature for relevant work since the aims and hypo-

Table 2.1   Four types of hypotheses

	Causal	Non-causal
Directional	more A causes more (or less) B e.g. greater attitude similarity causes greater interpersonal attraction	more A is related to more (or less) B e.g. greater attitude similarity is related to greater interpersonal attraction
Non-directional	A causes B e.g. attitude similarity causes interpersonal attraction	A is related to B e.g. attitude similarity is related to interpersonal attraction

theses help indicate what is relevant. Once the past research and writings relevant to the new research study have been identified with the help of clear aims and hypotheses, the introduction can be written using more convincing and coherent justifications for them. The aims and hypotheses clarify what variables will need to be measured. Similarly, the aims and hypotheses help guide the researcher towards appropriate research design. The data will support or not support the hypotheses, either wholly or partially. Finally the discussion of the results will primarily refer back to the aims and hypotheses. It is hardly surprising, then, to find that the aims and hypotheses of a study can be the lynchpin that holds a report together. If they are incoherent and confused then little hope can be offered about the value of the study.

BOX 2.1   DIRECTION, HYPOTHESES AND STATISTICAL ANALYSIS

It is important to differentiate between:

- Assessing the adequacy of the research hypothesis which underlies the research study in question.
- Testing the null hypothesis and alternate hypothesis in significance testing (or statistical inference) as part of the statistical analysis.

They are frequently confused. The hypothesis testing model in statistical analysis deals with a very simple question – are the trends found in the data simply the consequence of chance fluctuations due to sampling? Statistical analysis in psychology is guided by the Neyman–Pearson hypothesis testing model although it is rarely referred to as such and seems to be frequently just taken for granted. In the Neyman–Pearson hypothesis testing model there are two statistical hypotheses offered:

- That there is no relationship between the two variables that we are investigating – this is known as the *null hypothesis*.
- That there is a relationship between the two variables – this is known as the *alternate hypothesis*.

→

Box 2.1 continued

The researcher is required to choose between the null hypothesis and the alternate hypothesis. They must accept one of them and reject the other. Since we are dealing with probabilities, we do not say that we have proven the hypothesis or null hypothesis. In effect, hypothesis testing assesses the hypothesis that any trends in the data may be reasonably explained by chance due to using samples rather than all cases. The alternative is that the relationship found in the data represents a substantial trend which is not reasonably accountable for on the basis of chance.

To put it directly, statistical testing is only one aspect of hypothesis testing. We test research hypotheses in other ways in addition to statistically. There may be alternative explanations of our findings which perhaps fit the data even better, there may be methodological flaws in the research that statistical analysis is not intended to, and cannot, identify, or there may be evidence that the hypotheses only work with certain groups of participants, for example. So significance testing is only a minimal test of a hypothesis – there are many more considerations when properly assessing the adequacy of our research hypothesis.

Similarly, the question of direction of a hypothesis comes up in a very different way in statistical analysis. Once again, one should not confuse direction when applied to a research hypothesis with direction when applied to statistical significance testing. One-tailed testing and two-tailed testing are discussed in virtually any statistics textbook (e.g. Chapter 17 of our companion statistics text *Introduction to Statistics in Psychology* (Howitt and Cramer, 2005a) is devoted to this topic). Quite simply, one-tailed testing is testing a directional hypothesis whereas two-tailed testing is for testing non-directional hypotheses. However, there are exacting requirements which need to be met before applying one-tailed testing to a statistical analysis:

■ There should be very strong theoretical or empirical reasons for expecting a particular relationship between two variables.
■ The decision about the nature of the relationship between the two variables should be made in ignorance of the data.

These requirement are so demanding that very little research can justify the use of one-tailed testing. Psychological theory is rarely so well developed that it can make precise enough predictions about outcomes of new research, for example. Previous research in psychology has a tendency to manifest very varied outcomes. Hence, the difficulty of making precise predictions.

One-tailed (directional) significance testing will produce statistically significant findings more readily than two-tailed testing – so long as the outcome is in the predicted direction. Hence the need for caution about its incorrect use since we are applying a less stringent test. Two-tailed testing should be the preferred method in all but the most exceptional circumstances as described above.

The distinction between a research hypothesis (which is evaluated in a multitude of ways) and a statistical hypothesis (which can only be evaluated statistically) is very important. Any researcher who evaluates a research hypothesis merely on the basis of statistical hypothesis testing has only partially completed the task.

2.5 Difficulties in formulating aims and hypotheses

The aims or objectives of published studies are usually well defined and clear. They are, after all, the final stage of the research process – publication. It is far more difficult to be confident about the aims and hypotheses of a study that you are planning for yourself. One obvious reason for this is that you are at the start of the research process. Refining one's crude ideas for research into aims and hypotheses is not easy – there is a lot of reading, discussing, planning and other work to be done. You will usually have a rough idea of what it is that you want to do but you are not likely to think explicitly in terms of aims and hypotheses. Take some comfort in personal construct theory (Kelly, 1955) which suggests that humans act like scientists and construct theories about people and the nature of the world. You may recognise yourself behaving like this when you catch yourself thinking in ways such as 'if this happens, then that should happen'. For example, 'if I send a text message then he might invite me to his party in return'.

This kind of statement is not different from saying 'if someone has the same attitude as someone else, then they will be attracted to that person' or 'the more similar someone's attitude is to that of another person, the more they will be attracted to that individual'. These are known as conditional propositions and are clearly not dissimilar from hypotheses. This kind of thinking is not always easy to recognise. Take, for example, the belief or statement that behaviour is determined by one's genes. At first sight this may not appear to be a conditional or 'if . . . , then . . .' proposition. However, it can be turned into one if we restate it as 'if someone has the same genes as another person, they will behave in the same way' or 'the more similar the genes of people are, the more similar they will behave'.

There is another fundamental thing about developing aims and hypotheses for psychological research. If people are natural scientists testing out theories and hypotheses, they also need to have a natural curiosity about people and the world. In other words, research ideas will only come to those interested in other people and society. Research can effectively be built on your interests and ideas just so long as you remember that these must be integrated with what others have done starting with similar interests.

The comparative method

Characteristically, hypotheses in psychology imply a comparison between two or more groups. Sometimes this comparison is taken for granted in the expression of hypotheses so is not overtly stated. Unless one recognises this implicit comparison in hypotheses, it may prove difficult to formulate satisfactory ones and, furthermore, it may not be obvious that the appropriate research design should involve a comparison of two or more groups. Suppose we are interested in physical abuse in romantic relationships. One possible reason for such abuse is that one or both of the partners in the relationship are very possessive of the other person. So the violence may occur whenever a partner feels threatened by what the other person does or does not do. The research we carry out examines whether or not abusive partners are possessive. So the hypothesis is that abusive partners are possessive. We give out questionnaires measuring possessiveness to 50 people known to have physically abused their partner. Suppose we find that 70% of people in abusive relationships are possessive. What can we conclude on the basis of this? Well it is certainly true that most abusive people are possessive. However, we do not know how many people not in abusive relationships are also possessive. That is, when it is suggested that abusive people are possessive, there is an implication that non-abusive people are *not* possessive.

The problem does not stem from how we have tested our hypothesis but from our understanding of the hypothesis itself. What the hypothesis implies is that abusive partners are *more* possessive than non-abusive partners. Just by looking at abusive partners we cannot tell whether they are more possessive than non-abusive partners. It could be that 70% or even 90% of non-abusive partners were possessive. If this were the case, abusive partners are not more possessive than non-abusive partners. They may even be less possessive than non-abusive partners.

Had the hypothesis been put as 'There is a relationship between possessiveness and abuse' then the comparison is built in but may still not be entirely obvious to those starting research for the first time. Probably the best rule of thumb is the assumption that psychological hypotheses almost invariably include comparisons between groups of people.

2.6 Types of variables

So far we have been using the term variable without much by way of definition. Yet, as we have seen, the central component of the research hypothesis is the names of the variables involved – the relation between them is next. So we need to look at the concept of variable in some depth. A variable is any characteristic or quality that has two or more categories or values. Of course, what that characteristic or quality is has to be defined in some way by the researcher. By saying that a variable has two or more categories or values simply reminds us that a variable must vary by definition. Otherwise we call it a *constant*.

Measurement characteristics of variables

Measurement is the process of assigning individuals to the categories or values of the variable. Different variables have different measurement characteristics which need to be understood in order to effectively plan and execute research. The most important way in which variables differ is in terms of the nominal versus quantitative measurement.

Nominal variables (also known as qualitative, category or categorical variables)

Nominal variables are ones in which measurement consists of categorising cases in terms of two or more named categories. The number of different categories employed is also used to describe these variables:

■ *Dichotomous, binomial or binary variables* These are merely variables which are measured using just two different values. (The term dichotomous is derived from the Greek meaning equally divided or cut in two: dicho- is Greek for apart, separate or in two parts while -ous is Latin for characterised by.) For example, one category could be 'friend' while the other category would be anyone else.

■ *Multinomial variables* When a nominal variable has more than two values it is described as a multinomial, polychomous or polytomous variable. (Poly is Greek for many.) We could have the four categories of 'friend', 'family member', 'acquaintance' and 'strangers'.

Each value or category of a dichotomous or multinomial variable needs to be identified or labelled. For example, we could refer to the four categories friend, family member, acquaintance and stranger as category A, category B, category C and category D. We could also refer to them as category 1, category 2, category 3 and category 4. The problem with this is that the categories named in this way have been separated from their original labels – friend, acquaintance, stranger and enemy. This kind of variable may be known as a nominal, qualitative, category, categorical or frequency variable. Numbers are simply used as names or labels for the different categories. We may have to use numbers for the names of categories when analysing this sort of data on a computer. The only arithmetical operation that can be applied to dichotomous and multinomial variables is to count the frequency of how many cases fall into the different categories.

Quantitative variables

When we measure a quantitative variable, the numbers or values we assign to each person or case represent increasing levels of the variable. These numbers are known as scores since they represent amounts of something. A simple example of a quantitative variable might be social class (socio-economic status is a common variable to use in research). Suppose that social class is measured using the three different values of lower, middle and upper class. Lower class may be given the value of 1, middle class the value of 2 and upper class the value of 3. Hence, higher values represent higher social status. The important thing to remember is that the numbers here are being used to indicate different quantities of social class. Many quantitative variables (such as age, income, reaction time, number of errors or the score on a questionnaire scale) are measured using many more than three categories. When a variable is measured quantitatively, then the range of arithmetic operations that can be carried out is extensive – we can, for example, calculate the average value or sum the values.

The term dichotomous can be applied to certain quantitative variables as it was to some nominal variables. For example, we could simply measure a variable such as income using two categories – poor and rich which might be given the values 1 and 2. Quite clearly the rich have greater income than the poor so the values clearly indicate quantities. However, this is true of any dichotomous variable. Take the dichotomous variable sex or gender. For example, females may be given the value of 1 and males the value of 2. These values actually indicate quantity. A person who has the value 2 has more maleness than a person given the value 1. In other words, the distinction between quantitative and qualitative variables is reduced when considering dichotomous variables.

Independent and dependent variables

The concepts of independent and dependent variables are common in psychological writings. The distinction between the two is at its clearest when we consider the true experiment and, in an ideal world, would probably best be confined to laboratory and similar true experiments. The variable which is manipulated by the researcher is known as the independent variable. Actually it is totally independent of any other variable in a true experimental design since purely random processes are used to allocate participants to the different experimental treatments. Nothing in the situation, apart from randomness, influences the level of the independent variable. The variable which is measured (rather than manipulated) is the dependent variable since the experimental manipulation is expected to influence how the participants in the experiment behave. In other words, the dependent variable is subject to the influence of the independent variable.

The concepts of independent and dependent variables would appear to be quite simple – that is, the independent variable is the manipulated variable and the dependent variable is the measured variable which is expected to be influenced by the manipulated variable. It becomes rather confusing because the distinction between independent and dependent variable is applied to non-experimental designs. For example, the term independent variable is applied to comparisons between different groups. Thus, if we were comparing men and women in terms of their computer literacy then gender would be the independent variable. Computer literacy would be the dependent variable.

Of course, gender cannot be manipulated by the researcher – it is a fixed characteristic of the participant. Variables which cannot be or were not manipulated and which are characteristic of the participant or subjects are sometimes called *subject variables*. They include such variables as how old the person is, how intelligent they are, how anxious they are and so on. All of these variables may be described as the independent variable by some researchers. However, how can a variable be the independent variable if the causal direction of the relationship between two variables is not known? In non-experiments it may be better to use more neutral terms for these two types of variables such as predictor variable for the independent variable and criterion variable for the dependent variable. In this case we are trying to predict what the value is of the criterion variable from the values of the predictor variable or variables.

2.7 Operationalising concepts or variables

There is a crucial distinction to be made between a variable and the measure of that variable. Variables are concepts or abstractions which are created and refined as part of the advancement of the discipline of psychology. Gender is not a tick on a questionnaire, but we can measure gender by getting participants to tick male or female on a questionnaire. The tick on the questionnaire is an *indicator* of gender, but it is not gender. Operationalisation (Bridgman, 1927) is the steps (or operations) that we take to measure the variable in question.

Some researchers argue that the best way of defining the nature of our variables is to describe how they are measured. For example, there are various ways in which we could operationalise the concept or variable of anxiety. We could manipulate it by putting participants in a situation which makes them anxious and compare that situation with one in which they do not feel anxious. We could assess anxiety by asking them how anxious they are, getting other people to rate how anxious they seem to be, or measuring some physiological index of anxiety such as their heart rate. These are different ways of operationalising anxiety. If they all reflect what we consider to be anxiety we should find that these different methods are related to one another. So we would expect participants in a situation which makes them anxious to report being more anxious, be rated as being more anxious and to have a faster heart rate than those in a situation which does not make them anxious. If these methods are not related to one another, then they may not all be measuring anxiety.

Operationalisation has benefits and drawbacks. The benefit is that by defining a concept by the steps involved in measuring it, then the meaning of the concept could not be more explicit. The costs include that operationalisation places less onus on the researcher to explicate the nature of their concepts and encourages the concentration on measurement issues rather than conceptual issues. Of course, ultimately any concept used in research has to be measured using specific and specified operations. However, this should not be at the expense of careful consideration of the nature of the concepts involved.

2.8 Conclusion

It is almost a truism to suggest that the aims and hypotheses of research should be clear. This does not mean that the aims and hypotheses are obvious at the earliest stages of the research project. Since research is part of the ways in which psychological knowledge and ideas develop, it is almost inevitable that aims and hypotheses go through a developmental process. Reformulation of the aims and objectives of a study will commonly occur in the research planning stage – and sometimes after. All research is guided by aims, but hypotheses are only universal in certain types of research – especially true experiments – where it is possible to specify likely outcomes with a great deal of precision. Hypotheses are best included wherever possible since they represent the distillation of the researcher's thoughts about the subject matter. Sometimes, for non-experimental studies, the formulation of hypotheses becomes too cumbersome to be of value. Hence, many excellent studies in psychology will not include hypotheses.

The true experiment (e.g. the laboratory experiment) has many advantages in terms of the testing of hypotheses – its ability to randomise participants to conditions, the requirement of manipulating the independent variable rather than using already existing variables such as sex, and the control over variables. Although we have largely discussed the testing of a single hypothesis at a time, very little research in real life is so restricted. Most research studies have several aims and several hypotheses in the same study because we are usually interested in the way in which a number of different variables may be related to one another. It would also be more costly in terms of time and effort to investigate these hypotheses one at a time in separate studies.

In the penultimate section of the book on qualitative research methods, we will see that important research in psychology can proceed using a quite different approach to investigation in which the idea of specified aims and hypotheses is something of anathema. Nevertheless, much research in psychology either overtly or tacitly subscribes to hypothesis testing as an ideal. Chapter 15 overviews the theoretical basis to these different approaches to research.

Key points

■ Research studies have different general aims. Most seem to be concerned with testing causal propositions or hypotheses. Others may describe a phenomenon or intervention in detail, estimate how common a behaviour is in some population, evaluate the effects of an interventions or statistically summarise the results of similar studies. The aims or aims of a study should be clearly and accurately stated.

■ Studies which test causal propositions should describe clearly and accurately what these propositions are.

■ The research study should make a contribution to the topic. While research usually builds on previous research in an area, the contribution of the study should be original to some extent in the sense that the particular question addressed has not been investigated in this way before.

■ A hypothesis describes what the relationship is expected to be between two or more variables. The hypothesis should be stated in a causal form when the study is a true experiment. It should be stated in a non-causal form when the study is a non-experiment.

■ When suggesting that variables may be related to one another, we usually expect the variables to be related in a particular way or direction. When this is the case, we should specify in the hypothesis what this direction is.

■ The variable thought to be the cause may be called the independent variable and the variable presumed to be the effect the dependent variable. Some people feel that these two terms should be restricted to the variables in a true experiment. In non-experiments the variable assumed to be the cause may be called the predictor and the variable considered to be the effect the criterion.

■ To study the relationship between variables, variables have to be manipulated or measured. The way in which this is done is called the operational definition of the variable. Variables may be operationalised in different ways.

Activities

1. Choose a recent study that has been referred to either in a textbook you are reading or in a lecture that you have attended. What kind of aim or aims did the study have in terms of the aims mentioned in this chapter? What were the specific aims of this study? What kinds of variables were manipulated or measured? In other words, were they categorical or score variables? If the study involved testing hypotheses were the direction and the causal nature of the relationship specified? If the hypothesis was stated in a causal form was the design a true (i.e. randomised) one?

2. You wish to test the hypothesis that we are what we eat. How could you do this? What variables could you measure? What type of variable is each of them?

3 The problems of generalisation
Chance findings and sample size

Overview

- A number of factors are especially influential on the limits to generalisation from any data. The sampling procedures used and the statistical significance of the findings are very important. At the same time, psychologists generalise because psychology has a tendency towards universalism which assumes that what is true of one group of people is true of all people.

- Psychological research (as opposed to practice) is usually concerned with samples of people rather than specific individuals. This allows general trends to be considered at the expense of neglecting the idiosyncratic aspects of individuals.

- Much psychological research depends on the samples selected primarily because they are convenient for the researcher to obtain. The alternative would be random sampling from a clearly specified population.

- Characteristically, a great deal of psychological research is concerned with studying principles of human behaviour that are assumed to apply generally. As the generalisations being tested are assumed to be true of people in general, the necessity to ensure that the sample is representative is minimised.

- Statistical analysis is often concerned with answering the simple question of how safe it is to generalise from a particular study or sample of data. The usual model of statistical testing in psychology is based on postulating what would happen if the null hypothesis were true and then comparing this with what was actually obtained in the research.

- The probability of accepting that the results are not due to chance sampling if the null hypothesis were true is usually set at the 0.05 or 5% level. This means that the probability of the finding being due to chance when the null hypothesis is in fact true is 5 times out of 100, or less. Results that meet this criterion are called statistically significant, otherwise they are statistically non-significant.

- The bigger the sample the more likely it is that the results will be statistically significant – all other things being equal. Consequently, it is necessary to look at the size of the result as well as its statistical significance when evaluating its importance.

This chapter discusses in some detail the process of generalisation of research findings. This is a crucial step in any research. There are three important themes that need consideration:

■ The limitations placed on generalisation by the sampling methods used.
■ The limitations placed on generalisation by the strictures of statistical significance testing.
■ The lack of limitations placed on generalisation by the universalism of psychological theory.

3.1 Universalism

One of the characteristics of psychology is its tendency towards *universalism*. This is the fundamental assumption that the principles of human behaviour are the same for all people, all cultures and all societies. So when psychologists propose a hypothesis there is an implicit assumption that it is true of all people – unless it is stated or implied that the principle applies only to restricted groups of people. In other words, they are interested in making generalisations about behaviour that apply no matter the circumstances. Psychological principles are assumed to be laws of human behaviour anywhere. Increasingly psychologists question this idea of universalism and argue that a culturally specific approach to psychology is more realistic and productive (Owusu-Bempah and Howitt, 2000). Many of the principles put forward by psychologists are assumed to apply not only to people but also to other animals. Examples of this include classical conditioning theory (Pavlov, 1927) and operant conditioning theory (Skinner, 1938). Indeed, psychologists made extensive use of animals in their research because they believed that lessons learnt from animal research could be generalised to humans.

While universalism is characteristic of a great deal of psychological thinking, it is rarely, if ever, stated as such in modern psychology. It operates rather more covertly, but reveals itself in a number of different ways – such as when university students are used unquestioningly as participants in a great deal of academic research.

3.2 Sampling and generalisation

Many criticisms have been made of psychology for its restricted approach to sampling. Psychological research has sometimes been described as being the psychology of psychology students or sophomores (Rosenthal and Rosnow, 1969, p. 59). (A sophomore is a second year student in the USA.) This criticism only means something if the idea of universalism is being questioned – otherwise it would not matter since the laws of human behaviour could just as well be determined from studies using psychology students as any other group of participants.

Not all research has a sample of participants. The earliest psychological research tended to use the researcher themselves as the principal or only research participant. Consequently, experimental psychologists would explore phenomena on themselves. For example, Ebbinghaus (1913) studied memory or forgetting on himself. There are circumstances in which a single case may be an appropriate unit for study. Some psychologists advocate using single cases or relatively few cases in order to investigate changing a particular individual's behaviour (Barlow and Hersen, 1984). A single-case experimental study involves applying the independent variable at different random points in time. If the independent variable is having an effect then the participant should respond differently at the time that the independent variable is applied than when it is not. Its obvious major advantage is that it can be helpful when the particular sort of case is very rare. For example, if a particular patient has a very unusual brain condition then it provides a way of studying the effect of that condition. Clinicians working with a patient are an obvious set of circumstances in which this style of research might be helpful.

The problems with the approach are largely to do with the high demands on the participants' time and the usual problems associated with participants being aware of the nature of the design because it is apparent what is happening. This normally occurs when the researcher has responsibility for trying to change the participant's behaviour. Although this method has never been very common and appears to be becoming less so (Forsyth *et al.*, 1999), its use questions the extent to which research requires substantial samples of cases to be worthwhile or effective.

Representative samples and convenience samples

Most research studies are based on more than a few participants. The mean number of participants per study in articles published in 1988 in the *Journal of Personality and Social Psychology* was about 200 (Reis and Stiller, 1992). This is quite a substantial number of participants. So

- How big should a sample be in order for us to claim that our findings apply generally?
- How should samples be selected in order for us to maximise our ability to generalise from our findings?

If everyone behaved in exactly the same way we would only need to select one person to investigate – everyone else would behave exactly the same. Neither would the way in which we select the sample have any bearing on the outcome of the research.

People vary in any number of different ways. Take, for example, the number of hours people say they usually sleep a day. While most people claim to sleep between seven and eight hours, others claim that they sleep less than six hours and others that they sleep more than ten hours (Cox *et al.*, 1987, p. 129). In other words, there is considerable variation in the number of hours claimed. Furthermore, how much sleep a person has varies from day to day – one day it may be six hours and the next day eight hours. Differences between people and within a person are common for many measures.

The necessary size of the samples used in research may reflect the consequence of the findings of the research. Research for which the outcome matters may have more stringent requirements about sample size than research for which the outcome, whatever it is, is trivial. For example, what size sample would one require if the outcome of the study could result in counselling services being withdrawn by a health authority? What size sample would one require if the study is just part of the training of psychology students? What size sample would one require for a pilot study prior to a major investigation? While we might disagree about the exact sample size to use, we probably can all agree that larger samples are required for the study that might put the future of counselling at risk. The size of sample used is also affected by the need for precision about what is being measured. For example, it is generally the case that larger samples are employed when we are trying to estimate the frequency, or typical value, of a particular behaviour or characteristic in the population. If we wanted an estimate of the mean number of reported hours of sleep in, say, the elderly, then we are likely to use a bigger sample. On the other hand, if we want to know whether the number of hours slept is related to mental health then we may choose to use a smaller sample. The reason for this is that we only need to establish that sleep and mental health are related approximately – we are less concerned about the precise size of the relationship between the two. (If the aim is to produce an estimate of some behaviour for a population, then we will have more confidence in that estimate if the sample on which that estimate is based is selected in such a way so as to be representative of the population. Ways of selecting a representative sample will be discussed in Chapter 11 along with other sampling methods.)

Probably most sampling in psychological research is what is termed *convenience samples*. These are *not* random samples but groups of people that are relatively easy for the researcher to approach. In the case of university lecturers and students, the most convenient sample typically consists of students – often psychology students. What is convenient for one psychologist may not be convenient for another. For a clinical psychologist psychotherapy patients may be a more convenient sample than undergraduate students. West *et al.* (1992) noted that undergraduate students were the most common kind of participants used in studies published in 1988 in the *Journal of Personality and Social Psychology*. Eighty per cent of studies used undergraduate students, 12% adults in the community and 8% special populations such as medical patients.

Convenience samples are usually considered to be acceptable for much psychological research. Since psychological research often seeks to investigate whether there is a relationship between two or more variables, then a precisely defined sample may be unnecessary (Campbell, 1969, pp. 360–2). Others would argue that this is very presumptuous about the nature of the relationship between the two variables – especially that it is consistent over different sorts of people. For example, imagine that watching TV violence is related to aggressiveness in males, but inversely related to aggressiveness in females. By taking a sample of psychology students, who tend to be female, a convenience sample of university students will actually stack things in favour of finding that watching TV is associated with lower levels of aggressiveness.

Whether it is possible to generalise from a sample of psychology students, or even students, to the wider population is obviously an empirical question for any one topic of research. There may be particular reasons why a researcher decides that findings based on student samples might not generalise to other populations and so seeks other samples. On the other hand, there are many circumstances in which it would seem perverse to choose to research students rather than other groups. For example, if a researcher was interested in the comprehensibility of the police caution then using university students might seem less appropriate than using a sample of people with poor educational attainment. Obviously, if one is addressing an issue that is particular to a certain group such as children or psychotherapy patients, then it is important to select this group of people. In the long run, it would seem inappropriate if all research on a particular topic were carried out on students. Getting the balance right is a matter for the research community in general, not students learning to do psychology.

Often in psychological research, it is difficult to identify the population that is of concern to the researcher. Although common sense would suggest that the population of concern is that which is represented by the actual participants in the research, this often does not appear to be what is in the researcher's mind. Probably because psychologists tend to see research questions as general propositions about human behaviour rather than propositions about a particular type of person or specific population, they have a tendency to generalise beyond the population defined by the research sample. The difficulty is, of course, just when the generalisation should stop – if ever. Similarly, there tends to be an assumption that propositions are not just true at one point in time but true across a number of points in time. That is, psychological processes first identified more than a lifetime ago are still considered relevant today.

So there appears to be a distinction between the *population of interest* and the population defined clearly by the sample of participants utilised in the research. Of course, it would be possible to limit our population in time and space. We could say that our population is all students at Harvard University in 2004. However, it is almost certain that having claimed this we would readily generalise the findings that we obtain to students at other universities, for example. But we would be fooling ourselves because this would not be our population of interest – human beings in general. People may be samples from a particular group simply because of our resource constraints. For example, a researcher may select some, but not all, 16 year olds from a particular school to take part in research. When this happens, we may wish to do this on a random basis. While this would be a random sample and should be described as such, the population as defined by the sample would be very limited. Because of the very limited nature of the sampling, the results of the study may not be seen as being more informative than a study where this random selection procedure was not used.

The question of the appropriateness of sampling methods in most psychological research is a difficult one to raise. Psychological research rarely uses random sampling from a clearly defined population. Almost invariably a convenient sample of participants is employed. This is as true of the best and most influential psychological research as less auspicious and more mundane research. In other words, if precise sampling were the criterion for good research, psychology textbooks may just as well be put through the shredder. This is not to say that sampling in psychological research is good enough. There is a great deal to be desired on current practice. However, given the major justification lies in the generality of psychological principles, the practice probably will not change materially in the near future.

Another factor needs to be considered when evaluating the adequacy of psychological research methods. Participation rates in many sorts of research are very low. Participation rates refer to the proportion of people who actually take part in the research compared to the number asked to take part in the research – that is, supply usable data. Random sampling is considerably undermined by poor participation rates – it cannot be assumed that those who do *not* participate are a random sample of the people approached. They do not participate for a variety of reasons. These reasons may be systematically related to the research topic such as they are not interested in the topic of the research. In other words, issues to do with sampling are complex and difficult to evaluate. Simply using random selection methods does not ensure a random sample. In these circumstances, convenience samples may be much more attractive propositions than at first they appear.

3.3 Statistics and generalisation

Statistical analysis serves many important roles in psychology. There are numerous statistical techniques that help researchers explore the patterns in their data. Most students, however, are more familiar with what is known as 'inferential statistics' or, more likely, 'significance testing'. Significance testing is only one aspect of research but is a crucial one in terms of a researcher's willingness to generalise the trends that they find in their data. While students are encouraged to believe that statistical significance is an important criterion, it is just one of two really important things. The other is the size of the trend, difference, effect or relationship found in the research. The bigger that these are, then the more important the relationship.

Chance findings and statistical significance

When investigating any research question, one decides what will be an appropriate sample size largely on the basis of the size of the effect or association expected. The bigger the effect or association, the smaller the sample can be in purely statistical terms. This is because bigger effects are more likely to be statistically significant with small sample sizes. A statistically significant finding is one that is large enough that it is unlikely to be due to chance fluctuations due to sampling. (It should be stressed, the calculation of statistical significance is based on the null hypothesis that there is no trend in the data.) The conventionally accepted level of significance is the 5% or 0.05 level. This means that a finding as big as ours can be expected to occur by chance on 5 or fewer occasions if we tested that finding on 100 occasions (and the null hypothesis in fact true). A finding that occurs on more than 5 out of a 100 times is described as being statistically non-significant or not statistically significant. Note that the correct term is non-significant *not* that it is statistically insignificant, although authors sometimes write this. Insignificant is a misleading term since it implies that the finding is not statistically important – but that simply is not what is meant in significance testing. The importance of a finding is the strength of the relationship or difference between two variables or samples. Statistical significance testing merely refers to the question whether the trend is sufficiently large in the data that it is unlikely that it could be the result of chance factors due to the variability inherent in samples – that is there is little chance that the null hypothesis is correct.

Too much can be made of statistical significance if the size of the trend in the data is disregarded. For example, it has been argued that with very large samples, virtually any relationship will be statistically significant though the relationship may itself be a very small one. That is, a statistically significant relationship may, in fact, represent a very small trend in the data. Another way of putting this is that very few null hypotheses are true *if* one deals with very large samples and one will accept even the most modest of trends in the data.

The difference between statistical significance and psychological significance is at the root of the following question: Which is better – a correlation of 0.06 which is statistically significant with a sample of 1000 participants or a correlation of 0.8 that is statistically significant with a sample of six participants?

This is a surprisingly difficult question for many psychologists to answer.

While the critical value of 5% or 0.05 or less is an arbitrary cut-off point, nevertheless it is one widely accepted. However, there are circumstances in which this arbitrary criterion of significance may be replaced with an alternative value:

■ The significance level may be set at a value other than 5% or 0.05. If the finding had important consequences and we wanted to be more certain that our finding was not due to chance, we might set it at a more stringent level. For example, we may have developed a test that we found was significantly related at the 5% level to whether or not someone had been convicted of child abuse. Because people may want to use this test to help determine whether someone had, or was likely to, commit child abuse, we may wish to set the critical value at a more stringent or conservative level because we would not want to wrongly suggest that someone would commit child abuse. Consequently, we may set the critical value at, say, 0.1% or 0.001, which is 1 out of a 1000 times or less.

■ Where a number of effects or associations are being evaluated at the same time, this critical value may be set at less than the 5% or 0.05 level. For example, if we were comparing differences between three groups, we could make a total of three comparisons altogether. We could compare group 1 with group 2, group 1 with group 3, and group 2 with group 3. If the probability of finding a difference between any two groups is set at 5% or 0.05, then the probability of finding any of the three comparisons statistically significant at this level is three times as big, in other words 15% or 0.15. Because we want to maintain the overall significance level at 5% or 0.05 for the three comparisons, we could divide the 5% or the 0.05 by 3, which would give us an adjusted or corrected critical value of 1.67% (5/3 = 1.666) or 0.017 (0.05/3 = 0.0166). This correction is known as a Bonferroni adjustment. (See our companion statistics text, *Introduction to Statistics in Psychology* (Howitt and Cramer, 2005a), for further information.)

■ For a pilot study using a small sample and less than satisfactory measuring instruments, the 5% of 0.05 level of significance may be an unnecessarily stringent criterion. The size of the trends in the data (relationship, difference between means, etc.) is possibly more important. For the purposes of such a pilot study, the significance level may be set at 10% or 0.1 to the advantage of the research process. There may be other circumstances in which we might wish to be flexible about accepting significance levels of 5% or 0.05. For example, in medical research, imagine that researchers have found a relationship between taking hormone replacement therapy and the development of breast cancer. Say that we find this relationship to be statistically significant at the 8% or 0.08 level, would we willingly conclude that the null hypothesis is preferred or would we be unwilling to take the risk that the hypothesis linking hormone replacement therapy with cancer is in fact true. Probably not. The point is not that significance testing is at fault but that a whole range of factors impinge on what we do with our hypotheses.

However, students are well advised to stick with the 5% or 0.05 level as a matter of routine. One would normally have to make the case for varying this.

3.4 Directional and non-directional hypotheses again

When hypotheses are being developed, researchers usually have an idea of the direction of the trend, correlation or difference that they expect. For example, who would express the opinion that there is a difference between the driving skills of men and woman without expressing an opinion as to what that difference is – such as women are definitely worse drivers. We do not have such a view on the basis of a whim but on the basis of beliefs about the general worth, role and abilities of women compared to those of men. Researchers, similarly, often have expectations about the likely outcome of their research – that is, the direction of the trend in their data. It should also be patently obvious that in some cases there will be very sound reasons for expecting a particular trend in the data whereas in other circumstances no sound grounds can be put forward for our expectations.

In other words, often research hypotheses will be expressed in a directional form. In statistical testing, a similar distinction is made between directional and non-directional tests but the justifications are required to be exacting and reasoned (see Box 2.1, Chapter 2). In a statistical analysis, there are tough requirements before a directional hypothesis can be offered. These requirements are that there are very strong empirical or theoretical reasons for expecting the relationship to go in a particular direction and that researchers are ignorant of their data before making the prediction. It would be silly to claim to be making a prediction if one is actually just reporting the trend observed in the data. These criteria are so exacting that they probably mean that little or no student research should employ directional *statistical* hypotheses. Probably the main exceptions are where a student researcher is replicating the findings of a classic study, which has repeatedly been shown to demonstrate a particular trend.

The reason why directional statistical hypotheses have such exacting requirements is that conventionally the significance level is adjusted for the directional hypothesis. The directional hypothesis is referred to as one-tailed significance testing. The non-directional hypothesis is referred to as two-tailed significance testing. In two-tailed significance testing, the 5% or 0.05 chance level is split equally between the two possibilities – that the association or difference between two variables is either positive or negative. So if the hypothesis is that cognitive behaviour therapy has an effect then this would be supported by cognitive behaviour therapy either being better in the highest 2.5% or 0.025 of samples or worse in the lowest 2.5% or 0.025 of samples. Remember, that these probabilities are based on the null hypothesis that there is no effect of cognitive behaviour therapy one way or the other.

Put another way, a directional hypothesis is supported by weaker data than would be required by the non-directional hypothesis. The only good justification for accepting a weaker trend is that there is strong reason to think that it is correct – that is, either previous research has shown much the same trend or theory powerfully predicts a particular outcome. Given the often weak predictive power of much psychological theory, the strength of the previous research is probably the most useful of the two.

The problem with directional hypotheses is what happens when the researcher gets it wrong – that is the trend in the data is exactly the reverse of what is suggested in the hypothesis. There are two possibilities:

■ That the researcher rejects the hypothesis.

■ That the researcher rejects the hypothesis but argues that the reverse of the hypothesis has been demonstrated by the data. The latter is rather like having one's cake and eating it statistically speaking. If the original hypothesis had been supported using the less stringent requirements then the researcher would claim credit for that finding. If, on the other hand, the original hypothesis was actually substantially reversed by the data then this finding would now find favour. The reversed hypothesis, however, was deemed virtually untenable once the original directional hypothesis had been decided upon. So how can it suddenly be favoured when it was previously given no credence with good reason? The only conclusion must be that the findings were chance findings.

So the hypothesis should be rejected. The temptation, of course, is to forget about the original directional hypothesis and substitute a non-directional or reverse directional hypotheses. Both of these are totally wrong but who can say when even a researcher will succumb to temptation?

Possibly the only circumstances in which a student should employ directional *statistical* hypotheses is when conducting fairly exact replication studies. In these circumstances the direction of the hypothesis is justified by the findings of the original study. If the research supports the original direction then the conclusion is obvious. If the replication actually finds the reverse of the original findings then the researcher would be unlikely to claim that the reverse of the original findings is true since it only would apply to the replication study. The situation is one in which the original findings are in doubt as are the new findings since they are diametrically opposite.

One- versus two-tailed significance level

Splitting the 5% or 0.05 chance or significance level between the two possible outcomes is usually known as the two-tailed significance level because two outcomes are being considered. We do this if our hypothesis is non-directional as we have not specified which of the two outcomes we expect to find. Confining the outcome to one of the two possibilities is known as the one-tailed significance level because only one outcome is predicted. This is what we do if our hypothesis is directional where we expect the results to go in one direction.

To understand what is meant by the term 'tailed', we need to plot the probability of obtaining each of the possible outcomes that could be obtained by sampling *if the null hypothesis is assumed to be true*. This is the working assumption of hypothesis testing and reference to the null hypothesis is inescapable if hypothesis testing is to be understood. The technicalities of working out the distribution of random samples if the null hypothesis is true can be obtained from a good many statistics textbooks. The 'trick' to it all is employing the information contained in the actual data. This gives us information about the distribution of scores. One measure of the distribution of scores is the *standard deviation*. In a nutshell, this is a sort of average of the amount scores in a sample differ from the mean of the sample. It is computationally a small step from the standard deviation of scores to the standard error of the means of samples. Standard error is a sort of measure of the variation of sample means drawn from the population defined by the null hypothesis. Since we can calculate the standard error quite simply (it is the distribution of sample characteristics such as the sample mean), this tells us how likely each of the different sample means are. Not surprisingly, samples very different from the outcome defined by the null hypothesis are increasingly uncommon the more different they are from what would be expected on the basis of the null hypothesis.

This is saying little more than that if the null hypothesis is true, then samples that are unlike what would be expected on the basis of this null hypothesis are likely to be uncommon.

3.5 More on the similarity between measures of effect (difference) and association

Simple basic research designs in psychology are often analysed using the *t*-test and the Pearson correlation coefficient. The *t*-test is based on comparing the means (usually) of two samples and essentially examines the size of the difference between the two means. The

Pearson correlation coefficient is a measure of the amount of association or relationship between two variables. Generally speaking, they are regarded as two very different approaches to the statistical analysis of data. However, they are actually very closely related.

A *t*-test is usually used to determine whether an effect is significant in terms of whether the mean score of two groups differ. We could use a *t*-test to find out whether the mean depression score was higher in the cognitive behaviour therapy group than in the no treatment group. A *t*-test is the mean of one group subtracted from the mean of the other group and divided by what is known as the standard error of the mean:

$$t = \frac{\text{mean of one group} - \text{mean of the other group}}{\text{standard error of the mean}}$$

The standard error of the mean is a measure of the extent to which sample means are likely to differ. It is usually based on the extent to which scores in the data differ. There are different versions of the *t*-test. Some calculate the standard error of the mean and others calculate the standard error of the difference between two means.

The value of *t* can be thought of as the ratio of the difference between the two means to the degree to the variability of the scores in the data. If the individual scores differ widely, then the *t* value will be smaller than if they do not differ much. The bigger the *t* value is, the more likely it is to be statistically significant. To be statistically significant at the two-tailed 0.05 level, the *t* value has to be 2.00 or bigger for samples of more than 61 cases. The *t* value can be slightly less than 2.00 for bigger samples. The minimum value that *t* has to exceed to be significant at this level is 1.960, which is for an infinite number of cases. These figures can be found in the tables of a statistics text such as *Introduction to Statistics in Psychology* (Howitt and Cramer, 2005*a*).

Bigger values of *t* generally indicate a bigger effect (bigger difference between the sample means). However, this is affected by the sample size so this needs to be taken into consideration in addition. Bigger values of *t* also tend to indicate increasingly significant findings but this too is affected by sample size.

The Pearson's correlation shows the size of an association between two quantitative variables. It varies from −1 through 0 to 1:

■ A negative correlation means that lower values on one variable go together with higher values on the other variable.
■ A positive correlation means that higher values on one variable go together with higher values on the other variable.
■ A value of zero or close to zero means that there is no linear relationship between the two groups and the outcome measure.

Note that Pearson's correlation is typically used to indicate the association between two quantitative variables. Both variables should consist of a number of values, the frequencies of which take the shape of a bell approximately. The bell-shaped distribution is known as the normal distribution. (See the companion book *Introduction to Statistics in Psychology* (Howitt and Cramer, 2005*a*) or any other statistics textbook for a detailed discussion of precisely what is meant by a normal distribution.) Suppose, for example, we are interested in what the relationship is between how satisfied people are with their leisure and how satisfied they are with their work. Suppose the scores on these two measures vary from 1 to 20 and higher scores indicate greater satisfaction. A positive correlation between the two measures means that people who are more satisfied with their leisure are also more satisfied with their work. It could be that these people are generally positive or that

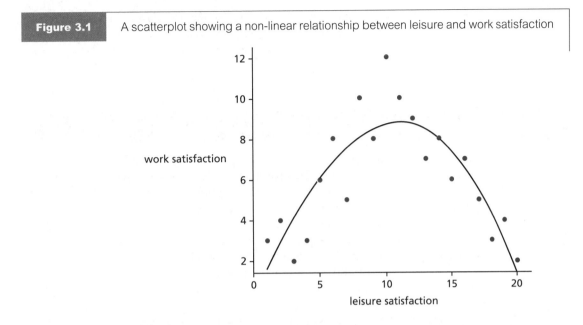

Figure 3.1   A scatterplot showing a non-linear relationship between leisure and work satisfaction

being satisfied in one area of your life spills over into other areas. A negative correlation indicates that people who are more satisfied with their leisure are less satisfied with their work. It is possible that people who are dissatisfied in one area of their life try to compensate in another area.

A correlation of zero or close to zero shows that either there is no relationship between these two variables or there is a relationship but it does not vary in a linear way. For example, people who are the most and least satisfied with their leisure may be less satisfied with work than people who are moderately satisfied with their lives. In other words, there is a curvilinear relationship between leisure and work satisfaction. The simplest and the most appropriate way of determining whether a correlation of zero or close to zero indicates a non-linear relationship between two variables is to draw a scattergram or scatterplot as shown in Figure 3.1. Each point in the scatterplot indicates the position of one or more cases or participants in terms of their scores on the two measures of leisure and work satisfaction.

The t values which compare the means of two unrelated or different groups of cases can be converted into a Pearson's correlation or what is sometimes called a point–biserial correlation, which is the same thing. The following formula is used to convert an unrelated t value to a Pearson's correlation (which is denoted by the letter r; and n is, of course, the sample size):

$$r = \sqrt{\frac{t^2}{t^2 + n - 2}}$$

Alternatively, we could calculate the value of r directly from the data. Suppose higher values on the measure of depression indicate greater depression and that the cognitive behaviour therapy group shows less depression than the no treatment group. If we code or call the no treatment group 1 and the cognitive behaviour therapy group 2, then we will have a negative correlation between the two groups and depression when we calculate the Pearson correlation value.

Because of the interchangeability of the concepts of correlation and tests of difference as shown, it should be apparent that we can speak of a difference between two groups or alternatively of a correlation between group membership and another variable.

3.6 Sample size and size of association

Now that we have provided some idea as to what statistical significance is and how to convert a test of difference into a correlation, we can discuss how big a sample should be in order to see whether an effect or association is statistically significant. The bigger the correlation is, the smaller the sample can be for that correlation to be statistically signific-ant. In Table 3.1 we have presented 11 correlations decreasing in size by 0.10 from ±1.00 to 0.00 and the size that the sample has to exceed to be significant at the one-tailed 5% or 0.05 level. So, for example, if we expect the association to be about 0.20 or more, we would need a sample of more than 69 for that association to be statistically significant. It is unusual to have an overall sample size of less than 16. The size of an effect may be expected to be bigger when manipulating rather than simply measuring a variable because this is what we are attempting to do in a true experiment. Consequently, sample sizes are generally smaller for true experiments than non-experiments.

When dealing with two groups it is important that the two groups are roughly equal in size. If there were only a few cases in one of the groups we could not be confident that the values for that group were a reasonable estimate for the population from which it was drawn. The conversion of a *t* value into a Pearson's correlation presupposes that the variation or variance in the two groups is also similar in size. The interpretation of a correlation assumes that the frequency of values are shaped like a bell. Where there are only two values, as in the case of two groups, this means that the two groups should be roughly similar in size. Therefore, it is important to check that this is the case.

A correlation of zero is never significant no matter how big the sample – since that is the value which best supports the null hypothesis. Correlations of 1.00 are very unusual as

Table 3.1 Size of sample required for a correlation to be statistically significant at the 5% or 0.05 level

Correlation (r)	Sample size (n)	Verbal label for size of correlation	Percentage of variance shared	Verbal label for size of shared variance
±1.00		perfect	100	perfect
±0.90	4		81	large
±0.80	6	large, strong or high	64	
±0.70	7		49	
±0.60	9	modest or moderate	36	
±0.50	12		25	
±0.40	18		16	
±0.30	32	small, weak or low	9	medium
±0.20	69		4	
±0.10	270		1	small
0.00		none	0	none

they represent a perfect straight line or linear relationship between two variables. This would happen if we correlated the variable with itself. You need to have a minimum sample of three to determine the statistical significance of a correlation. A correlation of 0.99 or more would be significant at the one-tailed 5% or 0.05 level if the sample was three. Consequently, no sample size has been given for a correlation of 1.00. These sample sizes apply to both positive correlations and negative ones. It is the size of the correlation that matters for determining statistical significance and not its sign.

The size of an association and its meaning

The size of a correlation is often described in words as well as in numbers. Correlations of 0.80 or above are usually talked of as being 'large', 'strong' or 'high'. This size of correlation may be obtained when we measure the same variable, such as depression, on two separate occasions two weeks apart. In such a case, we may say there was a strong correlation between the first and second test of depression. Correlations of 0.30 or less are usually spoken of as being small, weak or low. Correlations of this size are typically found when we measure different variables, such as depression and social support, on the same or different occasions. Correlations between 0.30 and 0.80 are commonly said to be moderate or modest. They are usually shown when we assess very similar measures, but which are not the same, such as how supportive one sees a partner as being and how satisfied one is with that relationship.

These labels may be misleading in that they may seem to be underestimating the strength of a correlation. The meaning of the size of a correlation is better understood if we square the correlation value – this gives us the *coefficient of determination*. So a correlation of 0.2 when squared gives a coefficient of determination of 0.04. This value represents the proportion of the variation in a variable that is shared with the variation in another variable. Technically this variation is measured in terms of a formula called variance. The way to calculate variance can be found in a statistics textbook such as the companion book *Introduction to Statistics in Psychology* (Howitt and Cramer, 2005*a*).

A correlation of 1.00, gives a coefficient of determination of 1.00, which means that the two variables are perfectly related. A correlation of zero produces a coefficient of determination of zero, which indicates that the variables are either totally separate or they do not have a straight-line relationship such as the relationship between work and leisure satisfaction in Figure 3.1. These proportions may be expressed as a percentage, which may be easier to understand. We simply multiply the proportion by 100 so 0.04 becomes 4 (0.04×100). The percentage of the variance shared by the correlations in Table 3.1 is shown in the third column of that table.

If we plot the percentage of variance shared against the size of the correlation as shown in Figure 3.2 we can see that there is not a straight line or linear relationship between the two but what is called an exponential relationship. The percentage of variance increases at a faster rate at higher than lower correlations. As the size of a correlation doubles, the corresponding size of the percentage of shared variance quadruples. To give an example of this, a correlation of 0.40 is twice as big as one of 0.20. If we express these correlations as the percentage of shared variance we can see that a percentage of 16 is four times as big as one of 4.

The verbal labels generally used to describe different sizes of the shared variance have tended to differ from those given to the correlations that correspond to them. Where the percentage of shared variance is about 1, the size of the effect or the association has been

| Figure 3.2 | Relationship between correlation and percentage of shared variance |

called 'small' (Cohen, 1988, pp. 24–7). Where it is about 5 it has been described as being 'medium'. Where it is more than about 10 it has been referred to as being 'large'. These judgements are obviously subjective or personal to some extent. What one psychologist considers to be a large effect, another might think of as being small. We are inclined to think that 10 may be considered medium and above 20 as large.

Justification for the use of these labels might come from considering just how many variables or factors may be expected to explain a particular kind of behaviour. Racial prejudice is a good example of such behaviour. It is reasonable to assume that racial prejudice is determined by a number of factors rather than just a single factor. The tendency towards authoritarianism has a correlation of 0.30 with a measure of racial prejudice (Billig and Cramer, 1990). This means that authoritarianism shares 9% of its variance with racial prejudice. On the face of things, this is not a big percentage of the variance. What if we had, say, another ten variables that individually and independently explained (accounted for) a similar proportion of the variance. Then we could claim a complete account of racial prejudice. The problem in psychology is finding out what these other ten variables are – or whether they exist. Actually a correlation of 0.30 is not unusual in psychological research and many other variables will explain considerably less of the variance than this.

But there is an alternative way of looking at this issue. That is to ask the value of a correlation of 0.30 – this is meaningless in absolute terms. In the above example, the purpose of the research was basically associated with an attempt to theorise about the nature of racial prejudice. In this context, the correlation of 0.30 would seem to imply that one's resources would be better applied to finding better explanations of racial prejudice than can be offered on the basis of authoritarianism. On the other hand, what if the researcher was interested in using cognitive behaviour therapy in suicide prevention. A correlation of 0.30 between the use of cognitive behaviour therapy and decline in the risk of suicide is a much more important matter – it actually amounts to a change in the probability of suicide prevention from 0.35 to 0.65 (Rosenthal, 1991). This in no sense is even a moderate finding – it is of major importance. In other words, there is a case against the routine use of labels when assessing the importance of a correlation coefficient.

There is another reason why we should be cautious about the routine application of labels to correlations or any other research result. Our measures are not perfectly reliable or valid measures of what they are measuring (see Chapter 13 for a detailed discussion of reliability and validity). Because they are often relatively poor measures of what they are intended to measure, they tend usually to underestimate the true or real size of the association. There is a simple statistical procedure for taking into account the unreliability of the measures called the correction for attenuation (see the companion book *Introduction to Statistics in Psychology*, Howitt and Cramer, 2005a, Chapter 31). Basically it gives us an idealised version of the correlation between two variables as if they were perfect measures. The formula for the corrected correlation is:

$$\text{corrected correlation} = \frac{\text{correlation between measures 1 and 2}}{\sqrt{\text{measure 1 reliability} \times \text{measures 2 reliability}}}$$

If the correlation between the two measures is 0.30 and their reliability is 0.75 and 0.60, respectively, the corrected correlation is 0.45:

$$\text{corrected correlation} = \frac{0.30}{\sqrt{0.75 \times 0.60}} = \frac{0.30}{\sqrt{0.45}} = \frac{0.30}{0.67} = 0.45$$

This means that these two variables share about 20% of their variance. If this is generally true, we would only need another four variables to explain what we are interested in. (Though this is a common view in the theory of psychological measurement, the adjustment actually redefines each of the concepts as the *stable* component of the variables. That is, it statistically makes the variables completely stable (reliable). This obviously is to ignore the aspects of a variable which are unstable – for example, why depression varies over time – which may be as interesting and important to explain as the stable aspects of the variable.)

How do we know what size of effect or association to expect if we are just setting out on doing our research:

■ Psychologists often work in areas where there has already been considerable research. While what they propose to do may never have been done before, there may be similar research. It should be possible from this research to estimate or guestimate how big the effect is likely to be.

■ One may consider collecting data on a small sample to see what size of relationship may be expected and then to collect a sample of the appropriate size to ensure that statistical significance is achieved if the trend in the main study is equal to that found in the pilot study. So if the pilot study shows a correlation of 0.4 between the two variables we are interested in, then we would need a minimum of about 24 cases in our main study. This is because by checking tables of the significance of the correlation coefficient, we find that 0.4 is statistically significant at the 5% level (two-tailed test) with a sample size of 24 (or more). These tables are to be found in many statistics textbooks – our companion statistics text, *Introduction to Statistics in Psychology* (Howitt and Cramer, 2005a), has all you will need.

■ Another approach is to decide just what size of relationship or effect is big enough to be of interest. Remember that very small relationships and effects are significant with very large samples. If one is not interested in small trends in the data then there is little point in depleting resources by collecting data from very large samples. The difficulty is deciding what size of relationship or effect is sufficient for your purposes. Since these purposes vary widely then no simple prescription may be offered. It is partly a matter of assessing the value of the relationship or effect under consideration. Then the consequences of getting things wrong need to be evaluated. (The risk of getting things wrong is higher with smaller relationships or effects, all other things being equal.) It is important not simply to operate as if statistical significance is the only basis for drawing conclusions from research.

It is probably abundantly clear by now that purely statistical approaches to generalisation of research findings are something of an impossibility. Alongside the numbers on the computer output is a variety of issues or questions that modify what we get out of the statistical analysis alone. These largely require thought about one's research findings and the need not to simply regard any aspect of research routine or mechanical.

3.7 Conclusion

Psychologists are often interested in making generalisations about human behaviour that they believe to be true of, or apply to, people in general – though they will vary in the extent to which they believe that their generalisations apply universally. If they believe that the generalisation they are testing is specific to a particular group of people they will state what that group of people is. Because all people do not behave in exactly the same way in a situation, many psychologists believe that it is necessary to determine the extent to which the generalisation they are examining holds for a number, or sample, of people. If they believe that the generalisation applies by and large to most people and not to a particular population, they will usually test this generalisation on a sample of people that is convenient for them to use.

The data they collect to test this generalisation will either be consistent or not consistent with it. If the data are consistent with the generalisation, the extent to which they are consistent will vary. The more consistent the data are, the stronger the evidence will be for the generalisation. The process of generalisation is not based solely on simple criteria about statistical significance. Instead it involves considerations such as the nature of the sampling, the adequacy of each of the measures taken, and an assessment of the value or worth of the findings for the purpose for which they were intended.

Key points

■ Psychologists are often concerned with testing generalisations about human behaviour that are thought to apply to all human beings. This is known as universalism since it assumes that psychological processes are likely to apply similarly to all people no matter their geographical location, culture or gender.

■ The ability of a researcher to generalise from their research findings is limited by a range of factors. These factors include the statistical significance of the findings, the representativeness of the sample used, participation and drop-out rates, and the strength of the findings.

■ Participants are usually chosen for their convenience to the researcher – e.g. they are easily accessible. A case can be made for the use of convenience samples on the basis that these people are thought for theoretical purposes to be similar to people in general. Nonetheless, researchers are often expected to acknowledge this limitation of their sample.

■ The data collected to test a generalisation or hypothesis will either be consistent with it or not consistent with it. The probability of accepting that the results or findings are consistent with the generalisation is set at 0.05 or 5%. This means that these results are likely to be due to chance 5 times out of 100 or less. Findings that meet this criterion or critical value are called statistically significant. Those that do not match this criterion are called statistically non-significant.

Activities

1. Choose a recent quantitative study that has been referred to either in a textbook you are reading or in a lecture that you have attended. What was the size of the sample used? Was a one- or a two-tailed significance level used and do you think that this tailedness was appropriate? What could the minimum size of the sample have been to meet the critical level of significance adopted in this study? What was the size of the effect or association, and do you think that this shows that the predictor or independent variable may play a reasonable role in explaining the criterion or dependent variable? Are there other variables that you think may have shown a stronger effect or association?

2. Choose a finding from just about any psychological study that you feel is important. Do you think that the principle of universalism applies to this finding. For example, does it apply to both genders, all age groups and all cultures? If not, then to which groups would you be willing to generalise the finding?

4 Research reports

The total picture

Overview

- The research report is the key means of communication for researchers. The laboratory report, projects, masters and doctoral dissertations, and journal articles all use a similar and relatively standard structure.

- Research reports are more than an account of how data were collected and analysed. They describe the entire process by which psychological knowledge develops.

- Research reports have certain conventions about style, presentation, structure and content. This conventional structure aids communication once the basics have been learnt.

- The research report should be regarded as a whole entity not a set of discrete parts. Each aspect – title, abstract, tables, text and referencing – contributes to how well the total report communicates.

- This chapter describes the detailed structure of a research report and offers practical advice on numerous difficulties.

Research is not just about data collection and analysis. The major purpose is to advance understanding of the subject matter – that is, to develop theory, concepts and information about psychological processes. The research report describes this process. Research is not the application of a few techniques without rhyme or reason. Equally, the research report is not a number of unarticulated sections but a fully integrated description of the process of developing understanding and knowledge in psychology. To fully appreciate a research report requires an understanding of the many different aspects of research. Not surprisingly, writing a research report is a demanding and sometimes confusing process.

Despite there being different types of research report (laboratory report, dissertation, thesis, journal article, etc.), a broadly standard structure is often employed. Accounts of research found in psychology journals – journal articles – are the professional end of the continuum. At the other end are the research reports or laboratory reports written by undergraduate students. In between there is the final year project, the masters dissertation and the doctoral dissertation. An undergraduate laboratory report is probably 2000 words, a journal article 5000 words, a final year project 10 000 words, a masters dissertation 20 000 – 40 000 words and a doctoral dissertation in Europe 80 000 words but shorter where the programme includes substantial assessment of taught courses. Although there is a common structure which facilitates the comprehension of research reports, this structure should be regarded as flexible enough to cope with a wide variety of contingencies. Psychology is a diverse field of study so it should come as no surprise to find conflicting ideas about what a research report should be. Some of the objections to the standard approach are discussed in the chapters on qualitative methods (Chapters 15–21).

There are two main reasons why research reports can be difficult to write:

■ The research report is complex with a number of different elements, each of which requires different skills. The skills required when reviewing the previous theoretical and empirical studies in a field are not the same as those involved in drawing conclusions from statistical data. The skills of organising research and carrying it out are very different from the skills required to communicate the findings of the research effectively.

■ When students first start writing research (laboratory) reports their opportunities to read other research reports – such as journal articles – are limited. There is a bit of a chicken-and-egg problem here. Until students have understood some of the basics of psychological research and statistics they will find journal articles very difficult to follow. At the same time, they are being asked essentially to write a report using much the same structure as a journal article. Hopefully, some of the best students will be the next generation of professional researchers writing the journal articles.

This chapter on writing the research report comes early in this book. Other books have it tucked-away at the end. But to read and understand research papers it helps to understand how and why a research report is structured the way it is. Furthermore writing a report should not be regarded as an afterthought but as central to the process of doing research. It may be regarded as the main objective of doing research. Apart from training and educational reasons, there is little point in doing research which is not communicated to others. The structure of the research report is a blueprint of the entire research process. For example, the review of previous research (literature review) would appear to be done first judging by most research reports – it follows the title and summary (abstract) after all. Nevertheless, most researchers would admit that they are still reading relevant publications even after the first draft of the report is completed. It cannot be stressed too much that the research report actually prioritises what should be done in research. In contrast, a tiny minority of researchers (see Chapter 20) reject the idea that the literature review should come first – some claim that only after the data has been collected and analysed should the previous research be examined to assess its degree of compatibility with the new findings. This is not sloppiness or laziness on their part. Instead, it is a desire to analyse data unsullied by preconceptions – but it does mean that building on previous research is not central to this alternative formulation. Put another way, a research report is largely the way it is because the methodology of psychology is the way it is. Departures from the standard practice serve to emphasise the nature of the characteristics of the psychological method.

The conventional report structure, then, gives us the building blocks of conventional research. Good research integrates all of the elements into a whole – a hotchpotch of unrelated thoughts, ideas and activities is *not* required. At the same time, research reports do not give every last detail of the process but a clear synthesis of the major and critical aspects of the research process. A research report contains a rather tidy version of events, of course, and avoids the messy detail of the actual process in favour of the key stages presented logically and coherently. Writing the research report should be seen as a constructive process which can usefully begin even at the planning stage of the research. That is, the research report is *not* the final stage of the research process but integral to it. If this seems curious then perhaps you should consider what many qualitative researchers do when analysing their textual data. They begin their analysis and analytic note-taking as soon as the first data become available. Such forethought and planning is a difficult requirement to fulfil but regard it as an ideal to be aimed at.

Something as complex as a research report may be subject to a degree of inconsistency. Journals, for example, publish detailed style instructions for those submitting material to them. The American Psychological Association (APA), for example, publish a substantial manual. There is no universal manual for student research reports so, not surprisingly, different lecturers and instructors have varying views of the detail of the structure and style of undergraduate student research reports. Different universities have different requirements for doctoral theses, for example. And the problem goes beyond this into professional research reports. A quick search of the Internet using the search term 'psychology research report' will locate numerous web sites giving advice and instruction about writing a research report. These sites far from speak with one voice. Nevertheless, there is a great deal of overlap or unanimity of approach. It is essential for a student to understand the local rules for the research report just as it is for the professional researcher to know what is acceptable to the journal to which they submit work for possible publication. Probably students will receive advice from their lecturers and instructors giving specific requirements. In this chapter, we have opted to use the style guidelines of the American Psychological Association. This helps prepare students for a possible future as a user and producer of psychological research. It should be remembered that research is increasingly regarded as an important skill for practitioners and not just academic psychologists. No longer is research confined to universities; practitioner research is commonplace.

4.1 Overall strategy of report writing

Structure

A psychological research report normally consists of the following sections:

■ *Title page* This is the first page and contains the title, the author, and author details such as their address, e-mail address, telephone and fax number. For a student report, this will be replaced with details such as student ID number, degree programme name, and module name.

■ *Abstract* This is the second page of the report and you may use the subheading 'Abstract' for clarity. The abstract is a detailed summary of the contents of the report.

■ *Title* This is another new page – the title is repeated from the first page but *no* details as to authorship are provided. This is to make it easier for editors to send out the manuscript for anonymous review by other researchers.

■ *Introduction*   This continues on the same page but normally the subheading 'Introduction' is omitted.

■ *Method*   This consists of the following sections at a minimum:
   – participants
   – materials, measures or apparatus
   – procedure.

■ *Results*   This includes statistical analyses, tables and diagrams.

■ *Discussion*   This goes into a detailed explanation of the findings presented under results. It can be quite conjectural.

■ *Conclusion*   These are usually contained within the discussion section and are not usually a separate sub-heading. Nevertheless, sometimes conclusions are provided in a separate section.

■ *References*   One usually starts a new page for these. It is an alphabetical (then chronological if necessary) list of the sources that one has cited in the body of the text.

■ *Appendices*   This is an optional section and is relatively rare in professional publications. Usually it contains material which is helpful but would be confusing to incorporate in the main body of the text.

This is the basic, standard structure which underlies the majority of research reports. However, sometimes other sections are included where appropriate. Similarly, sometimes sections of the report are merged *if* this actually improves clarity. The different sections of the structure are presented in detail later in this chapter.

   While these different components may be regarded as distinct elements of the report, that they are integrated into a whole is a characteristic of a skilfully written report. In practice, this means that even the title should characterise the entire report. With only a few words at your disposal for the title this is difficult but quite a lot can be done. Similarly the discussion needs to integrate with the earlier components such as the introduction to give a sense of completeness and coherence. The title is probably the first thing read so it is crucial to orientating the reader to the content of the report. The abstract (summary) gives an overview of all aspects of the research so clarity not only creates a good impression but helps reassure the reader that the report and the research it describes are of a high quality.

Overall writing style

Clarity is essential since there is a great deal of information contained within a research report. The material contained in the report should be geared to the major theme of the report. This is particularly the case with the introduction in which the research literature is reviewed. It is a bad mistake to simply review research in the chosen field and fail to integrate your choice with the particular aspects addressed by your research.

   A number of stylistic points should be remembered:

■ Keep sentences short and as simple as possible. Sentences of eight to ten words are probably the optimum. Check carefully for sentences over 20 words in length. The reader has forgotten the beginning of the sentence by the time the end is reached! With modern word processing it is possible to check for sentence length. In Microsoft Word, for example, the spelling and grammar check does this – and it is possible to get readability statistics by selecting the appropriate option. If you have the slightest problem about sentence length then you should consider using this facility. (Readability statistics are based on things like average sentence length. As such they provide a numerical indication of stylistic inadequacies.)

■ It is useful to use subheadings (as well as the conventional headings). The reason for this is that subheadings indicate precisely what should be under that subheading – and what should not be. *Even if you delete the subheadings before submitting the final report*, you will benefit by having a report in which the material is in meaningful order. If you think that your draft report is unclear, try to put in subheadings. Often this will help you spot just where the material has got out of order. Then it is a much easier job to put it right.

■ It is normally inappropriate to use personal pronouns such as 'I' and 'we' in a research report. However, care needs to be taken as this can lead to lengthy passive sentences. In an effort to avoid 'We gave the participants a questionnaire to complete.' the result can be the following passive sentence: 'Participants were given a questionnaire to complete.' It would be better to use a more active sentence structure such as 'Participants completed a questionnaire.' This is shorter by far. In the active sentence it is the subject that performs the action; for example, 'We [SUBJECT] wrote [VERB] the report [OBJECT]'. In a passive sentence the subject suffers the action, as in 'The report [SUBJECT] was written [VERB]'.

■ The dominant tense in the research report is the past tense. This is because the bulk of the report describes completed activities in the past (e.g. 'The questionnaire measured two different components of loneliness.'). That is, the activities completed by the researcher in the process of collecting, analysing and interpreting the data took place in the past and are no longer ongoing. But other tenses are sometimes used. The present tense is often used to describe the current beliefs of researchers (e.g. 'It is generally considered that loneliness consists of two major components . . .'). Put this idea into the past tense and the implications are clearly different (e.g. 'It was generally considered that loneliness consists of two major components . . .'). The future tense is also used sometimes (e.g. 'Clarification of the reasons for the relationship between loneliness and lack of social support will help clinicians plan treatment strategies.').

■ Remember that the tables and diagrams included in the report need to communicate as clearly and effectively as the text. Some readers will focus on tables and diagrams before reading the text since these give a quick overview what the research and the research findings are about. Too many tables and diagrams are not helpful and every table and diagram should be made as clear as possible by using headings and clear labels.

■ Avoid racist and sexist language, and other demeaning and otherwise offensive language about minority groups. The inclusion of this in a professional research report may result in the rejection of the article or substantial revision to eliminate such material. See Box 4.1.

■ Numbers are expressed as 27, 3, 7, etc. in most of the text except where they occur as the first words of the sentence. In this case, we would write; 'Twenty seven airline pilots and 35 cabin crew completed the alcoholism scale.'

■ It is a virtue to keep the report reasonably compact. Do not waffle or put in material simply because you have it available. It is not desirable to exceed word limits so sometimes material has to be omitted. It is not uncommon to find that excess length can be trimmed simply by judicious editing of the text. A quarter or even a third of words can be edited out if necessary.

■ Do *not* include quotations from other authors except in those cases where it undesirable to omit them. This is particularly the case when one wishes to dispute what a previous writer has written. In this instance, only by quoting the origin can its nuances be communicated.

■ Generally introductions are the longest section of a research report. Some authorities suggest about a third of the available space should be devoted to the introduction. Of course, adjustments have to be made according to circumstances. Research which collects data on numerous variables may need to devote more space to the results section.

■ A rule of thumb is to present the results of calculations to no more than two decimal places. There is a danger of spuriously implying a greater degree of accuracy than psychological data usually possess. Whatever you do, be consistent. You need to understand how to properly round to 2 decimals. Basically, if the original number ends with a figure of 5 or above then we round up, otherwise we round down. So 21.455 gives 21.46 rounded whereas 21.454 gives 21.45 rounded.

■ Psychological terms may not have a standard definition which would be accepted by all researchers. Consequently, you may find it necessary to define how you are using terms in your report. Always remember that definitions in psychology are rarely definitive and they are often problematic in themselves.

■ Layout: Double space your work and word-process it. Leave wide margins for comments. Use underlining or bold for headings and subheadings. The underlying assumption behind this is that the report is being reviewed by another person. A report which won't be commented upon would not require double spacing.

■ Check your paragraphs. Break up any very long paragraphs. Combine very short paragraphs especially those of just one or two sentences in length.

BOX 4.1 AVOIDING BIAS IN LANGUAGE

Racism, sexism, homophobia and hostility to minorities such as people with disabilities are against the ethics of psychologists. The use of racist and sexist language is to be avoided in research reports. Indeed, such language may result in the material being rejected for publication. We would stress that the avoidance of racist and sexist language cannot fully be reduced to a list of dos and don'ts. The reason is that racism and sexism can manifest themselves in a multiplicity of different forms and those forms may well change with time. For example, Howitt and Owusu-Bempah (1994) trace the history of racism in psychology and how the ways it is manifest have changed over time. While it is easy to see the appalling racism of psychology from a century ago, it is far harder to understand its operation in present day psychology. For detailed examples of how the writings of psychologists may reinforce racism see Owusu-Bempah and Howitt (1995) and Howitt and Owusu-Bempah (1990).

→

Box 4.1 continued

Probably the first step towards the elimination of racism and sexism in psychological research is for researchers to undergo racism and sexism awareness training. This is increasingly available in universities and many work locations. In this way, not only will the avoidance of offensive language be helped but, more important, the inadvertent propagation of racist and sexist ideas through research will be made much more difficult.

A few examples of avoidable language use follow:

■ Writing things like 'the black sample . . .' can readily be modified to the sample of black people . . .' or, if you prefer, 'the sample of people of colour . . .' In this way, the most important characteristic is drawn attention to – the fact that you are referring to people first and foremost who also happen to be black. You might also wish to ask why one needs to refer to the race of people at all.

■ Avoid references to the racial (or gender) characteristics of participants which are irrelevant to the substance of the report. For example, 'Female participant Y was a black lone-parent . . .'. Not only does this contain the elements of a stereotypical portrayal of black people as being associated with father absence and 'broken families', but the race of the participant may be totally irrelevant to what the report is about.

■ Do not refer to man, mankind or social man, for example. These terms do not make people think of man and woman but of men only. Words like 'people' can be substituted. Similarly referring to 'he' contributes to the invisibility of women and so such terms should not be used.

Of course, the use of demeaning and similar language is not confined to race and gender. Homophobic language and writings are similarly to be avoided. Equally, careful thought and consideration should be given when writing about any disadvantaged or discriminated against group. So people with disabilities should be treated with dignity in the choice of language and terms used. So, for example, the phrase 'disabled people' is not acceptable and should be replaced with 'people with disabilities'.

The website of the American Psychological Association contains in-depth material on these topics – race and ethnicity, gender and disabilities. Should your report touch on any of these, you are well advised to consult the Association's guidance. The following location deals with race and ethnicity and there are links to gender and disabilities:

<http://www.apastyle.org/race.html>

4.2 The sections of the research report in detail

Title

The title is *not* used as a heading or subheading. Often it is given twice – once on the title page and again just before the Introduction.

The title of a research report serves two main purposes:

■ To attract the attention of potential readers. This is especially the case for professional research reports since the potential reader probably comes across the title either in a database or by browsing through the contents of a journal.

■ To inform the reader of the major features of the research paper In other words, it amounts to a summary of the contents of the research report in no more than about 12 words (although 20 words might be used if necessary). This includes any subheading. It requires a good understanding of your research before you can write a good title. It is a good discipline to try to write a title even before you have finished the research. This may need honing into shape since initial attempts are often a little clumsy and too wordy. Enlist the help of others who are familiar with your research as they may be able to help you to rephrase your initial efforts. The key thing is that the reader gains a broad idea of the contents of the report from the title.

The following suggestions may help you write a clear and communicative title for your work:

■ Phrases such as 'A study of . . .', 'An investigation into . . .', and 'An experiment investigating . . .' would normally not be included in well written titles since they are not really informative and take up precious words. They should be struck out in normal circumstances.

■ Avoid clever or tricky titles which, at best, merely attract attention. So titles like 'The journey out of darkness' for a report on the effectiveness of therapy for depression fails the informativeness test. It may be a good title for a novel but not a psychological research report. Better titles might include 'Effectiveness of cognitive behavioural therapy in recovery from depression during long-term imprisonment'. This title includes a great deal of information compared with 'The journey out of darkness'. In our new title, we know that the key dependent variable is depression, that the population being researched is long-term prisoners, and that the key independent variable is cognitive behavioural therapy. Occasionally you may come across a title which is tricky or over-clever but nevertheless communicates well. For example, one of us published a paper with the title 'Attitudes do predict behaviour – in mails at least'. The first four words clearly state the overriding theme of the paper. The last four words do not contain a misprint but an indication that the paper refers to letter post. Another example is 'Deception among pairs: "Let's say we had lunch and hope they will swallow it!" ' All in all, the best advice is to avoid being this smart.

■ If all else fails, one can concentrate on the major hypothesis being tested in the study (if there is one). Titles based on this approach would have a rudimentary structure something like 'The effects of (variable A) on (variable B). Alternative,' The relationship between (variable A) and (variable B). A published example of this is 'The effects of children's age and delay on recall in a cognitive or structured interview'. The basic structure can be elaborated as in the following published example: 'Effects of pretrial juror bias, strength of evidence and deliberation process on juror decisions: New validity evidence of the juror bias scale scores'. The phrase 'Effects of . . .' may create some confusion. It may mean 'the causal effect of variable A on variable B' but not necessarily so. Often it means 'the relationship between variable A and variable B'. 'The effects of' and 'the relationship between' are sometimes used interchangeably. It is preferable to restrict 'Effects of' to true experiments and 'Relationships between' to non-experiments.

Abstract

The abstract is best given this heading in a student's report although this is not normally done in psychology journals. Since the abstract is a summary of many aspects of the research report, normally it is written after the main body of the report has been drafted. This helps prevent the situation in which the abstract refers to things *not* actually in the main body of the report. Since the abstract is crucially important, expect to write several drafts before it takes its final shape. The brevity of the abstract is one major reason for the difficulty.

The abstract is a (fairly detailed) summary of *all* aspects of the research report. It is usually limited to a maximum number of words. This maximum may vary, but limits of 100 to 200 words are typical. The APA recommends 120 words for journal articles. With space available for only ten to twenty short sentences, inevitably the summary has to be selective. Do *not* cope with the word limit by concentrating on just one or two aspects of the whole report – e.g. the hypotheses and the data collection method used would be insufficient on their own. When writing an abstract you should take each of the major sections of the report in turn and summarise the key features of each. There is an element of judgement in this but a well written abstract will give a good overview of the contents of the report.

It is increasingly common to find 'structured abstracts'. The structure may vary but a good structure is four subheadings:

Purpose
Methods
Results
Conclusions.

This structure ensures that the abstract covers the major components of the research.

Although this does not apply to student research reports, the abstract (apart from the title) is likely to be all that potential readers have available in the first instance. Databases of publications in psychology and other academic disciplines usually include the title and the abstract. Hence, the abstract is very important in a literature search – it is readily available to the researcher whereas obtaining the actual research report may require some effort. Most students and researchers will be able to obtain abstracts almost instantly by using Internet connections to databases. A badly written abstract may deter some researchers from reading the original research report and may cause others to waste effort obtaining a report which is not quite what they expected it to be. The clearer and more comprehensive the information in the abstract, the more effective will be the decision of whether or not to obtain the original paper.

The other function of the abstract is that it provides a structure for when one is reading the entire paper. In other words, the reader will know what to expect and this speeds up and simplifies the task of reading. Since first impressions are important, writing the abstract should not be regarded as a drudgery but an opportunity to establish the value of the research. Get it wrong, and the reader may get the impression that you are confused and muddled. Bad news if that person is giving you a grade or possibly considering your work for possible publication.

You will find examples of abstracts in any psychology journal and on the website associated with this textbook (www.pearsoned.co.uk/howitt).

BOX 4.2   IMPORTANT THINGS
TO SUMMARISE IN THE ABSTRACT

Ideally, the following should be outlined in the abstract but normally subheadings are *not* used except in structured abstracts though this rule may be broken if necessary. They are given here simply for purposes of clarity. They relate to the major subheadings of the report itself:

■ *Introduction*   This is a brief statement justifying the research and explaining the purpose followed by a short statement of the research question or the main hypotheses. The justification may be in terms of the social or practical utility of the research, its relevance to theory, or even the absence of previous research. The research question or hypotheses will also be given. Probably no more than 30% of the abstract will be such introductory material.

■ *Method*   This a broad orientation to the type of research that was carried out. Often a simple phrase will be sufficient to orient the reader to the style of research in question. So phrases like 'Brain activity was studied using PET (positron emission tomography) and FMRI (functional magnetic resonance imaging). . . .', 'A controlled experiment was conducted . . .', 'The interview transcripts were analysed using discourse analysis . . .', and 'A survey was conducted . . .' suggest a great deal about the way in which the research was carried out without being wordy.

■ *Participants*   This will consist of essential detail about the sample(s) employed. For example, 'Interview data from an opportunity sample consisting of young carers of older relatives was compared with a sample of young people entering the labour market for the first time, matched for age'.

■ *Procedure*   This should identify the main measures employed. For example, 'Loneliness was assessed using the shortened UCLA loneliness scale. A new scale was developed to measure social support'. By stipulating the important measures employed one also identifies the key variables. For an experiment, in addition it would be appropriate to describe how the different conditions were created (i.e. manipulated). For example, 'Levels of hunger were manipulated by asking participants to refrain from eating or drinking for 1 hour, 3 hours and 6 hours prior to the experiment'.

■ *Results*   There is no space in an abstract for elaborate presentations of the statistical analyses that the researcher may have carried out. Typically, however, broad indications are given of the style of analysis. For example, 'Factor analysis of the 20 item anxiety scale revealed two main factors', 'The groups were compared using a mixed-design ANOVA' or 'Binomial multiple regression revealed five main factors which differentiated men and women'. Now these statistical techniques may be meaningless to you at the moment but they will not be to most researchers. They refer to very distinct types of analysis so the terms are very informative to researchers. In addition, the major findings of the statistical analysis need to be reported. Normally this will be the important,

→

Box 4.2 continued

statistically significant features of the data analysis. Of course, sometimes the lack of significance is the most important thing to draw attention to in the abstract. There is no need and normally no space to use the succinct methods of the reporting of statistics in the abstract. So things like ($t = 2.43$, df $= 17$, $p < 0.05$) are rare in abstracts and best omitted.

■ *Discussion*   In an abstract, the discussion (and conclusions) needs to be confined to the main things that the reader should take away from the research. As ever, there are a number of ways of doing this. If you have already stated the hypothesis then you need do little other than confirm whether or not this was supported, given any limitations you think are important concerning your research, and possibly mention any crucial recommendations for further research activity in the field.

Introduction

Usually, the introduction to a report is *not* given a heading or subheading – to do so merely states the obvious. The introduction sets the scene for the research, the analysis and discussion which follow it. In effect, it is an explanation of why your chosen research topic deserved researching and the importance of the particular aspect of the topic you have chosen to focus on.

Explanations or justifications for a particular research topic include the following:

■ There is a need to empirically test ideas that have been developed in theoretical discussions of the topic. In other words, the advancement of theory may be offered as full or partial reasons for engaging in research.

■ There is a pressing concern over a particular issue which can be informed by empirical data. Often social research is carried out into issues of public concern but the stimulus may, instead, come from the concerns of organisations such as health services, industry and commerce, the criminal justice system, and so forth.

■ There is an unresolved issue arising out of previous research on a topic which may be illuminated by further research – especially research which constructively replicates the earlier research.

Just being interested in the topic is not a good or sufficient reason for doing research in academic terms. You should make the intellectual case for doing the research not the personal case for doing so.

The introduction contains a *pertinent* review of previous research and publications on the topic in question, partly to justify the new research. One explains the theoretical issues, the problems with previous research, or even the pressing public interest by reference to what other researchers have done and written before. Research is regarded as part of a collective enterprise in which each individual contribution is part and builds on the totality. The keyword is *pertinent* – or relevant – previous research and publications. Just writing vaguely about the topic of the research using any material that is to hand is not appropriate. The literature that you need to incorporate is that which most directly leads to the research that you have carried out and are about to describe later in the report. In other words, the literature review needs to be in tune with the general thrust of your research. That it is vaguely relevant is not a good reason for the inclusion of anything and you may well find that an unfocused review is counterproductive.

Students sometimes face problems stemming from their use of secondary sources – for example, a description given in a textbook. This may contain very little detail about, say, a particular study or theory. As a consequence, the student lacks information when they write about the study or theory. Often they introduce errors because they read into the secondary source things that they would not if they had read the original source. There is no easy way around this other than reading sources that cover the topic in depth. Ideally this will be the original source but some secondary sources are better than others.

The introduction should consistently and steadily lead to a statement of the aims of your research and to the hypotheses (though there is some research for which hypotheses are either not possible or are inappropriate). There is a difference between the aims and the hypotheses. Aims are broad, hypotheses more specific. For example, 'the aim of this study was to investigate gender differences in conversation' might include the hypothesis 'Males will interrupt more than females in mixed-gender dyads'.

It is usually suggested that the introduction should be written in the past tense. This may generally be the case but is not always so. The past perfect tense describes activities which were completed in the past. I ran home, the car broke down, the CD finished playing are all examples of the past tense. However, it is not always possible to use the past tense – sometimes to do so would produce silly or confusing writing. For example, the sentence 'The general consensus among researchers is that loneliness is a multifaceted concept' is in the present tense. The past tense cannot convey the same meaning. 'The general consensus among researchers was that loneliness is a multifaceted concept' actually implies that this is no longer the general consensus. Hence one needs to be aware of the pitfalls of the present tense for communicating certain ideas. However since most of the material in the introduction refers to completed actions in the past then most of it will be in the past tense. Sentences like, 'Smith and Hardcastle (1976) showed that intelligence cannot be adequately assessed using motor skills alone' refer to past events. Similarly, 'Haig (2004) argued for the inclusion of "waiting list" control groups in studies of the effectiveness of counselling' cannot be expressed well using a different tense.

Putting all of this together, a typical structure of an introduction is as follows:

■ A brief description of the topic of the research.
■ Key concepts and ideas should be explained in some detail or defined if this is possible.
■ Criticisms of aspects of the relevant research literature together with synthesis where the literature clearly leads to certain conclusions.
■ A review of the most important and relevant aspects of the research literature:
  – Theoretical matters pertinent to the research
  – Describe and discuss as necessary the key variables to be explored in your research

List your aims and hypotheses as summary statements at the end of the introduction.

Method

This is a major heading. The method section can be tricky to write since the overall strategy is to provide sufficient information for another researcher to replicate your study precisely. At the same time, the minutiae of the procedures that you carried out are not

BOX 4.3 ABBREVIATIONS

Abbreviations should be used with caution in a research report. Their main advantage is brevity. Before the days of computerisation, typesetting was very expensive, and the use of abbreviations saved some considerable expense. This is no longer really the case. Student writing rarely benefits from the use of abbreviations. If they are used badly or inappropriately, then they risk confusing the reader who may then feel that the student is confused.

The major disadvantage of abbreviations is that they hamper communications and readability. Ss, DV, *n*, Sd and SS are examples of abbreviations that sometimes were included in reports. The trouble is that we assume that the reader knows what the abbreviations refer to. If the reader is not familiar with the abbreviation then their use hampers rather than aids communication and clarity. The problem is not solved simply by stating the meaning of the abbreviation early in the report (e.g. The dependent variable (DV) was mental wonderment (MW)). The reader may not read your definition or they may forget the meaning of the abbreviation the next time it appears. Acronyms for organisations can similarly tax readers unnecessarily. This is because acronyms are commonly used by those involved with an organisation but an outside reader may be unfamiliar with their use. We recommend only using abbreviations in exceptional circumstances and where their use is conventional – as when you succinctly report your statistical findings (e.g. $t = 2.3$, df = 27, $p = 0.05$).

BOX 4.4 IVs AND DVs – INDEPENDENT AND DEPENDENT VARIABLES

In student research reports, it is common to identify what variable(s) is the IV (independent variable) and what variable(s) is the DV (dependent variable). This is much less common in professional research reports. In general, it is probably a useful thing for students new to research to do. However, it is something that few professional researchers do and, consequently, might best be left out as soon as possible. The problem in professional research is that the IVs and DVs are often interchangeable. This is especially the case in regression analyses. The independent variable is the variable which is expected to affect the value of the dependent variable. There is no necessary assumption that there is a causal link at all. In controlled experiments (see Chapter 7) the IV or independent variable is always the variable(s) defined by the experimental manipulation(s). So if the level of anger in participants is manipulated by the experimenter then anger level is the IV or independent variable. In an experiment, any variables which might be expected to be affected by varying the level of anger or any other independent variable is called a dependent variable (DV). The dependent variable is the one for which we calculate the means and standard deviations, etc. In a controlled or randomised experiment, the effect of the independent variable on the dependent variable is regarded as causal. In this case, the dependent variable is expected to have a direct effect on the scores of the dependent variable. In non-randomised research, all that is established is that there is an association or relationship between the independent and dependent variable.

included. Clearly getting the balance between what to include and what to omit is difficult. Too much detail and the report becomes unclear and difficult to read. Too little detail and significant aspects of the research may be difficult for other researchers to reproduce. Really the task is to describe your methods in sufficient detail that the reader has a clear understanding of what you did – they could probably replicate the research, more or less. In a sense it is rather like a musical score – broadly speaking the musicians will know what and how to play, but they will have to fill in some of the detail themselves.

Nevertheless, it is inevitable that the method section contains a greater density of detail than most other sections, which tend to summarise and take an overview.

The method section may include as many as six or more sections if the procedures are especially complex. These include:

■ participants (sometimes archaically referred to as subjects)
■ materials or apparatus (or even both)
■ procedure (always)
■ design (possibly)
■ stimuli (if these require detailed description)
■ ethical considerations (recommended).

Of these, design and stimuli would only be used if the research is especially complex in these respects – it is a matter of judgement whether to include them or not. One approach would be to include them in the early draft of your report. If they seem unnecessary or if you write very little under them (just a few sentences) then they can be combined quickly with a few mouse clicks on the word processor. An ethical considerations section is becoming increasingly common and is required in some professional writings. While students should not carry out any research which does not use well established, ethically-sound procedures, including an ethics section demonstrates that the ethical standing of the research has been considered.

Normally the methods heading is given as a major title, perhaps centralised and under-lined or in bold, the section headings are subheadings and are aligned to the left margin. It is usual to go straight from the methods heading to the participants subheading. No preamble is required.

Participants

This section should contain sufficient information so that the reader knows how many participants you had in total, how many participants were in each condition of the study, and sufficient detail about the characteristics of the participants to make it clear what the limitations on generalising the findings are likely to be. Given that much student research is conducted on other students, often the description will be brief in these cases. It is old-fashioned (and misleading; see Box 4.5) to refer to those taking part in your research as subjects. Avoid doing so. Once in a while the word subjects will occur in relation to particular statistical analyses which traditionally used the term (e.g. related-subjects analysis of variance).

We would normally expect to include the following information to describe the participants:

■ The total number of participants.
■ The numbers of participants in each of the groups or conditions of the study.
■ The gender distribution of the participants.

- The average age of the participants (group by group if they are not randomly allocated to conditions) together with an appropriate measure of the spread of the characteristic (e.g. standard deviation, variance or standard error – these are equally understandable to most researchers and more-or-less equivalent in this context).

- Major characteristics of the participants or groups of participants. Often this will be university students but other research may have different participant characteristics – e.g. pre-school children, visitors to a health farm, etc. These may also be presented in numerical form as frequencies.

- How the participants were contacted or recruited initially.

- How the participants were selected for the research. Rarely are participants formally sampled using random sampling in psychological research. Convenience sampling is much more common (see Chapter 11).

- It is good practice, but not common, to give some indication of refusal rates and drop out rates for the participants. Refusal rates are the numbers who are asked to take part in the research but say no. Drop-out rates are the numbers who initially take part in the research but for some reason fail to complete all of the stages. Sometimes this is known alarmingly as 'the mortality rate' or the 'experimental mortality'.

- Any inducements or rewards given to participants to take part in the study. So, for example, being given monetary rewards or course credits would be mentioned.

BOX 4.5 NO SUBJECTS – JUST PARTICIPANTS

One of the most misleading terms ever in psychology was the concept of 'subject'. Monarchs have subjects, psychologists do not. In the early days of psychological research, terms like reactors, observers, experimentees and individuals under experiment were used. Danziger (1985) points out that these early research studies used other professors, students and friends which may explain the lack of use of the slightly hostile term 'subjects'. Although the term subjects had a long history in psychological writing, the term is inadequate because it gives a false picture of the people who take part in research. The term implies a powerful researcher and a manipulated subject. Research has long-since dispelled this myth – people who take part in research are not passive but actively involve themselves in the research process. They form hypotheses about the researcher's hypotheses, for example. As a consequence they must be regarded as active contributors in the research process. In the 1990s, psychological associations such as the American Psychological Association and the British Psychological Society recommended/insisted on the modern terminology for their journals.

Materials/apparatus

The materials or apparatus section describes psychological tests, other questionnaire measures, laboratory equipment and other such resources which are essential components of the research. Once again the idea is to supply enough detail so that another researcher could essentially replicate the study and the reader gains a clear impression of the questionnaire, tests and equipment used. These requirements allow for a degree of individual interpretation, but experience at writing and considering other people's writings in research journals, especially, will help improve your style and hone the level of detail that you provide. Remember that the degree of detail you go into should be sufficient to help the reader contextualise your research but not so detailed that the wood cannot be seen for the trees. So trivial detail should be omitted – things like the make of the stopwatch used, the colour of the biro given to participants, and the physical dimensions of the research setting (laboratory, for example) – would not normally be given. However, where these minutiae are relevant then they should be included. If the study were, for example, into the effects of stress on feelings of claustrophobia then the physical dimensions of the laboratory would be very important. Provide the name and address of suppliers of extremely specialised laboratory equipment, for example, but not for commonplace items such as stopwatches. When using computers in psychological research, details of the software used to present experimental stimuli, for example, would normally be given.

It would also be usual to give details of any psychological tests employed. This would probably include the official name of the test, the number of items, broadly what sorts of items are employed, the response format, maybe information about its reliability and validity, and any adjustments or alterations you may have made to the psychological test. Of course, you may be developing your own psychological measures (see Chapter 12), in which case more detail should be provided about the items included in the questionnaire and so forth. It is unlikely that you would include the full test or measure in the description though this may be included in an appendix. The method section is normally the place where one outlines how questionnaires etc. were quantified or coded.

Remember that the materials and apparatus are related to the variables being measured and the procedures being employed. Hence, it is important to clearly structure this section so that the reader will gain a good understanding of the key aspects of the study. In other words, an organised description of the materials and apparatus communicates key features of the research procedures and design. Jumble this section and your reader will have trouble in understanding the research clearly.

Procedure

Under the subheading *Procedure* one describes the essential sequence of events through which you put participants in your research. The keyword is sequence and this implies a chronological order. It is a good idea to list the major steps in your research before writing the procedure. This will help you get the key stages in order – and proportional to their importance. The instructions given to participants in the research should be given and variations in the contents of these instructions (e.g. between experimental and control group) should be described. Do not forget to include debriefing and similar aspects of the research in this section.

Also you should mention any randomisation that was involved – random allocation to conditions, for example, or randomisation of the order of presentation of materials or stimuli.

It is difficult to recommend a length for the procedure section since studies vary enormously in their complexity of administration. A complex laboratory experiment may take rather more space to describe than a study of the differences in mathematical ability in male and female psychology students. Of course, a great deal of research uses procedures which are very similar to those of previous research studies in that field. By checking through earlier studies you should gain a better idea of what to include and exclude – this is not an invitation to plagiarise the work of others.

Finally, it may be appropriate to describe broadly the strategy of the statistical analysis especially, for example, if specialised computer programmes or statistics are employed.

Design

The additional subheading *Design* might be included if the research design is very complex. A diagram may be appropriate if it is difficult to explain in words alone. The design subheading may be desirable when one has a complex analysis of variance (ANOVA) design, for example (see Chapters 7 and 8).

Results

The results section also has a main heading. Like many other aspects of the report, it is largely written in the past tense. The results section is mainly about the outcome of the statistical analysis of your data. Statistical outcomes of your research are *not* the same as the psychological interpretation of your statistical findings. Statistical analysis is rather more limited than psychological analysis which involves the development of psychological knowledge and theory. Thus the outcomes of your analyses should normally be reported without conjecture about what they mean – you simply say what the findings *are*. That is, say that there is a difference in the means of two groups or a correlation between two variables. Draw no further inferences than that there is a relationship or a difference. Since the statistical analysis is often related to the hypotheses, it is perfectly appropriate to present the results hypothesis by hypothesis. It is also appropriate to indicate whether the statistical evidence supports or fails to support each of the hypotheses.

The results section will vary in length according, in part, to the numbers of variables and type of statistical analysis employed. It is not usual to go into a detailed description of the statistical tests used – just the outcome of applying them. There is no need to mention how the computations were done. If you used a statistical package such as SPSS (Statistical Package for the Social Services) then there is no need to mention this fact – or even that you did your calculations using a calculator.

One common difficulty occurs when the standard structure is applied to research which does not involve hypothesis or theory testing. That is, largely, when we are not carrying out laboratory experiments. Sometimes it is very difficult to separate the description of the results of the study from a discussion of those results (i.e. the next section). Ultimately, clarity of communication has to take precedence over the standard conventions and some blurring of the boundaries of the standard structure for reports may be necessary.

Statistical analyses, almost without exception in psychology, consist of two components:

■ Descriptive statistics which describe the characteristics of your data. For example, the means and standard deviations of all of your variables, where appropriate.

■ Inferential statistics which indicate the relationship between the variables in your analysis. These are used to assess the adequacy of your analysis. Statistics such as the correlation coefficient and *t*-test are examples of the sorts of inferential statistics that beginning researchers use.

Both descriptive and inferential statistics should be included in the results section though not to the extent that they simply cloud the issues. The statistical analysis is not a description of everything that you did with the data but the crucial steps in terms of reaching the conclusions that you draw.

Conventionally, the raw, unprocessed data are *not* included in the results section. The means, standard deviations and other characteristics of the variables are given instead. This convention is difficult to justify other than on the basis of the impracticality of including large data sets in a report. Students should always consider including their raw data in an appendix. All researchers should remember the ethical principle of the APA which requires that they should make available their data to any other researcher who has a legitimate reason to verify their findings.

Tables and diagrams are common in the results section. They are not decorations. They are a means of communicating one's findings to others. We suggest a few rules-of-thumb for consideration:

■ Keep the number of tables and diagrams to a minimum. If you include too many they become confusing. Worse still, they become irritating. For example, giving separate tables for many very similar variables can exhaust the reader. Far better to have fewer tables and diagrams but ones which can allow comparisons, say, between the variables in your study.

■ Always take care about titling and labelling your tables and diagrams. If the title and labels are unclear then the whole table or diagram becomes unclear. It is easy to use misleading or clumsy labels so check them.

■ Some readers will look at tables and diagrams before reading your text. So for them the quality of the tables and diagrams is even more important. Those used to statistical analyses will be drawn to such tables as they often are quicker to absorb than what you say about the data in the text.

■ Tables and diagrams should be numbered.

■ Tables and diagrams *must* be referred to in your text. At the very least you need to say what the table or diagram indicates – the important features of the table or diagram.

■ Tables and diagrams are readily created in SPSS, Excel and other computer programs. The difficulty is that the basic versions (the default options) of tables and diagrams are often unclear or in some other way inadequate. They need editing to make them sufficiently clear. Tables may need simplifying to make them more accessible to the reader. Much student work is spoilt by the use of computer generated tables and diagrams without modification. Think very carefully before using any unmodified output from a computer program.

A glance at any psychology research journal will indicate that relatively little space is devoted to presenting the key features of each statistical analysis. Succinct methods are used which provide the key elements of the analysis simply and clearly. These are discussed in detail in the companion book *Introduction to Statistics in Psychology*, Chapter 16 (Howitt and Cramer, 2005*a*). Basically the strategy is to report the statistical test used, the sample size or the degrees of freedom, and the level of statistical significance. So you will see things like:

$(t = 2.37, \mathrm{df} = 14, p = 0.05)$
$(t = 2.37, N = 16, p < 0.05)$
$(t = 2.37, \mathrm{df} = 1, p = 5\%)$

All of these are much the same. They give the statistic used, an indication of the sample size(s) or degrees of freedom (df), and the level of statistical significance.

Discussion

This is a main heading. The past tense will dominate the discussion section but you will also use the present and future tenses from time to time. It all depends on what it is you are writing about. The material in the discussion should not simply rehash that in the introduction. You may need to move material between the introduction and the discussion sections to ensure this. It may be a fairly arbitrary matter whether a previous study is included in the discussion rather than the introduction. A research report is no place to be repetitive.

If your study tested a hypothesis, then the discussion is likely to begin with a statement indicating whether or not your hypothesis was supported by the statistical analysis (i.e. the results). Remember that most statistical analyses are based on samples and so the findings are probabilistic not absolute. Consequently, researchers can only find their hypotheses to be supported or not supported. Research based on samples (i.e. all research) cannot definitely establish the hypothesis' truth or falsity since a different sample might produce different outcomes. Consequently it grates to read that the hypothesis was 'proved' or 'not proved'.

Your research findings should be related to those of previous research. They may completely, partially or not support those of previous studies. The differences between the current research and past research should be described as well as the similarities. Sometimes, previous research findings may cast light on the findings of your study. Where there is a disparity between the new findings and previous findings, attempts should be made to explain the disparity. Different types of sample, for example, may be the explanation though it may not be as simple as that. In the discussion section one has new findings as well as older ones from previous research. The task is to explain how our knowledge is extended or enhanced or complicated by the new findings. It may be that the new findings tend to support one interpretation of implications of the previous research rather than another. This should be drawn out.

Of course there may be methodological features which may explain the disparity between the new and older findings. Notice that we use the term methodological features rather than methodological flaws. The influence of methodological differences cuts both ways – your research may have problems and strengths but the previous research may have had other problems and strengths. Try to identify what these may be. Accuracy in identifying the role of methodological features is important since vague, unspecified suggestions leave the reader unclear as to what you regard as the key differences between studies. Try to identify the role of methodological features as accurately and precisely as you can – merely pointing out that the samples are different is not very helpful. Better to explain the ways in which the sample differences could produce the differences in the findings. That is, make sure that it is clear why methodological factors might affect the findings differentially. And, of course, it is ideal if you can recommend improvements to your methodology.

Try not to include routine commonplaces. The inclusion of phrases such as 'A larger sample size may result in different findings' is not much of a contribution – especially when you have demonstrated large trends in your data.

The discussion should not simply refer back to the previous research, it should include the theoretical implications which may be consequent on your findings. Perhaps the theory is not quite so rigorous as you initially thought. There may be implications of your findings. Perhaps you could suggest further research or practical applications.

Finally, the discussion should lead to your conclusions. This should be the main things that the reader should take away from your research. It is not normal to include a separate heading for the conclusions.

References

This a major heading and should start on a fresh page. Academic disciplines consider it important to provide evidence in support of all aspects of the argument that you are making. This can clearly be seen in research reports. The research evidence itself and your interpretation of it is perhaps the most obvious evidence for your argument. However, your report will make a lot of claims over and above this. You will claim that the relevant theory suggests something, that previous studies indicate something else, and so forth. In order for the reader of your report to be in a position to check the accuracy or truth of your claims, it is essential to refer them to the sources of information and ideas that you use. Simply suggesting that 'research has found that' or 'it is obvious that' is not enough. So it is necessary to identify the source of your assertions. This includes two main components:

■ You cite your sources in the text as, say, (Donovan and Jenkins, 1663). 'Donovan and Jenkins' gives the name of the authors and 1663 is the date of publication (dissemination) of the work. There are many systems in use for giving citations, but in psychology it is virtually universal to use this author–date system. It is known as the Harvard system but there are variants of this and we will use the American Psychological Association's version which is the basis of those employed throughout the world by other psychological associations.

■ You provide an alphabetical list of references by the surname of the first author. There is a standard format for the references though this varies according to whether it is a book, a journal article, an Internet source and so forth. The reference contains sufficient information for a reader to track down and, in most cases, obtain a copy of the original document.

The citation

While the citation in the text seems to be very straightforward, there are a number of things that you need to remember:

■ The citation should be placed adjacent to the idea which it supports. Sometimes confusion can be caused because the citation is placed at the end of a sentence which contains more than one idea. In these circumstances, the reader may be misled about which of the ideas the citation concerns. For that reason, think very carefully about where you insert the citation. You may choose to put it part-way through the sentence.

■ Citations should be to *your* source of information. So if you read the information in Smith (2004) then you should cite this as the source really. The trouble is that Smith (2004) may be a secondary source which is explaining, say, Freud's theory of neurosis, Piaget's developmental stages, or the work of some other theorist or researcher. Students rarely have time or resources to read all of the original publication from which the idea came although it is a good idea to try. So although uncommon in professional report writing, student research reports will often contain citations such as (Piaget, 1953, cited in Atkinson, 2005). In this way the ultimate source of the idea is acknowledged but the actual source is also given. To attribute to Atkinson ideas which the reader might recognise as those of Piaget would cause great confusion and would be misleading anyway. In your reference list you would list Atkinson (2005) and also Piaget (1953).

■ Citations with several authors are given as Smith *et al.* (1776) with the et al followed by a full stop to indicate an abbreviation.

BOX 4.6 CITING WHAT YOU HAVEN'T ACTUALLY READ!

The basic rules of citations are clear. You indicate the source of the idea in the text just like this (Conqueror, 1066) and then put where the information was found in the reference list. This is all very well in theory but in practice causes problems in relation to student work. The difficulty is that the student may only have read textbooks or other secondary sources and they may not be able to get their hands on Conqueror (1066). Now one could simply cite the textbook from which the information came but this has problems. If one cites the secondary source it reads like the secondary source was actually responsible for the idea which they were not. So what does the student do?

There are three, probably equally acceptable, ways of doing this in student work:

■ In the main body of the text give the original source first followed by 'cited in' then the secondary source (Conqueror, 1066, cited in Bradley, 2004). Then in the reference list simply list Bradley (2004) in full in the usual way. This has the advantage of keeping the reference list short.

■ In the main body of the text give the original source (Conqueror, 1066). Then in the reference list insert

Conqueror, W. (1066). Visual acuity in fatally wounded monarchs. *Journal of Monocular Vision Studies*, 5 (3), 361–72. Cited in Bradley, M. (2004). *Introduction to Historical Psychology* (Hastings: Forlorn Hope Press).

This method allows one to note the full source of both the primary information and the secondary information.

■ In the main body of the text give the original source (Conqueror, 1066). Then in the reference list insert

Conqueror, W. (1066). Cited in Bradley, M. (2004). *Introduction to Historical Psychology* (Hastings: Forlorn Hope Press).

This is much the same as the previous version but the full details of the original source are not given.

It might be wise to check which version your lecturer/supervisor prefers. Stick to one method and do not mix them up together in your work.

■ Student writing (especially where they have carried out a literature review) can become very stilted because they write things like 'Brownlow (1989) argued that children's memories are very different from those of adults. Singh (1996) found evidence of this. Perkins and Ottaway (2002) confirmed Singh's findings in a group of seven-year-olds.' The problem with this is that the sentence structure is repetitive and the person who you are citing tends to appear more important than their ideas. It is a good idea to keep this structure to a minimum and bring their contributions to the fore. For example: 'Memory in children is different from that of adults (Brownlow, 1989). This was initially confirmed in pre-school children (Singh, 1996) and extended to seven-year-olds by Perkins and Ottaway (2002).' Both versions contain similar information but the second illustrates a greater range of stylistic possibilities.

■ When you cite several sources at the same time (Brownlow, 1989; Perkins and Ottaway, 2002; Singh, 2002, 2003) do so in alphabetical order (and then date order if necessary).

■ Sometimes an author (or authors) has published more than one thing in a particular year and you want to cite all of them. There may be two papers by Kerry Brownlow published in 1989. To distinguish them, the sources would be labelled Brownlow (1989*a*) and Brownlow (1989*b*). The alphabetical order of the title of the books or articles determines which is '*a*' and which is '*b*'. In the references, we include the '*a*' and '*b*' after the date so that the sources are clearly distinguished. Remember to do this as soon as possible to save you from having to re-read the two sources later to know which contains what. If you were citing both sources then you would condense things by putting (Brownlow, 1989*a*, *b*).

■ It is important to demonstrate that you have read up-to-date material. However, do not try to bamboozle your lecturers by inserting citations which you have not read in a misguided attempt to impress. Your lecturer won't always be taken in. There are many tell-tale signs such as citing obscure sources which are not in your university library.

Many of the problems associated with citations and reference lists can be avoided by using a reference and citation computer program. EndNote, for example, is basically a database in which you enter essential details such as the authors, the date of publication, the title of the publication, and the source of the publication. One can also insert notes as to the work's contents. It is also possible to download details of publications from some Internet databases of publications which can save a lot of typing. If you do this properly and systematically, it is possible to use the program in conjunction with a word processing program to insert citations at appropriate places and to generate a reference list. Even more useful is that the program will do the citations and reference list in the style of a particular publication. You can easily choose another style for another publication. Figure 4.1 overleaf shows a screen shot from EndNote which illustrates something of the information that can be recorded (or even downloaded from the Web) by the user.

The main problem with these programs is their cost. Bona fide students may get heavily discounted rates. Increasingly universities have site licences for this sort of bibliographic software so check before making any unnecessary expenditure.

Reference list

References will be a main heading at the end of the report. There is a difference between a list of references and a bibliography. The reference list only contains the sources which you cite in the main body of your report. Bibliographies are *not* usually included in research reports. A bibliography lists everything that you have read which is pertinent to the research report – even if it is not cited in the text. Normally just include the references you cite unless it is indicated to you to do otherwise.

Items in reference lists are *not* numbered in the Harvard system, they are merely given in alphabetical order by surname of the author.

One problem with reference lists is that the structure varies depending on the original source. The structure for books is different from the structure for journal articles. Both are different from the structure for Internet sources. Unpublished sources have yet another structure. In the world of professional researchers, this results in massive style guides for

---

Figure 4.1   EndNote Screen Shot

---

citing and referencing. Fortunately, the basic style for references boils down to just a few standard patterns. However, house styles of publishers differ. The house style of Pearson for example, as seen in the references at the end of this book differs slightly from that recommended here. We would recommend that you obtain examples of reference lists from journal articles and books which correspond to the approved style. This constitutes a compact style guide.

Normally journal names are underlined as are book titles. This is a printer's convention to indicate that emphasis should be added. In the final printed version, it is likely that what is underlined will appear in italics. If preparing a manuscript for publication, this convention should be followed. If it is a report or thesis then it is appropriate for you to use italics for emphasis instead of the underline. This has the advantage of being less cluttered and has positive advantage for readers with dyslexia as underlining often makes the text harder to read.

The following is indicative of the style that you should adopt for different sorts of source:

Books
Author family name, author initials or first name, date of publication in brackets, stop/period, title of book with capitals as in example, stop/period, place of publication, colon, publisher details.

Howitt, D. (2002). *Forensic and Criminal Psychology*. Harlow: Pearson.

Journal articles
Author family name, author initials or first name, date of publication in brackets, stop/period, journal article title in lower case except for first word, stop/period, title of journal in italics or underlined, with capitals on first letter of first word and significant parts of the title, comma, volume of journal, comma, pages of journal.

Schopp, R. F. (1996). Communicating risk assessments: Accuracy, efficacy, and responsibility. *American Psychologist*, 9, 939–44.

Web sources

For a journal on the WWW then simply add the date retrieved and the source:

> Schopp, R. F. (1996). Communicating risk assessments: Accuracy, efficacy, and responsibility. *American Psychologist*, 9, 939–44. Retrieved 20 January 2003 from PsyKnow database.

This is a developing area and the style depends a little on the source. Search the American Psychological Association site for further information and details. The following contains current standards for electronic sources but, of course, it may change like all electronic sources:

> <http://www.apastyle.org/elecsource.html>

BOX 4.7   QUOTATIONS

The most straightforward approach to quotations is *never* to use them. It is generally best to put things in your own words. The use of quotations tends to cause problems because they are often used as a substitute for explaining and describing things yourself. The only legitimate use of quotations, we would suggest, is when the wording of the quotation does not lend itself to putting in your own words for some reason. Sometimes the nuances of the wording are essential. The use of a quotation really should always be accompanied by some commentary of your own. This might be a critical discussion of what the author said.

Quotations should always be clearly identified as such by making sure that they appear in quotation marks and indicating just where they appear in the original source. There are two ways of doing this. One is simply to put the page number into the citation: (Smith, 2004: 56). This means that the quotation is on page 56 of Smith (2004). Alternatively the pages can be indicated at the end of the quotation as (pp. 45–6) or (p. 47).

Appendix/appendices

In some types of publication appendices are a rarity. This is because they are space consuming. The main reason for using appendices is to avoid cluttering up the main body of the report with overlong detail which may confuse the reader and hamper good presentation. So, for example, it may be perfectly sensible to include your 50 item questionnaire in your report but common sense may dictate that it is put at the very end of the report in the section for appendices. In this case, it would be usual to give indicative examples of questions under materials. Similar considerations would apply to the multitude of tables that the statistical analysis may generate but which are too numerous to include in the results section. These too may be confined to the appendices. Remember:

■ To refer to the relevant appendix in the main text where appropriate.
■ To number and title the appendices appropriately in order to facilitate their location.
■ That you may be partly evaluated on the basis of the contents of your appendices. It is inappropriate simply to place a load of junk material there.

4.3 Conclusion

It should be evident that research reports require a range of skills to be effective. That is why they are amongst the most exacting tasks that any researcher can undertake. There seems to be a great deal to remember. In truth, few professional researchers would have all of the detail committed to memory. Not surprisingly, details frequently need to be checked. The complexity, however, can be very daunting for students who may feel overwhelmed by having so much to remember. It will clearly take time to be skilled at writing research reports. The key things are:

- Make sure that the text is clearly written with attention paid to spelling and grammar.
- Keep to the conventional structure (title, abstract, introduction, method, etc.) as far as is possible at the initial stages.
- Ensure that you cite your sources carefully and include all of them in the list of references.
- Carefully label and title all tables and diagrams.
- Remember that reading some of the relevant research literature will not only improve the quality of your report but also quickly familiarise you with the way in which professionals write about their research.

BOX 4.8 SOME ESSENTIALS OF THE RESEARCH REPORT AT A GLANCE

Title

- This is normally centralised and is often emphasised in bold.
- Should be informative about study.
- Usually no more than 12 words but sometimes longer.
- Avoid uninformative phrases such as 'A study of'.
- A good title will orient the reader to the contents of the research report.

Abstract or summary

- Usually 100 to 200 words long but this may vary. The APA standard is 120 words.
- The abstract is a summary of *all* aspects of the report. It should include key elements from the introduction, method, findings and conclusions.
- The abstract is crucial in providing access to your study and needs very careful writing and editing.

Introduction

- This is not normally given a heading in research reports, unless it is a very long thesis.
- Should be a focused account of why the research was needed. All material should be pertinent and lead to the question addressed by the research.
- Should contain key concepts and ideas together with any relevant theory.

→

Box 4.8 continued

■ Avoid using quotations unless their content is to be discussed in detail. Do not use them as a substitute for writing in your own words.
■ Consider using subheadings to ensure that the flow of the argument is structured. They can easily be removed once the report is complete.
■ Make sure that the argument leads directly to the aims of your research.

Method

■ This is a centralised, main heading.
■ Sections should include participants, materials or apparatus, procedure, possibly design in complex cases, stimuli and (recommended) ethical considerations.
■ It is difficult to judge the level of detail to include. Basically the aim is to provide enough detail that another researcher could replicate the study in its essence.
■ Do not regard the structure as too rigid. It is more important to communicate effectively than to include all sections no matter whether they apply or not.

Results

■ This is a centralised, main heading.
■ The results are intended to be the outcomes of the statistical analysis of the data. Quite clearly, this is not appropriate for many qualitative studies.
■ Do not evaluate the results or draw general conclusions in the results section.
■ Remember that tables and diagrams are extremely important and need to be very well done. They help provide a structure for the reader. So good titles, labelling and general clarity are necessary.
■ Do not leave the reader to find the results in your tables and diagrams. You need to write what the results are – you should not leave it to the reader to find them for themselves.

Discussion

■ The discussion is the discussion of the results. It is not the discussion of new material except in so far as the new material helps in understanding the results.
■ Do not regurgitate material from the introduction here.
■ Ensure that your findings are related back to previous research findings.
■ Methodological differences between your study and previous studies which might explain any disparities in the findings should be highlighted. Explain why the disparities might explain the different outcomes.
■ The discussion should lead to the conclusions you may wish to draw.

References

■ This is a centralised, main heading.
■ It is an alphabetical list of the sources that you cite in the text of the report.
■ A bibliography is *not* normally given. This is an alphabetical list of *all* the things that you have read when preparing the report.

→

Box 4.8 continued

- The sources are given in a standard fashion for each of journal articles, books, reports, unpublished sources and internet sites. Examples of how to do this are given on pages 74–5.
- Multiple references by the same author(s) published in a single year are given letters, starting with '*a*', after the date to distinguish each (e.g. 2004*a*, 2004*b*).

If you wish to cite sources which you have only obtained from secondary sources (i.e. you have not read the original but, say, read about it in textbooks) then you must indicate this. Box 4.6 gives several ways of doing this.

Appendix

- Appendix (or appendices) is a centralised, main heading.
- These are uncommon in published research reports largely because of the expense. However, they can be a place for questionnaires and the like. For student reports, they may be an appropriate place for providing the raw data.
- The appendices should be numbered (Appendix 1, Appendix 2, etc.) and referred to in the main text. For example, you may refer to the appropriate appendix by putting in brackets (see Appendix 5).
- As much work should go into the appendices as other components of the report. They should be clear, carefully structured and organised.

Tables and diagrams

- These should be placed in the text at appropriate points and their presence indicated in the text (with phrases such as 'see Table 3'). In work submitted for publication tables and diagrams are put on separate pages. Their approximate location in the text is indicated by the phrase 'Table 5 about here' inserted in the text and centralised.
- Tables and diagrams are key features of an effectively communicating report. There should be a balance between keeping their numbers low and providing sufficient detail.
- They should be numbered and given an accurate and descriptive title.
- All components should be carefully labelled – e.g. axes given titles, frequencies indicated to be frequencies and so forth.
- Avoid using a multitude of virtually identical tables by combining them into a clear summary table or diagram.
- Remember that well constructed tables and diagrams may be helpful to the reader as a means of giving an overview of your research.

Key points

- The research report draws together the important features of the research process and does not simply describe the details of the empirical research. As such, it brings the various aspects of the research process into an entirety. It is difficult to write because of the variety of different skills involved.

■ There is a basic, standard structure which underlies all research reports which allows a degree of flexibility. The detail of the structure is too great to remember in detail and style manuals are available for professional researchers to help them with this.

■ Although quality of writing is an important aspect of all research reports, there are conventions which should be followed in all but exceptional circumstances. For example, most of the report is written in the past tense, avoids the personal pronoun, and uses the active, not passive, voice.

■ A research report needs to document carefully the sources of the evidence supporting the arguments made. Citations and references are the key to this and should correspond to the recommended format.

■ All parts of the report should work to communicate the major messages emerging from the empirical research. Thus the title and abstract are as important in the communication as the discussion and conclusions.

Activities

1. Photocopy an article in a current psychology journal held in the library. Draw up a list of any disparities between this article and the conventional structure described in this chapter. Why did the author(s) make these changes?

2. Find a recent practical report that you have written. Using the material in this chapter, list some of the ways in which your report could be better.

5   The literature search

Overview

■ The literature search is an integral part of the research process. Pertinent research studies and theoretical papers obtained in this way provide the researcher with an overview of thinking and research in a particular area. Although time consuming, it is essential to developing ideas about the issues to be addressed and what more needs to be explored.

■ The literature search is best seen as a process of starting broadly but moving as rapidly as possible to a more narrow and focused search. One common strategy is to focus on the most recent research and writings on a topic. These contain the fruits of other researchers' literature searches as well as up to date information of where current research has taken us. The current literature is likely to alert us to what still needs to be done in the field. Of course, the major limitation of starting with current publications is that important ideas from earlier times become ignored and neglected.

■ Computers and computerised databases are the modern, highly efficient way of searching the research literature through electronic databases such as *Web of Science* and *PsycINFO*. Amongst a great deal of information of various sorts, they provide a brief abstract or summary of the publication. The abstract in the Web of Science is that of the article itself whereas this may not be the case in PsycINFO.

■ Abstracts, if well-written, contain a great deal of information which will provide a degree of detail about the research in question and the theoretical context. Usually abstracts contain enough information to help the reader decide whether or not to obtain the original article or report. Almost certainly local college and university libraries are unlikely to have anything other than a small fraction of these publications in stock. Consequently, it is necessary to obtain the article by some means from elsewhere. There are various ways of doing this, including visiting other libraries, e-mailing the author for a copy of the article, or getting the library to obtain a copy or photocopy of the article in question.

■ There are a number of reasons why it may be essential to obtain the original article. For example, it is the only way of obtaining an overview of the methods and procedures employed. Sometimes one may be suspicious of how sound the conclusions of the study are and may wish to evaluate, say, the statistical analysis carried out or consider possible flaws in the method.

■ One must keep a careful record of the publications that you consider important to your research. Although initially this is time consuming it is far less frustrating in the long run. There are a number of ways of doing this including computerised databases (such as RefWorks or EndNote), simple hand-written index cards or computer files to which material may be cut and pasted.

How the literature search is conducted depends a little on one's starting point. A professional researcher with a well established reputation will have much of the previous research and theory readily at their command. A beginning student will have little or no knowledge. If one knows very little about a topic, then a sensible first stage is to read some introductory material such as that found in textbooks. A relatively recent textbook is likely to cover fairly recent thinking on the topic although in brief overview form. At the same time, the textbook is likely to provide a fairly rapid access to a field in general. This is especially useful for students doing research for the first time in practical classes. Because it is readily to hand, material in the college or university library will be your first port of call. Getting material from elsewhere may take a little time and cause problems in managing your time – and getting your assignments in before the deadline. Of course, professional researchers regularly keep up to date – perhaps searching the new literature on a monthly basis.

It cannot be stressed too much that professional researchers are part of complex networks of individuals sharing ideas and interests. As such, information flows through a variety of channels and few researchers would rely exclusively on the sources described in this chapter. For one thing, no matter how efficient the system – and it is impressive – there is always a delay between research being done and the final report being published. This can be a year or two in many cases. So if one needs to be more up to date than that then one needs to rely on conferences and other sources of contact and information. This would be characteristic of the activities of most researchers.

Searching one's college or university library usually involves using its electronic catalogue system via computer terminals. As there are a number of such systems, these may differ across universities. Many British university libraries use the OPAC system (Online Public Access Catalogue). Leaflets about using the local system are likely to be available from the library, there may be induction or training sessions for new library users, or you may simply seek help from members of the library staff. If you have, say, a specific book in mind then its title and author will quickly help you discover where it is located in the library. However, if you simply are searching with a general keyword such as 'memory' or 'intelligence' then you are likely to find more entries or hits. Sometimes it may be quicker to go to the section of the library where items with particular keywords are likely to be held – though this is less systematic and others on the course may have beaten you there. Library classification systems need to be understood in general if one is to use this sort of method.

5.1 Library classification systems

There are two main systems for classifying and arranging non-fiction (mostly) books in a library. It is sufficient to know how to find the books in the library without having a detailed knowledge of the system used by your library.

■ One scheme is the Dewey Decimal Classification (DDC) system developed by Melvil Dewey in 1876 which is reputedly the world's most widely used library classification system, although not necessarily in university libraries (Chan & Mitchell, 2003; Dewey Services, n.d.). Each publication is given three whole numbers followed by several decimal places as shown in Table 5.1. These numbers are known as *call numbers* in both systems. The first of the three whole numbers indicates the classes of which there are 10 as shown in Table 5.2. So psychology mainly comes under 1 _ _ although certain areas fall into other classes. For example, abnormal or clinical psychology is classified under 6 _ _. The second whole number shows the divisions. Much of psychology comes under 1 5 _. The third whole number refers to the section. The decimal numbers indicate further subdivisions of the sections.

Table 5.1   Some psychology subcategories in the Dewey Decimal Classification

Number	Subject
150	psychology
150.1	philosophy and theory
150.19	systems, schools, viewpoints
150.192	existential, faculty, phenomenological, rational schools
150.193	functionalism, perception, movement, emotions, drives
150.194	reductionism
150.1943	behaviourism
150.19432	Watsonian behaviourism
150.19434	neobehaviourism

Table 5.2   Ten major classes of the Dewey Decimal Classification for cataloguing library material

Number (class)	Subject
000–099	computers, information and general reference
100–199	philosophy and psychology
200–299	religion
300–399	social sciences
400–499	language
500–599	science
600–699	technology
700–799	arts and recreation
800–899	literature
900–999	history and geography

■ The other main system for organising non-fiction material in a library is the Library of Congress classification system (Chan, 1999; Library of Congress Classification Outline, n.d.) which was developed by that library in the United States. Each publication is assigned one or two letters, signifying a category, followed by a whole number between 1 and 9999. There are twenty-one main categories labelled A to Z but excluding I, O, W, X and Y. These categories are shown in Table 5.3. Psychology largely comes under BF. Some of the numbers and categories under BF are presented in Table 5.4.

Table 5.3 Twenty-one major categories of the Library of Congress classification system for cataloguing non-fiction

Letter (category) Subject	Letter (category) Subject
A general works	M music
B philosophy, psychology, religion	N fine arts
C auxiliary sciences of history	P language and literature
D history: (general) and history of Europe	Q science
E history: America	R medicine
F history: America	S agriculture
G geography, anthropology, recreation	T technology
H social sciences	U military science
J political science	V naval science
K law	Z bibliography, library science, information
L education	resources

Table 5.4 Some psychology sub-categories in the Library of Congress classification system

Letter (category)	Number (sub-category)	Subject
BF	1–1999	psychology, parapsychology, occult sciences
	1–990	psychology
	38–64	philosophy, relation to other topics
	173–175.5	psychoanalysis
	176–176.5	psychological tests and testing
	180–198.7	experimental psychology
	203	Gestalt psychology
	207–209	psychotropic drugs and other substances
	231–299	sensation, aesthesiology
	309–499	consciousness, cognition

5.2 Electronic databases

Using the library catalogue in this way is clearly a rather haphazard process. It is totally dependent on what books (and other publications) are actually in the library. Consequently you may prefer to go directly to electronic databases (as opposed to catalogues). There are a number of different electronic databases that contain information relevant to psychology. Generally libraries have to pay for access to these. The web pages for your library will usually provide details as to what is available to you at your university or college. For those databases that are only available on the web, you will generally need to have a username and password. This is obtained from your library. Two databases that you may find especially useful are called *ISI Web of Science* and *PsycINFO*. ISI stands for Institute for Scientific Research though we will refer to this database as just the Web of Science. PsycINFO is short for Psychological Information and is produced by the American Psychological Association. Each of these has its advantages and disadvantages and it is worth becoming familiar with both of them (and others) if they are available. Both PsycINFO and Web of Science are essentially archives of summaries of research articles and other publications. These summaries are known as abstracts. Apart from reading the full article, they are probably the most complete summary of the contents of journal articles.

PsycINFO is more comprehensive in its coverage of the content of psychology journals than Web of Science. It goes back as far as 1872 (it was formerly known as Psychological Abstracts and available in bound copies) and contains summaries of the content of psychology books and sometimes individual chapters. Abstracts of books and chapters make up 11% of its database (PsycINFO Database Information, n.d.). However, it also includes abstracts of postgraduate dissertations called *Dissertation Abstracts International* which constitute 12% of the data. These abstracts are based on postgraduate work which has not been specially reviewed for publication unlike the vast majority of published research reports. The dissertations themselves are often the length of a short book and rather difficult to get access to – certainly they are difficult to obtain in a hurry. Consequently, their use is problematic when normal student submission deadlines are considered.

Web of Science contains the abstracts of articles published since 1981 and covers only those in journals that are thought to be the most important in a discipline (Institute for Scientific Information, 2002). It ranges through a number of disciplines and is not restricted to psychology. Moreover, it may be linked to the electronic catalogue of journals held by your library. If so, it will inform you about the availability of the journal in your library. This facility is very useful as there are a large number of psychology journals and your library will only subscribe to some of them.

Using Web of Science

Web of Science is currently accessed through Web of Knowledge. It is not possible in the limited space available to show you all its different facilities. Once you have tried out one or two basic literature searches you may wish to explore its other capabilities. In the United Kingdom, Web of Knowledge is based, or hosted, at the Manchester Information and Associated Services whose website address is <http://wok.mimas.ac.uk/>. Find out from your college library whether you can access it and, if so, how to do so. Once you are logged into Web of Knowledge and have selected ISI Web of Science, the home page shown in Figure 5.1 will appear.

Easy Search is sufficient in most cases. Select this option and the screen in Figure 5.2 appears. Options can be selected using the computer mouse. To restrict your search you

Figure 5.1	ISI Web of Science home page

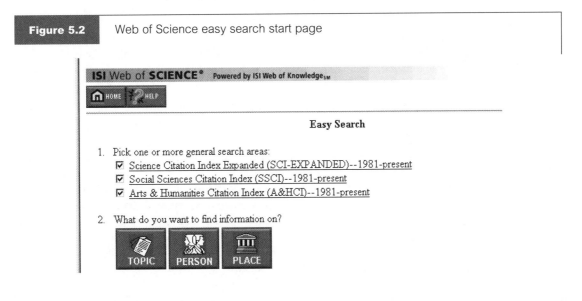

may wish to de-select the *Arts & Humanities Citation Index* and, possibly, the *Science Citation Index* by clicking on the box containing the tick mark. If too many inappropriate references come up when the number of databases is not restricted, then go back and limit your search.

Select the *Topic* icon which leads to the screen shown in Figure 5.3. Enter the key words or terms that describe the topic that you want to conduct the search on. If too many

Figure 5.2	Web of Science easy search start page

ISI Web of **SCIENCE**®   Powered by ISI Web of Knowledge$_{SM}$

🏠 HOME   ❓ HELP

Easy Search

1. Pick one or more general search areas:
    ☑ Science Citation Index Expanded (SCI-EXPANDED)--1981-present
    ☑ Social Sciences Citation Index (SSCI)--1981-present
    ☑ Arts & Humanities Citation Index (A&HCI)--1981-present

2. What do you want to find information on?

    TOPIC   PERSON   PLACE

Figure 5.3 Web of Science topic search start page

references are found, limit your search by adding further keywords. There is a help facility if you want more information on what to do. Suppose you want to find out what articles there are on the topic of interpersonal attraction and attitude similarity. You type in these terms in the box provided combining them with the word or search operator 'and'. Then press the *Return* key or select the *Search* option.

The first part of the first page of the *Summary* of the results of this search is shown in Figure 5.4. Of course, if you search using these terms now you will get newer publications than these as this example was done in 2004. Articles are listed in order of the most recent ones unless you have selected them in order of the highest relevance of the keywords. This option is shown in instruction 2 in Figure 5.3. With this option articles containing more of these terms and presenting them closer together are listed first.

Three kinds of information are provided for each article listed in the summary:

■ the last name of the authors and their initials
■ the title of the article
■ the abbreviated name of the journal together with the volume number, the issue number in parentheses, the first and last page numbers of the article, and the month and the year the issue was published.

For the first article shown in Figure 5.4, the authors are Quist and Crano. The title of the article is 'Assumed policy similarity and voter preference'. The journal is *Journal of Social Psychology*.

It would seem from its title that this article is not directly relevant to our topic as the title refers to voter preference. To see whether this is the case and to find out further details of this article we select the title which produces the *Full Record* shown in Figure 5.5 on page 88. The keywords we used are shown in bold. If we read the abstract we can see that the paper is about voters' preferences and not about personal relationships. The reason that this article was included is that one of the keywords used by the authors to describe the content of their article is 'interpersonal-attraction'. Attraction in this context refers to preference for a presidential candidate.

| Figure 5.4 | Web of Science first summary page of the results of easy search |

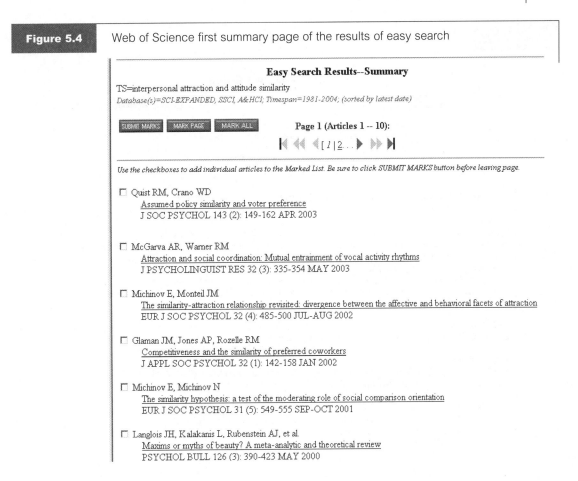

Web of Science includes the references although in a somewhat abbreviated form. To look at the references select *Cited References* near the top of the full record as shown in Figure 5.5.

To find out whether the journal was held in our library, we would select the *SFX* icon just underneath *Full Record* at the top of the page. This would produce the webpage shown in Figure 5.6 overleaf. If we selected the *Library Catalogue*, we could see whether our library held this journal and, if so, whether it held this volume. If we want to go back to the summary page, we select the *Summary* option just beneath *Easy Search* Results towards the top of the page.

There are several ways of saving this information. Perhaps the easiest method is to move the cursor to the start of the information you want to save, hold down the left button of the mouse and drag the cursor down the page until you reach the end of the information you want to save. The address is useful if you want to contact the authors. This area will be highlighted. Select the *Edit* option on the bar at the top of the screen which will produce a dropdown menu. Select *Copy* from this menu. Then paste this copied material into a Word file which will contain the details of the references on this topic.

Easy Search will give you a maximum of 100 references. For this example there were only 18 references as shown towards the upper left corner of Figure 5.5 where it says 'Article 1 of 18'. If there are more than 100 references which you want to look at, you need to go back to the home page as shown in Figure 5.1 and select *Full Search*. This will

---

Figure 5.5   Web of Science full record of an article

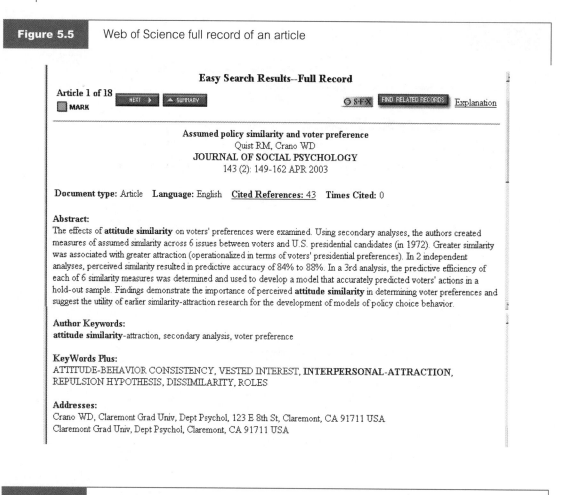

Figure 5.6   Web of Science SFX window

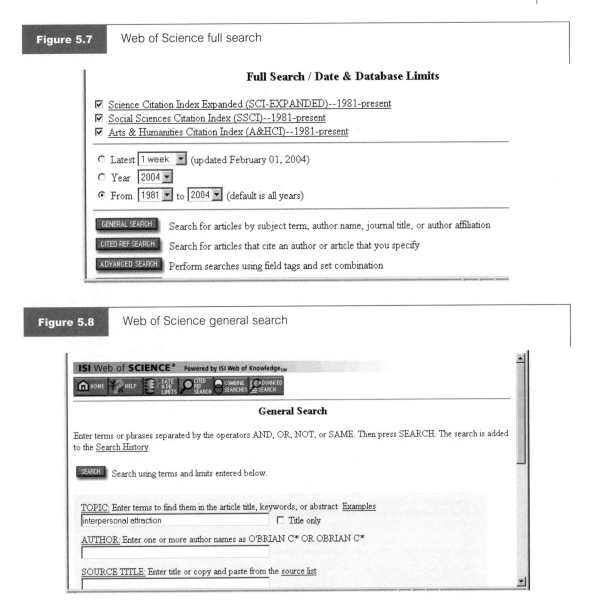

Figure 5.7 Web of Science full search

Figure 5.8 Web of Science general search

produce the screen in Figure 5.7. If we wanted to search references from the current time to the earliest year which is 1981 we leave the year setup as it is. To illustrate this procedure we need to use terms which will generate more than 100 references.

Select *General Search* which will produce the screen presented in Figure 5.8. Type in 'interpersonal attraction' in the box under *Topic* and select *Search*. When this was done, the search produced 217 references.

Using PsycINFO

PsycINFO operates somewhat differently from Web of Science. Its use is essential as its coverage of psychology is more complete. Although it may be accessed in CD form, it is more convenient to use it online which is the version we will illustrate. In the United Kingdom, PsycINFO is available at the following website: <http://www.bids.ac.uk/>. BIDS stands for Bath Information and Data Services. You may need to contact your college library to see if you can access it and, if so, how. After logging in, you may be presented with a list of databases like those shown in Figure 5.9. If you want all the databases select the empty box to the left of *PsycINFO Database* and just below *BIDS ERL Server*. If you do not want them all, choose those you want by selecting the empty box to the left of them. Then select *Start Searching* which will produce the screen in Figure 5.10.

We will again search using the terms 'interpersonal attraction' and 'attitude similarity'. So type in these terms in the empty box towards the top left corner of the screen, combining them with the word 'and'. Then press the *Return* key or select *Search*. This will produce the kind of list shown in Figure 5.11. Your list will, of course, be more up to date if you follow our steps now. Note that this list is somewhat different from that for Web of Science shown in Figure 5.4. However, the same three kinds of information are provided for each record or reference – the authors, the title of the reference and where it was published.

If you want to see the full record for a reference, select *Complete Record*. A major part of the complete record for the second reference by Klohnen and Shanhong is presented in Figure 5.12. Note that the record also contains the references included in the original article. This has been done from about 2000 onwards. To keep the details of a search it is probably easiest to select and copy the information you want and then paste it into a Word file as described for Web of Science.

| Figure 5.9 | PsycINFO databases |

| Figure 5.10 | PsycINFO search page |

| Figure 5.11 | PsycINFO list of records |

| Figure 5.12 | PsycINFO full record |

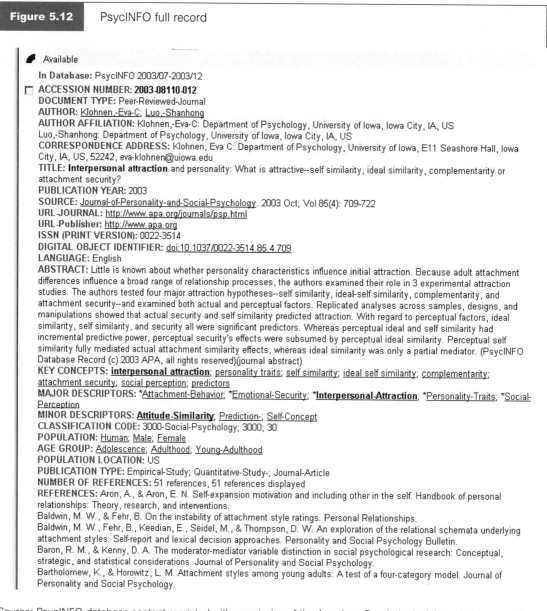

◢ Available

In Database: PsycINFO 2003/07-2003/12

☐ ACCESSION NUMBER: **2003-08110-012**
DOCUMENT TYPE: Peer-Reviewed-Journal
AUTHOR: Klohnen,-Eva-C; Luo,-Shanhong
AUTHOR AFFILIATION: Klohnen,-Eva-C: Department of Psychology, University of Iowa, Iowa City, IA, US
Luo,-Shanhong: Department of Psychology, University of Iowa, Iowa City, IA, US
CORRESPONDENCE ADDRESS: Klohnen, Eva C: Department of Psychology, University of Iowa, E11 Seashore Hall, Iowa City, IA, US, 52242, eva-klohnen@uiowa.edu
TITLE: **Interpersonal attraction** and personality: What is attractive--self similarity, ideal similarity, complementarity or attachment security?
PUBLICATION YEAR: 2003
SOURCE: Journal-of-Personality-and-Social-Psychology. 2003 Oct; Vol 85(4): 709-722
URL-JOURNAL: http://www.apa.org/journals/psp.html
URL-Publisher: http://www.apa.org
ISSN (PRINT VERSION): 0022-3514
DIGITAL OBJECT IDENTIFIER: doi:10.1037/0022-3514.85.4.709
LANGUAGE: English
ABSTRACT: Little is known about whether personality characteristics influence initial attraction. Because adult attachment differences influence a broad range of relationship processes, the authors examined their role in 3 experimental attraction studies. The authors tested four major attraction hypotheses--self similarity, ideal-self similarity, complementarity, and attachment security--and examined both actual and perceptual factors. Replicated analyses across samples, designs, and manipulations showed that actual security and self similarity predicted attraction. With regard to perceptual factors, ideal similarity, self similarity, and security all were significant predictors. Whereas perceptual ideal and self similarity had incremental predictive power, perceptual security's effects were subsumed by perceptual ideal similarity. Perceptual self similarity fully mediated actual attachment similarity effects, whereas ideal similarity was only a partial mediator. (PsycINFO Database Record (c) 2003 APA, all rights reserved)(journal abstract)
KEY CONCEPTS: interpersonal attraction; personality traits; self similarity; ideal self similarity; complementarity; attachment security; social perception; predictors
MAJOR DESCRIPTORS: *Attachment-Behavior; *Emotional-Security; *Interpersonal-Attraction; *Personality-Traits; *Social-Perception
MINOR DESCRIPTORS: Attitude-Similarity; Prediction-; Self-Concept
CLASSIFICATION CODE: 3000-Social-Psychology; 3000; 30
POPULATION: Human; Male; Female
AGE GROUP: Adolescence; Adulthood; Young-Adulthood
POPULATION LOCATION: US
PUBLICATION TYPE: Empirical-Study; Quantitative-Study-; Journal-Article
NUMBER OF REFERENCES: 51 references, 51 references displayed
REFERENCES: Aron, A., & Aron, E. N. Self-expansion motivation and including other in the self. Handbook of personal relationships: Theory, research, and interventions.
Baldwin, M. W., & Fehr, B. On the instability of attachment style ratings. Personal Relationships.
Baldwin, M. W., Fehr, B., Keedian, E., Seidel, M., & Thompson, D. W. An exploration of the relational schemata underlying attachment styles: Self-report and lexical decision approaches. Personality and Social Psychology Bulletin.
Baron, R. M., & Kenny, D. A. The moderator-mediator variable distinction in social psychological research: Conceptual, strategic, and statistical considerations. Journal of Personality and Social Psychology.
Bartholomew, K., & Horowitz, L. M. Attachment styles among young adults: A test of a four-category model. Journal of Personality and Social Psychology.

Source: PsycINFO database content reprinted with permission of the American Psychological Association, publisher of the PsycINFO database, all rights reserved.

5.3 Obtaining articles not in your library

There are a large number of journals published which are relevant to psychology. As the budgets of libraries are limited, your library will only subscribe to some of them. Furthermore, they may not have a complete set of a journal. Consequently, it is likely that some of the articles you are interested in reading will not be available in your library. If this occurs, there are at least five different courses of action you can take:

- You may have friends at other universities or there may be other universities near to where you live. You can check in their catalogue to see if they have the journal volume you need using the web pages of your local library in many cases.

- Libraries provide an inter-library loan service where you can obtain either a photocopy of a journal article or a copy of the issue in which the article was published. It is worth obtaining the issue if there is more than one article in that issue which is of interest to you. This service is not free and you may be expected to pay for some or all of these loans. You will need to check locally what arrangements are in place for using such a service. This service is relatively quick and you may receive the photocopied article in the post within a week of requesting it.

- Sometimes it may be worth travelling to a library such as the British Lending Library at Boston Spa in Yorkshire to photocopy these yourself. The number of articles you can request in a day at this library is currently restricted to 14 if you order five working days in advance or to 4 if you do not do this. It is worth checking before going – you will find contact details on the following website: <http://www.bl.uk/services>.

- Many journals now have a web-based electronic version which you may be able to access. Information about this may be available on your library's website.

- You may write to or e-mail the author (or one of the authors if there is more than one) of the paper and ask them to send you a copy of it. It should be quicker to e-mail the author than to mail them. Authors may have an electronic copy of the paper which they can send to you as an attachment to their reply. Otherwise you will have to wait for it to arrive by post. Some authors may have copies of their papers which you can download from their website. Perhaps the easiest way to find an author's e-mail address is to find out where they currently work by looking up their most recently published paper. This is readily done in Web of Science using the *Person* rather than the *Topic* option (see Figure 5.2). Then use an Internet search engine such as Google by typing in their name and the name of the institution. Since about 2001 PsycINFO provides the e-mail address of the author to whom correspondence on the article should be addressed as shown in the *Correspondence Address* of the full record in Figure 5.12. You need to include your postal address in your e-mail so that authors know where to send the paper should they not have an electronic copy.

BOX 5.1 JUDGING THE REPUTATION OF A PUBLICATION

There is a form of pecking-order for research journals in all disciplines and that includes psychology. To have an article published in *Nature* or *Science* signals something of the importance of one's work. Researchers are attracted to publishing in the most prestigious journals for professional advancement. Virtually every journal has a surfeit of material submitted to it so very good material may sometimes be rejected. The rejection rate of articles submitted for publication in journals is relatively high. In 2001, rejection rates varied from 34% for *Behavioral Neuroscience* to a 91% for

→

Box 5.1 continued

Psychological Review with an average of 72% across all the journals published by the leading American Psychological Association (American Psychological Association, 2002). Not unexpectedly, agreement between referees or reviewers about the quality of an article may be considerably less than perfect (Cicchetti, 1991). Quality, after all, is a matter of judgement. Authors may well find that an article rejected by one journal will be accepted by the next journal they approach.

The impact factor is a measure of the frequency with which the average article in a journal has been cited within a particular period. This may be regarded as a useful indicator of the quality of the journal. More prestigious journals should be more frequently cited than less prestigious ones. The Institute for Scientific Information which produces the Web of Science also publishes *Journal Citation Reports* annually in the summer following the year they cover. The impact factor of a particular journal may be found using these reports either online, on CD-ROM or on microfiche. The period looked at by the *Journal Citation Reports* is the two years prior to the year being considered (Institute for Scientific Information, 1994). For example, if the year being considered is 2004, the two years prior to that are 2002–3. The impact factor of a journal in 2004 is the ratio of the number of times in 2004 that articles published in that journal in 2002–3 were cited in that and other journals to the number of articles published in that journal in 2002–3:

$$\frac{\text{impact factor of}}{\text{journal 2004}} = \frac{\text{citations in 2004 of articles published in journal in 2002–2003}}{\text{number of articles published by journal in 2002–3}}$$

So, for example, if the total number of articles published in 2002 and 2003 was 200 and the number of citations of those articles in 2004 was 200, the impact factor is 1.00. The impact factor excludes what are called self-citations where authors refer to their previous articles.

Taking into account the number of articles published in a particular period controls for the size of the journal. If a journal publishes more articles than another journal, then that journal is more likely to be cited simply for that reason if all else is equal. This correction may not be necessary as it was found by Tomer (1986) that the corrected and the uncorrected impact factor correlates almost perfectly (0.97).

The impact factors for a selection of psychology journals for the years 1998 to 2002 are presented in Table 5.5. The impact factor varies across years for a journal. For example, for the *British Journal of Social Psychology* it increased from 1.00 in

Table 5.5   Impact factors for some psychology journals for 1998 to 2002

Journal	2002	2001	2000	1999	1998
British Journal of Social Psychology	1.59	1.43	1.35	1.10	1.00
Journal of Personality and Social Psychology	3.65	3.61	3.17	2.72	2.84
The Journal of Psychology	0.31	0.49	0.39	0.30	0.19
Journal of Social and Personal Relationships	0.68	0.73	0.56	0.59	0.71
The Journal of Social Psychology	0.38	0.33	0.29	0.28	0.24
Personality and Social Psychology Bulletin	1.76	1.25	1.21	1.18	1.75
Social Psychology Quarterly	1.26	1.27	1.28	1.40	1.49

→

Box 5.1 continued

1998 to 1.59 in 2002. It also differs between journals. For these journals in 2002, the highest impact factor is 3.65 for the *Journal of Personality and Social Psychology* and the lowest is 0.31 for *The Journal of Psychology*. An impact factor of about 1.00 means that the average article published in that journal was cited about once in the previous two years taking into account the number of articles published in that journal in those two years. The Web of Science only includes those journals that are considered to be the most important (Institute for Scientific Information, 2002).

However, even the Institute for Scientific Information which produces the impact factor measure says that the usefulness of a journal should not be judged only on its impact factor but also on the views of informed colleagues or peers (Institute for Scientific Information, 1994). The impact factor is likely to be affected by a number of variables such as the average number of references cited in a journal or the number of review articles that are published by a journal. The relationship between the citation count of a journal and the subjective judgement of its standing by psychologists has not been found to be strong.

For example, Buss and McDermot (1976) reported a rank-order correlation of 0.45 between the frequency of citations for 64 psychology journals in the period 1973–5 and a five-point rating made of those journals by the chairs or heads of 48 psychology departments in the United States in an earlier study by Mace and Warner (1973). This relationship was stronger at 0.56 when it was restricted to the ten most highly cited journals. In other words, agreement was higher when the less highly cited journals were excluded. Rushton and Roediger (1978) found a Kendall's tau correlation of 0.45 between the ratings of these journals by these departmental heads and their impact factor. Chairs of departments are an influential group of people in that they are often responsible for the selecting, giving tenure and promoting academic staff. However, it is possible that nowadays chairs are more aware of the impact factor and so that the relationship between the impact factor and the rating of the journal may be higher.

There appears not to be a strong relationship between the number of times a published paper is cited by other authors and either the quality or the impact of the paper as rated by about 380 current or former editors, associate editors and consulting editors of nine major psychology journals who had not published papers in those journals (Gottfredson, 1978). Because the distribution of the number of citations was highly skewed with most articles not being cited, the logarithm of the citation number was taken. The correlation between this transformed number was 0.22 for the quality scale and 0.36 for the impact scale. The number of times a paper is cited is given by Web of Science at the end of the line above the abstract in the full record of the article as shown in Figure 5.5. If you select *Times Cited*: you will see details of the papers that have cited this reference.

The lack of agreement about the quality of published papers was dramatically illustrated in a study by Peters and Ceci (1982) in which 12 papers which had been published in highly regarded American psychology journals were resubmitted to them 18 to 32 months later using fictitious names and institutions. Of the 38 editors and reviewers who dealt with these papers, only three realised that they were resubmissions. Of the nine remaining papers, eight were rejected largely on the grounds of having serious methodological flaws. This finding emphasises the importance of the reader being able to evaluate the worth of a paper by themselves and not to rely on the judgements of others.

5.4 Conclusion

The development of any discipline is the collective effort of numerous researchers acting to a degree independently. It is necessary for researchers to communicate their findings and ideas in publications such as journal articles. Similarly, researchers need to be able to access the work of other researchers in order to make an effective contribution to developing the field of research in question. Effectively searching the literature involves a number of skills. In this chapter we have concentrated on efficient searches of available databases. Of course, professional researchers have a wider variety of information sources available. For example, they go to conferences and hear of new work there, they get sent copies of reports by colleagues doing research elsewhere, and they have an extensive network of contacts through which news of research elsewhere gets communicated. Students have fewer options at first.

Searching the literature on a topic takes time and unless this is taken into account, students may have problems fitting it into their schedule. No one can expect that all materials will be available in their university or college library. There are ways of obtaining material which are increasingly dependent on the Web. If you are unfamiliar with the research on a particular topic, it may be helpful to find a recently published book which includes an introduction to that topic to give you some idea of what has been done and found. Electronic databases such as Web of Science and PsycINFO are a very convenient way to find out what has been published on a particular topic. These electronic databases provide short abstracts or summaries of publications which should give you a clearer idea of whether the publication is relevant to your needs. You may not always realise the importance or relevance of a paper. Consequently, it may be better to make a note of a paper even if it does not appear immediately relevant to your needs. This is easily done with the copy and paste functions of the computer software you are using. You need to learn to judge the value of a research paper in terms of what has been done rather than simply accepting it as being important because it has been published or has been published in what is reputedly a good journal.

Key points

■ The key to carrying out a successful literature research in any discipline lies in using the various available sources of information. Of these, modern research is most heavily dependent on the use of electronic databases such as Web of Science and PsycINFO. These are generally available in universities and elsewhere. Students will find them useful but often the materials available via their library catalogue will take priority because of their ease of availability.

■ The major databases essentially consist of abstracts or summaries of research publications including both journal articles and books. An abstract gives a fairly detailed summary of the research article and is an intermediate step to help the reader decide whether or not the complete article or book is required. In addition, these databases frequently contain enough information to enable the author to be contacted – sometimes this goes as far as including an e-mail address.

■ Databases are not identical and each can supplement the other. Furthermore, there may well be other sources of information that some researchers can profitably refer to. For example, the fields of biology, medicine, sociology and economics might provide essential information for researchers in some fields of psychology. Knowledge of these builds up with experience.

■ Abstracts and other information may be copied and pasted on one's computer. In this way it is possible to build up a record of the materials you feel will be useful to you.

■ There are numerous ways of obtaining published research. Increasingly the Internet and email are a rich source. It can be surprisingly easy to get in touch with academics all over the world. Many are quite happy to send copies of their work either in the mail or electronically.

Activities

1. If you do not already know this, find out what electronic databases are available in your library and how to access them. The best way of checking how good a system is and how to use it is to try it out on a topic that you are already familiar with. It should produce information you are already familiar with. If it does not do this, then you can try to find out how to locate this information in this system. Try out a few systems to see which suits your purposes best.

2. Many university libraries provide training in the use of their resources and systems. These are an excellent way of quickly learning about the local situation. Enquire at your library and sign up for the most promising. Afterwards try to turn your effort into better grades by conducting a more thorough search as preparation for your essays, practical reports and projects. Using information sources effectively is a valuable skill, and will be recognised and rewarded.

6 Ethics in research

Overview

- Psychological ethics are the moral principles that govern psychological activity. Research ethics are the result of applying these broader principles to research. Occasions arise when there is a conflict between ethical principles – ethical dilemmas – which are not simply resolved.

- Psychology's professional bodies (e.g. the American Psychological Association and the British Psychological Society) publish detailed ethical guidelines. They overlap significantly. This chapter is based on recent revisions of the ethical principles of these bodies.

- Deception, informed consent and confidentiality are commonly the focus of the debate about ethics. However, ethical issues stretch much more widely. They include responsibilities to other organisations, the law and ethical committees, circumstances in which photos and video recording are appropriate, and the publication of findings, plagiarism and fabricating data.

- Significantly, ethical considerations are the responsibility of all psychologists including students in training.

Quite simply, ethics are the moral principles by which we conduct ourselves. Psychological ethics, then, are the moral principles by which psychologists conduct themselves. It is wrong to regard ethics as being merely the rules or regulations which govern conduct. The activities of psychologists are far too varied and complex for that. Psychological work inevitably throws up situations which are genuinely dilemmas which no amount of rules or regulations could effectively police. Ethical dilemmas involve conflicts between different principles of moral conduct. Consequently psychologists may differ in terms of their position on a particular matter. Ethical behaviour is not the responsibility of each individual psychologist but a responsibility of the entire psychological community. Monitoring the activities of fellow psychologists, seeking the advice of other psychologists when ethical difficulties come to light and collectively advancing ethical behaviour in their workplace are all instances of the mutual concern that psychologists have about the conduct of the profession. Equally, psychological ethics cannot be entirely separated from personal morality.

The American Psychological Association's most recent ethical code was first published in 2002. It came into effect on the 1 June 2003. It amounts to a substantial ethical programme for psychological practitioners, not just researchers. This is important since unethical behaviour reflects on the entire psychological community. The collective strength of psychology lies largely in the profession's ability to control and monitor all aspects of the work of psychologists. The code, nevertheless, only applies to the professional activities of the psychologist – their scientific, professional and educational roles. For example, it requires an ethical stance in psychology teaching – so that there is a requirement of fidelity in the content of psychology courses such that they should accurately reflect the current state of knowledge. These newest ethical standards do not simply apply to members of the American Psychological Association but also to student affiliates/members. Ignorance of the relevant ethical standards is not a defence for unethical conduct and neither is failure to understand the standards properly. Quite simply, this means that all psychology students need a full and mature understanding of the ethical principles which govern the profession. It is not something to be left until the student is professionally qualified. Whenever scientific, professional and educational work in psychology is involved so too are ethics irrespective of the status. We have chosen to focus on the American Psychological Association's ethical guidelines as they are the most recent available but also because they consider more issues than any others. As such, they bring to attention matters which otherwise might be overlooked. We believe that it is no excuse to disregard them simply because they are not mentioned by one's own professional ethics.

What is the purpose of ethics? The answer to this may seem self-evident – that is, psychologists ought to know how to conduct themselves properly. But there is more to it than that. One of the characteristics of the professions (medicine being the prime example) is the desire to retain autonomy. The history of the emergence of professions such as medicine during the 19th century illustrates this well (Howitt, 1992*a*). Autonomy implies self-regulation of the affairs of members by the professional body. It is not possible to be autonomous if the activities of members are under the detailed control of legislation. So professions need to stipulate and police standards of conduct. There is another important reason why psychological work should maintain high ethical standards. The good reputation of psychology and psychologists among the general public, for example, is essential for the development of psychology. If psychologists collectively enjoyed a reputation for being dishonest, exploitative, prurient liars then few would employ their services or willingly participate in their research. Trust in the profession is essential.

Failure to adhere to sound ethical principles may result in complaints to professional bodies such as the American Psychological Association, British Psychological Society and so forth. Sanctions may be imposed on those violating ethical principles. Ultimately the final sanction is ending the individual's membership of the professional body, which may result in the individual being unable to practise professionally. Many organisations including universities have ethics committees that both supervise the research carried out by employees but also that of other researchers wishing to do research within the organisation. While this does provide a measure of protection for all parties (including the researcher), it should not be regarded as the final guarantee of good ethical practices in research.

6.1 APA ethics

The APA ethics are based on five general principles. These are:

■ *Principle A: Beneficence and nonmaleficence*   Psychologists seek to benefit and avoid harm to those whom they engage with professionally. This includes the animals used in research. Psychologists should both be aware of and guard against those factors which may result in harm to others. The list of factors is long and includes financial, social and institutional considerations.

■ *Principle B: Fidelity and responsibility*   Psychologists are in relationships of trust in their professional activities. They are thus required to take responsibility for their actions, adhere to professional standards of conduct, and make clear exactly their role and obligations in all aspects of their professional activities. In relation to research and practice, psychologists are not merely concerned with their own personal activities but with the ethical conduct of their colleagues (widely defined). It is worthwhile quoting word for word one aspect of the professional fidelity ethic: 'Psychologists strive to contribute a portion of their professional time for little or no compensation or personal advantage.'

■ *Principle C: Integrity – accuracy, honesty, truthfulness*   Psychologists are expected to manifest integrity in all aspects of their professional work. One possible exception to this is circumstances in which the ratio of benefits to harm of using deception is large. Nevertheless, it remains the duty of psychologists even in these circumstances to seriously assess the possible harmful consequences of the deception including the ensuing distrust. The psychologist has a duty to correct these harmful consequences. The problem of deception is discussed in more detail later.

■ *Principle D: Justice – equality of access to the benefits of psychology*   This means that psychologists exercise careful judgement and take care to enable all people to experience just and fair psychological practices. Psychologists should be aware of the nature of their biases (potential and actual). They should not engage in, or condone, unjust practices and need to be aware of the ways in which injustice may manifest itself.

■ *Principle E: Respect for people's rights and dignity*   According to the American Psychological Association, individuals have the rights of privacy, confidentiality and self-determination. Consequently, psychologists need to be aware of the vulnerabilities of some individuals that make it difficult for them to make autonomous decisions. Children are an obvious example. The principle also requires psychologists to be aware of and respect differences between cultures, individuals and roles. Age, culture, disability, ethnicity, gender, gender identity, language, national origin, race, religion, sexual orientation and socio-economic status are among these differences. Psychologists should avoid and remove biases related to these differences while being vigilant for, and critical of, those who fail to meet this standard.

Detailed recommendations about ethical conduct are provided on the basis of these principles. In this chapter we will concentrate on those issues which are especially pertinent to research.

6.2 Research ethics

Ethical issues are presented by the American Psychological Association's documentation in the order in which they are likely to be of concern to the researcher. Hence the list starts with the preparatory stages of planning research and culminates with publication.

Institutional approval

Much research takes place in organisations such as the police, prisons, schools and health services. Many, if not all, of these require formal approval before the research may be carried out in that organisation or by members of that organisation. Sometimes this authority to permit research is the responsibility of an individual (e.g. a headteacher) but, more likely, it will be the responsibility of a committee which considers ethics. It is incumbent on the researcher to obtain approval for their planned research. Furthermore, the proposal they put forward should be transparent in the sense that the information contained in the documentation and any other communication should accurately reflect the nature of the research. The organisation should be in a position to understand precisely what the researcher intends on the basis of the documentation provided by the researcher and any other communications. So any form of deceit or sharp practice such as lies, lying by omission and partial truths is unacceptable. Finally, the research should be carried out strictly in accordance with the protocol for the research as laid down by the researcher in the documentation. Material changes are not permissible and, if unavoidable, may require additional approval to remain ethical.

The next set of ethical requirements superficially seem rather different from each other. Nevertheless, they all relate to the general principle that participation in research should be a freely made decision of the participant. Undue pressure, fear, coercion and the like should not be present or implied. In addition, participants need to be understand just what they are subjecting themselves to by agreeing to be part of the research. Without this, they may inadvertently agree to participate in something which they would otherwise decline to do.

Informed consent to research

The general principle of informed consent applies widely and would include assessment, counselling and therapy as well as research. People have the right to have prior knowledge of just what they are agreeing to before agreeing to it. Only in this way is it possible for them to decide not to participate. Potential participants in research need to have the nature of the research explained to them in terms which they could reasonably be expected to understand. So the explanation given to a child may be different from that given to a university student. According to the ethical principles, sometimes research may be conducted without informed consent if it is allowed by the ethical code or where the law and other regulations specifically permit. (Although one might question whether research is ethical merely because the law permits it.)

The main provisions which need to be in place to justify the claim of informed consent are:

■ The purpose, procedures and approximate duration of the research should be provided to potential participants.

■ Participants should be made aware that they are both free to refuse to take part in the research and also free to withdraw from the research at any stage. Usually researchers accept that this freedom to withdrawal involves the freedom to withdraw any data provided up to the point of withdrawal. For example, the shredding of questionnaires and the destruction of recordings are appropriate ways of doing this if the withdrawing participant wishes. Or they may simply be given to the participant to dispose of as they wish.

■ The participant should be made aware of the possible outcomes or consequences of refusing to take part in the research or withdrawing. Frequently, there are no consequences but this is not always the case. For example, some organisations require that clients take part in research as part of the 'contract' between the organisation and client. Failure to take part in research might be taken as an indicator of non-cooperation. The sex offender undergoing treatment who declines to take part in the research might be regarded as lacking in contrition. Such judgements may have implications for the future disposal of the client. The researcher cannot be responsible for the original contract but they should be aware of the (subtle) pressure to participate and stress the voluntary nature of participation.

■ The participants should be informed of those aspects of the research which might influence their decision to participate. These include discomforts, risks and adverse outcomes. For example, one might include features of the study which might offend the sensibilities of the participant. Research on pornography in which pornographic images will be shown may offend the moral and/or social sensibilities of some participants.

■ Similarly, the participant should be informed of the benefits that may emerge from the research. A wide view of this would include benefits for academic research, benefits for the community, and even benefits for the individual participant. In this way, the potential participant is provided with a fuller picture of what the research might achieve which otherwise might not be obvious to them.

■ They should be told of any limits to the confidentiality of information provided during the research. Normally, researchers ensure the anonymity of the data that they collect and also the identity of the source of the data. But this is not always possible. For example, if one were researching sex offenders and they disclosed other offences of which authorities were unaware. It may be a requirement placed on the researcher that such undisclosed offences are reported to the authorities. In these circumstances, the appropriate course of action might be to indicate to participant that the researcher would have to report such previously undisclosed offences to the authorities.

■ Participants should be informed of the nature of any incentives being made to participate. Some participants may agree to take part as an act of kindness or because they believe that the research is important. If they are unaware of a cash payment, they may feel that their good intentions for taking part in the research are compromised when the payment is eventually offered.

■ Participants should be given contact details of someone whom they may approach for further details about the research and the rights of participants in the research. This information allows potential participants to ask more detailed questions and to obtain clarification. Furthermore, it has the benefit of helping to establish the bona fides of the research. For example, if the contact is a professor at a university, then this would help establish the reputability of the research.

Special provisions apply to experimental research involving potentially beneficial treatments which may not be offered to all participants (see Box 6.1).

BOX 6.1 INFORMED CONSENT IN INTERVENTION EXPERIMENTS

When a psychologist conducts *intervention research* there may be issues of informed consent. This does not refer to every experiment but those in which there may be significant advantages to receiving the treatment and significant disadvantages in *not* receiving the treatment. The treatment, for example, might be a therapeutic drug, counselling or therapy. Clearly, in these circumstances many participants would prefer to receive the treatment rather than not receive the treatment. If this were medical research it would be equivalent to some cancer patients being in the control group and dying because they are not given the newly developed drug that the experimental group benefits from. In psychological research, someone may be left suffering depression simply because they are allocated to the control group not receiving treatment. Due to these possibilities, the researcher in these circumstances should do the following:

■ The experimental nature of the treatments should be explained at the outset of the research.

■ It should be made clear that the services or treatments which will *not* be available should the participant be allocated to the control condition.

■ The method of assignment to the experimental or the control conditions should be explained clearly. If the method of selection for the experimental and control conditions is random then this needs to be explained.

■ The nature of the services or treatments available to those who choose *not* to take part in the research should be explained.

■ Financial aspects of participation should be clarified. For example the participant may be paid for participation, but it is conceivable that they may be expected to contribute to the cost of their treatment.

The classic study violating the above principles is known as the Tuskegee Experiment (Jones, 1981). Significantly, the study only involved black people as participants. They were suffering from syphilis at a time when this was a killer disease. The researchers, unbeknown to the participants, allocated them to experimental and control conditions. Hence those in the control had effective treatment withheld so were at serious health risk as a consequence. This may have been bad enough but there was worse. Even when it had become clear that the treatment was effective, the members of the control group were left to suffer from the disease because the researchers also wished to study its natural progression!

Informed consent for recordings and photography

Taking voice recordings, videos or photographs of participants is subject to the usual principle of informed consent. However, exceptions are stipulated in the ethical code:

- Informed consent is not necessary if the recording or photography takes place in a public place and is naturalistic (that is, there is no experimental intervention). This is ethical only to the extent that there is no risk of the inadvertent participants being identified personally or harmed by the recording or photography.

- If the research requires deception (and that deception is ethical) then consent for using the recording may be obtained retrospectively during the debriefing session in which the participant is given information about the research and an opportunity to ask questions. Deception is discussed below.

Circumstances in which informed consent may not *be necessary*

The ethical guidelines do not impose an invariant requirement of informed consent. They suggest circumstances in which it may be permissible to carry out research without prior consent of this sort. The overriding requirement is that the research could not be expected to (i.e. can be regarded as *not* likely to) cause distress or harm to participants. Additionally, at least *one* of the following should apply to the research in question:

- The study uses anonymous questionnaires or observations in a natural setting or archival materials – even then such participants should not be placed at risk of harm of any sort (even to their reputation) and confidentiality should be maintained.

- The study concerns jobs or related organisational matters in circumstances where the participant is under no risk concerning employment issues and the requirements of confidentiality are met.

- The study concerns 'normal educational practices, curricula or classroom management methods' in a context of an educational establishment.

The ethics also permit research not using informed consent *if* the law or institutional regulations permit research without informed consent. This provision of the ethical principles might cause some consternation. Most of us probably have no difficulty with the principle that psychologists should keep to the law in terms of their professional activities. Stealing from clients, for example, is illegal as well as unethical. However, there is a distinction to be made between what is permissible in law and what is ethical. A good example of this is the medical practitioner who has consenting sex with a patient. This may not be illegal and no crime committed in some countries. However, it is unethical for a doctor to do so and the punishment imposed by the medical profession is severe – possibly removal from the register of medical practitioners. There may be a potential conflict between ethics and the law. It seems to be somewhat lame to prefer the permission of the law rather than the constraints of the ethical standards.

Research with individuals in a less powerful/subordinate position to the researcher

Psychologists are often in a position of power relative to others. A university professor of psychology has power over his or her students. Clients of psychologists are dependent on the psychologists for help or treatment. Junior members of research staff are dependent on senior research staff and subordinate to them. It follows that some potential research participant may suffer adverse consequences as a result of refusing to take part in research or may be under undue pressure to participate simply because of this power differential. Any psychologist in such a position of power has an ethical duty to protect these vulnerable individuals from such adverse consequences. Sometimes, participation in research is a requirement of particular university courses or inducements may be given to participate in the form of additional credit. In these circumstances, the ethical recommendation is that fair alternative choices should be made available for individuals who do not wish to participate in research.

Inducements to participate

Financial and other encouragement to participate in research are subject to the following requirements:

■ Psychologists should not offer unreasonably large monetary or other inducements (e.g. gifts) to potential participants in research. In some circumstances such rewards can become coercive. One simply has to take the medical analogy of offering people large amounts of money to donate organs in order to understand the undesirability of this. While acceptable levels of inducements are not stipulated in the ethics, one reasonable approach might be to limit payments where offered to out-of-pocket expenses (such as travel) and a modest hourly rate for time. Of course, even this provision is probably out of the question for student researchers.

■ Sometimes professional services are offered as a way of encouraging participation in research. These might be, for example, counselling or psychological advice of some sort. In these circumstances, it is essential to clarify the precise nature of the services, including possible risks, further obligations and the limitations to the provision of such services. A further requirement, not mentioned in the APA ethics, might be that the researcher should be competent to deliver these services. Once again, it is difficult to imagine the circumstances in which students could be offering such inducements.

The use of deception in research

The fundamental ethical position is that deception should *not* be used in psychological research procedures. There are *no* circumstances in which deception is acceptable if there is a reasonable expectation that physical pain or emotional distress will be caused. However, it is recognised that there are circumstances in which the use of deception may be justified. If the proposed research has 'scientific, educational or applied value' (or the prospect of it) then deception may be considered. The next step is to establish that no effective alternative approach is possible which does not use deception. These are not matters which individual psychologists should regard themselves as their own personal arbiters. Consultation with disinterested colleagues is an appropriate course of action.

If the use of deception is the only feasible option, it is incumbent on the psychologist to explain the deception as early as possible. This is preferably immediately after the data have been collected from each individual, but it may be delayed until all of the data from all of the participants have been collected. The deceived participant should be given the unfettered opportunity to withdraw their data. Box 6.2 discusses how deception has been a central feature of social psychological research. The ethics of the British Psychological Society indicate that a distinction may be drawn between deliberate lies and omission of particular details about the nature of the research that the individual is participating in. This is essentially the distinction between lying by omission and lying by commission. You might wonder if this distinction is sufficient justification of anything. The British Psychological Society indicates that a key test of the acceptability is the response of participants at debriefing when the nature of the deception is revealed. If they express anger, discomfort or otherwise object to the deception then the deception was inappropriate and the future of the project should be reviewed. The BPS guidelines do not specify the next step however.

BOX 6.2 DECEPTION IN THE HISTORY OF SOCIAL PSYCHOLOGY

The use of deception has been much more characteristic of the work of social psychologists than any other branch of psychological research. Korn (1997) argues that this was the almost inevitable consequence of using laboratory methods to study social phenomena. Deception first occurred in psychological research in 1897 when Leon Solomons studied how we discriminate between a single point touching our skin and two points touching our skin at the same time. Some participants were led to believe that there were two points and others that there was just one point. Whichever they believed made a difference to what they perceived. Interestingly, Solomons told his participants that they might be being deceived before participation.

In the early history of psychology deception was indeed a rare occurrence, but so was any sort of empirical research. There was a gradual growth in the use of deception between 1921 and 1947. The *Journal of Abnormal and Social Psychology* was surveyed during this period. Fifty-two per cent of articles involved studies using misinformation as part of the procedure while 42% used 'false cover stories' (Korn, 1997). Little fuss was made about deception at this time. According to a variety of surveys of journals, the use of deception increased between 1948 and 1979 despite more and more questions about psychological ethics being asked. Furthermore, there appears to be no moderation in the scale of the sort of deceptions employed during this period. Of course, the purpose of deception in many cases is simply to hide the true purpose of the experiment. Participants threatened with a painful injection might be expected to behave differently if they believe this is necessary for a physiological experiment than if they know that the threat of the injection is simply a way of manipulating their stress levels.

Many of the classic studies in social psychology – ones still discussed in textbooks – used deceit of some sort or another. These did not necessarily involve trivial matters. In Milgram's studies of obedience in which participants were told that they were punishing a third party with electric shock, it appeared at one stage that the victim of the shock had been severely hurt. All of this was a lie and deception (Milgram, 1974). Milgram tended to refer to his deceptions as 'technical illusions' but this would appear to be nothing other than a euphemism. In studies by other researchers, participants believed that they were in an emergency situation when smoke was seeping into a

→

Box 6.2 continued

laboratory through a vent – again a deliberate deception (Latane and Darley, 1970). Deception was endemic and routine in social psychological research. It had to be, given the great stress on laboratory experimentation in the social psychology of the time. Without the staging of such extreme situations by means of deception, experimental social psychological research would be difficult if not impossible.

Sometimes the deceptions seem relatively trivial and innocuous. For example, imagine that one wished to study the effects of the gender of a student on the grades that they get for an essay. Few would have grave concerns about taking an essay and giving it to a sample of lecturers for marking, telling half of them that the essay was by a male and the other half the essay was by a woman. It would seem to be important to know through research whether or not there is a gender bias in marking which favours one gender over the other. Clearly there has been a deception – lie if one prefers – but it is one which probably does not jeopardise in any way the participant's psychological well-being though there are circumstances in which it could. Believing that you have endangered someone's life by giving them dangerous levels of electric shock is not benign but may fundamentally affect a person's ideas about themselves. In some studies, participants have been deceitfully abused about their abilities or competence in order to make them angry (Berkowitz, 1962).

How would studies like these stand up to ethical scrutiny? Well deception as such is not banned by ethical codes. There are circumstances in which it may be justifiable. Deception may be appropriate when the study has, or potentially has, significant 'scientific, educational or applied value' according to the APA ethical principles. Some might question what this means. For example, if we wanted to study the grieving process, would it be right to tell someone that the university had just been informed that their mother had just died? Grief is an important experience and clearly it is of great importance to study the phenomenon. Does that give the researcher carte blanche to do anything?

Deception is common in our society. The white lie is a deception, for example. Does the fact that deception is endemic in society justify its use in research? Psychologists are professionals who as a group do not benefit from developing a reputation as tricksters. The culture of deception in research may lead to suspicion and hostility towards participation in the research.

Debriefing

As soon as the research is over (or essential stages are complete), debriefing should be carried out. There is a mutual discussion between researcher and participant to fully inform the participant about matters such as the nature of the result, the results of the research and the conclusions of the research. The researcher should try to correct the misconceptions of the participant that may have developed about any aspect of research. Of course, there may be good scientific or humane reasons for withholding some information – or delaying the main debriefing until a suitable time. For example, it may be that the research involves two or more stages separated by a considerable interval of time. Debriefing participants after the first stage may considerably contaminate the results at the second stage.

BOX 6.3 ETHICS AND RESEARCH WITH ANIMALS

Nowadays, few students have contact with laboratory animals during their education and training. Many universities simply do not have any facilities at all for animal research. However, many students have active concerns about the welfare of animals and so may be particularly interested in the ethical provision for such research in psychology. It needs to be stressed that this is an area where the law in many countries has exacting requirements that may be even more stringent than those required ethically. The first principle is that psychologists involved in research with animals must adhere to the pertinent laws and regulations. This includes the means by which laboratory animals are acquired, the ways in which the animals are cared for, the ways in which the animals are used, and the way in which laboratory animals are disposed of or retired from research.

Some further ethical requirements are:

■ Psychologists both experienced and trained in research methods with laboratory animals should adopt a supervisory role for all work involving animals. Their responsibilities include consideration of the 'comfort, health and humane treatment' of animals under their supervision.

■ It should be ensured that all individuals using animals have training in animal research methods and the care of animals. This should include appropriate ways of looking after the particular species of animal in question and the ways in which they should be handled. The supervising psychologist is responsible for this.

■ Psychologists should take appropriate action in order that the adverse aspects of animal research should be minimised. This includes matters such as the animals' pain, comfort, freedom from infection and illnesses.

■ While in circumstances it may be ethically acceptable to expose animals to stress, pain or some form of privation of its bodily needs, this is subject to requirements. There must be no alternative way of doing the research. Furthermore, it should only be done when it is possible to justify the procedures on the basis of its 'scientific, educational or applied value'.

■ Anaesthesia before and after surgery is required to minimise pain. Techniques which minimise the risk of infection are also required.

■ Should it be necessary and appropriate to terminate the animal's life, this should be done painlessly and as quickly as possible. The accepted procedures for doing so should be employed.

One suspects that many will regard this list as inadequate. The list makes a number of assumptions – not the least being that it is ethically justifiable to carry out research on animals in certain conditions. But is this morally acceptable? Some might question whether cruelty to animals (and the unnecessary infliction of pain is cruel) is defensible in any circumstances. Others may be concerned about the lack of clarity in terms of when animal research is appropriate. Isn't any research defensible on the grounds of scientific progress? What does scientific progress mean? Is it achieved by publication in an academic psychology journal?

Debriefing cannot be guaranteed to deal effectively with the harm done to participants by deception. Whenever a researcher recognises that a particular participant appears to have been (inadvertently) harmed in some way by the procedures then reasonable efforts should be made to deal with this harm. It should be remembered that researchers are not normally qualified to offer counselling, and other forms of help and referral to relevant professionals may be the only appropriate course of action. There is a body of research on the effects of debriefing (e.g. Epley and Huff, 1998; Smith and Richardson, 1983).

6.3 Ethics and publication

The following few ethical standards for research might have particular significance for student researchers.

Ethical standards in reporting research

It is ethically wrong to fabricate data. Remember that this applies to students. Of course, errors may inadvertently be made in published data – this is most likely to be a computational or statistical error. The researcher, on spotting the error, should take reasonable efforts to correct this. Among the possibilities are corrections or retractions in the journal in question.

Plagiarism

Plagiarism is when the work of another person is used without acknowledgement and as if it was one's own work. Psychologists do *not* plagiarise. Ethical principles hold that merely occasionally citing the original source is insufficient to militate against the charge of plagiarism. So, copying chunks of other people's work directly is inappropriate even if they are occasionally cited during this. Of course, quotations clearly identified as such by the use of quotation marks, attribution of authorship, and citation of the source are normally acceptable. Even then, quotations should be kept short and within the limits set by publishers, for example.

Proper credit for publications

It is ethically inappropriate to stake a claim on work which one has not actually done or in some way contributed to substantially. This includes claiming authorship on publications. The principal author of a publication (the first-named) should be the individual who has contributed the most to the research. Of course, sometimes such a decision will be arbitrary where contributions cannot be ranked. Being senior in terms of formal employment role should not be a reason for principal authorship. Being in charge of a research unit is no reason for being included in the list of publications. There are often circumstances in which an individual makes a contribution but less than a significant one. This should be dealt with by a footnote acknowledging their contribution or some similar means. Authorship is not the reward for a minor contribution of this sort.

It is of particular importance to note that publications based on the dissertations of students should credit the student as principal (first) author. The issue of publication credit should be raised with students as soon as practicable by responsible academics.

Publishing the same data repeatedly

When data are published for the second or more time then the publication should clearly indicate the fact of republication. This is acceptable. It is not acceptable to repeatedly publish the same data as if for the first time.

The availability of data for verification

Following the publication of the results of research, they should be available for checking or verification by others competent to do so. This is not carte blanche for anyone to take another person's data for publication in some other form – that would require agreement. It merely is a safeguard for the verification of substantive claims made by the original researcher. The verifying psychologist may have to meet the costs of supplying the data for verification. Exceptions to this principle of verification are:

■ Circumstances in which the participant's confidentiality (e.g. anonymity) cannot be ensured.
■ If the data may not be released because another party has proprietary rights over the data which prevent their release.

6.4 Conclusion

Research ethics cover virtually every stage of the research process. The literature review, for example, is covered by the requirements of fidelity and other stages of the process have specific recommendations attached to them. It is in the nature of ethics that they do not simply list proscribed behaviours. Frequently they offer advice on what aspects of research require ethical attention and the circumstances in which exceptions to the generally accepted standards may be considered. They impose a duty on all psychologists to engage in consideration and consultation about the ethical standing of their research as well as that of other members of the psychological community. Furthermore, the process does not end prior to the commencement of data collection but requires attention and vigilance throughout the research process since new information may indicate ethical problems where they had not been anticipated.

One important thing about ethics is that they require a degree of judgement in their application. It is easy for students to seek rules for their research. For example, is it unethical to cause a degree of upset in the participants in your research? What if your research was into experiences of bereavement. Is it wrong to interview people about bereavement knowing that it will distress some of them? Assume that you have carefully explained to participants that the interviews are about bereavement. Is it wrong then to cause them any distress in this way? What if the research was just a Friday afternoon practical class on interviewing. Is it right to cause distress in these circumstances? What if it were a Friday workshop for trainee clinical psychologists on bereavement counselling. Is it any more acceptable? All of this reinforces the idea that ethics are fine judgements not blanket prohibitions for the most part.

The consideration of ethics is a fundamental requirement of the research process that cannot be avoided by any psychologist – including students at any level. It starts with not fiddling the data and not plagiarising. And what if your best friend fiddles the data and plagiarises?

Key points

- Psychological associations such as the American Psychological Association and the British Psychological Society publish ethical guidelines to help their members behave morally in relation to their professional work. Self-regulation of ethics is a characteristic of professions.

- Ethics may be based on broad principles, but frequently advice is provided in guidelines about their specific application, for example, in the context of research. So one general ethical principle is that of integrity meaning accuracy, honesty and truthfulness. This principle clearly has different implications to the use of deception in research from those when reporting data.

- Informed consent is the principle that participants in research should willingly consent to taking part in research in the light of a clear explanation by the researcher about what the research entails. At the same time, participants in research should feel in a position to withdraw from the research at any stage with the option of withdrawing any data that has already been provided. There are exceptions where informed consent is not deemed necessary – especially naturalistic observations of people who might expect to be observed by someone since they are in a public place.

- Deception of participants in research is regarded as problematic in modern psychology despite being endemic in some fields – particularly social psychology. Nevertheless, there is no complete ban on deception only the requirements that the deception is absolutely necessary since the research is important and there is no effective alternative deception-free way of conducting it. The response of participants during debriefing to the deception may be taken as an indicator of the risks inherent in that deception.

- The publication of research is subject to ethical constraints. The fabrication of data, plagiarism of the work of others, claiming the role of author on a publication to which one has only minimally contributed, and the full acknowledgement by first authorship of students' research work are all covered in recent ethical guidelines.

Activities

1. Are any principles of ethical conduct violated in the following examples? What valid arguments could be made to justify what occurs? These are matters that could be debated. Alternatively, you could list the ethical pros and cons of each before reaching a conclusion.

   (a) Ken is researching memory and Dawn volunteers to be a participant in the research. Ken is very attracted to Dawn and asks for her address and mobile phone number, explaining that she may need to be contacted for a follow-up interview. This is a lie as no such interviews are planned. He later phones her up for a date.

   (b) A research team is planning to study Internet sex offenders. They set up a bogus Internet pornography site – 'All tastes sex'. The site contains a range of links to specialised pages devoted to a specific sexual interest – bondage, mature sex, Asian women and the like. Visitors to the site who press these links see mild pornographic pictures in line with the theme of the link. The main focus of the researchers is on child pornography users on the internet. To this end they have a series of links labelled '12 year olds and under', 'young boys need men friends', 'schoolgirls for real', 'sexy toddlers' and so forth. These links lead nowhere but the researchers have the site programmed such that visitors to the different pages can be counted. Furthermore, they have a 'data miner' which implants itself onto the visitor's computer and can extract information from that computer and report back to the researchers. They use this information in order to send out an e-mail questionnaire concerning the lifestyle of the visitor to the porn site – details such as their age, interests, address and so forth as well as psychological tests. To encourage completion, the researchers claim that in return for completing the questionnaire, they have a chance of being selected for a prize of a Caribbean holiday. The research team is approached by the police who believe that the data being gathered may be useful in tracking down paedophiles.

   (c) A student researcher is studying illicit drug use on a university campus. She is given permission to distribute questionnaires during an introductory psychology lecture. Participants are assured anonymity and confidentiality, although the researcher has deliberately included questions about demographic information such as the participants' exact date of birth, their home town, the modules they are taking and so forth. However, the student researcher is really interested in personality factors and drug taking. She gets another student to distribute personality questionnaires to the same class a few weeks later. The same information about exact date of birth, home town, place of birth and so forth is collected. This is used to match each drugs questionnaire with that same person's personality questionnaire. However, the questionnaires are anonymous since no name is requested.

   (d) Professor Green is interested in fascist and other far-right political organisations. Since he believes that these organisations would not permit a researcher to observe them, he poses as a market trader and applies for and is given membership of several of these organisations. He attends the meetings and other events with other members. He is carrying out participant observation and is compiling extensive notes of what he witnesses for eventual publication.

(e) A researcher studying sleep feels that a young woman taking part in the research is physically attracted to him. He tries to kiss her.

(f) Some researchers believe that watching filmed violence leads to violence in real life. Professor Jenkins carries out a study in which scenes of extreme violence taken from the film *Reservoir Dogs* are shown to a focus group. A week later, one of the participants in the focus group is arrested for the murder of his partner on the day after seeing the film.

(g) A discourse analyst examines President Bill Clinton's television claim that he did not have sexual intercourse with Monica Lewinsky in order to assess discursive strategies that he employed and to seek any evidence of lying. The results of this analysis are published in a psychology journal.

(h) 'Kitty Friend complained to an ethics committee about a psychologist she read about in the newspaper who was doing research on evoked potentials in cat brains. She asserted that the use of domesticated cats in research was unethical, inhumane, and immoral' (Keith-Spiegel and Koocher, 1985, p. 35). The ethics committee chooses not to consider the complaint.

(i) A psychology student chooses to investigate suicidal thoughts in a student population. She distributes a range of personality questionnaires among her friends. Scoring the test she notices that one of her friends, Tom, has scored heavily on a measure of suicide ideation and has written at the end of the questionnaire that he feels desperately depressed. She knows that it is Tom from the handwriting which is very distinctive.

(j) Steffens (1931) describes how along with others he studied the laboratory records of a student of Wilhelm Wundt, generally regarded as the founder of the first psychological laboratory. This student went on to be a distinguished professor in America. Basically the student's data failed to support aspects of Wundt's psychological writings. Steffens writes that the student

> . . . *must have thought . . . that Wundt might have been reluctant to crown a discovery which would require the old philosopher [Wundt] to rewrite volumes of his lifework. The budding psychologist solved the ethical problem before him by deciding to alter his results, and his papers showed how he did this, by changing the figures item by item, experiment by experiment, so as to make the curve of his averages come out for instead of against our school. After a few minutes of silent admiration of the mathematical feat performed on the papers before us, we buried sadly these remains of a great sacrifice to loyalty, to the school spirit, and to practical ethics.* [p. 151]

PART 2
Quantitative research methods

7 The basic laboratory experiment

Overview

■ The laboratory experiment has a key role in psychological research in that it allows the investigation of causal relationships between variables. In other words, it identifies whether one variable affects another in a cause and effect sequence.

■ Essentially an experiment involves systematically varying the level of the variable that is thought to be causal then measuring the effect of this variation on the measured variable while holding all other variables constant.

■ The simplest experimental design used by psychologists consists of two conditions. One condition has a higher level of the manipulated variable than the other condition. The former condition is sometimes known as the experimental condition while the condition having the lower level is known as the control condition. The two experimental conditions also may be referred to as the independent variable. The researcher assesses whether the scores on the measured variable differ between the two conditions. The measured variable is often referred to as the dependent variable.

■ If the size of the effect differs significantly between the two conditions and all variables other than the manipulated variable have been held constant, then this difference is most likely due to the manipulated variable.

■ There are a number of means by which the researcher holds all of the variables constant other than the independent and dependent variables. These include: randomly assigning participants to the different conditions (which ensures equality in the long run), carrying out the study in the controlled setting of a laboratory where hopefully other factors are constant, and making the conditions as similar as possible for all participants except as far as they are in the experimental or control condition.

■ In *between-subjects designs* participants are randomly assigned to just *one* of the conditions of the study. In *within-subjects designs* the same participants carry out all conditions. Rather than being randomly assigned to just one condition, they are randomly assigned to the different orders in which the conditions are to be run.

■ Random assignment of participants only guarantees that in the long run that the participants in all conditions start off similar in all regards. For any individual study, random assignment cannot ensure equality. Consequently, some experimental designs use a prior measure of the dependent variable (the measured variable) which can be used to assess how effective the random assignment has been. The experimental and control groups should have similar (ideally identical) mean scores on this pre-measure. This prior measure is known as a pre-test while the measurement after the experimental manipulation is known as a post-test. The difference between the pre-test and post-test provides an indication of the change in the measured variable.

■ A number of disadvantages of the basic laboratory experiment should be recognised. The artificiality of the laboratory experiment is obvious so it is always possible that the experimental manipulation and the setting fail to reflect what happens in more natural or realistic research settings. Furthermore, the number of variables that can be manipulated in a single experiment is limited which can be frustrating when one is studying a complex psychological process.

When used appropriately, the randomised laboratory experiment is one of the most powerful tools available to researchers. This does not mean that it is always or even often the ideal research method. It simply means that the laboratory is an appropriate environment for studying many psychological processes – particularly physiological, sensory or cognitive processes. The use of the laboratory to study social processes, for example, is not greeted with universal enthusiasm. Nevertheless, many studies in psychology take place in a research laboratory using true or randomised experimental designs. Any psychologist, even if they never carry out a laboratory experiment in their professional careers, needs to understand the basics of laboratory research. Otherwise a great deal of psychological research will pass over their heads.

It is essential to be able to differentiate between two major sorts of research designs:

■ Experiments in which different participants take part in different conditions are known variously as between-subjects, between-participants, independent-groups, unrelated-groups or uncorrelated-groups designs. A diagram of a simple between-subjects design with only two conditions is shown in Figure 7.1*a*.

■ Designs in which the same participants take part in all (or sometimes some) of the various conditions are called within-subjects, within-participants, repeated-measures, dependent-groups, related-groups or correlated-groups designs. A diagram of a simple within-subjects design with only two conditions is presented in Figure 7.1*b*.

An example of a between-subjects design would be a study that compared the number of errors made entering data into a computer spreadsheet for a sample of people listening to loud popular music with the number of errors made by a different control sample listening to white noise at the same volume. That is to say, two different groups of people are compared. An example of a within-subjects design would be a study of the number of keyboard errors made by a group of 20 secretaries, comparing the number of errors when music is being played to when music is not being played. That is to say, the performance of one group of people is compared in two different circumstances.

One of the reasons why it is important to distinguish between these two broad types of design is that they use rather different methods of analysis. For example, they use different statistical tests. The first design which uses different groups of participants for each

Figure 7.1	(a) Between-subjects designs with two conditions; (b) Within-subjects design with two conditions

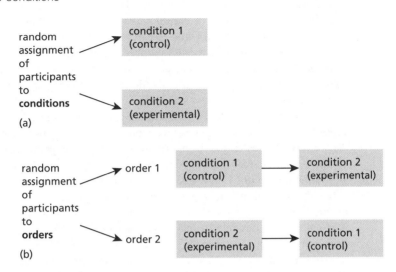

condition would require an unrelated statistical test (such as the unrelated or uncorrelated *t*-test). The latter design in which the same group of participants take part in every condition of the experiment would require a related statistical test (such as the related or correlated *t*-test).

Although it is perfectly feasible to do experiments in a wide variety of settings, a custom designed research laboratory is usually preferred. There are two main reasons for using a research laboratory:

■ *Practicalities*   A study may require the use of equipment or apparatus that may be too bulky or too heavy to move elsewhere, or needs to be kept secure because it may be expensive or inconvenient to replace.

■ *Experimental control*   In an experiment it is important to try to keep all factors constant other than the variable or variables that are manipulated. This is obviously easier to do in a room or laboratory that is custom designed for the task and in which all participants take part in the study. The lighting, the temperature, the noise and the arrangement of any equipment can all be kept constant. In addition, other distractions such as people walking through or talking can be excluded. You will often find great detail about the physical set up of the laboratory where the research was done in some reports of laboratory experiments.

The importance of holding these extraneous or environmental factors constant depends on how strong the effect of the manipulated variable is on the measured variable. Unfortunately, the researcher is unlikely to know in advance what their effect is in some cases. To the extent that the extraneous variable seems not to, or has been shown not to, influence the key variables in the research, one may consider moving the research to a more appropriate or convenient research location. For example, if you are carrying out a study in a school, then it is unlikely that that school will have a purpose built psychology laboratory for you to use. You may find yourself in a small room which is normally used for other purposes. If it is important that you control the kind or the level of the noise in the room, then you could be able to do this by playing what is called 'white noise' through earphones worn by each participant. If it is essential that the study takes place in a more carefully controlled setting, then the pupils will need to come to your laboratory. The essential point to realise is that the setting of the study may be less critical than its design.

It should be stressed that while researchers may aim for perfection, most research is to a degree a compromise between a number of considerations. The perfect research study has probably never been designed and is probably an oxymoron – that should not stop you trying for the best possible, but it should be remembered when your research seems not to be able to reach the highest standard.

Because of the important role it plays in psychological research, we introduced the concept of a true experiment in Chapter 1 on the role and nature of research in psychology. As we saw, studies employing a true or randomised experimental design were the most common kind of study published in the *Journal of Personality and Social Psychology* in 1996 (Sherman *et al.*, 1999). They constituted 55% of all the studies sampled in that year. While this journal may favour this design, this high percentage may seem surprising for an area where it is more difficult to manipulate concepts of central concern. For example, it is not usually possible to manipulate personality characteristics such as extraversion or whether or not a participant has a criminal record. The proportion of studies using a true or randomised experimental design is higher in areas such as learning, perception, cognition and memory, which have traditionally been called experimental psychology because of the use of this design.

7.1   Characteristics of the true or randomised experiment

The most basic laboratory experiment is easily demonstrated. Decide on an experimental and control group and allocate participants to one or other on the basis of a coin toss. Put the experimental group through a slightly different procedure to the control group. This is known as the experimental manipulation and corresponds to a variable which the researcher believes might affect responses on another variable called the dependent variable. After the data have been collected, the researcher examines the average score for the two conditions to see whether or not there is a substantial difference between them. For many purposes, such a simple design will work well.

In order to be able to run experiments satisfactorily one needs to understand the three essential characteristics of the true or randomised experiment – and more:

- ■ Experimental manipulation.
- ■ Standardisation of procedures – that is the control of all variables other than the independent variable.
- ■ Random assignment to conditions or order.

We will consider each of these in turn.

Experimental manipulation

Only the variable that is assumed to cause or affect another variable is manipulated (varied). This manipulated variable is often referred to as the *independent variable* because it is assumed to be varied independently of any other variable. If it is not manipulated independently, then any effect that we observe may be due to those other variables. An example of an independent variable is alcohol. If we think that alcohol increases the number of mistakes we make and we are interested in seeing whether this is the case, alcohol (or more strictly speaking, the level or amount of alcohol) is the independent variable which we manipulate. The variable that is presumed to be affected by the independent or manipulated variable is called the *dependent variable* because it is thought to be dependent on the independent variable. It is the variable that we measure. In this example, the dependent variable is the number of mistakes made in a task such as walking along a straight line.

In the most basic true or randomised experiment, we would only have two *conditions* (also known as *levels of treatment* or *groups*). In one condition, a lower amount of alcohol would be given the participant while in the other condition the participant receives a higher level of alcohol. The amount of alcohol given would be standard for all participants in a condition. So, in condition 1 the amount might be standardised as 8 millilitres (ml). This is about the amount of alcohol in a glass of wine. In the second condition the amount may be doubled to 16 ml. If the size of the effect varies directly with the amount of alcohol given, then the more the two groups differ then the bigger the effect.

Why did we choose to give both groups alcohol? After all, we could have given the experimental group alcohol but the control group no alcohol at all. Both groups are given alcohol in the hope that by doing so participants in both groups are aware that they have consumed alcohol. Participants receiving alcohol probably realise that they have been given alcohol. Unless the quantity of alcohol was very small, participants are likely to detect it. So two things have happened – they have been given alcohol and they are also aware that they have been given alcohol. However, if one group received no alcohol then, unless we deliberately misled them, members of this group will not believe that they have taken alcohol. So we would not know whether the alcohol or the belief that they had been given alcohol was the key causal variable. Since the effects of alcohol are well known, participants believing that they have taken alcohol may behave accordingly. By giving both groups alcohol, both groups will believe that they have taken alcohol. The only thing that varies is the key variable of the amount of alcohol taken. In good experimental research the effectiveness of the experimental manipulation is often evaluated. This is discussed in Box 7.1 overleaf. In this case, participants in the experiment might be asked about whether or not they believed that they had taken alcohol in a debriefing interview at the end of the study.

The condition having the lower quantity of alcohol is referred to as the *control condition*. The condition having the higher quantity of alcohol may be called the *experimental condition*. The purpose of the control condition is to see how participants behave when they receive less of the variable that is being manipulated.

In theory, if not always in practice, the experimental and control conditions should be identical in every way but for the variable being manipulated. It is easy to overlook differences. So, in our alcohol experiment participants in both groups should be given the same quantity of liquid to drink. But it is easy to overlook this if the low alcohol group are, say, given one glass of wine and the high alcohol group two glasses of wine. If the participants in the control condition are not given the same amount to drink, then alcohol is not being manipulated independently of all other factors. Participants in the experimental condition would have been given more to drink while participants in the control condition would have been given less to drink. If we find that reaction time was slower in the experimental condition than in the control condition, then we could not be certain whether this difference was due to the alcohol or the amount of liquid drunk. This may seem very pernickety

BOX 7.1 CHECKS ON THE EXPERIMENTAL MANIPULATION

It can be a grave mistake to assume that simply because an experimental manipulation has been introduced by the researcher that the independent variable has actually been effectively manipulated. It might be argued that if the researcher finds a difference between the experimental and control conditions on the dependent variable that the manipulation must have been effective. Things are not that simple.

Assume that we are investigating the effects of anger on memory. In order to manipulate anger, the researcher deliberately says certain pre-scripted offensive comments to the participants in the experimental group whereas nice things are said to the participants in the control group. It is very presumptuous to assume that this procedure will work effectively without subjecting it to some test.

For example, the participants might well regard the offensive comments as a joke rather than an insult so the manipulation may make them happier rather than angrier. Alternatively, the control may find the nice comments of the experimenter to be patronising and become somewhat angry as a consequence. It would be advantageous to demonstrate that the experimental manipulation has actually worked. One relatively simple thing to do in this case would be to get participants to complete a questionnaire about their mood containing a variety of emotions, such as angry, happy, sad, etc., which the participant rates. In this way it would be possible to assess whether the experimental group was indeed angrier than the control group following the anger manipulation. Alternatively, at the debriefing session following participation in the experiment, the participants could be asked about how they felt after the experimenter said the offensive or nice things. This check would also demonstrate that the manipulation had had a measurable effect on the participant's anger levels.

Sometimes it is appropriate, as part of pilot work trying out one's procedures prior to the study proper, to establish the effectiveness of the experimental manipulation as a distinct step in its own right. Researchers need to be careful not to assume that simply because they obtain statistically significant differences between the experimental and control conditions that this is evidence of the effectiveness of their experimental manipulation. If the experimental manipulation has had an effect on the participants but not the one intended, it is vital that the researcher knows this. Otherwise, the conceptual basis for their analysis may be inappropriate. For example, they may be discussing the effects of anger when they should be discussing the effects of happiness.

In our experience, checks on the experimental manipulation are relatively rare in published research and are, probably, even rarer in student research. Yet such checks would seem to be essential. As we have seen, the debriefing session can be an ideal opportunity to interview participants about this aspect of the study along with its other features. The most thorough researchers may also consider a more objective demonstration of the effectiveness of the manipulation as above when the participants' mood was assessed.

in this case but dehydration through having less liquid may have an effect on behaviour. The point of the laboratory experiment is that we try to control as many factors as it possible. Of course, variations in the volume of liquid drunk could be introduced into the research design in order to discover what the effect of varying volume is on errors.

Standardisation of procedures

A second essential characteristic of the true experiment is implicit in the previous characteristic. That is, all factors should be held constant apart from the variable(s) being investigated. This is largely achieved by standardising all aspects of the procedures employed. Only the experimental manipulation should vary. We have already seen the importance of this form of control when we stressed in our alcohol study that the two conditions should be identical apart from the amount of alcohol taken. So participants in both conditions were made aware that they will be given alcohol and that they are given the same amount of liquid to drink.

There are other factors which we should try to hold constant which are not so obvious. The time of day the study is carried out, the body weight of the participants, the amount of time that has lapsed since they have last eaten and so forth are all good examples of this. Such standardisation is not always easy to achieve. For example, what about variations in the behaviour of the experimenter during an experiment? If the experimenter's behaviour differs systematically between the two groups then experimenter behaviour and the effects of the independent variable will be confounded. We may confuse the variability in the behaviour of the experimenter with the effects of different quantities of alcohol. There have been experiments in which the procedure is automated so that there is no experimenter present in the laboratory. For example, tape-recorded instructions to the participants are played through loudspeakers in the laboratory. In this way, the instructions can be presented identically in every case and variations in the experimenter's behaviour eliminated.

Standardisation of procedures is easier said than done but remains an ideal in the laboratory experiment. It is usual for things like the instructions to participants to be written out as a guide for the experimenter when running the experiment. One of the difficulties is that standardisation has to be considered in relation to the tasks being carried out by participants. So it is impossible to give advice that would apply in every case. Because of the difficulty in standardising all aspects of the experiment, it is desirable to randomly order the running of the experimental and control conditions. For example, we know that cognitive functions vary according to the time of day. It is very difficult to standardise the time of day that an experiment is run. Hence it is desirable to randomly decide which condition the participant who arrives at 2.30 p.m. will be in, which condition the participant who arrives next will be in, and so forth. In this way there will be no systematic bias for one of the conditions of the experiment to be run at different times of the day from the other conditions.

Random assignment

Random assignment is the third essential feature of an experiment. There are two main procedures according to the type of experimental design:

■ Participants are put in the experimental or control condition at random using a proper randomisation procedure (which may be simply the toss of a coin – heads the experimental group, tails the control group.) There are other methods of randomisation as we will see. Random assignment to conditions is used when the participants only take part in one condition.

■ Alternatively, if participants undertake more than one condition (in the simplest case both the experimental and control conditions), then they are randomly assigned to the different orders of those two conditions. With just two conditions there are just two possible orders – experimental condition first followed by control condition second, or control condition first followed by experimental condition second. Of course, with three or more conditions then there are rapidly increasing numbers of possible orders.

It is easy to get confused about the term *random*. Random assignment requires the use of a proper random procedure. This is not the same thing at all as a haphazard or casual choice. By random we mean that each possible outcome has an equal chance of being selected. We do not want a selection process which systematically favours one outcome rather than another. (For example, the toss of a coin is normally a random process but it would not be if the coin had been doctored in someway so that it lands heads up most of the time.) There are a number of random procedures which may be employed. We have already mentioned the toss of a coin but will include it in the list of possibilities again as it is a good and simple procedure:

■ With two conditions or orders you can toss a coin where the participant will be assigned to one of them if the coin lands 'heads' up and to the other if it lands 'tails' up.

■ Similarly, especially if there is more than two conditions, you could throw a die.

■ Write the two conditions or orders on two separate index cards or slips of papers, shuffle them without seeing them and select one of them.

■ Use random number tables where, say, even numbers represent one condition or order and odd numbers represent the other one.

■ Sometimes a computer can be used to generate a sequence of random numbers. Again you could use an odd number for the experimental group and an even number for allocating the participant to the control group (or vice versa).

One can either go through one of these randomisation procedures for each successive participant or you can draw up a list in advance for the entire experiment. However, there are two things that you need to consider:

■ You may find that you have 'runs' of the same condition such as six participants in sequence all of which are in, say, the control group. If you get runs like this you may find, for example, that you are testing one condition more often at a particular time of day. That is, despite the randomisation, the two conditions are not similar in all respects. For example, these six participants may all be tested in the morning rather than spread throughout the day.

■ Alternatively, you may also find that the number of participants in the two conditions or orders is very different. There is even a remote possibility that all your participants are assigned to one condition or order.

Randomisation only equates things in the long run, In the short run, it merely guarantees that there is no systematic bias in the selection. In the short term, chance factors may nevertheless lead to differences between the conditions.

There is no need to go into technical details, but if it is possible to have equal numbers in each condition of an experimental design then you should try to do so. Most statistical tests work optimally in these circumstances. If equal numbers are impossible then so be it. However, there are ways in which one can ensure that there are equal numbers of particip-ants in each condition. For example, one can employ *matched* or *block randomisation*. That is, the first participant of every pair of participants is assigned at random using a specified procedure while the second participant is assigned to the remaining condition or order. So, if the first participant has been randomly assigned to the control condition, the second participant will be allocated to the experimental condition. If you do this, you will end up with equal numbers of participants in the two conditions or orders if you have an equal number of participants. Box 7.2 discusses how you can pair off participants to ensure that the different groups have similar characteristics.

In the between-subjects design (in which participants serve in just one condition of the experiment), any differences between the participants are usually controlled by random assignment. The prime purpose of this is to avoid systematic biases in the allocation of participants to one or other condition. If the experimenter merely decided on the spot which group a participant should be in then all sorts of 'subconscious' factors may influ-ence this choice and perhaps influence the outcome of the experiment as a consequence.

BOX 7.2   MATCHING

One way of ensuring that the participants in the experimental and control group are similar on variables which might be expected to affect the outcome of the study is to use matching. Participants in an experiment will vary in many ways so there may be occasions when you want to ensure that there is a degree of consistency. For instance, some participants may be older than others unless we ensure that they are all the same age. However, it is difficult, if not impossible, to control for all possible individual differences. For example, some participants may have had less sleep than others the night before or gone without breakfast. Some might have had more familiarity with the type of task to be carried out than others and so on.

We could try to hold all these factors constant by making sure, for example, that all participants were female, aged 18, weighed 12 stone (76 kilograms), had slept 7 hours the night before and so on. But this is far from easy. It is generally much more practicable to use random assignment. To simplify this illustration, we will think of all these variables as being dichotomous or only having two categories such as female/male, older/younger, heavier/lighter and so on. If you look at Table 7.1, you will see that we have arranged our participants in order and that they fall into sets of individuals who have the same pattern of characteristics on these three variables. For example, the first three individuals are all female, older and heavier. This is a matched set of individuals. We could choose one of these three at random to be in the experimental condition and another at random to be in the control condition. The third individual would not be matched with anyone else so they cannot be used in

→

Box 7.2 continued

Table 7.1 Sex, age and weight details for 24 participants

Number	Sex	Age	Weight
1	female	older	heavier
2	female	older	heavier
3	female	older	heavier
4	female	older	lighter
5	female	older	lighter
6	female	older	lighter
7	female	younger	heavier
8	female	younger	heavier
9	female	younger	heavier
10	female	younger	lighter
11	female	younger	lighter
12	female	younger	lighter
13	male	older	heavier
14	male	older	heavier
15	male	older	heavier
16	male	older	lighter
17	male	older	lighter
18	male	older	lighter
19	male	younger	heavier
20	male	younger	heavier
21	male	younger	heavier
22	male	younger	lighter
23	male	younger	lighter
24	male	younger	lighter

our matched study. We could then move on to the next set of matched participants and select one of them at random for the experimental condition and a second for the control condition.

You might like to try this with the rest of the cases in Table 7.1 which consists of information about the sex, the age and the weight of 24 people who we are going to randomly assign to two groups.

Matching is a useful tool in some circumstances. There are a few things that have to be remembered if you use matching as part of your research design:

■ The appropriate statistical tests are those for related data. So a test like the related *t*-test or the Wilcoxon matched pairs test would be appropriate.

■ Variables which correlate with both the independent and dependent variables are needed for the matching variables. If a variable is unrelated to either one or both of the independent or dependent variables then there is no point in using it as a matching variable. It could make no difference to the outcome of the study.

■ The most appropriate variable to match on is most probably the dependent variable measured at the start of the study.

For example, without randomisation it is possible that the researcher allocates males to the experimental group and females to the control group – and does not even notice what they have done. If there is a gender difference on the dependent variable, the results of the experiment may confuse the experimental effect with the bias in participant selection.

7.2 More advanced research designs

We have stressed that there is no such thing as a perfect research design that can be used irrespective of the research question and circumstances. If there were such a thing then not only would this book be rather short but research would probably rank in the top three most boring jobs in the world. Research is intellectually challenging because it is problematic. The best research that any of us can do is probably a balance between a wide range of different considerations. In this chapter we are essentially looking at the simplest laboratory experiment in which we have a single independent variable. But even this basic experimental design gathers levels of complexity as we try to plug the holes in the simple design. The simplest design, as we are beginning to see, has problems. One of these problems is that if a single study is to be relied on, then the more that we can be certain that the experimental and control conditions are similar prior to the experimental manipulation the better. The answer is obvious – assess the two groups prior to the experimental manipulation to see whether they are similar on the dependent variable. This is a good move but, as we will see, it brings with it further problems to solve. It should be stressed that none of what you are about to read reduces the importance of using random allocation procedures for participants in experimental studies.

Pre-test and post-test sensitisation effects

The pre-test is a way of checking whether random assignment has in fact equated the experimental and control groups prior to the experimental manipulation. It is crucial that the two groups are similar on the dependent variable prior to the experimental manipulation. Otherwise it is not possible to know whether the differences following the experimental manipulation are due to the experimental manipulation or due to pre-existing differences between the groups on the dependent variable.

The number of mistakes is the dependent variable in our alcohol-effects example. If members of one group make more mistakes than do members of the other group before drinking alcohol, then they are likely to make more mistakes after drinking alcohol. For example, if the participants in the 8 ml alcohol condition have a tendency to make more errors regardless of whether or not they have had any alcohol, then they may make more mistakes after drinking 8 ml of alcohol than the participants who have drunk 16 ml.

This situation is illustrated in Figure 7.2 overleaf. In this graph the vertical axis represents the number of mistakes made. On the horizontal axis are two marks which indicate participants' performance before drinking alcohol and after drinking alcohol. The measurement of the participant's performance before receiving the manipulation is usually called the pre-test and the measurement after receiving the manipulation the post-test. The results of the post-test are usually placed after those of the pre-test in graphs and tables as time is usually depicted as travelling from left to right.

Figure 7.2	Performance differences before the manipulation

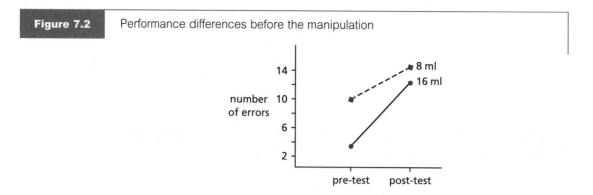

Without the pre-test measure, there is only the measure of performance after drinking alcohol. Just looking at these post-test measures, people who drank 8 ml of alcohol made more mistakes than those who drank 16 ml. In other words drinking more alcohol seems to have resulted in making fewer mistakes (and not more mistakes as we might have anticipated). This interpretation is incorrect since, by chance, random assignment to conditions resulted in the participants in the 8 ml condition being those who tend to make more mistakes. Without the pre-test we cannot know this, however.

It is clearer to see what is going on if we calculate the difference between the number of mistakes made at pre-test and at post-test (simply by subtracting one from the other). Now it can be seen that the increase in the number of mistakes was greater for the 16 ml condition $(12 - 4 = 8)$ than for the 8 ml condition $(14 - 10 = 4)$. In other words, the increase in the number of mistakes made was greater for those drinking more alcohol.

We can illustrate the situation summarised in Figure 7.2 with the fictitious raw data in Table 7.2 where there are three participants in each of the two conditions. Each participant is represented by the letter P with a subscript from 1 to 6 to indicate the six different participants. There are two scores for each participant – the first for the pre-test and the second for the post-test. These data could be analysed in a number of different ways. Among the better of these would be the mixed-design analysis of variance. This statistical test is described in some introductory statistics texts such as the companion

Table 7.2   Fictitious data for a pre-test–post-test two-group design

		Pre-test	Post-test
Condition 1	P_1	9	13
	P_2	10	15
	P_3	11	14
Sum		30	42
Mean		30/3 = 10	42/3 = 14
Condition 2	P_4	3	12
	P_5	4	11
	P_6	5	13
Sum		12	36
Mean		12/3 = 4	36/3 = 12

book *Introduction to Statistics in Psychology* (Howitt and Cramer, 2005*a*). However, this requires more than a basic level of statistical sophistication. Essentially, though, you would be looking for an interaction effect. A simpler way of analysing the same data would be to compare the differences between the pre-test and post-test measures for the two conditions. An unrelated *t*-test would be suitable for this.

Experimental designs which include a pre-test are referred to as a pre-test–post-test design while those without a pre-test are called a post-test-only design. There are two main advantages of having a pre-test:

■ As we have already seen, it enables us to determine whether randomisation has worked.

■ It allows us to determine whether or not there has been a change in performance between pre-test and post-test. If we just have the post-test scores, we cannot tell whether there has been a change in those scores and what that change is. For example, the post-test scores may show a decline from the pre-test. Without the pre-test, we may suggest incorrectly that the independent variable is increasing the scores on the dependent variable.

Look at the data shown in the graph in Figure 7.3. Concentrate on the post-test scores and ignore the pre-test. That is, pretend that we have a post-test-only design for the moment. Participants who had drunk 16 ml of alcohol made more errors than those who had drunk 8 ml. From these results we may conclude that drinking more alcohol increases the number of mistakes made. If the pre-test number of errors made were as shown in Figure 7.3, this interpretation would be incorrect. If we know the pre-test scores we can see that drinking 16 ml of alcohol decreased the number of errors made ($10 - 14 = -4$) while drinking 8 ml of alcohol had no effect on the number of errors ($6 - 6 = 0$). Having a pre-test enables us to determine whether or not randomisation has been successful and what, if any, was the change in the scores. (Indeed, we are not being precise if we talk of the conditions in a post-test-only study as increasing or decreasing scores on the dependent variable. All that we can legitimately say is that there is a difference between the conditions.)

Whatever their advantages, pre-tests have disadvantages. One common criticism of pre-test designs is that they may alert participants as to the purpose of the experiment and consequently influence their behaviour. That is, the pre-test affects or sensitises participants in terms of their behaviour on the post-test (Lana, 1969; Solomon, 1949; Wilson and Putnam, 1982). Again we might extend our basic research design to take this into account. We need to add to our basic design groups which undergo the pre-test and other groups

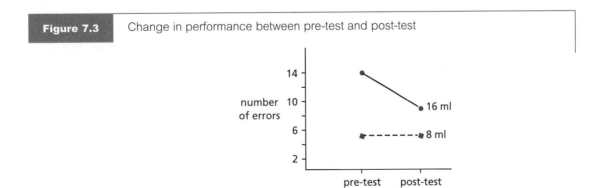

Figure 7.3   Change in performance between pre-test and post-test

Figure 7.4 Solomon's (1949) four-group design

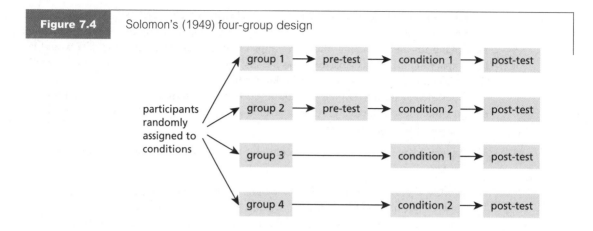

which do not. Solomon (1949) called this a four-group design since at a minimum there will be two groups (an experimental and control group) that include a pre-test and two further groups that do not have a pre-test as shown in Figure 7.4.

One way of analysing the results of this more sophisticated design is to tabulate the data as illustrated in Table 7.3. This contains fictitious post-test scores for three participants in each of the four conditions. The pre-test scores are *not* given in Table 7.3. Each participant is represented by the letter P with a subscript consisting of a number ranging from 1 to 12 to denote there are 12 participants.

The analysis of these data involves combining the data over the two conditions. That is, we have a group of six cases which had a pre-test and another group of six cases which did not have the pre-test. The mean score of the group which had a pre-test is 8 whereas the mean score of the group which had no pre-test is 2. In other words we are ignoring the effect of the two conditions at this stage. We have a pre-test sensitisation effect if the means for these two (combined) conditions differ significantly. In our example, there may be a pre-test sensitisation effect since the mean score of the combined two conditions with

Table 7.3   Fictitious post-test scores for a Solomon four-group design

	Had pre-test	Had no pre-test	Row means
Condition 1	$P_1 = 4$ $P_2 = 5$ $P_3 = 6$	$P_7 = 0$ $P_8 = 1$ $P_9 = 2$	
Sum	15	3	18
Mean	15/3 = 5	3/3 = 1	18/6 = 3
Condition 2	$P_4 = 10$ $P_5 = 11$ $P_6 = 12$	$P_{10} = 2$ $P_{11} = 3$ $P_{12} = 4$	
Sum	33	9	42
Mean	33/3 = 11	9/3 = 3	42/6 = 7
Column sums	48	12	
Column means	48/6 = 8	12/6 = 2	

the pre-test is 8 which is higher than the mean score of 2 for the two conditions without the pre-test combined. If this difference is statistically significant we have a pre-test sensitisation effect. (The difference in the two means could be tested using an unrelated t-test. Alternatively, one could use a two-way analysis of variance. In this case we would look for a pre-test–no pre-test main effect.)

Of course, it is possible that the pre-test sensitisation effect is different for the experimental and control conditions (conditions 1 and 2):

■ For condition 1 we can see in Table 7.3 that the difference in the mean score for the group with the pre-test and the group without the pre-test is $5 - 1 = 4$.

■ For condition 2 we can see that the difference in the mean score for the group with the pre-test and the group without the pre-test is $11 - 3 = 8$.

In other words, the mean scores of the two conditions with the pre-test and the two conditions without the pre-test appear to depend on, or interact with, the condition in question. The effect of pre-test sensitisation is greater for condition 1 than for condition 2. The difference between the two in our example is quite small, however. This differential effect of the pre-test according to the condition in question would be termed a pre-test/condition interaction effect. [We could test for such an interaction effect using a two-way analysis of variance. How to do this is described in some introductory statistics texts such as the companion volume *Introduction to Statistics in Psychology* (Howitt and Cramer, 2005*a*). If the interaction between the pre-test and the experimental condition is statistically significant, we have a pre-test sensitisation interaction effect.]

If you are beginning to lose the plot in a sea of numbers and tables, perhaps the following will help. Pre-test sensitisation simply means that participants who are pre-tested on the dependent variable tend to have different scores on the post-test from the participants who were not pre-tested. There are many reasons for this. For example, the pre-test may simply coach the participants in the task in question. However, the pre-test/condition interaction means that the effect of pre-testing is different for the experimental and the control conditions. Again there may be many reasons why the effects of pre-testing will differ for the experimental group. For example, participants in the experimental group may have many more clues as to what the experimenter is expecting to happen. As a consequence, they may change their behaviour more in the experimental condition compared to the control condition.

Pre-test sensitisation in itself may not be a problem whereas if it interacts with the condition to produce different outcomes it is problematic:

■ A pre-test sensitisation interaction effect causes problems in interpreting the results of a study. We simply do not know with certainty if the effect is different in the different conditions. Further investigation would be needed to shed additional light on the matter. If we are interested in understanding this differential effect we need to investigate it further to find out why it has occurred.

■ A pre-test sensitisation effect without a pre-test sensitisation interaction effect would not be a problem if we are simply interested in the relative effect of an independent variable and not its absolute effect. For example, it would not be a problem if we just wanted to know whether drinking a greater amount of alcohol leads to making more errors than drinking a smaller amount. The size of the difference would be similar with a pre-test to without one. On the other hand, we might be interested in the absolute number of errors made by drinking alcohol. For example, we may want to recommend the maximum amount of alcohol that can be taken without affecting performance as a driver. In these circumstances it is important to know about pre-test sensitisation effects if these result in greater errors. In this case we would base our recommendation on the testing condition which resulted in the greater number of errors.

If one wishes to use a pre-test but nevertheless reduce pre-test sensitisation effects to a minimum then there are things which could be done:

■   Try to disguise the pre-test by embedding it in some other task or carrying it out in a different context.

■   Increase the length of the interval between the pre-test and the manipulation so that the pre-test is less likely to have an effect on the post-test. So if the pre-test serves as a practice for the post-test measure, then a big interval of time may result in a reduced practice effect.

■   If the effects of the manipulation were relatively short-lived we could give the 'pre-test' after the post-test. For example, if we were studying the effects of alcohol on errors then we could test the participants a couple of hours later when the effects of alcohol would have worn away. The two groups could be tested to see if they made similar numbers of errors once the effects of alcohol had dissipated.

While there are many studies which use a pre-test and a post-test measure fruitfully, the same is not true of the Solomon four-groups design. Such studies are scarce. That is, while it is important to be aware of pre-test sensitisation effects, we know of very few published studies which have tested for pre-test sensitisation effects.

Within-subjects design

Where the same participants take part in all conditions, this effectively controls for many differences between participants. For example, we may have a participant who makes numerous errors irrespective of condition. Because this person is in every condition of the experiment, the pre-existing tendency for them to make a lot of errors will apply equally to every condition of the experiment. In other words, they would make more errors in every condition. The effects, say, of alcohol will simply change the number of errors they make differentially. The advantage of the within-subjects design is that it provides a more sensitive test of the difference between conditions because it controls for differences between individuals. Having a more sensitive test and having the same participants take part in all conditions means that, ideally, fewer participants can be used in a within-subjects than in a between-subjects design.

The extent to which this is the case depends on the extent to which there is a correlation between the scores in the experimental and control conditions. Many of the statistical tests appropriate for within-subjects designs will give an indication of this correlation as well as a test for the significance of the difference between the two conditions. This is discussed in more detail in Chapter 12 of our companion statistics text, Introduction to Statistics in Psychology *(Howitt and Cramer, 2005a). It is also discussed in Box 7.3 on page 136. So long as the correlation is significant then there is no problem. If it is not significant then the test of the difference between the two means may well be not very powerful.*

| **Figure 7.5** | Fatigue effect in within-subjects design |

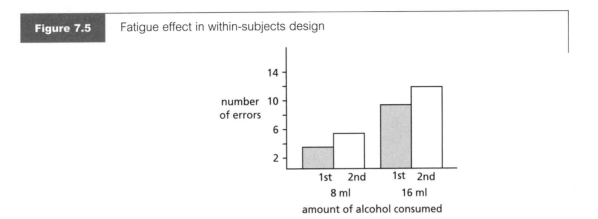

In a within-subjects design the effects that may occur as a result of doing the conditions in a particular order must be controlled. In a design consisting of only two conditions, these order effects are dealt with by counterbalancing the two orders so that both orders occur equally frequently. This counterbalancing is important since the data may be affected by any of a number of effects of order. The main ones are:

■ *Fatigue or boredom*   Participants may become progressively more tired or bored with the task they are performing. So the number of mistakes they make may be greater in the second than in the first condition, regardless of which condition, because they are tired. An example of a fatigue effect is illustrated in the bar chart in Figure 7.5 for the effect of two different amounts of alcohol on the number of mistakes made. The vertical axis shows the number of errors made. The horizontal axis shows the two conditions of 8 ml and 16 ml of alcohol. Within each condition, the order in which the conditions were run is indicated. So '1st' means that that condition was run first and '2nd' that that condition was run second. We can see that there is a similar fatigue effect for both conditions. More errors are made when the condition is run second than when it is run first. In the 8 ml condition 6 errors are made when it is run second compared to 4 when it is run first. The same difference holds for the 16 ml condition where 12 errors are made when it is run second compared to 10 when it is run first.

■ *Practice*   Participants may become better at the task they are carrying out. So the number of mistakes they make may be less in the second than in the first condition, regardless of which condition, because they have learned to respond more accurately. Sometimes the term 'practice effect' is used to cover both learning as described here and fatigue or boredom.

■ *Carryover, asymmetrical transfer or differential transfer*   Here the effect of an earlier condition affects a subsequent one but not equally for all orders. (One can refer to this as an interaction between the conditions and the order of the conditions.) For example, if the interval between the two alcohol conditions is close together, the carryover effect of drinking 16 ml of alcohol first may be greater on the effect of drinking 8 ml of alcohol second than the carryover effect of drinking 8 ml of alcohol first on the effect of drinking 16 ml of alcohol second. This pattern of results is illustrated in Figure 7.6. When the 8 ml condition is run second the number of mistakes

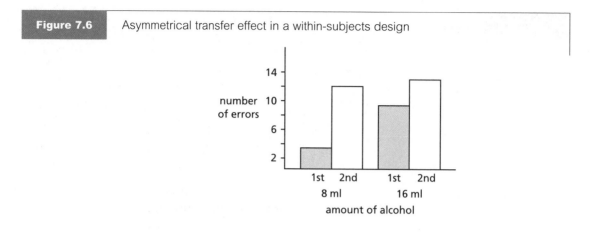

Figure 7.6 Asymmetrical transfer effect in a within-subjects design

made is much greater (12) than when it is run first (4) and is almost the same as the number of mistakes made when the 16 ml condition is run first (10). When the 16 ml condition is run second the number of mistakes made (13) is not much different than when it is run first. This asymmetrical transfer effect reduces the overall difference between the 8 and 16 ml conditions. If one finds such an asymmetrical transfer effect then it may be possible to make adjustments to the research design to get rid of them. In the alcohol example, one could increase the amount of time between the two conditions. In this way, the alcohol consumed in the first condition may have worked its way out of the blood system. Of course, this has disadvantages. It might involve participants returning to the laboratory at a later time rather than the entire study being run at the same time. This increases the risk that participants may not return. Worse still, you may find that participants in one of the conditions may fail to return at different rates from participants in the other condition.

Of course, this implies that counterbalanced designs are not always effective at balancing any effects of order. They clearly do balance out order effects in circumstances in which there is no significant interaction between the conditions and the order in which the conditions are run. If there is a significant interaction between the conditions and the order in which they are run, we need to describe what this interaction is. We can illustrate the interaction summarised in Figure 7.6 with the fictitious raw data in Table 7.4 where there are three participants who carry out the two different orders in which the two conditions are run. Each participant is signified by the letter P with a subscript consisting of two whole numbers. The first number refers to a particular participant and varies from 1 to 6 as there are six participants. The second number represents the two conditions. We could analyse these data with a mixed analysis of variance. This statistical test is described in some introductory statistics texts such as the companion text *Introduction to Statistics in Psychology* (Howitt and Cramer, 2005a).

With counterbalancing, it is obviously important that equal numbers of participants are included in each condition. The random assignment of participants to different orders in a within-subjects design is necessary to ensure that the orders are exactly the same apart from the order in which the conditions are run. For example, in our study of the effects of

Table 7.4   Fictitious scores for a within-subjects design with two conditions

	Condition 1	Condition 2
Condition 1 first	$P_{1,1} = 3$	$P_{1,2} = 11$
	$P_{2,1} = 4$	$P_{2,2} = 10$
	$P_{3,1} = 5$	$P_{3,2} = 9$
Sum	12	30
Mean	12/3 = 4	30/3 = 10
Condition 1 second	$P_{4,1} = 11$	$P_{4,2} = 13$
	$P_{5,1} = 12$	$P_{5,2} = 12$
	$P_{6,1} = 13$	$P_{6,2} = 14$
Sum	36	39
Mean	36/3 = 12	39/3 = 13

alcohol on the number of errors made it is important that the proportion of people who are inclined to make more errors is the same in the two different orders. So if the proportion is not the same, then there may be a difference between the two orders which may result in a significant interaction effect.

If there is a significant interaction effect in a counterbalanced design, the analysis becomes a little cumbersome. Essentially, one regards the study as having two different parts – one part for each different order. The data from each part (order) are then analysed to see what is the apparent effect of the experimental treatment. If the same conclusions are reached for the different orders, then all is well as far as one's findings are concerned. Things become difficult when the conclusions from the different orders are not compatible with each other. Also note that this also effectively reduces the maximum sample size and so takes away the advantage of a within-subjects design.

Of course, researchers using their intelligence would have anticipated the problem for a study such as this in which the effects of alcohol are being studied. To the extent that one can anticipate problems due to the order of running through conditions then one would be less inclined to use a within-subjects design. This is a case where noting problems with counterbalanced designs identified by researchers investigating similar topics to one's own may help decide whether a within-subjects design should be avoided.

Stable individual differences between people are controlled in a within-subjects design by requiring the same participants to carry out all conditions. Nevertheless, it remains a requirement that assignment to different orders is done randomly. Of course, this does not mean that the process of randomisation has not left differences between the orders. This may be checked by pre-testing participants prior to the different first conditions to be run. One would check whether the pre-test means were the same for those who took condition 1 first as for those who took condition 2 first. In other words, it is possible to have a pre-test–post-test within-subjects design. It would also be possible to extend the Solomon four-group design to investigate not only the effects of pre-testing but also the effects of having participants undertake more than one condition.

BOX 7.3   STATISTICAL SIGNIFICANCE

Statistical significance is one of those ideas that many students have difficulty with. So it can be usefully returned to from time to time so that the ideas are reinforced. We can explain the concept of statistical significance with the experiment on the effects of alcohol on errors. Suppose that we find in our study of the effects of alcohol on making errors that the participants who drink less alcohol make fewer errors than those who drink more alcohol. We may find that we obtain the results shown in Table 7.5. All the participants who drink less alcohol make fewer errors than those who drink more alcohol.

The mean number of errors made by the participants who drink less alcohol is 2 compared with a mean of 5 for those who drink more alcohol. The absolute difference between these two means, which ignores the sign of the difference, is 3 $(2 - 5 = 3)$. (To be precise, this should be written as $(|2 - 5| = 3)$, which indicates that the absolute value of the difference should be taken.) Can we conclude from these results that drinking more alcohol causes us to make more mistakes?

We cannot draw this conclusion without determining the extent to which we may find this difference simply by chance as it is possible to obtain a difference of 3 by chance. If this difference has a probability of occurring by chance of 5% or 0.05 or less we can conclude that this difference is quite unusual and unlikely to be due to chance and represents a real difference between the two conditions. If this difference has a probability of occurring by chance of more than 5% or 0.05, we would conclude that this difference could be due to chance and so does not represent a real difference between the two conditions. It needs to be stressed that the 5% or 0.05 significance level is just a conventional and generally accepted figure. It indicates a fairly uncommon outcome if differences between groups were simply due to chance factors resulting from sampling.

We can demonstrate the probability of this difference occurring by chance in the following way. Suppose that it is only possible to make between 1 and 6 mistakes on this task. (We are using this for convenience, it would be more accurate in terms of real statistical analysis to use the same figures but arranged in a bell-shaped or normal distribution in which scores of 3 and 4 are the most common and scores

Table 7.5   Fictitious data for a two-group between-subjects post-test only design

	Post-test
Condition 1	$P_{1,1} = 1$
	$P_{2,1} = 2$
	$P_{3,1} = 3$
Sum	6
Mean	$6/3 = 2$
Condition 2	$P_{4,2} = 4$
	$P_{5,2} = 5$
	$P_{6,2} = 6$
Sum	15
Mean	$15/3 = 5$

→

Box 7.3 continued

of 1 and 6 were the most uncommon.) If we only have three participants in each condition and the results were simply determined by chance, then the mean for any group would be the mean of the three numbers selected by chance. We could randomly select these three numbers in several ways. We could toss a die three times. We could write the six numbers on six separate index cards or slips of paper, shuffle them, select a card or slip, note down the number, put the card or slip back, shuffle them again and repeat this procedure three times. We could use a statistical package such as SPSS. We would enter the numbers 1 to 6 in one of the columns. We would then select *Data, Select Cases . . . , Random sample of cases, Sample . . . , Exactly*, and then enter one case from the first six cases. We would note down the number of the case selected and repeat this procedure twice.

As we have two groups we would have to do this once for each group, calculate the mean of the three numbers for each group and then subtract the mean of one group from the mean of the other group. We would then repeat this procedure 19 or more times. The results of our doing this 20 times are shown in Table 7.6.

Table 7.6   Differences between the means of three randomly selected numbers varying between 1 and 6

	Condition 1				Condition 2				
	P_{11}	P_{21}	P_{31}	Mean	P_{42}	P_{52}	P_{62}	Mean	Difference
1	1	3	2	**2.00**	2	3	1	**2.00**	0.00
2	5	1	2	**2.67**	5	5	4	**4.67**	−2.00
3	6	1	4	**3.67**	6	1	6	**4.33**	−0.67
4	6	3	6	**5.00**	5	6	6	**5.67**	−0.67
5	1	5	3	**3.00**	6	3	1	**3.33**	−0.33
6	1	2	4	**2.33**	1	3	6	**3.33**	−1.00
7	3	6	2	**3.67**	6	3	5	**4.67**	−1.00
8	1	2	5	**2.67**	5	5	4	**4.67**	−2.00
9	6	2	3	**3.67**	2	4	4	**3.33**	0.33
10	6	1	1	**2.67**	6	3	3	**4.00**	−1.33
11	4	4	6	**4.67**	2	3	1	**2.00**	2.67
12	1	6	2	**3.00**	2	5	2	**3.00**	0.00
13	2	5	5	**4.00**	5	3	6	**4.67**	−0.67
14	2	1	2	**1.67**	6	5	1	**4.00**	−2.33
15	4	6	3	**4.33**	6	5	6	**5.67**	−1.33
16	2	4	5	**3.67**	6	1	3	**3.33**	0.33
17	2	5	4	**3.67**	5	1	5	**3.67**	0.00
18	2	2	2	**2.00**	1	6	6	**4.33**	−2.33
19	2	1	2	**1.67**	3	1	5	**3.00**	−1.33
20	6	3	6	**5.00**	2	2	2	**2.00**	3.00

The mean for both the first two groups is 2.00 so the difference between them is zero. As the six numbers are equiprobable, the mean of three of these numbers selected at random is likely to be 3.5. This value is close to the mean for the 40 groups which is 3.52. However, the means can vary from a minimum of 1 [(1 + 1 + 1)/3 = 1] to a maximum of 6 [(6 + 6 + 6)/3 = 6].

→

Box 7.3 continued

The distribution of the frequency of an infinite number of means will take the shape of an inverted U or bell as shown by the normal curve in Figure 7.7 which has been superimposed onto the histogram. Of the 40 means in Table 7.6 the smallest is 1.67 and the largest is 5.67. The distribution of these means approximates the shape of an inverted U or bell as shown in the histogram in Figure 7.7. The more samples of three scores we select at random, the more likely it is that the distribution of the means of those samples will resemble a normal curve. The horizontal width of each rectangle in the histogram is 0.50. The first rectangle, which is on the left, ranges from 1.50 to 2.00 and contains two means of 1.67. The last rectangle which is on the right, varies from 5.50 to 6.00 and includes two means of 5.67.

If the means of the two groups tend to be 3.5, then the difference between them is likely to be zero. They will vary from a difference of -5 ($1 - 6 = -5$) to a difference of 5 ($6 - 1 = 5$) with most of them close to zero as shown by the normal curve superimposed on the histogram in Figure 7.8. Of the 20 differences in means in Table 7.6 the lowest is -2.33 and the highest is 3.00. If we plot the frequency of these differences in means in terms of the histogram in Figure 7.8 we can see that its shape approximates that of a normal curve. If we plotted an infinite number or a very large number of such differences then the distribution would resemble a normal curve. The horizontal width of each rectangle in this histogram is 1.00. The first rectangle, which is on the left, ranges from -3.00 to -2.00 and contains two differences in means of -2.33. The last rectangle which is on the right, varies from 2.00 to 3.00 and includes two differences in means of 2.67 and 3.00.

We can see that the probability of obtaining by chance a difference as large as -3.00 is quite small. One test for determining this probability is the unrelated *t*-test. This test is described in most introductory statistics texts including our companion volume *Introduction to Statistics in Psychology* (Howitt and Cramer, 2005*a*). If the variances in the scores for the two groups are equal or similar, the probability of the unrelated *t*-test will be the same as a one-way analysis of variance with two groups. If we had strong grounds for thinking that the mean number of errors would be smaller for those who drank less rather than more alcohol, then we could confine our 5% or 0.05 probability to the left tail or side of the distribution which covers this possibility. This is usually called the one-tailed level of probability. If we did not have good reasons for predicting the direction of the results, then we are saying that the number of errors made by the participants drinking less alcohol could be either less or more than those made by the participants drinking more alcohol. In other words, the difference between the means could be either negative or positive in sign. If this was the case, the 5% or 0.05 probability level would cover the two tails or sides of the distribution. This is normally referred to as the two-tailed level of probability. To be significant at the two- rather than the one-tailed level, the difference in the means would have to be bigger as the 5% or 0.05 level is split between the two tails so that it covers a more extreme difference. If the difference between the two means is statistically significant, which it is for these scores, we could conclude that drinking less alcohol results in making fewer errors.

Our companion statistics text, *Introduction to Statistics in Psychology* (Howitt and Cramer, 2005*a*), presents a more extended version of this explanation for the correlation coefficient and the *t*-test.

→

Box 7.3 continued

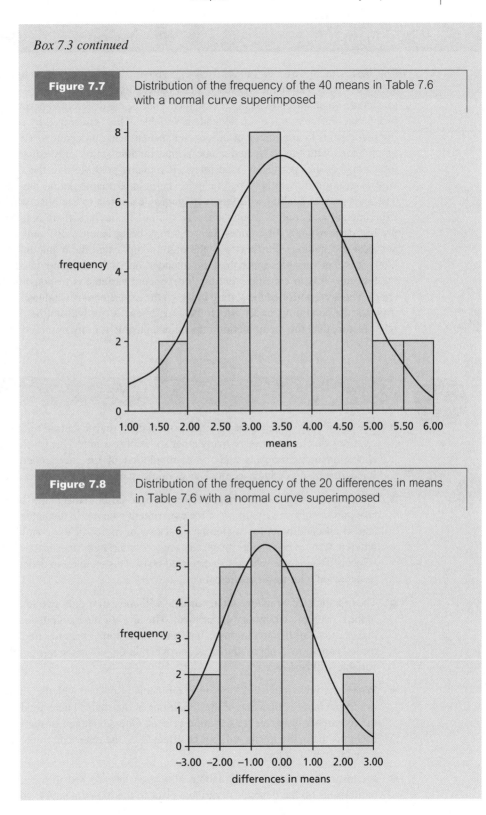

Figure 7.7 Distribution of the frequency of the 40 means in Table 7.6 with a normal curve superimposed

Figure 7.8 Distribution of the frequency of the 20 differences in means in Table 7.6 with a normal curve superimposed

7.3 Conclusion

The basics of the true or randomised experiment are simple. The major advantage of such a design is that that it is easier to draw conclusions about causality since care is taken to exclude other variables as far as possible. That is, the different experimental conditions bring about differences on the dependent variable. This is achieved by randomly allocating participants to conditions or orders and standardising procedures. There are a number of problems with this. The major one is that randomisation only equates groups in the long run. For any particular experiment, it remains possible that the experimental and control group differ initially before the experimental manipulation has been employed. The main way of dealing with this is to employ a pre-test to establish whether or not the experimental and control groups are very similar. If they are, there is no problem. If the pre-test demonstrates differences then this may bring about a different interpretation of any post-test findings. Furthermore, the more complicated the manipulation is, the more likely it is that variables other than the intended one will be manipulated. Consequently, the less easy it is to conclude that the independent variable is responsible for the differences. The less controlled the setting in which the experiment is conducted, the more likely it is that the conditions under which the experiment is run will not be the same and that other factors than the manipulation may be responsible for any observed effect.

Key points

- The laboratory experiment has the potential to reveal causal relationships with a certainty which is not true of many other styles of research. This is achieved by random allocation of participants and the manipulation of the independent variable while standardising procedures as much as possible to control other sources of variability.

- The between-subjects and within-subjects designs differ in that in the former participants take part in only one condition of the experiment whereas in the latter participants take part in all conditions (or sometimes just two or more) of the conditions. These two different types of designs are analysed using rather different statistical techniques. Within-subjects designs use related or correlated tests. This enables statistical significance to be achieved with fewer participants.

- The manipulated or independent variable will consist of only two levels or conditions in the most basic laboratory experiment. The level of the manipulated variable will be higher in one of the conditions. This condition is sometimes referred to as the experimental condition as opposed to the control condition where the level of the manipulated variable will be lower.

- Within-subjects (related) designs have problems associated with the sensitisation effects of serving in more than one of the conditions of the study. There are designs that allow the researcher to detect sensitisation effects. One advantage of the between-subjects design is that participants will not be affected by the other conditions as they will not have taken part in them.

- Pre-testing to establish that random allocation has worked in the sense of equating participants on the dependent variable prior to the experimental treatment sometimes works. Nevertheless, pre-testing may cause problems due to the sensitising effect of the pre-test. Complex designs are available which test for these sensitising effects.

■ The extent to which random assignment has resulted in participants being similar across either conditions or orders can be determined by a pre-test in which participants are assessed on the dependent variable before the manipulation is carried out.

■ Any statistical differences between the conditions in the dependent variable at post-test are very likely to be due to the manipulated variable if the dependent variable does not differ significantly between the conditions at pre-test and if the only other difference between the conditions is the manipulated variable.

Activity

Design a basic randomised experiment to test the hypothesis that unemployment leads to crime. After thinking about this you may find it useful to see whether and how other researchers have tried to study this issue using randomised designs. How are you going to operationalise these two variables? Is it possible to manipulate unemployment and how can you do so? If you are going to carry out a laboratory experiment you may have to operationalise unemployment in a more contrived way than if you carry out an experiment in a more natural or field setting. How can you reduce the ethical problems that may arise in the operationalisation of these variables? How many participants will you have in each condition? How will you select these participants? Will you pre-test your participants? Will you use a between- or a within-subjects design? How will you analyse the results? What will you say to participants about the study before and after they take part?

8 Advanced experimental design

Overview

■ Few laboratory experiments consist of just an experimental and control group. The information obtained from such a study would be very limited for the time, money and effort expended. The simple experimental group–control group is often extended to include perhaps four or five different conditions. Naturally it is important that every condition of an experiment should be justifiable. A typical justification is that each group will produce a different outcome relative to the other groups.

■ Most behaviours are multiply affected by a range of factors (i.e. variables). Consequently, it can be advantageous to study several factors at the same time. In this way the relative effects of the factors can be compared. The number of variables that can be manipulated in a study should be kept to an optimum. Typically no more than two or three should be used. If more are employed, the interpretation of the statistical findings becomes extremely complex and, possibly, misleading.

■ The factors that are studied may include those which cannot be randomised (or manipulated) such as gender, age and intelligence. These are sometimes referred to as subject variables.

■ It is common for researchers to use more than one dependent variable. This is because the independent variables may have a range of effects and also because using a number of measures of the dependent variable can be informative. Where there are several dependent variables it may be worthwhile controlling for any order effects amongst these variables by varying the order. This can be done systematically using a *Latin square*.

■ Latin squares are also used to systematically vary the order of the conditions run in a within-subjects design where there are a number of different conditions.

■ Planned and unplanned comparisons in factorial designs have rather different requirements in terms of statistical analysis. Comparisons planned in advance of data collection have distinct advantages, for example, in terms of the ease of making multiple comparisons.

■ Quite distinct from any of the above, the advanced experimenter should consider including means of controlling for potential nuisances in the research design.

The use of placebos, double blind procedures, and the like help may make the methodology more convincing. Quasi-controls to investigate the experience of participants in the research might be regarded as good practice as, in part, they involve discussions after the study between participant and researcher as part of a process of understanding the findings of the research.

In this chapter we will extend our understanding of experimental design in two ways. We will consider more complex experimental designs in which there are two or more independent variables. This leads to a degree of efficiency in terms of the amount of information which can be obtained from a single study. Circumstances in which more than one dependent variable is used are also considered. Then we will look at aspects of experimental design which, unless carefully considered, may result in problems in the interpretation of the findings of the research. Some of these are conventionally termed experimenter effects and come under the general rubric of the social psychology of the laboratory experiment.

The simple two-groups design – experimental and control group – provides the researcher with relatively little information for the effort involved. The design may be extended by using a greater variety of conditions but, perhaps more likely, the single independent variable is extended to two or three independent variables, perhaps more.

■ Just having two conditions or levels of an independent variable, such as the amount of alcohol consumed (as in the example used in the previous chapter), tells us little about the shape of the relationship between the independent and the dependent variable. Is the relationship a linear one or curvilinear? What kind of curvilinear relationship is it? Having a number of levels of the dependent variable helps us to identify the nature of the trends.

■ Does the independent variable interact with other independent or subject variables? For example, is the effect of alcohol on the number of errors made similar for a subject variable such as gender or for an independent variable such as task complexity or does it differ according to sex and task complexity?

■ Does the independent variable affect more than one dependent variable? For example, does alcohol affect the number of errors made on a number of different tasks?

These three main ways of extending the basic two-group design are discussed below.

8.1 Multiple levels of an independent variable

Multiple levels of the independent variable occur when there are three or more different levels of that variable. This is sometimes described as having several levels of the treatment. An example of this is to be found in Figure 8.1 overleaf. The independent variable may vary in one of two different ways – quantitative or qualitative:

■ Quantitative would be, for example, when the amount of alcohol consumed in the different conditions can be arranged in order of size. In general the order is from smaller quantities to larger ones ordered either across or down a table or across a graph such as Figure 8.1.

Figure 8.1 Number of errors as a function of amount of alcohol consumed

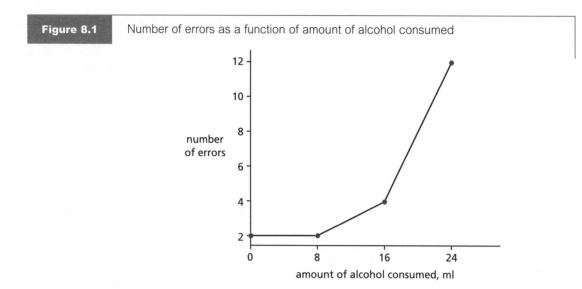

■ Qualitative would be, for example, when we study the effects of the kind of music being played in the different conditions. There is generally no one way in which the levels or categories can be ordered in terms of amount. The categories will reflect a number of different characteristics such as the date when the music was recorded, the number of instruments being played and so forth. In other words, qualitative is the equivalent of a nominal, category or categorical variable. When studying the effect of a qualitative variable which varies in numerous ways, it is not possible to know what features of the qualitative variable produces any differences that are obtained.

Multiple comparisons

The analysis of designs with more than two conditions is more complicated than one with only two conditions. For one reason, there are more comparisons to make the more conditions there are. If there are three levels or conditions we can compare:

■ condition 1 with condition 2,
■ condition 1 with condition 3, *and*
■ condition 2 with condition 3.

That is, a total of up to three comparisons. With four conditions, there are six comparisons we can make. With five conditions there are ten comparisons and so on. Whether or not one makes all possible comparisons depends on the purpose of one's research. The temptation is, of course, to do all possible comparisons. In research, however, the justification for whatever number of comparisons are to be made should be made clearly.

The more comparisons we make, so the likelihood increases of finding some of these comparisons to be statistically significant by chance. If these comparisons are completely independent of each other, the probability of finding one or more of these comparisons statistically significant can be calculated with the following formula:

$$\text{probability of statistically significant comparison} = 1 - (1 - 0.05)^{\text{number of comparisons}}$$

where 0.05 represents the 5% or 0.05 significance level. With three comparisons, this probability or significance level is about 14% or 0.14 [$1 - (1 - 0.05)^3 = 0.14$]. With four comparisons it is 19% or 0.19 $[1 - (1 - 0.05)^4 = 0.26]$. With five comparisons it is 23% or 0.40 $[1 - (1 - 0.05)^5 = 0.23]$ and so on. This probability is known as the *familywise* or *experimentwise* error rate because we are making a number, or family, of comparisons from the same study or experiment.

Data which consist of more than two conditions or more than two independent variables, would normally be analysed by a group of tests known collectively as the analysis of variance (ANOVA). However, there may not always be a need to do this. If we had good grounds for predicting which conditions would be expected to differ from each other and the direction of those differences, then an overall or omnibus test such as an analysis of variance may be unnecessary (e.g. Howell, 2002, p. 372; Keppel and Wickens, 2004, p. 116). An omnibus test simply tells us whether overall the independent variable has a significant effect but it does not tell us which conditions are actually different from each other. Regardless of whether we carry out an omnibus test, the conditions we expect to differ still have to be compared. These comparisons have been called planned or a priori comparisons. [*A priori* is Latin for 'from what is before'.] We can use a test such as a simple *t*-test to determine which conditions differ from each other provided that we test a limited number of comparisons (e.g. Howell, 2002, pp. 375–6; Keppel and Wickens, 2004, p. 116). If we make a large number of comparisons, then we should make an adjustment for the familywise error rate. The point is that if we plan a few comparisons we have effectively pinpointed key features of the situation. The more comparisons we make then the less precision is involved in our planning. Hence the need to make adjustments when we have a high proportion of all of the possible comparisons to make.

The more common situation, however, is when we lack good reasons for expecting a particular difference or for predicting the direction of a difference. The procedure in these circumstances is to employ an omnibus statistical test such as an analysis of variance. If this analysis is significant overall, unplanned, post hoc or a posteriori comparisons can be carried out. These comparisons determine which conditions differ significantly from each other. *Post hoc* is Latin for 'after this' and *a posteriori* is Latin for 'what comes after'. With the post hoc test, it is necessary to adjust the significance of the statistical test to take into account the number of comparisons being made. The simplest way to do this is to divide the 0.05 level by the number of comparisons to be made. This is known as a Bonferroni adjustment or test. So with three comparisons, the adjusted level is about 0.0167 (0.05/3 = 0.0167). With four comparisons it is 0.0125 (0.05/4 = 0.0125) and so on. Be careful! What this means is that a comparison has to be statistically significant at this adjusted level to be reported as being statistically significant at the 0.05 level of significance. So if we make four comparisons, only differences which are statistically significant at the 0.0125 level can be reported as being significant at the 0.05 level. It is easier to do this with SPSS output since the exact probability found for a comparison simply has to be multiplied by the number of comparisons to give the appropriate significance level. The finding is only significant if the *multiplied* exact significance is below 0.05. This is discussed in the companion text *Introduction to Statistics in Psychology* (Howitt and Cramer, 2005*a*).

The Bonferroni test is a conservative test if we are comparing all the conditions because at least one of the comparisons will not be independent of the others. Conservative basically means less likely to give statistically significant results. Suppose we wanted to compare the mean scores for three conditions which are 2, 4 and 8, respectively. If we work out the differences for any two of the comparisons, then we can derive the difference for the third comparison by subtracting the other two differences from each other. For instance, the differences between conditions 1 and 2 (4 − 2 = 2) and conditions 1 and

3 (8 − 2 = 6) are 2 and 6, respectively. If we subtract these two differences from each other (6 − 2 = 4) we obtain the difference between conditions 2 and 3 (8 − 4 = 4), which is 4. In other words, if we know the differences for two of the comparisons, we can work out the difference for the third comparison.

So, in this situation, the Bonferroni test is a conservative test in the sense that the test assumes three rather than two independent comparisons are being made. The probability level is lower for three comparisons (0.05/3 = 0.017) than for two comparisons (0.05/2 = 0.025), and so is less likely to occur.

There is some disagreement between authors about whether particular multiple comparison tests such as the Bonferroni test should be used for a priori or post hoc comparisons. For example, Howell (2002, p. 403) suggests that the Bonferroni test should be used for making planned or a priori comparisons while Keppel and Wickens (2004, p. 115) recommend that this test be used for making a small number of unplanned or post hoc comparisons! The widely used statistical package SPSS also lists the Bonferroni test as a post hoc test. There are also tests for determining the shape of the relationship between the levels of a quantitative independent variable and the dependent variable, which are known as trend tests (e.g. Kirk, 1995).

In many instances such disagreements in the advice of experts will make little or no difference to the interpretation of the statistical analysis – that is the findings will be unaffected. Since multiple comparison tests are quickly computed using SPSS and other statistical packages, it is easy to try out a number of multiple comparison tests. Only in circumstances in which they lead to radically different conclusions do you really have a problem. These circumstances are probably rare and equally probably mean that some comparisons which are significant with one test are marginally non-significant with another. In these circumstances, if would be appropriate to highlight the problem.

8.2 Multiple dependent variables

Sometimes researchers may wish to use a number of different measures of the dependent variable within a single study. For example, we can assess the effects of alcohol on task performance in terms of both the number of errors made and the speed with which the task is carried out. Performance on a number of tasks such as simple reaction time, complex reaction time, attention span and distance estimation could be studied. One could, of course, carry out separate studies for each of these different measures of performance. However, it would be more efficient to examine them in the same study. In these circumstances, it may be important to control for potential order effects in the measurement of the various dependent variables. Univariate analysis of variance (ANOVA) is not appropriate for analysing these data since it only deals with one dependent variable. Multivariate analysis of variance (abbreviated to MANOVA) is used instead since it deals with multiple dependent variables. A description of MANOVA can be found in books dealing with advanced statistics (e.g. Tabachnick and Fidell, 2001).

There are circumstances where one would not use MANOVA. Sometimes a researcher will measure tasks like reaction time several times in order to sample the participant's performance on this task. These data are better dealt with by simply averaging to give a mean score over the several trials of what is the same task. There would be nothing to gain from treating these several measures of the same thing as multiple dependent variables.

8.3 Factorial designs

A study which investigates more than one independent variable is known as a factorial design – see Table 8.1. Variables like gender may be referred to as subject variables. These are characteristics of the participants which cannot be independently manipulated (and randomly assigned). Gender, age and intelligence are good examples of subject variables. They are also referred to as independent variables if they are seen as potential causes of variations in the dependent variable.

Table 8.1   A simple factorial design investigating the effects of alcohol and gender on performance

	Females	Males
8 ml alcohol		
16 ml alcohol		

Terms like two-way, three-way and four-way are frequently mentioned in connection with factorial research designs. The word 'way' really means factor or independent variable. Thus a one-way design means one independent variable, a two-way design means two independent variables, a three-way design means three independent variables and so forth. The phrase is also used in connection with the analysis of variance. So a two-way analysis of variance is an appropriate way of analysing a two-way research design. The number of factors and the number of levels within the factors may be indicated by stating the number of levels in each factor and by separating each of these numbers by an '×' which is referred to as 'by'. So a design having two factors with two levels and a third factor with three levels may be called a $2 \times 2 \times 3$ factorial design. The analysis of factorial designs is usually through the use of analysis of variance (ANOVA). There are versions of ANOVA that cope with virtually any variation of the factorial design. For example, it is possible to have related variables and unrelated variables as independent variables in the same design (i.e. a mixed ANOVA).

When quantitative subject variables such as age, intelligence or anxiety are to be used in a factorial design and analysed using ANOVA, they can be categorised into ranges or groups of scores. Age, for example, may be categorised as ages between 18 and 22, 23 and 30, 30 and 40, and so on. The choice of ranges to use will depend on the nature of the study. Some researchers may prefer to use the subject variable as a covariate in an analysis of covariance design (ANCOVA). The use of ranges is particularly helpful if there is a non-linear relationship between the subject variable and the dependent variable. This would be assessed by drawing a scatterplot of the relationship between the subject variable and the dependent variable. If the relationship between the two seems to be a curved line then there is a non-linear relationship between the two.

There is an alternative way of analysing complex factorial designs which is to use multiple regression. This statistical technique identifies the pattern of independent variables which best account for the variation in a dependent variable. This readily translates to an experimental design which too has independent and dependent variables. If there are any subject variables in the form of scores then they may be left as scores. (Though this requires that the relationship between the subject variable and the dependent variable is linear.) Qualitative variables (i.e. nominal, category or categorical variables) may also be included as predictors. They may need to be converted into *dummy variables* if the qualitative variable has more than two categories. A good description of dummy variables is provided by Cohen and Cohen (1983), and they are explained also in the companion text *Introduction to Statistics in Psychology* (Howitt and Cramer, 2005*a*). Basically, a dummy variable involves taking each category of a nominal variable and making it into a new variable. Participants are simply coded as having the characteristic to which the category refers or not. For example, if the category variable is cat, dog and other (the question is 'What is the participant's favourite animal?') then this can be turned into two dummy variables such as cat and dog. Participants are coded as choosing cat *or not and* choosing dog *or not*. There is always one less dummy variable than the number of categories. Participants choosing other will be those who have not chosen cat and dog.

The advantages of using multiple regression to analyse multifactorial designs include:

■ The subject variables are not placed into fairly arbitrary categories.
■ The variation (and information) contained in the subject variable is not reduced by turning the subject variable into a small number of categories or ranges of scores.

There are three main advantages to using a factorial design:

■ It is more efficient, or economical, in that it requires fewer cases or observations for approximately the same degree of precision or power. For example, a two-factor factorial design might use just 30 participants. To achieve the same power running the two-factor factorial design as two separate one-factor designs, twice as many participants would be needed. That is, each one-factor design would require 30 participants. In the multifactorial design, the values of one factor are averaged across the values of the other factors. That is to say, the factorial design essentially can be considered as several non-factorial designs. Hence, the economy of numbers.

■ Factorial designs enable greater generalisability of the results in that a factor is investigated over a wider range of conditions. So, for example, we have looked at the effects of alcohol under two levels of noise rather than, say, a single one, and in females and males rather than in just one of these two groups.

■ A third advantage is that a factorial design allows us to determine whether there is an interaction between two or more factors in that the effect of one factor depends on the effect of one or more other factors. Box 8.1 deals with interactions.

BOX 8.1   THE NATURE OF INTERACTIONS

One of the consequences of employing multifactorial designs is that the combined influences of the variables on the dependent variable may be identified. An interaction is basically a combination of levels of two or more variables which produces effects on the dependent variable which cannot be accounted for by the separate effects of the variables in question. Interactions must be distinguished from main effects. A main effect is the influence of a variable acting on its own – not in combination with any other variable. Interactions can only occur when there are two or more independent variables.

Interactions may be most easily grasped in terms of a graph such as Figures 7.2 and 7.3 where the vertical axis represents the dependent variable, the horizontal axis

→

Box 8.1 continued

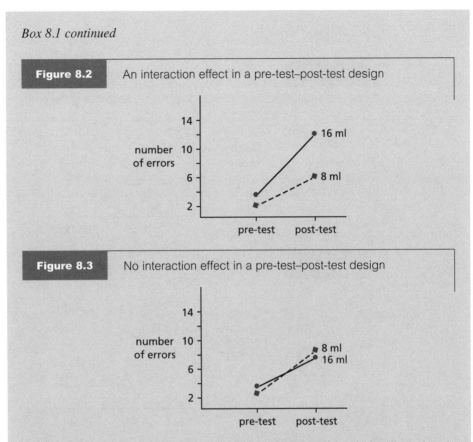

| Figure 8.2 | An interaction effect in a pre-test–post-test design |

| Figure 8.3 | No interaction effect in a pre-test–post-test design |

represents one of the independent variables and the lines connecting the points in the graph represent one or more other independent variables. In Figures 8.2 and 8.3 the vertical axis represents the number of errors made, the horizontal axis represents the time of testing, pre-test and post-test, and the two lines the two alcohol conditions, 8 and 16 ml.

An interaction effect may have occurred if the lines in the graph are out of parallel. Interactions have occurred when the lines diverge or converge (or both) as can be seen in these two graphs. In these two graphs the effect of differing amounts of alcohol appears to depend on the time of testing. In other words there seems to be an interaction between the amount of alcohol consumed and the time of testing. In both figures the difference between the two amounts of alcohol is greater at pre-test than post-test. In terms of a true or randomised pre-test–post-test experimental design we would hope that the pre-test scores were similar, as illustrated in Figure 8.2, as this is the main purpose of randomisation but this does not always happen.

In Figure 8.2 there still appears to be an interaction but the difference between the two amounts of alcohol is greater at post-test than at pre-test. Drinking 16 ml of alcohol has a greater effect on the number of errors made than 8 ml of alcohol which is what we would anticipate. In pre-test–post-test experimental designs this is the kind of interaction effect we would expect if our independent variable had an effect.

The absence of an interaction between time of testing and alcohol is illustrated in Figure 8.3 as the two lines representing the two alcohol conditions are more or less parallel. There also appears to be a main effect for the time of testing in that the

→

Box 8.1 continued

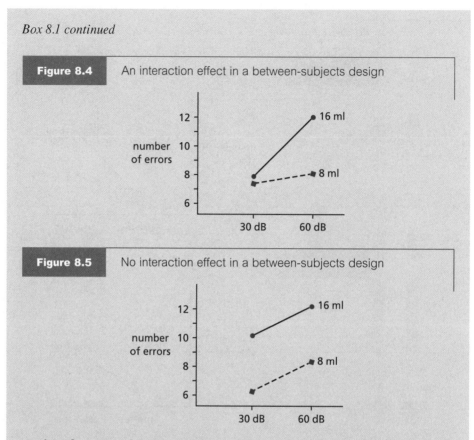

Figure 8.4 An interaction effect in a between-subjects design

Figure 8.5 No interaction effect in a between-subjects design

number of errors made at post-test seem to be greater than the number made at pre-test, but there does not seem to be a difference between the two alcohol conditions.

Figure 8.4 shows an apparent interaction effect for a between-subjects factorial design which consists of the two factors of amount of alcohol and level of noise. The difference in the number of errors made between the two alcohol conditions is greater for the 60 dB condition than the 30 dB condition.

Figure 8.5 illustrates the lack of an interaction effect for these two factors. The difference in performance between the two alcohol conditions appears to be similar for the two noise conditions.

There are circumstances where one should be very careful in interpreting the results of a study. These are circumstances such as those illustrated in Figure 8.4. In this diagram we can see that the only difference between the conditions is the 16 ml/60 dB condition. All other three conditions actually have a similar mean on the numbers of errors. This is clearly purely an interaction with no main effects at all. The problem is that the way the analysis of variance works means it will tend to identify main effects which simply do not exist. That is because to get the main effects, two groups will be combined (the two 30 dB groups and the two 60 dB groups for instance). In other words, at least part of the interaction will be subsumed under the main effects.

It is not possible to determine whether there is an interaction between two or more factors simply by looking at the plot of the scores on a graph. It is necessary to establish that this is a statistically significant interaction by carrying out a test such as an analysis of variance.

There are special problems facing a researcher designing a related design study. If participants are to be studied in every possible condition of the study then the order ought to be counterbalanced such that no order is more common than any other order. These designs are known as Latin square designs. These are discussed in Box 8.2.

BOX 8.2 LATIN SQUARES TO CONTROL ORDER EFFECTS

In a within-subject design you need to control for order effects by running the levels or conditions in different orders. The more conditions you have, the more orders there are for running those conditions. With three conditions called A, B and C, there are six different orders: ABC; ACB; BAC; BCA; CAB; and CBA. With four conditions there are 24 possible orders. With five conditions there are 120 possible orders and so on. We can work out the number of potential orders by multiplying the number of conditions by each of the numbers that fall below that number. For three conditions this is $3 \times 2 \times 1$ which gives 6. For five conditions it is $5 \times 4 \times 3 \times 2 \times 1$ which gives 120. Often there are more possible orders than actual participants. Suppose, for example, you only required 12 participants in a within-subjects design which has four conditions. In this situation, it is not possible to run all 24 possible orders. To determine which orders to run, one could randomly select 12 out of the 24 possible orders. However, if you do this, you could not guarantee that each condition would be run in the same ordinal position (for example, the first position) the same number of times and that each condition precedes and follows each condition once. In other words, you could not control for these order effects. The way to control for these order effects is to construct a Latin square.

A Latin square has as many orders as conditions. So a Latin square with four conditions will have four orders. To make a Latin square, perform the following steps:

■ Create a random order of the conditions. This random order will be used to generate the other orders in the Latin square. There are several ways to create this initial random order. Suppose there are four conditions labelled A, B, C and D. One way is to write each letter on a separate slip of paper or index card, thoroughly shuffle the papers or cards and choose a sequence. (Randomisation is dealt with on p. 124.)

■ Suppose the starting random order from step 1 is BACD. Sequentially number the conditions in this random order starting with 1. For this example, B = 1, A = 2, C = 3 and D = 4.

■ To create the first order in the Latin square, put the last number or condition (*N*) in the third position as follows:

   1, 2, 4, 3

which corresponds to the conditions as initially lettered B, A, D, C. If we had more than four conditions, then every subsequent unevenly numbered position (e.g. 5, 7 and so on) would have one less than the previous unevenly numbered position as shown in Table 8.2.

→

Box 8.2 continued

Table 8.2 Position of unevenly numbered conditions in the first order of a Latin square

Order number	1	2	3	4	5	6	7	8	9	10
Condition number	1	2	N	3	$N-1$	4	$N-2$	5	$N-3$	6

■ To create the second order in the Latin square add 1 to each number apart from the last number N, which now becomes 1. So, in terms of our example with four conditions, the order is:

    $2 (1 + 1), 3 (2 + 1), 1 (N), 4 (3 + 1)$

which corresponds to the conditions as first lettered A, C, B, D.

■ To create further orders we simply proceed in the same way by adding 1 to the previous numbers except that the last number (4) becomes the first number (1). So, the order of the third row in our example becomes:

    $3 (2 + 1), 4 (3 + 1), 2 (1 + 1), 1$

which corresponds to the conditions as originally lettered C, D, A, B.
    Our Latin square will look as follows

B, A, D, C
A, C, B, D
C, D, A, B
D, B, C, A

We can see that each of the four letters only occurs once in each of the four orders or four columns of the square. Each letter is preceded and followed once by every other letter. For example, B is preceded once by C, A and D in the second, third and fourth rows, respectively. It is also followed once by A, D and C in the first, second and last rows, respectively.

■ If there is an odd number of conditions, then two Latin squares are constructed. The first square is created as just described. The second square is produced by reversing the order of each of the rows in the first square so that the first condition becomes the last and the second condition becomes the second to last and so on. So, if we have five conditions and the first row of our initial Latin square is:

    C, A, D, E, B

the first row of our reversed Latin square becomes:

    B, E, D, A, C.

With five conditions we would have 10 rows or orders.

■ Participants are randomly assigned to each order. The number of participants for each order should be the same.

The Latin square could be used for controlling the order in which we measure the dependent variable when there are several of these being measured in a particular study.

8.4 The psychology and social psychology of the laboratory experiment

There is no doubt that the design of effective experiments is problematic. Some of the most troublesome issues in psychology experiments are not about the detail of design or the statistical analysis, but a consequence of the psychology laboratory being a social setting in which people interact and, it has to be said, in less than normal circumstances. Generically this can be referred to as the psychology and social psychology of the laboratory experiment. These issues are largely about the interaction between the participants and the experimenter, and the experimental procedures. Their consequence is to somewhat muddy the interpretation and validity of laboratory experiments. These are not recent ideas. Some stretch back into the history of psychology and most can be traced back 40 or 50 years. Some see these features as making experimentation untenable as the fundamental method of psychological research, others regard them as relatively trivial, but interesting, features of experimental research.

Placebo effect

Placebo effects have long been recognised in the evaluation of drugs and clinical treatments (Rivers, 1908). Careful attempts are made to control placebo effects in clinical trials though somewhat similar effects in other fields of psychological research may be left uncontrolled (Orne, 1959, 1969). A drug has two aspects – what the medication looks like and the active ingredients that it contains. Long ago, the medical researcher Beecher (1955) noted that participants who believed they were receiving the active medication but were in fact receiving bogus medication (which lacked the active ingredient) nevertheless showed similar effects to those who received the active ingredient. One possible explanation is that they have expectations about the effectiveness of the drug. The treatment that does not contain the component whose effectiveness is being evaluated is called a placebo or placebo treatment. Placebo is Latin for 'I shall be pleasing or acceptable'. The treatment is called a placebo because it is given to patients to please them into thinking that they are being treated.

In clinical trials of the effectiveness of drugs or clinical treatments, participants are told that either they are being given the treatment (even though they are not) or that they may receive either the placebo or the treatment but they are not told which they are receiving. In other words, they may not be aware of (that is they may be 'blind' to) the treatment they are receiving. Furthermore, the person administrating the study should, ideally, be ignorant of what is actually happening to the participant. It is believed that the person responsible for, say, giving out the treatment may unconsciously convey to the participant information about which sort of treatment they are receiving. If the administrator does not know what treatment is being given, then no subtle cues may be communicated about whether or not the placebo was given, for example. In other words, it may be ideal if the administrator is not aware of, or is blind to, the treatment they are giving. This is known as a 'double-blind' – which means both the participants in the research and the administrator of the research are ignorant of whether the active or the placebo treatment has been given.

Sheldrake (1998) surveyed experimental papers that were published in important journals in a number of fields. One feature of this survey was the low frequency of the use of blind experimental procedures. Blind procedures were by far the most common in the field of parapsychology, where over four out of five studies used blind procedures. This is important since parapsychological research (i.e. into supernatural phenomena) is one type of research about which there is a great deal of scepticism. Hence the need for researchers in this field to employ the most exacting research methods since critics are almost certain to identify methodological faults. Equally clearly, some fields of research do not equally fear similar criticisms – or else blind procedures would be rather more common. So there may be an important lesson – that the more likely one's findings are likely to be controversial, the greater the need for methodological rigour in order to avoid public criticism.

Experimenter effects

In all of the concern about experimental design and statistical analysis, it is easy to overlook some important parameters of the experimental situation. If we concentrate on what participants do in an experiment we may ignore what effect the researcher is having. There is some evidence that the role of the researcher is not that of a neutral and unbiased collector of scientific data. Instead there is evidence that different characteristics of the experimenter may affect the outcome of the research. Some of these characteristics would include factors like the race and gender of the researcher. But there are other features of experimenters which are shared by experimenters in general. An important one of these is that experimenters generally have a commitment to their research and the outcomes of their research. Rosnow (2002) indicates something of the extent to which the experimenter can influence the accuracy of the observations they record. For example, in an overview of a sizeable number of studies involving the observations of several hundreds of researchers, something like one in every hundred observations are incorrect when measured against objective standards. Some of the inaccuracy appears to be just that – but given that about two-thirds of the errors tended to support the experimenters' hypotheses then it would appear fair to accept that there is a small trend for researchers to make errors which favour their position on a topic (Rosenthal, 1978). Whether or not these 'consistent' errors are sufficient to determine the findings of studies overall is difficult to assess. However, even if they are insufficient acting alone, there is a range of other influences of the researcher which may be compounded with recording errors.

Of course, here we are talking about non-intentional errors of which the researchers would probably be unaware. Furthermore, we should not assume that biases solely exist at the level of data collection. There are clearly possibilities of the literature review or the conclusions including some form of systematic bias. One of the best ways of dealing with these is to be always sceptical of the claims of other researchers and check out key elements of their arguments including those of Rosenthal. That is the essence of the notion of the scientific method anyway.

Experimenter expectancy effect

Rosenthal (1963, 1969) raised another potential problem in experimental studies. The idea is that experimenters may unintentionally influence participants into behaving in the way that the experimenter wants or desires. Barber (1973, 1976) described this as the experimenter unintentional expectancy effect. A typical way of investigating this effect involves student experimenters. Participants in the study are asked to rate the degree of success shown in photographs of several different people (Rosenthal and Rubin, 1978). Actually the photographs had been chosen because previous research had shown them to be rated at the neutral midpoint of the success scale. In this study, the student experimenters were deceived into believing either that previous research had shown the photographs to be rated as showing success or that the previous research had shown the photographs to be showing failure. However, of the 119 studies using this experimental paradigm (procedure), only 27% found that student experimenters were affected by their expectations based on the putative previous research. So in most cases there was no evidence for expectancy effects. Nevertheless, if over a quarter of studies found evidence of an effect, then it should always be considered a possibility when designing research. Very few studies have included control conditions to determine to what extent they may occur when the focus of the study is not the examination of expectancy effects.

Demand characteristics

Orne (1962, 1969) suggested that when participating in an experiment, participants are influenced by the totality of the situation which provides cues that essentially convey a hypothesis for the situation and perhaps indications of how they should behave. In many ways, the concept of demand characteristics cannot be separated from the notion of helpful and cooperative participants. Orne, for example, had noticed that participants in research when interviewed afterwards make statements indicating that they are aware that there is some sort of experimental hypothesis and that they, if acting reasonably, should seek to support the researcher in the endeavour. So, for example, a participant might say 'I hope that was the sort of thing you wanted.' or 'I hope that I didn't mess up your study.' The demand characteristics explanation takes account of the totality of cues in the situation – it is not specifically about the experimenter's behaviour. The prime focus is on the participants and the influence of the totality of the situation on them. He proposed that certain features or cues of the experimental situation, including the way that the experimenter behaves, may lead the participant to behave in certain ways. These cues are called the demand characteristics of the experiment. This effect is thought to be largely unconscious in that participants are not aware of being affected in this way. Of course, some might question this as the cognitive processes involved seem quite complex. Orne only gives a few examples of studies where demand characteristics may be operating but these examples do not seem to quite clinch the matter.

One study examined sensory deprivation effects. The question was whether the apparent effects of deprivation of sensory stimulation for several hours could be simply the result of the participants' expectations that their behaviour should be adversely affected (Orne and Scheibe, 1964). In one condition participants underwent various procedures which indicated that they may be taking part in a study which had deleterious effects. For example, they were given a physical examination and were told that if they could not stand being in the condition any longer they could press a red 'panic' button to release them from the situation. In the other condition participants were put in exactly the same physical situation but were simply told that they were acting as the controls in a sensory deprivation study. The effects of these two conditions were examined in terms of 14 different measures (an example of a study using multiple dependent variables). However, there were significant differences in only three of the 13 measures where this difference was in the predicted direction.

It has to be stressed that Orne did not regard demand characteristics as just another nuisance source of variation for the experimenter to control. Indeed, the demand characteristics could not be controlled for, for example, by using sophisticated control conditions.

Instead the demand characteristics needed to be understood using one major resource – the participants in the study themselves. Rosnow (2002) likens the role of demand characteristics to the greengrocer whose thumb is always on the scale. The bias may be small but it is consistent and in no sense random.

Orne's solution was to seek out information which would put the researcher on a better track to understanding the meaning of their data. Quasi-control strategies were offered which essentially change the status of the participants in the research from that of the subject to a role which might be described as co-investigators. In the post-experiment interview, once the participant has been effectively convinced that the experiment is over, the experimenter and participant are free to discuss all aspects of the study in which things like the meaning of the study as experienced by the participant may be explored. Of course, the participant needs to understand that the experimenter has concerns about the possibility of demand characteristics influencing behaviour in the experiment.

An alternative to this is to carry out a pre-inquiry. This is a mind game really in which the participants are asked to imagine that they are participating in the actual study. The experimental procedures are described to the participants in the mind experiment in a great deal of detail. The participant is then asked to describe how they believe that they would behave in these circumstances. Eventually, the experimenter is in a position to compare the conjectures about behaviour in the study with what actually happens in the study. An assessment may be made of the extent to which demand characteristics may explain the participants' actual behaviours. The problem is, of course, that the behaviours cannot be decisively identified as the consequence of demand characteristics.

Imagine an experiment (disregarding everything you learnt in the ethics chapter) in which the experimental group has a lighted cigarette placed against their skin whereas the control group has an unlighted cigarette place against their skin. In a quasi-control pre-inquiry, participants will probably anticipate that the real participants will show some sort of pain reaction. Would we contemplate explaining such responses in the real experiment as the result of demand characteristics? Probably not. But what, for example, if in the actual experiment the participants in the lighted cigarette condition actually showed no signs of pain? In these circumstances the demand characteristics explanation simply is untenable. What, though, if the pre-inquiry study found that participants expected that they would remain stoical and stifle the expression of pain? Would we not accept the demand characteristics explanation in this case? This would surely clarify the meaning of the findings of a study in which participants know that they are participants of a study.

There are a number of demonstrations by Orne and others that participants in experiments tend to play the role of good participants. That is, they seem especially willing to carry out tasks which, ordinarily away from the laboratory, they would refuse to do or question. So it has been shown that participants in a laboratory will do endless press-ups simply at the request of the experimenter. This situation of 'good faith' in which the participant is keen to serve the needs of the experiment may not always exist and it is a very different world now from when these studies were originally carried out in the middle of the 20th century. But this could be accommodated by the notion of demand characteristics.

Not surprisingly, researchers have investigated demand characteristics experimentally, sometimes using aspects of Orne's ideas. Demand characteristics have been most commonly investigated in studies manipulating feelings of elation and depression (Westermann *et al.*, 1996).

Velten (1968) examined the effect of demand characteristics by having participants in the control conditions read various information about the corresponding experimental condition. For example, by describing the procedure used in this condition, by asking participants to behave in the way they think that participants in that condition would behave, and by asking them to act as if they were in the same mood as that condition was designed to produce. Velten found no evidence for the effect of demand characteristics. Participants in the elation condition rated their mood as significantly less depressed than those in the elation demand characteristics condition and participants in the depression condition rated their mood as significantly more depressed than those in the depression demand characteristics condition.

What to conclude? Orne-style quasi-control studies have one feature that would be valuable in any study – that is, participants and researcher get together as equals to try to understand the experience of participants in the research. Out of such interviews, information may emerge which can help the researcher understand their data. Not to talk to research participants is a bit like burying one's head in the sand to avoid exposure to problems. Researchers should want to know about every aspect of their research – whether or not this knowledge is comfortable. On the other hand, studies into the effects of demand characteristics often produce at best only partial evidence of their effects as we saw above. That is, quasi-participants who simply experience descriptions of the experimental procedures rarely if ever seem to reproduce the research findings in full. Whether such 'partial replications' of the findings of the original study are sufficient to either accept or reject the notion of demand characteristics is difficult to arbitrate on.

The important lesson learnt from the studies of the social psychology of the laboratory experiment is the futility of regarding participants in research as passive recipients of stimuli which affect their behaviour. The old-fashioned term subject seems to encapsulate this view better than anything. The modern term participants describes the situation more accurately.

8.5 Conclusion

Most true or randomised experimental designs include more than two conditions and measure more than one dependent variable. Where the design consists of a single factor, the number of conditions is limited and may generally consist of no more than four or five conditions. The number of factors that are manipulated in a true or randomised design should also be restricted and may usually comprise no more than two or three manipulated variables. The reason for this advice partly rests on the difficulty of carrying out studies with many independent variables – the planning of them introduces many difficulties. Furthermore, the statistical analysis of very complex factorial designs is not easy and may stretch the statistical understanding of many researchers to the limit. For example, numerous complex interactions may emerge which are fraught with difficulties of interpretation.

Hypotheses often omit consideration of effects due to basic demographic factors such as gender and age. Nevertheless, factorial designs can easily and usefully include such factors when numbers of participants permit. Of course, where the participants are, for example, students, age variation may be too small to be worthy of inclusion. Alternatively, where the numbers of females and males are very disproportionate it may also be difficult to justify looking for gender differences.

It is wise to make adequate provision in terms of participant numbers for trends to be statistically significant. Otherwise a great deal of effort is wasted. A simple but good way of doing this is to examine similar studies to inform yourself about what may be the minimum appropriate sample size. Alternatively, by running a pilot study a more direct estimate of the likely size of the experimental effect can be made and a sample size chosen which gives that size of effect the chance of being statistically significant. The way in which the results of factorial randomised designs are analysed can also be applied to the analysis of qualitative variables in non-randomised designs such as surveys, as we shall see in the next chapter.

A pilot study is also an opportunity for exploring the social psychological characteristics of the experiment being planned. In particular, it can be regarded as an opportunity to interview participants about their experience of the study. What they have to say may confirm the appropriateness of your chosen method but it, equally, may provide food for thought and a stimulus to reconsider some of the detail of the planned experiment.

Key points

- Advanced experimental designs extend the basic experimental group–control group paradigm in a number of ways. Several experimental and control groups may be used. More than one independent variable may be used and several measures of the dependent variable.

- Because considerable resources may be required to conduct a study, the number of conditions run must be limited to those which are considered important. It is not advisable to simply extend the number of independent variables since this can lead to problems in interpreting the complexity of the output. Further studies may be needed when the interpretation of the data is hampered by a lack of sufficient information.

- Multifactorial designs are important since they are not only efficient in terms of the numbers of participants needed, but they can help identify interactions between the independent variables in the study. Furthermore, the relative influences of the various factors is revealed in a factorial design.

- Research which has insufficient cases to detect the effect under investigation is a waste of effort. The numbers in the cells of an experimental design need to be sufficient to determine that an effect is statistically significant. Previous similar studies may provide indications of appropriate sample sizes or a pilot study may be required to estimate the likely size of the effect of the factors. From this, the minimum sample size to achieve statistical significance may be assessed.

- As with most designs, it is advantageous if the cells of a design have the same number of cases. This, for factorial designs, ensures that the effects of the factors are independent of one another. The extent to which factors are not independent can be determined by multiple regression. Many statistical tests work optimally with equal group sizes.

- Placebos and double-blind procedural controls should be routinely used in the evaluation of the effects of drugs to control for the expectations that participants and experimenters may have about the effects of the drugs being tested. Some of these procedures are appropriate in a variety of psychological studies.

■ In general, it would seem that few researchers incorporate checks on demand characteristics and other social psychological aspects of the laboratory experiment. This may partly be explained by the relative lack of research into such effects in many areas of psychological research. However, since it is beneficial to interview participants about their experiences of the experimental situation, it is possible to discuss factors such as demand characteristics and expectancy effects with participants as part of the joint evaluation of the research by experimenter and participants.

Activities

1. Answer the following questions in terms of the basic design that you produced for the exercise in Chapter 7 to investigate the effect of unemployment on crime. Can you think of reasons for breaking down the independent variable of unemployment into more than two conditions? If you can, what would these other conditions be? Are there ways in which you think participants may be affected by the manipulation of unemployment which are not part of unemployment itself? In other words, are there demand-type characteristics which may affect how participants behave? If there are, how would you test or control these? Which conditions would you compare and what would your predictions be about the differences between them. Is there more than one way in which you can operationalise crime? If there are, would you want to include these as additional measures of crime? Are there any subject or other independent variables that you think are worth including? If there are, would you expect any of these to interact with the independent variable of unemployment?

2. What is your nomination for the worst experiment of all time for this year's Psycho Awards? Explain your choice. Who would you nominate for the experimenter's hall of fame and why?

9 Cross-sectional or correlational research
Non-manipulation studies

Overview

■ Various terms describe research that, unlike the true or randomised experiment, does not involve the deliberate manipulation of variables. These terms include correlational study, survey study, observational study and non-experiment.

■ Non-manipulation study is the most accurate and most generic term to describe this type of study as there are problems with the others.

■ There are many reasons why laboratory/experimental research cannot fulfil all of the research needs of psychology. Sometimes important variables simply cannot be manipulated effectively. Laboratory experiments can handle only a small number of variables at any one time which makes it difficult to compare variables in terms of their relative influence. One cannot use experiments to investigate patterns or relationships among a number of variables.

■ Cross-sectional designs are typical of most psychological research. In cross-sectional designs, the same variable is only measured on one occasion for each participant. The question of causality cannot be tested definitively in cross-sectional designs though the relationships obtained are often used to support potential causal interpretations. These designs, however, help determine the direction and the strength of the association between two or more variables. Furthermore, the extent to which this association is affected by controlling other variables can also be assessed.

The most common alternative to the true or randomised experiment is variously referred to as a non-experimental, correlational, passive observational, survey or observational study. There are inadequacies with each of these terms. An experiment has the implication of some sort of intervention in a situation in order to assess the consequences of this intervention. This was more or less its meaning in the early years of psychological research. Gradually the experiment in psychology took on the more formal characteristics of randomisation, experimental and control groups, and control of potentially confounding sources of variation. However, in more general terms, an experiment is generally defined along the lines of being a test or trial (Allen, 1992) which does not necessarily involve all of the formal expectations of the randomised psychology experiment. In this more general context, we could be interested in testing whether one variable, such as academic achievement at school, is related to another variable, such as parental income. However, this would be a very loose use of language in psychology and the key requirement of the manipulation of a variable is the defining feature. This is clear, for example, when Campbell and Stanley (1963, p. 1) state that an experiment is taken to refer to 'research in which variables are manipulated and their effects upon other variables observed'. It should be clear from this that a non-experiment in psychology refers to any research which does not involve the manipulation of a variable. However, it may be better to state this directly by referring to a non-manipulation rather than a non-experimental study.

Campbell and Stanley (1963, p. 64) use the term correlational to describe designs which do not entail the manipulation of variables. Today it is a very common term to describe this sort of research. Later, however, Cook and Campbell (1979, p. 295) point out that the term correlational actually describes a statistical technique not a research design. So correlational methods can be used to analyse the data from an experiment just as they can be used in many other sorts of quantitative research. A particular set of statistical tests have traditionally been applied to the data from experiments (e.g. t-tests, analyses of variance). However, it is perfectly feasible to analyse the same experiment with a correlation coefficient or multiple regression. Remember that the common distinction between correlation and differences between means is more apparent than real (see Box 9.1). Data from non-experimental studies can frequently be analysed using the statistical techniques common in reports of experiments – t-tests and analyses of variance, for example. We would most probably apply a two-way analysis of variance to determine whether the scores on a measure of depression varied according to the gender and the marital status of participants. Although researchers would not normally do this, the same data could be analysed using multiple regression techniques. In other words, analysis of variance and multiple regression are closely linked.

BOX 9.1   REMINDER: TESTS OF CORRELATION VERSUS TESTS OF DIFFERENCE

Although at first there may seem to be a confusing mass of different statistical techniques, many of them are very closely related as they are based on the same general statistical model. For example, both a Pearson's product moment correlation (r) and an unrelated t-test for data with similar variances can be used to determine the relationship between a dichotomous variable such as gender and a continuous variable such as scores on a measure of depression. Both these tests will give you the same significance level when applied to the same data. The relationship between the two tests is

$$r = \sqrt{\frac{t^2}{t^2 + \mathrm{df}}}$$

where df stands for the degrees of freedom. The degrees of freedom are two less the total number of cases.

The dichotomous variable could equally be the experimental condition versus the control condition. Hence the applicability of both tests to simple experiments. The dichotomous variable is coded 1 and 2 for the two different values whether the gender variable is being considered or the independent variable of an experiment (this is an arbitrary coding and could be reversed if one wished).

Although it never gained popularity, Cook and Campbell (1979, p. 296) suggested the term *passive observational* to describe a non-manipulation study. The adjective passive implies that the study does not involve a manipulation in this context. However, to refer to most research procedures as being passive reflects the situation very poorly. For instance, observation itself is often thought of as active rather than passive. However, like other forms of human perception, there is a degree of selectivity in terms of what is being observed (Pedhazur and Schmelkin, 1991, p. 142). Furthermore, even the value of the term 'observational' in this context is problematic since it can be applied to the data collection methods in experiments and other types of research equally. As observation can be used in a true or randomised experiment, this term does not exclude randomised studies. Cook and Campbell (1979, p. 296) themselves objected to using the term observational study because it would apply to what they called quasi-experiments which did not involve randomisation.

The term survey is also not particularly appropriate either. It too refers to a method of data collection which typically involves asking people questions. It also has the connotation of drawing precise sample from a population such as in stratified random sampling (see p. 191). Many studies in psychology have neither of these features and yet are not randomised experiments.

In view of the lack of a satisfactory term, we have given in to the temptation to use non-manipulation study to refer to this kind of study. This term is less general than non-experimental, refers to the essential characteristic of an experiment and does not describe a method of data collection. However we realise we are even less likely than Cook and Campbell (1979, p. 295) 'to change well-established usage'. In the majority of the social sciences, the distinction would not be very important. In psychology it is important for the simple reason that psychology alone has a strong commitment to laboratory experiment. Of course, medicine and biology do have a tradition of strict experimentation and may have similar problems over terminology.

9.1 Cross-sectional designs

The most basic design for a cross-sectional study involves just two variables. These variables may both be scores, may both be nominal categories, or there may be a mixture of nominal and score variables. For example, we could examine the relationship between gender and a diagnosis of depression. In this case both variables would consist of two binary values – male versus female, diagnosed as depressed versus not diagnosed as depressed. Such basic designs would provide very limited information which can restrict their interest to researchers. They are probably too simple to warrant the time and effort expended when they could benefit from the collection of a wider variety of data with possibly little or no more effort. This would be the more usual approach.

So, ideally, you should think in terms of a minimum of three variables for a cross-sectional study but realistically there are advantages in extending this further. The reason for considering a minimum of three variables is that the third variable introduces the possibility of introducing controls for potentially confounding variables or investigating possible intervening variables. There is often every advantage of introducing more variables and more than one measure of the same variable. This is *not* an invitation to throw into a study every variable that you can think of and have a means of measuring. The reasons for adding in more than the minimum number of variables is that the additional information they yield has the potential to clarify the meaning of the relationship between your primary variables of interest. Ideally this is a careful and considered process in which the researcher anticipates the possible outcomes of the research and adds in additional variables which may contribute positively to assessing just what the outcome means. Merely throwing in everything is likely to lead to more confusion rather than clarification.

The cross-sectional design is as difficult to execute as any other form of study, including the laboratory experiment. The skills required to effectively carry out field work are not always the same as those for doing experiments, but they are in no sense less demanding. Indeed, when it comes to the effective statistical analysis of cross-sectional data, this may be more complex than that required for some laboratory experiments. The reason for this is that non-manipulation studies employ statistical controls for unwanted influences whereas experimental studies employ procedural controls to a similar end. Furthermore, the cross-sectional study may be more demanding in terms of numbers of participants simply because the relationship between the variables of interest is generally smaller than would be expected in a laboratory experiment. In the laboratory, it is possible to maximise the obtained relationships by controlling for the 'noise' of other variables. In a cross-sectional design, we would expect the relationships between variables to be small and a correlation of about 0.30 would be considered quite a promising trend by many researchers. For a correlation of this size to be statistically significant at the two-tailed 5% or 0.05 level would require a minimum sample size of over 40.

The need for statistical controls for the influence of third variables in cross-sectional and all non-manipulation studies makes considerable demands on the statistical knowledge of the researcher. Many of the appropriate statistics are not discussed in many introductory statistics texts in psychology. One exception to this is *Introduction to Statistics in Psychology* (Howitt and Cramer, 2005*a*). Given the complexity of some of the statistical techniques together with the substantial numbers of variables that can be involved means that the researcher really ought to use a computer program capable of analysing these sorts of data well. The companion computing text *Introduction to SPSS in Psychology* (Howitt and Cramer, 2005*b*) will help you make light work of this task.

Because many variables which are of interest tend to be correlated with each other, samples have to be larger when the relationship between three or more variables are investigated together. It is difficult to give an exact indication of how big a sample should be because this depends on the size of the associations that are expected, but in general the size of the sample should be more than 60.

9.2 The case for non-manipulation studies

There are a number of circumstances which encourage the use of non-manipulation studies just as there are other circumstances in which the randomised laboratory experiment may be employed to better effect:

■ *Naturalistic research settings* Generally speaking, randomised experiments have a degree of artificiality which varies but is probably mostly present. Although there have been a number of successful attempts to employ randomised experiments in the 'field' (natural settings), these have been relatively few and risked losing the advantages of the laboratory experiment. Consequently, given that research is a matter of choices, many psychologists prefer not to do randomised experiments at all. There are arguments on all sides, but research is a matter of balancing a variety of considerations and that balance will vary between researchers and across circumstances.

■ *Manipulation not possible* It is not always possible, practical or ethical to manipulate the variable of interest. This would be the case, for example, if you were interested in looking at the effects of divorce on children. In this situation you could compare children from parents who were together with children from parents who were divorced. However, divorce cannot be assigned at random by the researcher.

■ *Establishing an association* You may wish to see whether there is a relationship between two or more variables before committing resources to complex experiments designed to identify causal relationships between those variables. For example, you may wish to determine whether there is an association between how much conflict there is in a relationship and how satisfied people are in that relationship before seeing whether reducing conflict increases satisfaction with the relationship. Finding an association does not mean that there is a causal relationship between two variables. This could be an example of where a third variable is confusing things. For example, low income may make for stressful circumstances in which couples are in conflict more often and are less satisfied with their relationship because shortage of cash makes them less positive about life in general. In this example, this confounding factor of income makes it appear that conflict is causally related to dissatisfaction when it is not. Conversely, the failure to find an association between two variables does not necessarily mean that those variables are not related. The link between the variables may be suppressed by other variables. For instance, there may be an association between conflict and dissatisfaction, but this association may be suppressed by the presence of children. Having children may create more conflict between partners, but may also cause them to be more fulfilled as a couple.

■ *Natural variation* In experiments, every effort is made to control for variables which may influence the association between the independent and dependent variables. In a sense, by getting rid of nuisance sources of variation, the key relationship will be revealed at its strongest. But what if your desire is to understand what the relationship is when these other factors are present, as they normally would be in real life? For example, when manipulating a variable you may find that there is a very strong association between the dependent variable and the independent variable but this association may be weaker when it is examined in a natural setting.

■ *Comparing size of associations* You may want to find out which of a number of variables are most strongly associated with a particular variable. This may help decide which ones would be the most promising to investigate further or which ones need controlling in a true experiment. For example, if you wanted to develop a programme for improving academic achievement at school, it would be best to look at those variables which were most strongly related to academic achievement rather than those which were weakly related to it.

■ *Prediction and selection* You may be interested in determining which variables best predict an outcome. These variables may then be used for selecting the most promising candidates. For example, you may be interested in finding out which criteria best predict which prospective students are likely to be awarded the highest degree marks in psychology and use these criteria to select applicants.

■ *Explanatory models*   You may want to develop what you consider to be an explanatory model for some behaviour and to see whether your data fit that model before checking in detail whether your assumptions about causes are correct. For example, you may think that children with wealthier parents perform better academically than children with poorer parents because of differences in the parents' interest in how well their children do academically. It may be that children with wealthier parents have parents who show more interest in their academic progress than children with poorer parents. As a consequence, children of wealthier parents may try harder and so do better. If this is the case, parental interest would be a mediating or intervening variable which mediates or intervenes between parental wealth and academic achievement.

■ *Structure*   You may be interested in determining what the structure is of some characteristic such as intelligence, personality, political attitudes or love. For example, you may be interested in seeing whether there is a general factor of intelligence or whether there are separate factors of intelligence such as memory, verbal ability, spatial ability and so on.

■ *Developing or refining measures*   You may want to develop or refine a measure in which you compare your new or refined measure with some criterion. For instance, you may want to refine a measure of social support. More social support has been found to be related to less depression so you may wish to see whether your refined measure of social support correlates more strongly with depression than the original measure.

■ *Temporal change*   You may wish to see whether a particular behaviour changes over time and, if it does, to what variables those changes are related. For example, has the incidence of divorce increased over the last 50 years and, if so, with what factors is that increase associated?

■ *Temporal direction of associations*   You may wish to determine what the temporal direction of the association is between two variables. For example, does parental interest in their child's academic achievement at school affect their achievement or is the causal direction of this association the other way round with the child's academic achievement influencing the parents' interest in how well their child is doing academically? Of course both these casual sequences may be possible. An association where both variables affect each other is variously known as a bi-directional, bilateral, non-recursive, reciprocal or two-way association.

Chapter 10 discusses methods of researching changes over time.

9.3 Key concepts in the analysis of cross-sectional studies

There are a number of conceptual issues in the analysis of cross-sectional studies which need to be understood as a prelude to the more purely statistical matters.

Varying reliability of measures

The concept of reliability is quite complex and is dealt with in detail in Chapter 13. There are two broad types of reliability. The first type is the internal consistency of a psychological scale or measure (i.e. how well the items correlate with the other items ostensibly measuring the same thing). This may be measured as the split-half reliability but is most often measured as Cronbach's (1951) alpha which is a more comprehensive index than that of split-half reliability. The other type of reliability is the stability of the measure over time. This is commonly measured using test–retest reliability. All of these measures vary from 0 to 1.00 just like a correlation coefficient. Generally speaking a reliability of about 0.80 would be regarded as satisfactory.

The crucial fact about reliability is that it limits the maximum correlation a variable may have with another variable. The maximum value of the correlation of a variable with a reliability of 0.80 with any other variable is 0.80 – that is, the figure for reliability. The maximum value that the correlation between two variables may have is the square root of the product of the two reliabilities. That is, if one reliability is 0.80 and the reliability of the other measure is 0.50 then the maximum correlation between these two variables is 0.63 ($\sqrt{(0.80 \times 0.50)} = \sqrt{0.40} = 0.632$). Remember that is the maximum and that we suggested that quite a good correlation between two variables in a cross-sectional study might be 0.30. So that correlation might be stronger than it appears if it were not for the influence of the lack of reliability of one or both of the variables.

If one knows the reliabilities (or even one reliability) then it is quite easy to correct the obtained correlation for the unreliability of the measures. One simply divides the correlation coefficient by the square root of the product of the two variables. So in our example, the correlation is 0.30 divided by the square root of 0.80×0.50. This gives $0.30/\sqrt{0.40} = 0.30/0.63 = 0.48$. This is clearly indicative of a stronger relationship than originally found.

While such statistical adjustments are a possibility and very useful if one has the reliabilities, this is not always the case. The other approach is to ensure that one's measures have the best possible opportunity for being reliable. This might be achieved, for example, by standardising one's procedures to eliminate unnecessary sources of variability. So, for example, if different interviewers ask about a participant's age in different ways then this will be a source of unnecessary variation (and consequently unreliability). For example, 'What age are you now?', 'About what age are you?' and 'Do you mind telling me your age?' might produce a variety of answers simply because of the variation of wording the question. For example, 'Do you mind telling me your age?' might encourage the participant to claim to be younger than they are simply because the question implies the possibility that the participant might be embarrassed to reveal their age.

Another problem for student researchers is the ever increasing sophistication of the statistics used by professional researchers when reporting their findings. For example, the statistical technique of structural equation modelling is quite commonly used to correct for reliability. Structural equation modelling is also known as analysis of covariance structures, causal modelling, path analysis and simultaneous equation modelling. In their survey of statistical tests reported in a random sample of papers published in the *Journal of Personality and Social Psychology*, Sherman and his colleagues (1999) found that 14% of the papers used this technique in 1996 compared with 4% in 1988 and 3% in 1978. A brief introduction to structural equation modelling may be found elsewhere (e.g. Cramer, 2003a; Pedhazur and Schmelkin, 1991). For the example above, structural equation modelling gives a standardised coefficient which has the same value as the correlation corrected for unreliability. We cannot imagine that undergraduate students would use this technique except when closely supervised by an academic but postgraduate students may well be expected to use it.

The third variable issue

The confounding variable problem is the classic stumbling block to claiming causal relationships in non-experimental research. The problem is really twofold. The first aspect is that we cannot be sure that the relationship between two variables cannot be explained by the fact that both of them are to a degree correlated with a third variable; these relationships may bring about the original correlation. This, remember, is in the context of trying to establish whether variable A is the *cause* of variable B. The other problem is that it is very difficult to anticipate quite what the effect of a third variable is – it actually can increase correlations as well as decrease them. Either way it confuses the meaning of the correlation between variables A and B.

Suppose we find that the amount of support in a relationship is positively related to how satisfied partners are. The correlation is 0.50 as shown in Figure 9.1. Further suppose that the couple's income is also positively related to both how supportive the partners are and how satisfied they are with the relationship. Income is correlated 0.60 with support and 0.40 with satisfaction. Because income is also positively related to both support and satisfaction it is possible that part or all of the association between support and satisfaction is accounted for by income. To determine if this is the case, we partial out the influence of income. One way of doing this is to use partial correlation. This is the terminology in statistics for what psychologists would normally called controlling for a third variable. That is, partialling = controlling.

Partialling is quite straightforward computationally. The basic formula is relatively easy to compute. Partialling is discussed in detail in the companion book *Introduction to Statistics in Psychology* (Howitt and Cramer, 2005a). However, we recommend using SPSS or some other package since this considerably eases the burden of calculation and risk of error when controlling for several variables at the same time. It is also infinitely less tedious.

The (partial or first-order) correlation between support and satisfaction is 0.35 once income has been partialled out. This is a smaller value than the original (zero order) correlation of 0.50. Consequently, income explains part of the association between support and satisfaction. If we want to determine whether the partial correlation is significant then the simple procedure for doing this is to use hierarchical multiple regression.

The following formula is used to partial out one variable where A refers to the first variable of support, B to the second variable of satisfaction and C to the third or confounding variable of income:

$$r_{AB.C} = \frac{r_{AB} - (r_{AC} \times r_{BC})}{\sqrt{(1 - r_{AC}^2) \times (1 - r_{BC}^2)}}$$

Figure 9.1	Correlations between support, satisfaction and income

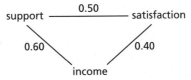

Figure 9.2 Partialling leading to a change in sign of the association between support and satisfaction

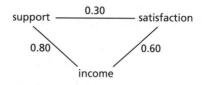

We can substitute the correlations in Figure 9.1 in this formula:

$$r_{AB.C} = \frac{0.50 - (0.60 \times 0.40)}{\sqrt{(1 - 0.60^2) \times (1 - 0.40^2)}} = \frac{0.260}{0.733} = 0.35$$

Sometimes the influence of the third variable is to make the association between the two main variables bigger than it actually is. The sign of the partial correlation can also be opposite to that of the original correlation (Cramer, 2003b). This radical change occurs when the correlation has the same sign as, and is smaller than, the product of the other two correlations. An example of this is shown in Figure 9.2. The correlation between support and satisfaction is 0.30. The signs of all three correlations are positive. The product of the other two correlations is 0.48 ($0.60 \times 0.80 = 0.48$) which is larger than the correlation of 0.30 between support and satisfaction. When income is partialled out, the correlation between support and satisfaction becomes -0.38. In other words, when income is removed, more support is associated with less rather than greater satisfaction. Different types of third variables are discussed in detail in Chapter 10.

Restricted variation of scores

This is probably the most technical of the considerations which lower the correlation between two variables. Equally, it is probably the least well recognised by researchers. A good example of a reduced correlation involves the relationship between intelligence and creativity in university students. University students have a smaller range of intelligence than the general population because they have been selected for university as they are more intelligent. The correlation between intelligence and creativity is greater in samples where the range of intelligence is less restricted.

To be formal about this, the size of the correlation between two variables is reduced when:

■ the range or variation of scores on one variable is restricted *and*
■ when the scatter of the scores of two variables about the correlation line is fairly constant over the entire length of that line (e.g. Pedhazur and Schmelkin, 1991, pp. 44–5).

A correlation line is the straight line which we would draw through the points of a scatter-gram (i.e. it is a regression line) but the scores on the two variables have been turned into z-scores or standard scores. This straight line best describes the linear relationship between these two variables (see, for example, Figure 9.3). If the scatter of scores around the correlation line is not consistent, then it is not possible to know what the size of the correlation is as this will vary according to the scatter of the scores.

Figure 9.3	Scattergram with a correlation line

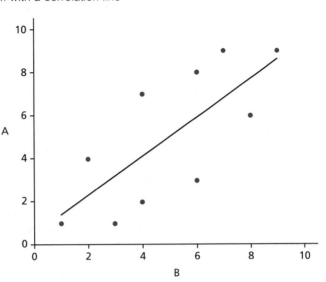

The effects of restricting range can be demonstrated quite easily with the small set of 10 scores shown in Table 9.1. The two variables are, respectively, called A and B. The scores of these two variables are plotted in the scattergram in Figure 9.3 which also shows the correlation line through them. Although the set of scores is small we can see that they are scattered in a consistent way around the correlation line. The correlation for the 10 scores is about 0.74. If we reduce the variation of scores on B by selecting the five cases with scores either above or below 5, the correlation is smaller at about 0.45. The correlation is the same in these two smaller groups because the scatter of scores around the correlation is the same in both of them.

Of course, you need to know whether you have a potential problem due to the restricted range of scores. You can gain some idea of this if you know what the mean or the standard deviation of the unrestricted scores is:

■ If the mean score is much higher (or lower) than the mean score of unrestricted scores, then the variation in scores is more likely to be restricted as the range for scores to be higher (or lower) than the mean is reduced. For example, the mean score for the two variables in Table 9.1 is 5.00. The mean score for the five cases scoring higher

Table 9.1   Scores on two variables for ten cases

Cases	A	B	Cases	A	B
1	1	1	6	6	8
2	1	3	7	7	4
3	2	4	8	8	6
4	3	6	9	9	7
5	4	2	10	9	9

than 5 on variable B is 7.20 [$(6 + 8 + 6 + 7 + 9)/5 = 36/5 = 7.20$]. As the mean for these five scores is higher than the mean of 5.00 for the ten cases, the potential range for these five scores to be higher is less than that for the ten scores.

■ The standard deviation (or variance) is a direct measure of variance. If the standard deviation of a set of scores is less than that for the unrestricted scores, then the variance is reduced. The standard deviation for variable B of the ten scores is about 2.63, whereas it is about 1.30 for the five scores both above and below the mean score of 5.

It is important to understand that generally in your research the effects of the range of scores may be of no consequence. For example, if one is interested in the relationship between creativity and intelligence in university students then there is no problem. However, it would be a problem if one were interested in the general relationship between intelligence and creativity. In this case, the restriction on the range of intelligence in the university sample might be so great that no significant relationship emerges. It is misleading to conclude from this that creativity is not related to intelligence since it may well be in the general population. Equally, you may see that studies, ostensibly on the same topic, may appear to yield seemingly incompatible findings simply because of the differences in the samples employed.

Another implication, of course, is of the undesirability of using restricted samples when exploring general psychological processes. The study of university students as the primary source of psychological data is not bad simply because of the restrictions of the sampling but also because of the restrictions likely on the distributions of the key variables.

There is more information on statistics appropriate to the analysis of cross-sectional designs in Chapter 10. Multiple regression and path analysis are discussed there and can help the researcher take full advantage of the fullness of the data which cross-sectional and other non-manipulation designs can provide.

9.4 Conclusion

There are numerous examples of research which cannot meet the requirements of the randomised controlled experiment. Indeed, psychology is somewhat unusual in its emphasis on laboratory experiments compared with other social science disciplines. We have used the term non-manipulation design for this sort of study though we acknowledge the awkwardness of this and the many other terms for this type of design. Non-manipulation designs are also used to determine the size of the association between variables as they occur naturally. Studies using these designs generally involve testing more cases than true or randomised experiments because the size of the associations or effects are expected to be weaker. Most of these studies use a cross-sectional design where cases are only measured on one occasion (Sherman *et al.*, 1999). Although the causal order of variables cannot generally be determined from cross-sectional designs, these studies often seek to explain one variable in terms of other variables. In other words, they assume that one variable is the criterion or dependent variable while the other variables are predictor or independent variables.

Key points

■ The main alternative to controlled and randomised experiments is the cross-sectional or non-manipulation study. There are numerous problems with the available terminology. We have used the term non-manipulation study.

■ Non-manipulation studies enable a large number of variables to be measured relatively easily under more natural conditions than a true or randomised study. This allows the relationships between these variables to be investigated. The cost is that these studies can be complex to analyse especially when questions of causality need to be raised.

■ The more unreliable measures are, the lower the association will be between those measures. Adjustments are possible to allow for this.

■ Partial correlation coefficients which control for third variable effects are easily computed though a computer is probably essential if one wishes to control for several third variables.

■ Restricting the range of scores on one of the variables will reduce the correlation between two variables.

Activities

1. Design a non-manipulation study that investigates the hypothesis that unemployment may lead to crime. How would you measure these two variables? What other variables would you investigate? How would you measure these other variables? How would you select your participants and how many would you have? What would you tell participants the study was about? How would you analyse the results?

2. What would be the difficulties of studying the hypothesis that unemployment may lead to crime in the psychology laboratory?

10 Longitudinal studies

Overview

■ Longitudinal studies study phenomena at different points in time.

■ A panel or prospective study involves studying the same group of participants on two or more distinct occasions over time.

■ Ideally exactly the same variables are measured on all occasions, although you will find studies where this is not achieved.

■ Longitudinal studies may be used to explore the temporal ordering or sequence of these variables (i.e. patterns of variation over time). This is useful in determining whether the association is two-way rather than one-way – that is, both variables mutually affecting each other although possibly to different degrees.

■ The concepts of internal and external validity apply particularly to longitudinal studies. The researcher needs to understand how various factors such as history and changes in instrumentation may threaten the value of a study.

■ Cross-lagged correlations are the correlations between variable X and variable Y when these variables are measured at different points in time. A lagged correlation is the correlation between variable X measured at time 1 and variable X measured at time 2.

■ Multiple regression and path analysis are important statistical techniques in the analysis of complex non-manipulation studies. The extra information from a longitudinal study adds considerably to their power.

Longitudinal studies offer the important advantage that they assess patterns in change over time. This enables a fuller interpretation of data than is possible with cross-sectional designs of the sort discussed in Chapter 9. It would appear self-evident that the study of change in any psychological variable over time is important in its own right. So, for example, it is clearly important to study how human memory changes (or does not change) during the life cycle. Change is so characteristic of humans that researchers would be failing in their obligations if they did not study change over time. Despite this, there is a quite distinct rationale for studying change over time which has much less to do with temporal changes. Remember that one of the criteria by which cause and effect sequences may be assessed is that the cause must precede the effect and the effect must follow the cause. Longitudinal studies by their nature allow the assessment of the relationship between two variables over a time period. In other words, one of the attractions of longitudinal studies is that they may help to sort out issues of causality. Hence, you may find causality to be the central theme of many longitudinal studies to the virtual exclusion of the process of actually studying change over time for its own sake.

Most frequently, variables are only measured once in studies. These are referred to as cross-sectional studies as the variables are measured across a section of time. These designs were discussed in detail in Chapter 9. Studies in which variables are measured several times at distinct intervals have been variously called longitudinal, panel or prospective studies. However, each of these terms implies a somewhat different type of study. For example, a panel study involves a group of participants (a panel) which is studied at different points in time. On the other hand, a longitudinal study merely requires that data be collected at different points in time.

So there are various kinds of longitudinal designs depending on the purpose of the study. Designs where the same people are tested on two or more occasions are sometimes referred to as *prospective studies* (Engstrom *et al.*, 1963) or *panel studies* (Lazarsfeld, 1948). This type of design was used to study American presidential elections. As you can imagine, because American elections take place over a number of months every four years, voters are subject to a great deal of media and other pressure. Some change their minds about the candidates, some change their minds about the parties they were intending to vote for. Some change their minds again later. So there are enormous advantages in being able to interview and re-interview the same group of participants at different points during the election. The alternative would be to study the electorate at several different points during the election but using different samples of the electorate each time. This causes difficulties since although it is possible to see what changes over time, it is not possible to relate these changes to what went before easily. So such a design might fail to provide the researcher with information about what sort of person changed their minds under the influence of, say, the media and their peers.

There would be enormous benefit in being able to study criminals in the long term. Some such studies have been done. For example, Farrington (1996) has studied the same delinquent children from early childhood through adulthood. As can be imagined, the logistical difficulties are enormous. Another example is the study of criminals who start their criminal careers late on in life. This is much more problematic to study and, as a consequence, little studied. If you wished to study the criminal careers of late onset criminals then an enormous sample of children would be required. Some may turn out to be late onset criminals but the vast majority would not. It is obviously easier to start with a sample of delinquents and study their progress than to try to obtain a sample of children, some of whom will turn criminal late in life. Hence the rarity of such studies (see Howitt, 2002, Chapter 5, for an example; though this does not begin in childhood).

Retrospective studies are ones in which information is sought from participants about events that happened prior to the time that they were interviewed. Usually this also involves the collection of information about the current situation. Of course, it is perfectly possible to have a study which combines the retrospective design and the prospective design. The sheer logistical requirements of longitudinal studies cannot be overestimated. Following a sample of delinquent youth from childhood into middle age has obvious organisational difficulties. Furthermore, the timescale is very long – possibly as long as a typical academic career – so alternatives may have to be contemplated. So, for example, the timescale can be truncated in real time by carrying out retrospective interviews with the offenders as adults to find information about their childhood. These adults can then be studied into middle age. However, their recollections may not be accurate. Not surprisingly, longitudinal research is uncommon.

BOX 10.1 THREATS TO INTERNAL AND EXTERNAL VALIDITY

The concepts of internal and external validity originate in the work of Campbell and Stanley (1963). They are particularly important and salient to longitudinal studies.

Internal validity is concerned with the question of whether or not the relationship between two variables is causal. That is, does the study help the researcher identify the cause and effect sequence between the two variables? It also refers to the situation where there is no empirical relationship between two variables. The question is, then, whether this means that there is no causal relationship or whether there is a relationship which is being hidden due to the masking influence of other variables. Cook and Campbell (1979) list a whole range of what they refer to as 'threats to internal validity'. Some of these are listed below and described briefly:

■ *History* Changes may occur between a pre-test and a post-test which are nothing to do with the effect of the variable of interest to the researcher. In laboratory experiments participants are usually protected from these factors. Greene (1990) was investigating the influence of eyewitness evidence on 'juries' under laboratory conditions. She found that a spate of news coverage of a notorious case where a man had been shown to be unjustly convicted on the basis of eyewitness evidence affected things in the laboratory. Her 'juries' were, for a period of time, much less likely to convict on the basis of eyewitness testimony.

■ *Instrumentation* A change over time may be due to changes in the measuring instrument over time. In the simplest cases, it is not unknown for researchers to use different versions of a measuring instrument at different points in time. But the instrumentation may change for other reasons. For example, a question asking how 'gay' someone felt would have had a very different meaning 40 years ago from today.

■ *Maturation* During the course of a longitudinal study a variety of maturation changes may occur. Participants become more experienced, more knowledgeable, less energetic and so forth.

■ *Mortality* People may drop out of the study. This may be systematically related to the experimental condition or some other characteristics. This will not be at random and may result in apparent changes when none have really occurred.

■ *Statistical regression* If groups of people are selected to be, say, extremely high and extremely low on aggression at point 1 in time, then their scores on aggression at point 2 in time will tend to converge. That is, the high scorers get lower scores than before and the low scorers get higher scores than before. This is purely a statistical artefact known as regression to the mean.

→

Box 10.1 continued

■ *Testing* People who are tested on a measure may be better on that measure when they are retested later simply because they are more familiar with its contents or because they have had practice.

External validity is closely related to the issue of generalisation discussed in detail in Chapter 3. It has to do with generalising findings to other groups of individuals, other geographic settings and other periods of time.

10.1 Panel designs

Panel or prospective studies are used to determine the changes that take place in people over time. For example, in the late 1920s in the United States there were a number of growth or developmental studies of children such as the Berkeley Growth Study (Jones *et al.*, 1971). This study was started in 1928 and was designed to investigate the mental, motor and physical development in the first 15 months of life of 61 children. It was gradually expanded to monitor changes up to 54 years of age. In Britain the National Child Development Study was begun in 1958 when data were collected on 17 000 children born in the week of 3–9 March (Ferri, 1993). This cohort has been surveyed on six subsequent occasions at ages 7, 11, 16, 23, 33 and 41/42. Most panel studies are of much shorter duration.

Figure 10.1 gives a simple example of a panel design. Data are collected at two different points in time on the same sample of individuals. One variable is the supportiveness of one's partner and the other variable is relationship satisfaction. The question is does supportiveness lead to relationship satisfaction? In Figure 10.1 there are essentially *two* measures of that relationship measured at the same time. That is, there is a relationship between supportiveness and satisfaction measured at time 1 and another measured at time 2. These relationships assessed at the same time are known as cross-sectional or *synchronous correlations*. Generally speaking, they are just as problematic as any other cross-sectional correlations to interpret.

There is another sort of relationship to be found in Figure 10.1. This is known as a *cross-lagged* relationship. A lag is, of course, a delay. The cross-lagged relationships in this case are the correlation of supportiveness at time 1 with satisfaction at time 2, and the correlation of satisfaction at time 1 with supportiveness at time 2.

| **Figure 10.1** | A two-wave panel design |

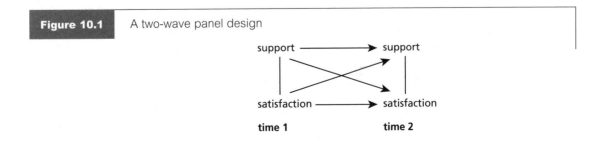

time 1   time 2

So perhaps we find that supportiveness$_{time1}$ is correlated with satisfaction$_{time2}$. Does this correlation mean that supportiveness causes satisfaction? It would be congruent with that idea but there is something quite simple that we can do to lend the idea support. That is, we can partial out (control for) satisfaction$_{time1}$. If we find that by doing so, the correlation between supportiveness$_{time1}$ and satisfaction$_{time2}$ reduces to zero then we have an interesting outcome. That is, satisfaction$_{time1}$ is sufficient to account for satisfaction$_{time2}$.

Of course, there is another possibility which has not been eliminated. That is, there is another causal sequence in which satisfaction may be the cause of supportiveness. At first this may seem less plausible, but if one is satisfied with one's partner then they are probably seen as more perfect in many respects than if one is dissatisfied. Anyway, this relationship could also be tested using cross-lagged correlations. A correlation between satisfaction$_{time1}$ with supportiveness$_{time2}$ would help establish the plausibility of this causal link. However, if we control for supportiveness$_{time1}$ and find that the correlation declines markedly or becomes zero, then this undermines the causal explanation in that supportiveness at time 1 is related to supportiveness at time 2.

The cross-lagged correlations should generally be weaker than the cross-sectional or synchronous correlations at the two times of measurement because changes are more likely to have taken place during the intervening period. The longer this period, the more probable it is that changes will have occurred and so the weaker the association should be. This also occurs when the same variable is measured on two or more occasions. The longer the interval, the lower the test–retest or auto correlation is likely to be. If both cross-lagged correlations have the same sign (in terms of being positive or negative) but one is significantly stronger than the other, then the stronger correlation indicates the temporal direction of the association. For example, if the association between support at time 1 and satisfaction at time 2 is more positive than the association between satisfaction at time 1 and support at time 2, then this difference implies that support leads to satisfaction.

There are several problems with this sort of analysis:

■ The size of a correlation is affected by the reliability of the measures. Less reliable measures produce weaker correlations. Consequently, the reliability of the measures need to be taken into account when comparing correlations.

■ The difference between the two cross-lagged correlations does not give an indication of the size of the possible causal association between the two variables. For example, the cross-lagged correlation between support at time 1 and satisfaction at time 2 will most probably be affected by satisfaction at time 1 and support at time 2. To determine the size of the cross-lagged association between support at time 1 and satisfaction at time 2 controlling for satisfaction at time 1 and support at time 2 we would have to partial out satisfaction at time 1 and support at time 2.

■ This method does not indicate whether both cross-lagged associations are necessary in order to provide a more satisfactory explanation of the relationship. It is possible that the relationship is reciprocal but that one variable is more influential than the other.

The solution to the above problems lies in using *structural equation modelling* and so this is the preferred method for this kind of analysis. It takes into account the unreliability of the measures. It provides an indication of the strength of a pathway taking into account its association with other variables. It also offers an index of the extent to which the model fits the data and is a more satisfactory fit than models which are simpler subsets of it. There are various examples of such studies (e.g. Cramer *et al.*, 1996; Fincham *et al.*, 1997; Krause *et al.*, 1989).

10.2 Different types of third variable

Conceptually there is a range of different types of third variable. They are only distinguishable in terms of their effect and, even then, this is not sufficient. We will illustrate these different types by reference to the issue of whether the supportiveness of one's partner in relationships leads to greater satisfaction with that partner.

Intervening or mediating variables

A variable which reduces the size of the correlation between two other variables may act as an explanatory link between the other two variables. In these circumstances it is described as an intervening or mediating variable. Making the distinction between a confounding and an intervening variable is not usually easy to do theoretically. With cross-sectional data it is not possible to establish the causal or the temporal direction between two variables. Nonetheless, researchers may suggest a direction even though they cannot determine this with cross-sectional data. For example, they may suggest that having a supportive relationship may lead to greater satisfaction with that relationship when it is equally plausible that the direction of the association may be the other way round or that the direction may be both ways rather than one way.

Suppose that we think that the direction of the association between supportiveness and satisfaction goes from support to satisfaction. With a variable which can change, like income, it is possible to argue that it may act as an intervening variable. For example, having a supportive partner may enable one to earn more which, in turn, leads to greater satisfaction with the relationship. It is easier to argue that a variable is a confounding one when it is a variable which cannot change like age or gender. Support cannot affect age or gender, and so this kind of variable cannot be an intervening one. However, many variables in the social sciences can change and so are potential intervening variables.

Suppressor variables

Another kind of confounding variable is one that appears to suppress or hide the association between two variables so that the two variables seem to be unrelated. This type of variable is known as a suppressor variable. When its effect is partialled out, the two variables are found to be related. This occurs when the partial correlation is of the opposite sign to the product of the other two correlations and the other two correlations are moderately large. When one of the other correlations is large, the partial correlation is large (Cramer, 2003b). Typically the highest correlations are generally those in which the same variable is tested on two occasions that are not widely separated in time. When both the other correlations are large, the partial correlation is greater than 1.00! These results are due to the formula for partialling out variables and arise when correlations are large, which is unusual.

There appear to be relatively few examples of suppressor effects. We will make up an example to illustrate one in which we suppose that support has been found to have a zero correlation with satisfaction with that relationship, although this is unlikely to be the case. Both support and satisfaction are positively related to how loving the relationship is, as shown in Figure 10.2. If we partial out love, we find that the partial correlation

Figure 10.2   Example of a suppressed association

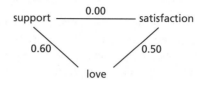

between support and satisfaction is −0.43. In other words we now have a moderately large correlation between support and satisfaction whereas the original or zero-order correlation was zero. This partial correlation is negative because the product of the other two correlations is positive.

Moderating variables

The size or the sign of the association between two variables may vary according to the values of a third variable, in which case this third variable is known as a moderating variable. For example, the size of the association between support and satisfaction may vary according to the gender of the partner. It may be stronger in men than in women. For example, the correlation between support and satisfaction may be 0.50 in men and 0.30 in women. If this difference in the size of the correlations is statistically different, we would say that gender moderates the association between support and satisfaction.

If we treated one of these variables, say support, as a dichotomous variable and the other as a continuous variable, we could display these relationships in the form of a graph, as shown in Figure 10.3. Satisfaction is represented by the vertical axis, support by the horizontal axis and gender by the two lines. The difference in satisfaction between women and men is greater for those with more support than those with less support. In other words, we have an interaction between support and gender like the interactions described for experimental designs. A moderating effect is an interaction effect.

If the moderating variable is a continuous rather than a dichotomous one, then the cut-off point used for dividing the sample into two groups may be arbitrary. Ideally the two groups should be of a similar size, and so the median score which does this can be

Figure 10.3   Graph showing the association between support and satisfaction moderated by gender

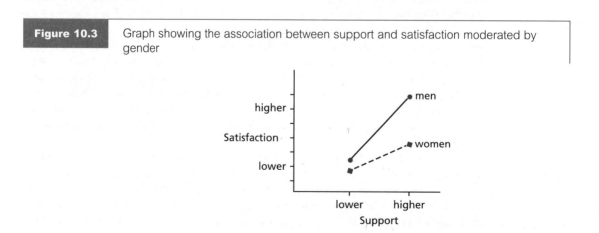

used. Furthermore, the natural variation in the scores of a continuous variable is lost when it is converted into a dichotomous variable. Consequently, it is better to treat a continuous variable as such rather than to change it into a dichotomous variable.

The recommended method for determining the statistical significance of an interaction is to conduct a hierarchical multiple regression (Baron and Kenny, 1986). The two main variables or predictors, which in this example are support and gender, are entered in the first step of the regression to control for any effects they may have. The interaction is entered in the second step. The interaction is created by multiplying the two predictors together provided that neither of these are a categorical variable with more than two categories. If this interaction is significant, there is a moderating effect as this means that the interaction accounts for a significant proportion of the variance in the criterion, which in this example is satisfaction. The nature of the interaction effect needs to be examined. One way of doing this is to divide the sample into two based on the median of the moderating variable, produce a scatterplot of the other two variables for the two samples separately and examine the direction of the relationship in the scatter of the two variables.

10.3 Analysis of non-experimental designs

It should be clear by now that the analysis of non-experimental designs is far from simple both conceptually and statistically. Furthermore, the range and scope of studies are far wider than we have suggested so far. Subsumed under this heading is every study which does not meet the requirements of a randomised experimental design. Quite clearly it is unlikely that any single chapter can cover every contingency. So you will find in many of the remaining chapters of this book a whole range of different styles of non-experimental data collection and analysis methods. To the extent that they are quantitative studies, then they share a number of characteristics in terms of analysis strategies. In this section, we will briefly review two of these as examples. They are both dealt with in detail in the companion statistics text, *Introduction to Statistics in Psychology* (Howitt and Cramer, 2005*a*). Although, some such designs may be analysed using the related *t*-test and the related analysis of variance, for example, the variety of measures usually included in such studies generally necessitates the use of more complex statistics designed to handle the multiplicity of measures.

Multiple regression

Multiple regression refers to a variety of methods which identify the best pattern of variables to distinguish between higher and lower scorers on a key variable of interest. For example, multiple regression would help us identify the pattern of variables which differentiates between different levels of relationship satisfaction. Using this optimum pattern of variables, it is possible to estimate with a degree of precision just how much satisfaction a person would feel given their precise pattern on the other variables. This could be referred to as a model of relationship satisfaction.

Another way of looking at it is to regard it as being somewhat like partial correlation. The difference is that multiple regression aims to understand the components which go to make up the scores on the key variable – the criterion or dependent variable. In this case, the key variable is relationship satisfaction. There is a sense in which multiple regression proceeds simply by partialling out variables one at a time from the scores on relationship satisfaction. How much effect on the scores does removing income, then social class, then supportiveness have? If we know the sizes of these effects, we can evaluate the possible importance of different variables on relationship satisfaction.

Technically, rather than use the partial correlation coefficient, multiple regression uses the part correlation coefficient or semi-partial correlation coefficient. The proportion of variance attributable to or explained by income or supportiveness is easily calculated. The proportion is simply the square of the part or semi-partial correlation. (This relationship is true for many correlation coefficients too.) We use the part or semi-partial correlation because it is only one variable that we are adjusting (relationship satisfaction). Partial correlation actually adjusts two variables, which is not what we need.

The part correlation between support and satisfaction partialling out income for the correlations shown in Figure 9.1 is 0.33 which squared is about 0.11. What this means is that support explains an additional 11% of the variance in satisfaction to the 16% already explained by income. The following formula is used to calculate the part correlation in which one variable is partialled out where B refers to satisfaction, A to support and C to income:

$$r_{BA.C} = \frac{r_{BA} - (r_{BC} \times r_{AC})}{\sqrt{(1 - r_{AC}^2)}}$$

If we insert the correlations of Figure 9.1 into this formula, we find that the part correlation is 0.33:

$$\frac{0.50 - (0.40 \times 0.60)}{\sqrt{(1 - 0.60^2)}} = \frac{0.26}{0.80} = 0.33$$

Multiple regression has three main uses:

■ To predict what the likely outcome is for a particular case or group of cases. For example, we may be interested in predicting whether a convicted prisoner is likely to re-offend on the basis of information that we have on them.

■ To determine what the size, sign and significance of particular associations or paths are in a model which has been put forward to explain some aspect of behaviour. For example, we may wish to test a particular model which seeks to explain how people become involved in criminal activity. This use is being increasingly taken over by the more sophisticated statistical technique of structural equation modelling.

■ To find out which predictors explain a significant proportion of the variance in the criterion variable such as criminal activity. This third use differs from the second in that generally a model is not being tested.

There are three main types of multiple regression for determining which predictors explain a significant proportion of the variance in a criterion:

■ *Hierarchical or sequential multiple regression* In this, the group of predictors are entered in a particular sequence. We may wish to control for particular predictors or sets of predictors by putting them in a certain order. For example, we may want to control for basic socio-demographic variables such as age, gender and socio-economic status before examining the influence of other variables such as personality or attitudinal factors.

- ■ *Standard multiple regression* All of the predictors are entered at the same time in a single step or block. This enables one to determine what the proportion of variance is that is uniquely explained by each predictor in the sense that it is not explained by any other predictor.

- ■ *Stepwise multiple regression* In this, statistical criteria are used to select the order of the predictors. The predictor that is entered first is the one which has a significant and the largest correlation with the key variable (the criterion or dependent variable). This variable explains the biggest proportion of the variation of the criterion variable because it is the largest correlation. The predictor that is entered second is the one which has a significant correlation and the largest part correlation with the criterion. This, therefore, explains the next biggest proportion of the variance in the criterion. This part correlation partials out the influence of the first predictor on the criterion. In this way, the predictors are made to contribute independently to the prediction. The predictor that is entered next is the one that has a significant and the next highest part correlation with the criterion. This predictor partials out the first two predictors. If a predictor that was previously entered no longer explains a significant proportion of the variance, it is dropped from the analysis. This process continues until there is no predictor that explains a further significant proportion of the variance in the criterion.

One important feature of multiple regression needs to be understood otherwise we may fail to appreciate quite what the outcome of an analysis means. Two or more predictors may have very similar correlations or part correlations with the criterion, but the one which has the highest correlation will be entered even though the difference in the size of the correlations is tiny. If the predictors themselves are highly related then those with the slightly smaller correlation may not be entered into the analysis at all. Their absence may give the impression that these variables do not predict the criterion when they do. Their correlation with the criterion may have been slightly weaker because the measures of these predictors may have been slightly less reliable. Consequently, when interpreting the results of a stepwise multiple regression, it is important to look at the size of the correlation between the predictor and the criterion. If two or more predictors are similarly correlated with the criterion, it is necessary to check whether these predictors are measuring the same rather than different constructs.

An understanding of multiple regression is very useful as it is commonly and increasingly used. Sherman and his colleagues (1999) found that 41% of the papers they randomly sampled in the *Journal of Personality and Social Psychology* used it in 1996 compared with 21% in 1988 and 9% in 1978.

Path analysis

A path is little more than a route between two variables. It may be direct but it can be indirect. It can also be reciprocal in that two variables mutually affect each other. For a set of variables, there may be a complex structure of paths, of course. Figure 10.4 has examples of such paths and various degrees of directness. Multiple regression can be used to estimate the correlations between the paths (these are known as path coefficients).

Figure 10.4 A path diagram with six variables

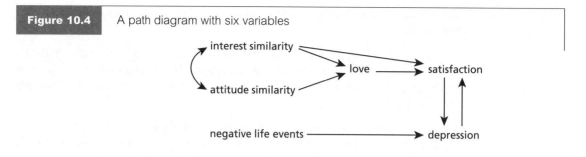

However, structural equation modelling is increasingly used instead. This has three main advantages over multiple regression:

■ The reliabilities of measures is not taken into account in multiple regression but they are in structural equation modelling. As explained earlier, reliability places a strict upper limit on the maximum correlation between any two variables.

■ Structural equation modelling gives an index of the extent to which the model provides a satisfactory fit to the data. This allows the fit of a simpler subset of the model to be compared to the original model to see if this simpler model provides as adequate a fit as the original model. Simpler models are generally preferred to more complicated ones as they are easier to understand and use.

■ Structural equation modelling can explain more than one outcome variable at the same time like the two presented in the path diagram of Figure 10.4.

The path diagram or model in Figure 10.4 seeks to explain the association between depression and satisfaction with a romantic relationship in terms of the four variables of attitude similarity, interest similarity, love and negative life events. The path diagram shows the assumed relationship between these six variables. The temporal or causal sequence moves from left to right. The direction of the sequence is indicated by the arrow of the line. So interest similarity leads to love which in turn leads to satisfaction. There is a direct association between interest similarity and satisfaction, and an indirect association which is mediated through love. In other words, interest similarity has, or is assumed to have, both a direct and an indirect effect. The association between satisfaction and depression is a reciprocal one as the arrows go in both directions. Being satisfied results in less depression and being less depressed brings about greater satisfaction. The lack of a line between two variables indicates that they are not related. So attitude similarity is not related to negative life events, depression or satisfaction. The curved line with arrows at either end shows that interest similarity and attitude similarity are related but that they are not thought to affect each other. Ideally we should try to develop a model such as we have done here to explain the relationships between the variables we have measured in our study.

10.4 Conclusion

Where the primary aim is to determine the temporal ordering of variables a panel or prospective study is required. In these, the same participants are studied on two or more occasions. The main variables of interest should be measured on each of these occasions so that the size of the temporal associations can be compared. Statistical analysis for non-manipulation studies is generally more complicated than that of true or randomised studies. This is especially the case when causal or explanatory models are being tested. Familiarity with statistical techniques such as multiple regression is advantageous for a researcher working in this field.

Key points

■ Panel or prospective designs measure the same variables in the same cases on two or more occasions. It is possible to assess whether variables mutually influence each other.

■ Longitudinal studies may be especially influenced by a number of threats to their internal validity and external validity. For example, because of the time dimension involved the participants may simply change because they have got a little older.

■ There are a number of types of variables which may play a role in the relationship between two variables. These include intervening variables and suppressor variables. Conceptually it is important to distinguish between these different sorts of third variables although they are very similar in practice.

■ The complexity of these designs encourage the use of complex statistical techniques such as multiple regression and path analysis.

Activities

1. Draw a path diagram for the following:

   ■ Couples who are similar fall in love more intensely.
   ■ They marry but tend to grow apart and stop loving each other.

2. Couples who love each other tend to have better sexual relationships with each other. It is found that once couples have a baby, the physical side of their relationship declines. What sort of variable is the baby?

11 Sampling and population surveys

Overview

- When we want to make inferences about a finite population such as the people of Britain, ideally we should obtain a representative sample of that population.

- The size of the sample to use is determined by various factors. How confident we are that the results of the sample represent those in the population is usually set at the 95% or 0.95 level although it might be set higher. The bigger the variation is in the characteristic that we are interested in estimating, the bigger the sample has to be. The smaller we want the sampling error or margin of error to be, the larger the sample has to be.

- Probability sampling is where every unit or element in the population has an equal and a known probability of being selected.

- Where the population is spread widely, multi-stage sampling may be used where the first stage is to select a limited number of areas from which further selections will be made.

As we have seen, when psychologists test a generalisation or hypothesis they always do so on a relatively limited sample of people – usually those who are convenient to recruit. These people are typically students (West *et al.*, 1992). Ideally, a more varied representative sample of people would be preferred. The time, effort and expense of recruiting such a sample are deterrents. Research psychologists are usually under some pressure to conduct their research as quickly and economically as possible. Obtaining a more representative sample of participants would hinder their work. To the extent that one believes that the generalisation being tested applies widely, then one would be disinclined to test a more representative sample. If you thought that different groups of people behaved differently, then you may include these groups in your study to see if this was the case. However, even in these circumstances a sample with very different characteristics might be just as useful as a more representative sample.

The issue of whether or not the assumption that findings apply widely ought to be more controversial in psychology. Just to indicate something of the problem, there have been very carefully controlled laboratory studies which have produced diametrically opposite findings from each other. For example, using more sophisticated students from the later years of their degree has on occasion produced findings very different from the findings of a study using first year students (Page and Scheidt, 1971). Probably this problem is best addressed by considering what is known about the behaviour of different groups of people in relation to the topic in question. Past research, for example, may indicate little or no evidence that different samples produce very different findings. In that case, the researcher may feel confident enough to use a convenience sample for their research.

Researchers should know how representative samples may be obtained even if only as a possible ideal. Furthermore, some studies have as their aim to make statements about a representative sample of people. People who are interested in how the general public behave may be less inclined to pay much attention to the results of a study which is solely based on students. Sociologists, for example, have lampooned psychology, sometimes unfairly, for its dependency on university students. Studies which have found similar results in a more representative samples lend extra credibility.

11.1 National surveys

Most of us are familiar with the results of the national opinion polls which are frequently reported in the media. However, national studies are extremely uncommon in psychological research. Using them would be an advantage but not always a big one. Generally, there is no great need to collect data from a region or country unless you are interested in how people in that region or country generally behave. Researchers from other social sciences, medical science and similar disciplines are more likely to carry out national surveys than psychologists. This is partly because these scientists are more interested in trends at the national and regional levels. Nonetheless the results of these surveys are often of relevance to psychologists.

It is not uncommon for such surveys to be placed in an archive accessible to other researchers. For example, in Britain many social science surveys are archived at the Economic and Social Research Council (ESRC). The data-sets that are available there for further or secondary analysis are listed at the following website: <http://www.data-archive.ac.uk/>.

Major studies include the British Crime Survey, British Social Attitudes and the National Child Development Study. International data-sets are also available. Students are not allowed direct access to these data-sets but they may be obtained via a lecturer who has an interest in them and the expertise to analyse them. This expertise includes an ability to use a statistical computer package such as SPSS which is widely used and taught to students. There are books which show you how to use SPSS such as the companion computing text, *Introduction to SPSS in Psychology* (Howitt and Cramer, 2005b).

11.2 Sample size and population surveys

When carrying out research, an important consideration is to estimate how big a sample is required. For surveys, this depends on a number of factors:

- How big the population is.
- How many people you will be able to contact and what proportion of them are likely to agree to participate.
- How variable their responses are.
- How confident you want to be about the results.
- How accurate you want your estimate to be compared with the actual population figure.

Not everyone who is sampled will take part. Usually in national sampling some sort of list of members of the population is used. This is known as the *sampling frame*. Lists of the electorate or telephone directories are examples of such lists thought they both have obvious inadequacies. Some of the sample will have moved from their address to an unknown location. Others may not be in when the interviewer calls even if they are visited on a number of occasions. Others refuse to take part. It is useful to make a note of why there was no response from those chosen to be part of the sample. The *response rate* will differ depending on various factors such as the method of contact and the topic of the research. The response rate is likely to be higher if the interviewer visits the potential participant than if they simply post a questionnaire. The most probable response rate may be estimated from similar studies or from a pilot or exploratory study.

How variable the responses of participants are likely to be can be obtained in similar ways. It is usually expressed in terms of the *standard* deviation of values which is similar to the average extent to which the values deviate from the mean of the sample.

Confidence interval

When one reads about the findings of national polls in the newspapers, statements like this appear: 'The poll found that 55% of the population trust the government. The margin of error was plus or minus 2%.' Of course, since the finding is based on a sample then we can never be completely confident in the figure obtained. Usually the confidence level is set at 95% or 0.95. The interval is an estimate based on the value obtained in the survey (55% of the population) and the variability in the data. The variability is used to estimate the range of the 95% of samples that are most likely to be obtained if our data were precisely the same as the values in the entire population. The single figure of 55% trusting the government is known as a *point estimate* since it gives a single value. Clearly the confidence interval approach is more useful since it gives some indication of the imprecision we expect in our data. This is expressed as the margin of error.

One could think of the confidence interval being the range of the most common sample values we are likely to obtain if we repeated our survey many times. That is, the 95 most common sample values if we repeated the study 100 times. If this helps you to appreciate the meaning of confidence intervals then all well and good. Actually it is not quite accurate since it is true only if our actual original sample data are totally representative of the population. This is not likely to be the case of course, but in statistics we operate with best guesses not certainties. If the confidence interval is set at 95% or 0.95 it means that the population value is likely to be in the middle 95% of possible sample means given by random sampling.

The confidence level is related to the notion of statistical significance that was introduced in Chapter 3. A detailed discussion of confidence intervals may be found in Chapter 34 of the companion text *Introduction to Statistics in Psychology* (Howitt and Cramer, 2005a). Confidence intervals apply to any estimate based on a sample. Hence, there are confidence intervals for virtually all statistics based on samples. Both statistical significance and the confidence level are concerned with how likely it is that a result will occur by chance. Statistical significance is normally fixed at 5% or 0.05. This means that the result will be obtained on 5 times out of 100 or less. If we find that a result is statistically significant it means that the result is so extreme that it is unlikely to occur by chance. A statistically significant finding is one which is outside of the middle 95% of samples defined by the confidence interval.

Sampling error (margin of error) and sample size

How accurately one's data reflect the true population value is dependent on something known as sampling error. Samples taken at random from a population vary in terms of their characteristics. The difference between the mean of your sample and the mean of the population of the sample is known as the *sampling error*. If several samples are taken from the same population their means will vary by different amounts from the value in the population. Some samples will have means that are identical to that of the population. Other samples will have means which differ by a certain amount from the population value. The variability in the means of samples taken from a population is expressed in terms of a statistical index known as the *standard error*. This is a theoretical exercise really as we never actually know what the population mean is – unless we do research on the entire population. Instead we estimate the mean of the population as being the same as the mean for our sample of data. This estimate may differ from the population mean, of course, but it is the best estimate we have. It is possible to calculate how likely the sample mean is to differ from the population mean by taking into account the variability within the sample (the measure of variability used is the standard deviation of the sample). The variability within the sample is used to estimate the variability in the population which is then used to estimate the variability of sample means taken from that population.

If we want to be 95% or 0.95 confident of the population mean, then we can work out what the sampling error is using the following formula where t is the value for this confidence level taking into account the size of the sample used (Cramer, 1998, pp. 107–8):

$$\text{sampling error} = t \times \frac{\text{standard deviation}}{\sqrt{\text{sample size}}}$$

The standard deviation is calculated using the data in our sample. The sample size we are considering is either known or can be decided upon. The appropriate t value can be found in the tables of most introductory statistics textbooks such as the companion text *Introduction to Statistics in Psychology* (Howitt and Cramer, 2005a).

If we substitute values for the standard deviation and the sample size, we can see that the sampling error becomes progressively smaller the larger the sample size. Say, for example, that the standard deviation is about 3 for scores of how extraverted people are (Cramer, 1991). For a sample size of 100 people, the t value for the 95% confidence level is 1.984 and so the sampling error is about 0.60:

$$\text{sampling error} = 1.984 \times \frac{3}{\sqrt{100}} = 1.984 \times \frac{3}{10} = \frac{5.952}{10} = 0.5952 = 0.60$$

If the mean score for extraversion for the sample was about 16, then the sample mean would lie between plus or minus 0.60 on either side of 16 about 95% of the time for samples of this size. So the mean would lie between 15.40 ($16 - 0.60 = 15.40$) and 16.60

(16 + 0.60 = 16.60). These values would be the 95% or 0.95 confidence limits. The confidence interval is the range between these confidence limits which is 1.20 (16.60 − 15.40 = 1.20). The confidence interval is simply twice the size of the sampling error (0.60 × 2 = 1.20). It is usually expressed as the mean plus or minus the appropriate interval. So in this case the confidence interval is 16.00 ± 0.60.

If the sample size is 400 people instead of 100, the *t* value for the 95% confidence level is slightly smaller and is 1.966. The sampling error for the same standard deviation is also slightly smaller and is about 0.29 instead of about 0.60:

$$1.966 \times \frac{3}{\sqrt{400}} = 1.966 \times \frac{3}{20} = \frac{5.898}{20} = 0.2949 = 0.29$$

In other words, the sampling error in this case is about half as small for a sample of 400 as for a sample of 100.

We can also see that if the variation or standard deviation of the variable is greater, then the sampling error will be greater. If the standard deviation was 6 instead of 3 with this sample and confidence level, then the sampling error would be about 0.59 instead of about 0.29:

$$1.966 \times \frac{6}{\sqrt{400}} = 1.966 \times \frac{6}{20} = \frac{11.796}{20} = 0.5898$$

The sampling error is sometimes known as the margin of error and may be expressed as a percentage of the mean. If the mean of the extraversion scores is 16 and the sampling error is about 0.60, then the sampling error expressed as a percentage of this mean is 3.75% (0.60/16 × 100 = 3.75). If the sampling error is about 0.29, then the sampling error given as a percentage of this mean is about 1.81% (0.29/16 × 100 = 1.8125). A margin of error of 2% for extraversion means that the mean of the population will vary between 0.32 (2/100 × 16 = 0.32) on either side of 16 at the 95% confidence level. In other words, it will vary between 15.68 (16 − 0.32 = 15.68) and 16.32 (16 + 0.32 = 16.32).

Suppose that we want to estimate what sample size is needed to determine the population mean of extraversion for a population of infinite size at the 95% confidence level with a margin of error of 2%. We apply the following formula where 1.96 is the *z* value for the 95% confidence level for an infinite population:

$$\text{sample size} = \frac{1.96^2 \times \text{sample standard deviation}^2}{\text{sampling error}^2}$$

If we substitute the appropriate figures in this formula, we can see that we need a sample of 346 to determine this:

$$\frac{1.96^2 \times 3^2}{0.32^2} = \frac{3.84 \times 9}{0.10} = \frac{34.56}{0.10} = 345.60$$

If the margin of error was set at a higher level, then the sample size needed to estimate the population characteristic would be smaller. If we set the margin of error at, say, 5% rather than 2%, the sampling error would be 0.80 (5/100 × 16 = 0.80) instead of 0.32 and the sample required would be 54 instead of 346.

$$\frac{1.96^2 \times 3^2}{0.80^2} = \frac{3.84 \times 9}{0.64} = \frac{34.56}{0.64} = 54.00$$

Remember that the above formula only deals with a situation in which we have specified a particular margin of error. It has very little to do with the typical situation in psychology in which the researcher tests to see whether or not a relationship differs significantly from no relationship at all.

Sample size for a finite population

The previous formula assumes that we are dealing with an infinitely large population. When dealing with big populations, this formula is sufficient for calculating the size of the sample to be used. When the populations are fairly small, we do not need as many people as this formula indicates. The following formula is used for calculating the precise number of people needed for a finite rather than an infinite population where n is the size of the sample and N is the size of the finite population (Berenson and Levine, 1999, p. 392)

$$\text{adjusted } n = \frac{n \times N}{n + (N - 1)}$$

We can see this if we substitute increasingly large finite populations in this formula while the sample size remains at 346. This has been done in Table 11.1. The first column shows the size of the population and the second column the size of the sample needed to estimate a characteristic of this population. The sample size can be less than 346 with finite populations of less than about 250 000.

Table 11.1 Sample size for varying finite populations with 95% confidence level, 2% sampling error and standard deviation of 3

Population size	Sample size
1 000	257
5 000	324
10 000	334
100 000	345
250 000	346
infinite	346

When carrying out a study we also need to take account of the response rate or the number of people who will take part in the study. It is unlikely that we will be able to contact everyone or that everyone we contact will agree to participate. If the response rate is, say, 70%, then 30% will not take part in the study. Thus, we have to increase our sample size to 495 people (346/0.70 = 494.29). A 70% response rate for a sample of 495 is 346 (0.70 × 495 = 346.50). Often response rates are much lower than this.

11.3 Types of probability sampling

Clearly, the characteristics of very large populations can be estimated from fairly small samples. The problem is ensuring that the sample is representative of the population if you want to generalise your results to that population. A distinction is made between *probability* and *non-probability sampling*:

■ Probability sampling is typically used when we have a clearly defined and accessible population which we want to make inferences about or when we want to know how characteristic a behaviour is of a particular population, such as the people of Britain.

■ Non-probability sampling is normally used in psychological research. This is because we are generally not interested in getting precise population estimates of a particular feature or characteristic in psychology. In psychology, the emphasis in research tends to be on relationships between variables and whether or not this relationship differs significantly from a zero relationship.

The advantage of probability sampling is that every person or element in the population has an equal and known probability of being selected. Suppose we want to use probability sampling to select 10% or 100 people out of a total population of 1000 people. In accordance with the concept of random sampling, everyone in that sample should have an equal probability of 0.10 of being selected (100/1000 = 0.10). The simplest procedure is to give each member of the population a number from 1 to 1000 and draw a hundred of these numbers at random.

There are various ways of drawing a sample of 100 numbers representing the 100 people we need for the probability sampling:

■ We could use a statistical package such as SPSS. We would enter the numbers 1 to 1000 in one of the columns. We would then select *Data*, *Select cases . . .* , *Random sample of cases*, *Sample . . .* , *Exactly*, and then enter 100 cases from the first 1000 cases. The 100 numbers that were selected would be the 100 people in the sample.

■ We could write the numbers 1 to 1000 on 1000 index cards or slips of paper, shuffle them and then select 100 cards or slips of papers. These 100 numbers would represent the people in our sample.

■ We could use a table of random numbers which can be found in the back of many introductory textbooks on statistics. These tables usually consist of rows and columns of pairs of numbers such as 87 46 and so on. The 1000th person is represented by the number 000. Each person in the population has a distinct three digit number. So we need a way of selecting three-digit numbers from the table of random numbers. There are no rules for this and you can decide on your own system. One could simply choose a random starting point in the table (eyes shut, using a pin) and record the first three digits after this as the first random selection. The person corresponding to this number is the first participant selected to be in the sample. The next three digits would give the number of the second member of the sample and so forth. Of course, one could go backwards through the table if one chose. If we select the same number more than once, we ignore it as we have already selected the individual represented by that number. Our sample of 100 individuals would be complete once we had selected 100 sets of three numbers from the table. As long as one is consistent, one can more or less decide on whatever rule one wishes for selecting numbers.

This form of probability sampling is called *simple random sampling*. An alternative procedure is to select every 100th person on the list. We have to decide what our starting point is going to be which can be any number from 1 to 100 and which we can choose using some random procedure. Let us suppose it is 67. This would be the first person we select.

We then select every 100th person after it, such as 167, 267, 367 and so on. This procedure is known as *systematic sampling*. The advantage of systematic sampling is that it is simpler to use with a printed list such as a register of electors. It is quicker than random sampling and has the advantage that people close together on the list (e.g. couples) will not be selected. Its disadvantage is that it is not random. The list may not be arranged in what is effectively a random order. So long as the complete list is sampled from (as the above method will ensure), there are unlikely to be problems with systematic sampling. However, if the researcher simply took every, say, 75th case then those at the end of the list could not be included in the sample.

Neither simple random sampling nor systematic sampling ensure that the sample will be representative of the population from which the sample was taken. For example, if the population contained equal numbers of females and males, say 500 of each, it is possible that the sample will contain either all, or a disproportionate number, of females or males. It may be important that the sample is representative of the population in respect of one or more characteristics such as gender. This is achieved by dividing the population into groups or strata representing that characteristic, such as females and males. Then the random sampling is essentially done separately for each of these two groups. In terms of our example of selecting a sample of 100 people, we would select 50 from the 500 females and 50 from the 500 males. This form of sampling is known as *stratified random sampling* or just *stratified sampling*.

As the proportion of females in the sample (0.50) is the same as the proportion of females in the population (0.50), this kind of stratified sampling may be called proportionate stratified sampling. It may be distinguished from *disproportionate stratified sampling* in which the sampling is not proportionate to the size of the group in the population. Disproportionate stratified sampling is used when we want to ensure that a sufficient number of people are sampled of whom there are relatively few in the population. For example, we may be keen to determine the behaviour of unemployed people in our population of 1000 people. Suppose there are only 50 unemployed people in our population. If we used proportionate stratified sampling to select 10% or 100 people from our population, then our sample of unemployed people is 5 $(10/100 \times 50 = 5)$ which is too few to base any generalisations on. Consequently, we may use disproportionate stratified sampling to obtain a bigger sample of unemployed people. Because the number of unemployed people is small, we may wish to have a sample of 25 of them in which case the proportion of unemployed people is 0.50 $(25/50 = 0.50)$ instead of 0.10 $(5/50 = 0.10)$. As our overall sample may be still limited to 100 people, the number of people in our sample who are not unemployed is now 75 instead of 95. So, the proportion of people who are not unemployed is slightly smaller than 0.10 and is about 0.08 $(75/950 = 0.0789)$.

One of the problems with stratified sampling is that relevant information about the characteristic in question is needed. For a characteristic such as gender then this is easily obtained from a person's title (Mr, Miss, Ms or Mrs) but this is the exception rather than the rule. Otherwise, more work is involved in obtaining information about that characteristic prior to sampling.

If our population is dispersed over a wide area we may use what is called *cluster sampling* in order to restrict the amount of time taken to draw up the sampling list or for interviewers to contact individuals. For example, if we wanted to carry out a probability survey of all British students it would be difficult and time-consuming to draw up a list of all students from which to select a sample. What we might do instead is to select a few universities from around the country and sample all the students within those universities. The universities would be the group or cluster of students which we would sample. The clusters need not be already existing ones. They may be created artificially. For example, we may impose a grid over an area and select a number of squares or cells within that area. The advantage of cluster sampling is that it saves time and money. Its disadvantage is that it is likely to be less representative of the population because the people within a cluster are likely to be more similar to one another. For example, students at one university may be more inclined to come from fee-paying rather than state schools or to be female rather than male.

Another form of probability sampling is called *multi-stage sampling* in which sampling is done in a number of stages. For example, we could have a two-stage sample of university students in which the first stage consists of sampling universities and the second stage of sampling students within those universities.

It should be noted that the formula for calculating sampling error for proportionate stratified sampling and cluster sampling differs somewhat from that given earlier in this chapter which was for simple random sampling (Moser and Kalton, 1971, pp. 87, 103). Compared to simple random sampling, the sampling error is likely to be smaller for proportionate stratified sampling and larger for cluster sampling. This means that the sample can be somewhat smaller for proportionate stratified sampling but somewhat larger for cluster sampling than for simple random sampling.

The *representativeness of a sample* can be evaluated against other information about the population from which it was drawn. For example, in trying to determine whether our sample is representative of the British population we can compare it with census or other national data on characteristics such as gender, age, marital status and employment status. It should be noted that these other sources of information will not be perfectly accurate and will contain some degree of error themselves.

BOX 11.1 EXAMPLE OF A NATIONAL REPRESENTATIVE SURVEY

The British Social Attitudes Survey is a good example of the use of a representative sample in research which may be of relevance to psychologists. The detail is less important to absorb than the overall picture of the meticulous nature of the process and the need for the researcher to make a number of fairly arbitrary decisions. This survey has been carried out more or less annually since 1983. The target sample for the 2001 survey was 6200 adults aged 18 or over living in private households (Park *et al.*, 2003, pp. 231–2). The *sampling list* or *frame* was the Postcode Address File. This is a list of addresses (or postal delivery points) which is compiled by, and which can be bought from, the Post Office. The multi-stage sampling design consisted of three stages of selection:

■ selection of postcode sectors
■ selection of addresses within those postcode sectors
■ selection of an adult living at an address.

The postcode sector is identified by the first part of the postcode. It is LE11 3 for Loughborough, for example. Any sector with fewer than 1000 addresses was combined with an adjacent sector. Sectors north of the Caledonian Canal in Scotland

→

Box 11.1 continued

were excluded due to the high cost of interviewing there. The sectors were stratified into:

- 37 sub-regions
- three equal-sized groups within each sub-region varying in population density *and*
- ranking by the percentage of homes that were owner-occupied in England and Wales and where the head of the household was in a non-manual occupation in Scotland.

The sampling frame may look something like that shown in Table 11.2 (Hoinville & Jowell, 1978, p. 74).

Table 11.2 Part of sampling frame for the British Social Attitudes Survey

Region 01	Percentage owner or non-manual occupiers
Highest density group	
Postcode sector	65%
Postcode sector	60%
⋮	
Postcode sector	40%
Intermediate density group	
Postcode sector	78%
Postcode sector	75%
⋮	
Postcode sector	60%
Lowest density group	
Postcode sector	79%
Postcode sector	74%
⋮	
Postcode sector	55%
⋮	
Region 37	
⋮	

The total number of postcode sectors in the United Kingdom is about 9750 (Postal geography, n.d.) from which two hundred sectors were selected. The probability of selection was made proportional to the number of addresses in each sector. The reason for using this procedure is that the number of addresses varies considerably between postcode sectors. If postcode sectors have an equal probability of being selected, the more addresses a postcode sector has, the smaller the chance or probability is that an address within that sector will be chosen. So not every address has an equal probability of being selected for the national sample.

To ensure that an address within a sector has an equal probability of being chosen, the following procedure was used (Hoinville and Jowell, 1978, p. 67). Suppose we have six postcode sectors and we have to select three of these sectors. The number

→

Box 11.1 continued

Table 11.3   Example of sampling sectors with probability proportional to size

Sector	Size	Cumulative size	Points	
1	4000	0–4000	2 334	2nd point
2	6000	4 001–10 000	9 334	random start
3	5000	10 001–15 000		
4	2000	15 001–17 000	16 334	3rd point
5	3000	17 001–20 000		
6	1000	20 001–21 000		

of addresses in each sector is shown in Table 11.3. Altogether we have 21 000 addresses. If we use systematic sampling to select these three sectors, then we need to choose the random starting point or address from this number. We could do this using a five-digit sequence in a table of random numbers. Suppose this number was 09334. If we add the number of addresses cumulatively as shown in the third column of Table 11.3, then the random starting point is in the second postcode sector. So this would be the first postcode sector chosen randomly.

In systematic sampling we need to know the sampling interval between the addresses on the list. This is simply the total number of addresses divided by the number of samples (21 000/3 = 7000). As the random starting point is greater than 7000, a second point is 7000 below 9334 which is 2334 (9334 − 7000 = 2334). This point falls within the first postcode sector which is the second postcode sector to be selected. A third point is 7000 above 9334 which is 16 334 (9334 + 9000 = 16 334). This point falls within the fourth postcode sector which is the third postcode sector to be chosen. So these would be our three sectors.

Thirty-one addresses were systematically selected in each of the 200 postcode sectors chosen. This gives a total of 6200 addresses (31 × 200 = 6200). A random start point was chosen in each sector and 31 addresses selected at equal fixed intervals from that starting point. The numbers of adults aged 18 and over varies at the different addresses. A person was selected at random at each address using a computerised random selection procedure.

Response rates were affected by a number of factors:

■ About 10% of the addresses were out of the scope of the survey (for example, they were empty, derelict or otherwise not suitable).
■ About 28% of the 6200 refused to take part when approached by the interviewer.
■ About 5% of the 6200 could not be contacted.
■ About 4% of the original 6200 did not respond for some other reason.

This means that the response rate for the final survey was 53% of the original sample of 6200. This is quite a respectable figure and many surveys obtain much lower return rates. Of course, the non-participation rate may have a considerable impact on the value of the data obtained. There is no reason to believe that non-participants are similar to participants in their attitudes.

11.4 Non-probability sampling

The cost, effort and time involved in drawing up a representative or probability sample are clearly great. A researcher without these resources may decide to use a quota sample instead. In a *quota sample* an attempt is made to ensure different groups are represented in the proportion in which they occur within that society. So, for example, if we know that 5% of the population are unemployed, then we may endeavour to ensure that 5% of the sample are unemployed. If our sample consists of 100 people, we will look for 5 people who are unemployed. Because we have not used probability sampling then we may have a systematically biased sample of the unemployed. The numbers of people in the different groups making up our sample do not have to be proportionate to their numbers in society. For example, if we were interested in looking at how age is related to social attitudes, we may choose to use equal numbers of each age group no matter their actual frequencies in the population.

Where we need to collect a sample of very specific types of people then we may use *snowball sampling*. So this would be an appropriate way of collecting a samples of drug addicts, banjo players or social workers experienced in highly publicised child abuse cases. Once we have found individuals with the necessary characteristic we ask them whether they know of anyone else with that characteristic who may be willing to take part in our research. If that person names two other people and those two people name two further individuals then our sample has snowballed from one individual to seven.

In general, psychologists would assume a sample to be a non-random one unless it is specifically indicated. If it is a random sample, then it is necessary to describe in some detail the particular random procedure used to generate that sample. In most psychological research the sample will be a convenience one and it may be sufficient to refer to it as such.

11.5 Socio-demographic characteristics of samples

National samples usually gather socio-demographic information about the nature of the sample studied. Which characteristics are described depends on the kind of participants and the purpose of the study. If the participants are university students, then it may suffice to only describe the number of female and male students and the mean and standard deviation of their age either together or separately. If a substantial number or all of the participants are not students, then it is generally necessary to provide further socio-demographic information on them such as how well educated they are, whether they are working and what their social status is. These socio-demographic characteristics are not always easy to categorise, and the most appropriate categories to use may vary over time as society changes and according to the particular sample being studied. When deciding on which characteristics and categories to use, it is useful to look at recent studies on the topic and see what characteristics were used. Two social-demographic characteristics which are problematic to define and measure are social status and race or ethnicity.

In the United Kingdom one measure of social status is the current or the last job or occupation of the participant (e.g. Park *et al.*, 2003, pp. 235–7). The latest government scheme for coding occupations is the Standard Occupational Classification 2000

(Great Britain Office for National Statistics, 2000). The previous version was the Standard Occupational Classification 1990 (OPCS, 1991). The main socio-economic grouping based on the latest scheme is the National Statistics Socio-Economic Classification which consists of the following eight categories:

1   Employers in large organisations, higher managerial and professional occupations
2   Lower managerial and professional occupations
3   Intermediate occupations
4   Small employers and own account workers
5   Lower supervisory and technical occupations
6   Semi-routine occupations
7   Routine occupations
8   Never worked and long-term unemployed.

Previous schemes include the Registrar General's Social Class, the Socio-Economic Group and the Goldthorpe (1987) schema. There is a computer program for coding occupations based on the Standard Occupational Classification 1990 called Computer-Assisted Standard Occupational Coding (CASOC). This can be obtained from Her Majesty's Stationery Office (HMSO) but may not be available for use at every institution.

A measure of race may be included to determine how inclusive the sample is and whether the behaviour you are interested in differs according to this variable. The 2001 British Social Attitudes Survey measured race with the following question and response options (Park *et al.*, 2003, p. 297). The percentage of people choosing these categories is shown before each option.

To which one of these groups do you consider you belong?	
Black: of African origin	0.6%
Black: of Caribbean origin	1.3%
Black: of other origin (please state)	0.1%
Asian: of Indian origin	1.5%
Asian: of Pakistani origin	0.6%
Asian: of Bangladeshi origin	0.1%
Asian: of Chinese origin	0.2%
Asian: of other origin (please state)	0.6%
White: of any European origin	92.3%
White: of other origin (please state)	0.8%
Mixed origin (please state)	0.6%
Other (please state)	0.7%

Only 0.1%, or 3, of the 3287 people in the sample did not know which category they fell in and only 0.6% or 20 people did not answer this question.

11.6 Conclusion

Most psychological research is based on convenience samples which are not selected randomly and which often consist of students. The aim of this type of research is often to determine whether the support for an observed relationship is statistically significant. It is generally not considered necessary to ascertain to what extent this finding is characteristic of a particular population. Nonetheless where this is possible, it is useful to know to what degree our findings may be typical of a particular population. Consequently, it is important to understand what the basis is for selecting a sample which is designed to be representative of a population. Furthermore, in some cases, the population will be limited in size so that it is possible with relatively little effort to select a sample randomly. For example, if we are interested in examining the content of, say, recorded interactions or published articles, and we do not have the time or the resources to analyse the whole content, then it is usually appropriate to select a sample of that content using probability sampling. The great advantages of probability sampling is that the sample is likely to be more representative of the population and that the sampling will not be affected by any biases we have of which we may not even be aware.

Key points

- A random or probability sample is used to estimate the characteristics of a particular finite population. The probability of any unit or element being selected is equal and known.

- The population does not necessarily consist of people. It may comprise any unit or element such as the population of articles in a particular journal for a certain year.

- The size of the sample to be chosen depends on various factors such as how confident we want to be that the results represent the population, how small we want the sampling error to be, how variable the behaviour is and how small the population is. Bigger samples are required for higher confidence levels, smaller sampling errors, more variable behaviour and bigger populations.

- Fairly small samples can be used to estimate the characteristics of very large populations. The sample size does not increase directly with the population size.

- Where the population is widely dispersed, cluster sampling and multi-stage sampling may be used. In the first stage of sampling a number of clusters such as geographical areas (e.g. postcode sectors) may be chosen from which further selections are subsequently made.

- Where possible the representativeness of the sample needs to be checked against other available data about the population.

- Where the sample is a convenience one of undergraduate students, it may suffice to describe the number of females and males, and the mean and standard deviation of their ages. Where the sample consists of a more varied group of adults, it may be necessary to describe them in terms of other socio-demographic characteristics such as whether or not they are employed, the social standing of their occupation and their racial origin.

Activities

1. How would you randomly select ten programmes from the day's listing of a major TV channel to which you have ready access?

2. How would you randomly select three 3-minute segments from a 50 minute TV programme?

3. How would you randomly select ten editions of a major Sunday newspaper from last year?

PART 3
Fundamentals of testing and measurement

12 Psychological tests: Their use and construction

Overview

- Psychological tests and measures are commercially available, can be sometimes found in the research literature or may be created by the researcher. The construction of a psychological test is relatively easy using statistical packages.

- Tests used for clinical and other forms of assessment of individuals need to be well standardised and carefully administered. Measures used for research purposes only do not have to have the same degree of precision to be useful.

- Psychologists tend to prefer 'unidimensional' scales which are single dimensional 'pure' measures of the variable in question. However, multidimensional scales may be more useful for practical rather than research applications.

- Item analysis is the process of 'purifying' the measure. Item–total correlations simply correlate each individual item with the score based on the other items. Those items with high correlations with the total are retained. An alternative is to use factor analysis which identifies clusters of items that measure the same thing.

Standardised tests and measures are the major tools used extensively in psychological work with clients (e.g. clinical psychology, occupational psychology). They are also frequently used in research. In many ways standardised tests and measures are very characteristic of psychology. The term *standardised* can mean several things:

- That consistency of results is achieved by the use of identical materials, prescribed administration procedures and prescribed scoring procedures. That is to say, variability in the ways in which different psychologists administer the test or measure is minimised. Way back in 1905 when Alfred Binet presented the world's first psychological scale – one to measure intelligence – he was adamant about the detail of the assessment setting. For example, he suggested an isolated, quiet room in which the child was alone with the test administrator and, ideally, an adult familiar to the child to help reassure the child. However, the familiar adult should be 'passive and mute' and not intervene in any way (Binet, 1905).

- That the consistency of interpretation of the test is maximised by providing normative or standardisation data for the test or measure. This means that the test or measure has been administered to a large, relevant sample of participants. In this way, it is possible to provide statistical data on the range and variability of scores in such a sample. As a consequence, the psychologist is able to compare the scores of their participants with those of this large sample. These statistical data are usually referred to as the norms (or normative data) but they are really just the standard by which individual clients are judged. Often tables of *percentiles* are provided which indicate for any given score on the test or measure, the percentage of individuals with that score or a lower score (see the companion book *Introduction to Statistics in Psychology*, Howitt and Cramer, 2005*a*). Norms may be provided for different genders and/or age groups, and so forth.

Standardised tests and measures are available for many psychological characteristics including attitudes, intelligence, aptitude, ability, self-esteem, musicality, personality and so forth. Catalogues of commercially available measures are published by a number of suppliers. These may be quite expensive, elaborate products. Their commercial potential and practical application partly explains the cost. For example, there is a big market for tests and measures for the recruitment and selection of employees by businesses, especially in the USA. Selection interviews are not necessarily effective ways of assessing the abilities and potential of job applicants. Standardised selection tests assessing aptitude for various types of employment may help improve the selection process. They have been used in enormous numbers in the USA, in particular. By helping to choose the best employee, the costs of training staff and replacing those who are unsuited to the work are minimised.

Similarly there are commercially available tests and measures designed for work with clinical patients or school children. In these contexts, tests and measures may be used as screening instruments in order to identify potential difficulties in individuals. For example, if there were a simple effective test for dyslexia then it could be given to classes of children en masse in order to identify individuals who may require further assessment and treatment/support for dyslexia.

Although many of these commercially available tests and measures are employed in research, they are often designed primarily with the needs of practitioners in mind. They may not always be the ideal choice for research:

■ They are often expensive to buy. Given that research tends to use large samples, the cost may be prohibitive.

■ They are often expensive to administer. Many commercial tests and measures are administered on a one-to-one basis by the psychologist. They may also require training in their use which is a further cost. Some tests may take as much as two hours or more to administer, and this is not only a further cost, but may also be a deterrent to individuals from participating in the research.

■ They are often intended for use with special populations. The tests and measures used by clinical psychologists, for example, may be helpful in identifying schizoid thought tendencies in psychiatric settings but have no value when applied to non-clinical populations.

■ Some of the tests and measures are restricted in their circulation, such as to qualified clinical psychologists. Students, especially, may have no access to them. University departments, though, often have a variety of tests for use by students under the supervision of a member of staff.

■ There is no guarantee that there is a test or measure available for the variables that the researcher needs to measure.

As a consequence, researchers may need to consider constructing new tests or measures rather than relying on commercially available ones. There are many *research instruments* which have been developed which are not available through commercial sources. These can often be founded in relevant journal articles, books, websites or directly from their author. Identifying these tests and measures will entail a review of the literature in the research field in question. Research studies in your chosen field will often describe or make use of these research instruments. One advantage of using the same measures as other researchers is that they are recognised by the research community as effective measures. Care needs to be taken, however, since the purposes of your research may not be exactly the same as that of previous researchers or the instrument may be unsuitable for other reasons. For example, the research instrument may have been designed for a different culture or a different age group. Hence it may need some modification to make it suitable for the particular group on which you wish to use it. There are circumstances in which the research instrument appears so unsatisfactory that the researcher decides to create an entirely new instrument.

The mechanics of test construction are fairly straightforward and, with the availability of SPSS and other computer packages, it is feasible to produce bespoke measuring instruments even as part of student research.

12.1 The concept of a scale

Psychologists frequently refer to scales in relation to psychological tests and measures. In general English dictionaries, the term 'scale' is defined as a graded classification system. This will probably suffice to understand the use of the concept in test construction. That is, individuals are numerically graded in terms of their scores on the measure. Two important ways of creating such graded scales are:

■ Providing a series of test or measurement items which span the range from lowest to highest. So, if a measure of intelligence is required, a whole series of questions is provided which vary in terms of their difficulty. The most difficult question that the participant can answer is an indicator of their level of intelligence. The difficulty of an item is assessed simply by working out the percentage of a relevant sample who answer the question correctly. This approach was applied to the assessment of attitudes using the Thurstone Scale. For example, in order to measure racial attitudes a series of statements is prepared from the least racist to the most racist. The items are judged by a panel of judges in terms of the extent of the racism in the statement. The most hostile item that a participant agrees with is an indicator of their level of racism. This is known as the 'method of equal-appearing intervals' because the test constructor endeavours to make the items cover all points of the possible range evenly.

■ A much more common way of constructing psychological tests and measures operates on a quite distinct principle, although the outcomes of the two methods are often substantially the same. In the method of summated scores the researcher develops a pool of items to measure whatever variable is to be measured. The final score is based on the sum of the items. Usually, an additional criterion is introduced which is that the items should correlate with the total scores on the test or measure. We will return to this in the next section. It is the most commonly used method.

Psychological tests and measures are frequently described as unidimensional or multi-dimensional. A *unidimensional* scale is one in which the correlations of the items with each other are determined as a result of a single underlying dimension. This is analogous to measuring the weights of 30 people using ten different sets of bathroom scales – there will be strong intercorrelations between the weights as assessed by different sets of bathroom scales. A *multidimensional* scale has two or more underlying dimensions which result in a pattern of intercorrelations between the items in which there are distinct clusters or groups of items which tend to intercorrelate with each other but not with other items so well or not at all. This is analogous to measuring the weights of 30 people using ten different sets of bathroom scales and their heights using five different tape measures. In this case, we would expect for the sample of people:

- Strong intercorrelations of their weights as measured using the different sets of bathroom scales.
- Strong intercorrelations of the heights as measured with the five different tape measures.
- Poor intercorrelations between the ten sets of bathroom scale measures and the five sets of tape measure measures.

This is simply because our 15 different measures (analogous to 15 different items on a questionnaire) are measuring two different things – weight and height.

Which of these is the best? The short answer is that for most purposes of *research* the ideal is a unidimensional scale since this implies a relatively 'pure' measurement dimension. That is, a unidimensional scale can be thought of as aiming to measure a single concept. However, multidimensional scales are sometimes more useful in practical situations. For example, a multidimensional measure of intelligence is likely to predict success at university better than a unidimensional one. This is because university performance is determined by a variety of factors (e.g. maths ability, comprehension, motivation and so forth). Consequently a measure based on a variety of factors is more likely to be predictive of university success.

Measurement in psychology is beset with a number of fundamental and generally unavoidable problems. Many of these are to do with the weakness or imprecision of measurement in psychology. In the physical world, a centimetre is a standard, well established and precisely measurable amount. Psychological variables cannot be measured with the same degree of precision. Every psychological measure that we know of suffers from a degree of variability – that is to say, the measurement will vary somewhat each time it is taken – apparently in an unsystematic or random fashion. If we measure age by asking participants their age, we might expect a degree of imprecision – some participants may deliberately lie, others will have forgotten their age, we may mishear what they say, and so forth. This occurs when we are measuring something as easy to define as age so one can imagine that the problem is worse when measuring a difficult to define (or unclear) concept as self-esteem, happiness or cognitive distortions.

Since psychological concepts are often not precisely definable, psychologists tend to measure concepts using a variety of test or measurement items rather than a single item. The idea is that by using a number of imprecise measures of the concept in question, the aggregate of these measures is likely to be a better measure than any of the constituent individual items.

There is nothing wrong with using a single item to measure a psychological variable – one would not measure age by using a 20-item age scale, for example. However, we would use a long scale to measure a less clear variable such as happiness. So the use of scaling is really confined to circumstances in which you wish to get a decent measure of a variable that is difficult to measure. Thus, you would not use scaling if you wished to measure gender or age. A single question will generally produce high quality and highly valid answers to these questions.

Its a bit like finding out the cost of the tube fare to Oxford Street in London by asking lots of friends. Probably none of your friends knows the precise fare, but several would have a rough idea. By combining several rough estimates together by averaging, the probable outcome is a reasonable estimate of the train fare. Obviously it would be better to use a more accurate measure (e.g. phone the railway company) but this is not possible the rough estimates would do. In other words, there is an objective reality (the actual fare that you will pay) but you cannot find that out directly. This is much the same as psychological variables – there may be an objective reality of happiness but we can only measure it indirectly using an aggregate of imprecise measures.

12.2 Scale construction

At this point, it is important to stress that psychological tests and measures are not created simply on the back of statistical techniques. Ideally, the psychologist constructing a measure will be familiar with the relevant theory and research concerning the thing to be measured. They may also be familiar with related concepts, the opinion of experts, and information from samples of individuals about how they understand and experience aspects of the concept. For example, just what is depression like experientially? Such information concerning the concept can contribute to a more insightful and pertinent set of items to begin the research. The following are worth emphasising:

■ Every effort should be made to specify the nature of the concept we wish to measure – just what do we mean by loneliness, depression or staff burnout, for example? Often by reflecting on this we begin to realise that potentially there may be many different features of the concept which we need to incorporate into the *pool of items* from which we will develop the test or measure.

■ Even after we have developed our understanding of the concept as well as we can, we may find it impossible to phrase a single question to assess it. Take loneliness, is a question such as 'How many friends do you have?' a good measure of loneliness? It depends on many things – what an individual classifies as a friend, whether loneliness is determined by the number rather than the quality of friendships, the age of the individual, since an elderly person may have fewer friends simply as a consequence of bereavements, and so forth. In short, there are problems in turning a variable into a measure of that variable. This does not mean that the question is useless as a measure of the concept, merely that it is not a particularly accurate measure.

■ Variables do not exist in some sort of rarefied form out there in the real world. They are notions which psychologists and other researchers find extremely useful in trying to understand people. So sometimes it will appear appropriate to a researcher to measure a range of things which seem closely related. For example, loneliness might be considered to involve a range of aspects – few friendships, feelings of isolation, no social support, geographical isolation and so forth.

Once a pool of items for potential inclusion has been developed, the next stage is to administer the first draft of the test to a suitable and as substantial a sample of individuals as possible. Advice on how to formulate questions is to be found in Box 12.1. Let us assume that we have gone through that process and have a list of such items. For illustrative purposes we have ten different items but the list would probably be 30 or 40 items. We have decided to attempt to measure *honesty*. Our ten items are:

Item 1   I am an honest person.
Item 2   I have frequently told little lies so as not to offend people.
Item 3   If I found money in the street I would hand it in to the police.
Item 4   I have never told even the slightest untruth.
Item 5   I would always return the money if I knew that I had been given too much change in a shop.
Item 6   I would never make private phone calls from work.
Item 7   I have shoplifted.
Item 8   It is always best to tell the truth even if it hurts.
Item 9   I usually tell the boss what I think they would like to hear even if it is not true.
Item 10 If I were to have an affair, I would never tell my partner.

Several things are readily apparent about this list:

■ There is a wide range of items which seem to be measuring a variety of things. Probably all of the items are measuring something that may be regarded as honesty (or lack of it).

■ Some of the items are positively worded in terms of honesty (e.g. items 1, 6 and 8). That is, agreeing with these items is indicative of honesty. Other items are negatively worded in that *disagreeing* with them is indicative of honesty (e.g. items 7, 9 and 10). Often positively and negatively worded items are both included deliberately in order to help deal with 'response sets'. Briefly, it has been established that some people tend to agree with items no matter the content of the item. Thus they have a tendency to agree with an item but also *agree* with an item worded in the opposite direction. That is they might agree with the statement that 'I am an honest person' and also agree with the statement that 'I am not an honest person'. One way of dealing with this is to use both positively and negatively worded items – mixing items for which agreement is indicative of the variable with those for which disagreement is indicative of the variable. Many questionnaires can be found which do *not* do this.

You must remember to reverse score *the negatively worded items – if scored in the same way as the positively worded items then the positively worded items would be cancelled out by the negatively worded ones.*

■ One of the items (item 4: I have never told even the slightest untruth) seems unlikely to be true of any human. Items like this are sometimes included in order to assess faking 'good' or 'social desirability' – that is, trying to give an impression of meeting social standards even unobtainable ones. On the other hand, it is possible that the researcher has simply written a bad item. That is, if everyone disagrees with an item then it cannot discriminate between people in terms of, in this case, honesty. Useful items need to demonstrate variability (variance) among participants in the research.

A careful reading through of the items seems to suggest that there are at least two different sorts of honesty being measured – one is *verbal honesty* (not lying, basically) and the other *is not stealing*. It could well be that this questionnaire is multidimensional in that it is

BOX 12.1 WRITING ITEMS FOR QUESTIONNAIRES

Writing questions or items for a psychological measure requires one to focus on one key matter – trying to concoct items that are as unambiguous and clear as possible. The other main criterion has to be that they seem to measure a range of aspects of the topic. Of course, these are not simple matters to achieve and it is easy to rush the job and create an unsatisfactory measure. One needs to understand the topic at as many levels as possible. For example, what do you think the important things are likely to be? Then what do people you know regard as important aspects of the topic? Then what does a focus group or some other group of research participants talk about when they are asked to discuss the topic? How have previous researchers attempted to measure a similar topic? What does the empirical evidence indicate about the major dimensions of the topic? What does theory say about the topic?

Once again the important lesson is to research and explore the topic in a variety of ways. Only in this way can you acquire the depth of knowledge to create a good measure. To be frank, anyone can throw together a list of questions, it requires commitment and work to write a good questionnaire. If possible, put together elements from all of the resources that you have. Finally, do not forget that once you have the questionnaire, there are a number of processes that you will need to go through to assess its adequacy. These include item analysis, reliability assessment and perhaps validity assessment. These processes contribute to the adequacy of the measure and may help you eliminate inadequate items or excess items.

Nevertheless, here are a few tips:

- Use short and simple sentence structures.
- Short everyday words are better than long ones.
- Avoid complex or problematic grammar, such as the use of double negatives. For example, 'You ain't seen nothing yet.'
- Leading questions which suggest the expected answer should be avoided largely because of the limiting effect this will have on the variability of the answers. For example, 'Most people think it essential to vote in elections. Do you agree?'.
- Choose appropriate language for the likely participants – what would be appropriate to ask a group of high court judges may be inappropriate to a group of nursery children.
- Tap as many resources for items and questions as feasible.
- Accept that you cannot rely on yourself alone as a satisfactory source of questions and ideas for questions.
- People similar to the likely participants in your research are a good starting point for ideas.
- Relax – expertise in question and item writing is a rare commodity. Most researchers mix trial and error with rigorous item analysis as a substitute.

You may wish to consult Chapter 14 on coding data in order to appreciate the variety of ways in which the researcher can structure the answers further.

measuring two distinct things. The usual way of assessing this is by examining empirically whether the people who are verbally honest also tend not to steal. Basically this is a matter of correlating the different items one with another.

Scaling – or the process of developing a psychological scale – deals with the ways in which items are combined in order to get a better measure of a concept than could be achieved using a single item. The common methods of psychological scaling employed by most modern researchers are built on one of two general principles:

■ If we sum the scores on the individual items of a test or measure to give the *total score*, then each of the individual items should correlate with this total score if the items are measuring the same thing as each other. *Items which do not correlate with the total score are simply not measuring what the majority of the other items are measuring and may be eliminated from the scale.* This is also known as the *item–whole* approach to scale construction.

■ If items on the scale are measuring the same thing then they should correlate substantially with each other (and the total score as well for that matter). Items which measure very different things will correlate with each other either very poorly or not at all. This is the basis of internal consistency approaches to scale construction as well as the *factor analytic* methods. These are discussed later in this chapter. With a multi-dimensional scale, sometimes you will find distinct groups of items which correlate well with each other but not with other groups of items.

We will consider each of these approaches in turn. They are known as *item analysis* techniques. See Box 12.2.

Item–whole or item–total approach to scale construction

The purpose of item analysis is to eliminate bad items that do not measure the same thing as the scale in general. These are not laborious statistical techniques if one uses a computer program, although historically much time would have been spent doing the same task. So what would we expect our data to show if we had managed to produce a good measure of, say, honesty? Remember that we are doing little more than simply adding up the answers to a range of questions about honesty to give a total score:

■ The item–whole method of item analysis involves calculating a total score for honesty. The most obvious way of doing this is simply to add up (for each individual in the sample) the total of their scores on the (ten) individual items. (Don't forget to reverse score items as appropriate.) In this way, you have a total score on the scale for each participant. If the items are measuring the same thing then the total should also be measuring the same thing as the individual items. This total score is also referred to as the *whole*-scale score.

■ If the total (or whole-scale score) consists of the sum of several items which individually measure the same thing as the total score (but not so well), then scores on individual items should correlate with the total score on the scale. If an item does not correlate with the whole-scale score (total score) then that item is clearly measuring something different from what the scale is measuring. It can safely be eliminated.

By dropping items, a shorter and probably more consistent scale will be obtained.

BOX 12.2   ITEM ANALYSIS

Item analysis refers to the process of examining each item on the scale in order to identify its good features and inadequacies. The main things which are involved are:

■ Items which show little variation over the sample should be dropped. This is because such items contribute little or nothing to variations in the total score on the test. Low variability may be assessed by calculating a measure of variation (e.g. variance, standard error or standard deviation) or by examining a histogram of the scores on each item.

■ Ideally, all items should show similar levels of variation and as much variation in response as possible. If the items do *not* have similar variability then problems may arise if one simply sums the scores on the items on the scale to get a total. If the items do not have similar variabilities, then the proper procedure would be to turn the scores on the individual items into standard scores (see the companion book *Introduction to Statistics in Psychology* (Howitt and Cramer, 2005*a*, Chapter 5). In some psychological tests and measures, you will find that certain items are given extra scoring weight. This is to take into account this very problem. All other things being equal, an item with large variability would be preferred over one with low variability.

■ Items which are omitted (not replied to) or are commented on by a number of participants should be considered for dropping from the scale. Comments and omissions are indicative that the participants are having difficulty knowing the meaning of the item. Rephrasing the item is an option but this means that the scale should be re-administered to a new sample.

■ The final stage of item analysis is to examine the consistency with which the individual items contribute to whatever is being measured by the total scale. Item–whole correlation and factor analytic approaches to doing this are discussed in the main body of the text.

Another way of doing much the same thing is to take extreme groups on the whole or total test. That is, we could take the top 25% of scores and the bottom 25% of scores on the entire scale. Items which are answered very differently by high scorers on the entire scale compared to low scorers are good items and should be retained. Items which are answered similarly by high scorers and low scorers are not discriminating and may be dropped from the scale. There is no advantage of this method over using item–whole correlations.

Table 12.1 overleaf contains, among other things such as the average of scores on the full scale, the item–total correlations for our honesty scale. What does it tell us? The first thing to note is that all of the relationships are positive ones or very close to zero in one case. If there were any substantial negative relationships, especially sizeable ones, then that item has probably been scored the wrong way round. That is, it might be a negatively worded item which has not been reversed scored. The researcher needs to check that this is indeed the case. Wrongly scored items should be rescored in the opposite direction. (This can be easily done using recoding procedures such as those in SPSS.) The

Table 12.1   Item–total correlation

	Scale mean if item deleted	Scale variance if item deleted	Corrected item–total correlation
Honest	26.00	40.33	0.38
Offend	25.38	37.76	0.43
Street	25.77	37.36	0.46
Untruth	25.69	35.23	0.74
Change	26.00	37.00	0.56
Phone	25.31	36.40	0.55
Shoplift	25.85	36.97	0.69
Hurts	25.23	44.86	−0.04
Boss	25.38	37.76	0.43
Affair	25.54	37.94	0.36

calculations have all to be redone because the total score will be incorrect – one more good reason for using a computer.

The most important function of the item–whole correlation coefficients, though, is that they show us which of the items correlate poorly with the total score – that is, the items which correlate weakly with whatever it is that the scale measures. Looking at Table 12.1, it is clear that some of the items correlate rather better with the total score than others. If we wished to shorten the scale (though this one is not very long), then the obvious items to drop are the ones which relate poorly to the total score. The items which have good correlations with the total score are retained for inclusion in the final scale – by doing so we increase the likelihood that all of our remaining items are measuring much the same thing. This is a matter of judgement, of course, but is easily reversible if it seems that too many items have been omitted. However, since items have been dropped then the total score and the item–whole correlations have to be recalculated. Again, computers make this a fairly minimal chore.

Item 8 on the honesty scale ('It is always best to tell the truth even if it hurts') is the obvious item to drop first given its near zero correlation with the total of items.

So as a reminder, just what has dropping items achieved?

■ One result is that the scale becomes a more refined measure of whatever it is that it measures. That is to say, remaining items increasingly tend to measure the same thing.

■ The scale is shortened – this may be very important in some research contexts because participants may be more prepared to complete a short measure than a long measure, for example. Be careful though since a short scale will may not be as reliable as a longer scale (see Chapter 13 for a discussion of reliability) all other things being equal.

What constitutes a good item–whole correlation cannot be defined in absolute terms. It would be unwise to retain items which fail to meet the minimum criterion of statistical significance. For tests and measures developed solely for the purpose of research with substantial samples of participants, tests and measures with just a few items may be preferred simply because they place less demand on participants. There is a trade-off between length of the test or measure and the number of participants in the study. The greater the number of participants then the shorter the scale may be.

A small refinement

Item–total correlation analysis may be refined especially when the scale consists of relatively few items. This modification involves correlating the item with the total score *minus* the score on that particular item. Put another way, this is merely the correlation of the item with the sum of all of the *other* items. Because the item–whole correlations include the correlation of the item with itself, then this figure will always be inflated somewhat. The extent of the inflation depends on the number of items contributing to the total score on the test – the fewer the items then the greater the impact of any one item. So by dropping the item in question from the total score on the test or measure, we get a better indicator. This amount of inflation of the correlation is probably negligible when we have a lot of items; it is more influential when we have few items. The adjustment is straightforward and is recommended as the preferred approach. Computer programs such as SPSS will do both versions of the analysis so there is virtually no additional effort required.

This form of item analysis is very much a process and not a single step. By reducing the number of items one at a time, the value and influence of each variable may be assessed. The researcher simply removes items from the scale in order of their item–whole correlations. The item with the lowest item–whole correlation at any stage is normally the next candidate for omission. Box 12.3 explains another approach – how Cronbach's (1951) alpha coefficient may be used similarly to shorten scales and to increase measurement consistency.

BOX 12.3 USING CRONBACH'S ALPHA TO SHORTEN SCALES AND INCREASE CONSISTENCY OF ITEMS

There is another way of eliminating items which are not measuring what the scale measures particularly well. This is based on (Cronbach's) coefficient alpha. This is dealt with in more detail in Chapter 13. It can be regarded for now as an index of the consistency with which all of the items on the scale measure whatever the scale is measuring. It is possible (using a computer program such as SPSS) to compute the alpha coefficients of the test. There is an option which computes the alpha coefficients of the test with each of the items omitted in turn. This means that there will be as many alpha reliabilities as items in the test. Items which are not measuring the same thing as the other items may be dropped without affecting the size of the alpha reliability coefficient much – simply because they are adding nothing to the consistency of the test adversely. (This is by definition since if they added something to the consistency of the test, removing them would lower the reliability of the test.)

The researcher simply looks through the list of alpha coefficients, and the lowest alpha reliability is selected. The item which was dropped from this alpha may be omitted from the scale as this item is not a good measure of what the scale itself measures. This process is repeated for the 'new' scale and an item dropped. Eventually a shortened scale will emerge which has a sufficiently high alpha coefficient. One of 0.8 or so is usually regarded as satisfactory.

Cronbach's alpha coefficient is also known as the alpha reliability (see Chapter 13).

BOX 12.4 REMINDER: PHI AND POINT–BISERIAL CORRELATION COEFFICIENTS

Before computers, psychological test construction required numerous, time-consuming calculations. The phi and point–biserial correlation coefficients were developed as ways of speeding up the calculations by using special formulae in special circumstances. These formulae are now obsolete because computers can do the calculations quickly and easily – see the companion text *Introduction to Statistics in Psychology* (Howitt and Cramer, 2005*a*).

The phi coefficient is merely the Pearson correlation coefficient calculated between two binary (binomial or yes/no) variables. Many psychological tests have this form – one simply agrees or disagrees with the test item. So the phi coefficient provided a quicker way of calculating a correlation matrix between the items on a test.

The point–biserial correlation is merely the Pearson correlation calculated between a binary (yes/no) test variable and a conventional score. Thus item–whole (item–total) correlations could be calculated using the point–biserial correlation. One variable being the binomial (yes/no) item and the other variable being the total score on the test.

The factoring approach

The item-analysis approach described above is important since it is the basis of many common psychological tests and measures. There is an alternative – factor analysis – which is much more feasible than in the past because of the availability of high speed computers. Factor analysis was developed early in the history of modern psychology as a means of studying the structure of intelligence (and consequently measures of intelligence). Its primary uses are in the context of psychological test and measure construction. Once it was a specialised field but now it is readily available and calculated in seconds using statistical packages such as SPSS.

Firstly, in factor analysis the computer calculates a matrix of correlations between all of the items on the test or measure. (This is provided in Table 12.2.) Then mathematical routines are calculated which detect patterns in the relationships between items on the psychological test. These patterns are presented in terms of factors. A factor is simply an empirically based hypothetical variable which consists of items which are strongly associated with each other. Usually, there will be several factors which emerge in a factor analysis. The precise number depends on the data and it can be that there is simply one significant or dominant factor. More practical details on factor analysis can be found in the two companion texts *Introduction to Statistics in Psychology* (Howitt and Cramer, 2005*a*) and *Introduction to SPSS in Psychology* (Howitt and Cramer, 2005*b*).

Each individual test item has some degree of association with each of the major patterns (i.e. the factors found through factor analysis). This degree of association ranges from a zero relationship through to a perfect relationship. In factor analysis, the relationship of a test item to the factor is expressed in terms of a correlation coefficient. These correlation coefficients are known as *factor loadings*. So a factor loading is the correlation coefficient between an item and a factor. Usually there will be more than one factor but

Table 12.2   Correlation matrix for ten-item honesty scale

	Honest	Offend	Street	Untruth	Change	Phone	Shoplift	Hurts	Boss	Affair
Honest	1	−0.169	0.540	0.583	0.553	0.431	0.476	0.239	−0.169	−0.283
Offend	−0.169	1	−0.037	0.196	−0.027	0.046	0.303	0.090	0.999	0.676
Street	0.540	−0.037	1	0.554	0.464	0.583	0.448	−0.004	−0.037	0.082
Untruth	0.583	0.196	0.554	1	0.771	0.720	0.703	−0.077	0.196	0.208
Change	0.553	−0.027	0.464	0.771	1	0.553	0.717	0.035	−0.027	0.078
Phone	0.431	0.046	0.583	0.720	0.553	1	0.341	−0.288	0.046	0.504
Shoplift	0.476	0.303	0.448	0.703	0.717	0.341	1	0.144	0.303	0.164
Hurts	0.239	0.090	−0.004	−0.077	0.035	−0.288	0.144	1	0.090	−0.314
Boss	−0.169	0.999	−0.037	0.196	−0.027	0.046	0.303	0.090	1	0.676
Affair	−0.283	0.676	0.082	0.208	0.078	0.504	0.164	−0.314	0.676	1

not necessarily so. So each test item has a loading on each of several factors. This is illustrated for our honesty scale in Table 12.3. This table is a factor-loading matrix – it gives the factor loadings of each of the test items on each of the factors. Since they are correlation coefficients, factor loadings can range from −1.0 through 0.0 to +1.0. They would be interpreted as follows:

- A factor loading of 1.0 would indicate a perfect correlation of the item with the factor in question. It is unlikely that you will get such a factor loading.

- A factor loading of 0.8 would be a high value and you would often find such values in a factor analysis. It means that the item correlates well with the factor though less than perfectly.

- A factor loading of 0.5 would be a moderate value for a factor loading. Such factor loadings are of interest but you should bear in mind that a correlation of 0.5 actually means that only 0.25 of the variation of the item is accounted for by the factor. (See Chapter 3 of this book and the companion text *Introduction to Statistics in Psychology* (Howitt and Cramer, 2005*a*).)

Table 12.3   Factor loadings for honesty scale

	Factor 1	Factor 2	Factor 3
Honest	0.641	−0.520	0.260
Offend	0.278	0.904	0.276
Street	0.700	−0.261	0.009
Untruth	0.919	−0.007	−0.003
Change	0.818	−0.262	0.005
Phone	0.777	−0.002	−0.492
Shoplift	0.797	0.003	0.331
Hurts	−0.002	−0.119	0.873
Boss	0.278	0.904	0.276
Affair	0.353	0.794	−0.370

■   A factor loading of 0.2 generally speaking should be regarded as very low and indicates that the item is poorly related to the factor.

■   A factor loading of 0.0 means that there is no relationship between that item and the factor. That is, none of the variation in the item is associated with that factor.

■   Negative (−) signs in a factor loading should be interpreted just as a negative correlation coefficient would be. If the item were to be reverse scored, then the sign of its factor loadings would be reversed. So a negative factor loading may simply indicate an item which has not been reverse scored.

All of this may seem to be number crunching rather than psychological analysis. However, the end point of factor analysis is to put a psychological interpretation on the factors. This is done in a fairly straightforward manner though it does require a degree of creativity on the researcher's part. The factor loadings actually refer to items which are usually presented verbally. It is possible to take the items with high factor loadings and see what the pattern is which defines the factor. This merely entails listing the items which have high loadings with factor 1, first of all. If we take our cut-off point as 0.5 then the items which load highly on factor 1 in descending order of size are:

■   Item 4 (loading = 0.919) 'I have never told even the slightest untruth.'
■   Item 5 (loading = 0.818) 'I would always return the money if I knew that I had been given too much change in a shop.'
■   Item 7 (loading = 0.797) 'I have shoplifted.'
■   Item 6 (loading = 0.777) 'I would never make private phone calls from work.'
■   Item 3 (loading = 0.700) 'If I found money in the street I would hand it in to the police.'

Remember that some of the items would have been reverse scored so that a high score is given to the honest end of the continuum.

The next step is to decide what is the common theme in these high loading items. This simple step may be enough for you to say what the factor is. It can be helpful to compare the high loading items on a factor with the low loading items – they should be very different. The success of this process depends as much on the insight of the researcher about psychological processes as it does on their understanding of the mechanics of factor analysis.

Looking at the items which load highly on the first factor, mainly they seem to relate to matters of theft or white-collar crime (abusing the phone at work). So we might wish to label this factor as 'financial honesty' but there may be better descriptions. Further research may cause us to revise our view but in the interim this is probably as good as we can manage.

The process is repeated for each of the factors in turn. It is conventional to identify the factors with a brief title.

Just what can be achieved with factor analysis?

■   It demonstrates the number of underlying dimensions to your psychological test.

■   It allows you to dispense with any items which do not load highly on the appropriate factors – i.e. the ones which do not seem to be measuring what the test is designed to measure. In this way, it is possible to shorten the test.

■   It is possible to compute factor scores. This is easy with SPSS – see the companion text *Introduction to SPSS in Psychology* (Howitt and Cramer, 2005*b*). A factor score is merely a score based on the participants' responses to the test items which load heavily on the various factors. So instead of being a score on the test, a factor score is a score on one of the factors. One advantage of using factor scores is that they are standardised scores unaffected by differences in the variance of each of the items. As an alternative, it is possible to take the items which load heavily on a factor and derive a score by totalling those items. This is not so accurate as the factor score method. A disadvantage of using factor scores is that they are likely to vary from sample to sample.

■ Factor analysis generates variables (factors) which are pure in the sense that the items which load highly on a factor are all measuring the same underlying thing. This is not true of psychological tests created by other means.

12.3 Item analysis or factor analysis?

We have described item analysis and factor analysis. In many ways they seem to be doing rather similar jobs. Just what is the difference between the two in application?

■ Factor analysis works using the intercorrelations of all of the items with one another. Item analysis works by correlating the individual items with the total score. Factor analysis is more subtle as a consequence – since the total score obtained by adding together items in item analysis might actually include two or more somewhat distinct sets of items (though they are treated as if they were just a single set).

■ Factor analysis allows the researcher to refine their conceptualisation of what the items on the test measure. That is, the factors are fairly refined entities which may allow psychological insight into the scale. Item analysis merely provides a fairly rough way of ridding a scale of bad items which are measuring somewhat different things from those measured by the scale. In that sense it is much cruder.

It should be mentioned that extremely refined scales may not be as effective at measuring complex things as rather cruder measures. For example, we could hone our honesty scale down by factor analysis such that we have just one measure. The trouble is that honest behaviour, for example, may be multiply determined such that a refined measure does not predict honesty very well. In contrast, a cruder measure that measures different aspects of honesty may do quite a good job at predicting honest behaviour simply because it is measuring more aspects of honesty. In other words, there may be a difference between a test useful for the development of psychological theory and a test which is practically useful for the purpose of, say, clinical, educational or forensic practice.

12.4 Other considerations in test construction

Of course, this chapter just outlines some of the central features of psychological test construction. There are numerous other considerations that warrant attention:

■ There should be instructions for the participants about the completion of the test and, usually, instructions for the researcher to indicate the standard methods of administering the test. These instructions can be extremely detailed and for some tests fairly complex manuals are provided.

■ Tests intended for administration to individuals as part of a psychological assessment may contribute significantly to decisions made about the future of that individual. In these circumstances precision is of major importance. Often the researcher will provide tables of norms which is data on how the general (or some other) population score on the test. In this way, a particular clinical client may be compared with other individuals in the test. Norms, as they are called, are often presented as percentiles which are the cut-off points for the bottom 10%, bottom 20% bottom 50% of scores in that population. Norms may be subdivided by features such as gender or age for greater precision in the comparison.

■ Tests for research purposes do not require the same degree of precision or development as tests for practical purposes. This does not mean that the same high standards that are needed for clinical work are inappropriate, merely that for research involving a substantial number of participants sometimes circumstances will demand that a weaker or less precise test is used.

12.5 Conclusion

Writing appropriate and insightful items to measure psychological characteristics can be regarded as a skill involving a range of talents and abilities. In contrast, the creation of a worthwhile psychological scale based on these items is relatively simple once the basics are appreciated. The modern approach based on factor analysis using high speed computers can be routinely applied to data requiring scaling. Since factor analysis identifies the major dimensions underlying the intercorrelations of the items of the test, the outcome of the process may a unidimensional scale or a multidimensional scale according to the choices made by the researcher. It is up to the researcher whether the items are selected which would constitute a single dimension or whether more than one dimension is retained. Scaling basically works to make the items of the scale consistent with each other and to remove any which are not consistent with the others. However, at the end of the process we will have, hopefully, a scale high on internal consistency. This does not mean that the scale is anything other than internally consistent. There is another important job to be done – that is, to assess the fitness of the measure for its purpose. This is largely a question of its validity but to some extent also one of its reliability. These are dealt with in Chapter 13.

Key points

■ Standardised tests are available for assessment purposes. They may be suitable for research purposes also but not necessarily so. They may be too long, too time consuming or in some other way not fully appropriate to the purpose of the research. Hence a researcher may find it necessary to develop new measures.

■ Many psychological characteristics are difficult to measure with precision using any single item or question. Consequently, it is common to combine several items in order to obtain a more satisfactory measure. This involves selecting sets of items which empirically appear to be measuring much the same thing. This process is known as item analysis.

■ The most common methods of item analysis are item–whole (or item–total) correlations and factor analysis. The item–whole method simply selects items which correlate best with the sum of the items. That is, items which measure the same thing as the total of the items are good items. Factor analysis is a set of complex mathematical procedures which identifies groups of items which empirically are highly intercorrelated with each other. A factor then is the basis of a single dimensional scale.

■ There are other skills required in scale construction such as the ability to write good items, though the processes of item analysis may well get rid of badly worded items because they do not empirically relate well to other items.

■ Some items need to be reverse scored if they are worded in the opposite direction to the majority of items.

■ Internal consistency of items does not in itself guarantee that the scale can be vouchsafed as a useful measure of the thing it is intended to measure.

Activities

1. We made up the data for the honesty scale. Why don't you carry out the research properly? Take our items, turn them into a questionnaire, get as many people as possilble to fill it in, and once that is done analyse them using SPSS. This is quite easy if you use the companion text *Introduction to SPSS in Psychology* (Howitt and Cramer, 2005*b*). Was our made-up data anything like your data?

2. Try extending our honesty scale by including items which measure extra facets of honesty which were not included in our original. How satisfactory empirically is your new scale? How could you assess its validity?

13 Reliability and validity
Evaluating the value of tests and measures

Overview

■ Reliability and validity are the means by which we evaluate the value of psychological tests and measures.

■ In addition, objectivity indicates the extent to which different administrators of the test would get the same outcome when testing a particular participant or client.

■ Reliability is about (a) the consistency of a measure over time and (b) the consistency of the items within the measure. Validity concerns the evidence that the measure actually measures what it is intended to measure.

■ Both reliability and validity are multifaceted concepts and there are a number of approaches to each. For example, validity ranges from a measure's correlation with similar measures through to a thorough empirical and theoretical assessment of how the measure performs in relation to other variables.

■ Reliability and validity are *not* inherent characteristics of measures. They are affected by the context and purpose of the measurement. So, for example, a measure that is valid for one purpose may not be valid for another purpose.

We have created our measure using the item analysis procedures described in Chapter 12. What next? Usually the answer is to assess the reliability and validity of the measure. There are several different sorts of reliability and validity which need to be differentiated. Reliability includes internal, test–retest and alternate-forms reliabilities. Validity includes face, content, concurrent and construct validity. These different types of reliability and validity are not different ways of assessing the same thing but different ways of assessing different aspects of reliability and validity. A measure produced using the item-analysis methods described in Chapter 12 may be useful for many purposes, but what these are depends partly on the reliability and validity of the measure. Many psychological measures, for example, consist of a list of questions which, at best, can only partially capture the characteristics of the things to which they refer. Depression, for instance, cannot be fully captured by the words used to measure it. Consequently, the question of just how well a test or measure captures the essence of a particular concept needs to be asked.

There are a number of criteria to consider. These apply to both the assessment of individuals and measures being used for research purposes:

■ *Objectivity*   The test or measure should yield similar outcomes irrespective of who is administering the measure – though this is only true with trained personnel who know just how the test should be administered. The opposite of objectivity is subjectivity – that is the outcome of the measure will depend on who is administering the test. There are some measures which are more reliant on the judgement of the administrator (e.g. Hare's psychopathology scale) than others. Training may be more intense in the use of such scales.

■ *Reliability*   This term has a number of distinct meanings as we will see later. One important meaning is reliability or consistency of the measure at different points in time or across different circumstances. If one realistically expects a psychological characteristic to remain relatively stable over time, the measure used for this characteristic should be relatively stable. A measure of dyslexia which one month indicates that ten children in a school class may have a problem of dyslexia but the next month picks out ten totally different children from the same class would not be reliable. Since dyslexia is a stable characteristic, then the test is patently useless. A reliable test would pick out more or less the same group of children as potentially dyslexic no matter when the test was administered. Of course, if the psychological characteristic is relatively unstable – perhaps a person's mood such as how happy they feel – then we would not expect that measure to be particularly stable. Such a measure may be stable in the short term – i.e. with a similar mood on Monday morning compared with Monday afternoon – but unstable from week to week. There are relatively few measures which involve unstable characteristics so generally reliability over time is regarded as important in psychology.

■ *Validity*   Broadly speaking, this refers to the extent to which a measure assesses what it is claimed to measure. There are a variety of ways of assessing validity – none of which are identical to any of the others. The types of question raised in judging validity range from whether the items in the measure appear to assess what they are intended to measure (face validity) to whether the measure of variable A is capable of distinguishing variable A from, say, variables C and D (discriminative validity).

The different types of reliability and validity will be dealt with in detail in subsequent sections.

The concepts of reliability and validity need to be understood in relation to reasonable expectations about the characteristics of a good measure of the psychological concepts in question. We have seen that this is not quite the same as suggesting that a good measure will maximise reliability and validity – although often they will. Reliability and validity are not in-built qualities of psychological measures. Reliability and validity will vary with the context and purpose of the measurement, and among different samples of participants. Measurements designed purely for research purposes can be useful despite relatively low levels of reliability and validity. On the other hand, tests designed for the assessment of individuals in, say, clinical or educational settings of necessity have to have much higher levels of reliability and validity since they are used to assess individuals. The inadequacies of measures for research purposes can be partially compensated for by having larger sample sizes though this may be problematic in itself. Different criteria apply to research and individual assessment. In other words, there may be measuring instruments that are adequate for research purposes but unsatisfactory for assessing individuals and vice versa. The reasons for this include:

■ Research is almost always based on a sample of individuals rather than a particular case. That means that a psychological test that discriminates between groups of people may be useful for research purposes despite being hopelessly imprecise for the assessment of individuals. A forensic psychologist, for example, may need to assess the intelligence of an offender to determine whether their intellectual functioning is so low as to render them incapable of a plea because s/he is incapable of understanding relevant concepts.

■ It takes quite a long period of time and substantial effort to maximise the reliability and validity of a measure. Measures may be required for variables which have not yet been adequately researched. The upshot of this is that the researcher may be left with a choice between constructing a new measure for research purposes or using a poorly documented measure simply because it is available.

■ Even if there appears to be a satisfactory measure already available, one should not assume that it is satisfactory without carefully examining the measure and research on it or using it. For example, depression as a clinical syndrome may be different from depression as it is experienced by people in general. To use a clinical measure, then, may be problematic if the research is on depression in non-clinical samples since the test was intended for extreme (clinical) groups, and may not discriminate among non-clinical individuals.

■ Measures useful for the assessment of individuals often take a lot of time to administer: perhaps more than two hours for a major test. This amount of time may not be available to the researcher who is dealing with large samples. Hence, a less good measure might be the pragmatic choice.

Where does one find out information concerning the properties of ready-made psychological tests? The following are the main sources of information about psychological measures:

■ The instruction manual for the test (if there is one). Students may find that their department has a collection of tests and measures for teaching and research purposes.

■ Books or journal articles about the measure. Published research on a particular measure may be accessed through normal psychological databases (see Chapter 5). The published research may be extensive or sparse – it largely depends on the measure in question.

■ Catalogues of published tests. These are obtainable from test publishers. Many university departments of psychology would hold copies of such catalogues.

■ Increasingly, the Internet is a useful source – some tests are published on it.

Of course, exercise caution – what may be seen as a perfectly satisfactory test or measure by others may be flawed from your perspective.

13.1 Reliability of measures

This section reviews the major types of reliability. All reliability concerns the consistency of the measure but the type of consistency varies in the different types of reliability. The broad types of consistency dealt with are internal consistency and consistency over different measurements, such as different points in time. Internal consistency was discussed in Chapter 12. There are several measures of internal consistency which can be readily computed using programs such as SPSS – Cronbach's (1951) coefficient alpha and split-half reliability are examples. Stability across measures involves the stability of the measure over different versions of the test or across different points in time. Consistency over time has to be evaluated in the light of the interval between administrations of the test. Reliability over a one week period will be greater than reliability for the same measure over a month.

Internal reliability

Internal reliability indicates how consistently *all* of the items in a scale measure the concept in question. If a scale is internally reliable, any set of items from the scale could be selected and they will provide a measure that is more or less the same as any other group of items taken from that scale. One traditional way of calculating internal reliability is to calculate scores on half of the items in the test and correlate these scores with those for the same individuals on the remainder of the test. Such procedures form the basis of several measures of internal reliability. Alpha reliability may be construed as just a variant on this theme:

■ *Split-half reliability*   The first half of the items on the test are summed then the second half of the items summed (for each participant). The Pearson correlation between the two halves is calculated – this is referred to as the split-half reliability (though a correction for length of the scale is sometimes applied such that the reliability is for the full-length scale).

■ *Odd–even reliability*   The two halves are created differently for this. One half is the odd numbered items (e.g. items 1, 3, 5, 7, etc.) and the other half is the even numbered items (e.g. items 2, 4, 6, 8, etc). The correlation between these two sets of scores is the odd–even reliability. Once again, an adjustment for the length of the scale is often made.

■ *Alpha reliability (Cronbach's alpha)*   Split-half and odd–even reliability are dependent on which items are selected for inclusion in the two halves. Alpha reliability improves on this merely by being an average of every possible half of the items correlated with every possible other half of the items. Thus alpha reliability is the average of all possible split-half reliabilities. Since alpha reliability takes all items into account and all possible ways of splitting them, then the alpha reliability gives the best overall picture. Fortunately, the calculation of alpha reliability can be achieved more directly using an analysis of variance based method. This is described in the companion text *Introduction to Statistics in Psychology* (Howitt and Cramer, 2005a). All of these forms of reliability are easily calculated using SPSS.

These measures of internal reliability or consistency have a minor drawback – that is, they are the internal reliability of halves of the items rather than a measure of the internal reliability of the entire scale. It is possible to estimate the reliability of the entire scale by employing what is known as the Spearman–Brown formula. In general, what this does is to indicate the reliability of a scale longer or shorter than the actual scale length. Thus it can be used to estimate the reliability of the full scale, or it could be used to estimate what the reliability of an even shorter scale would be. (If one can achieve the desired level of reliability with a short scale then this may be preferred.) The procedure is given in the companion book *Introduction to Statistics in Psychology* (Howitt and Cramer, 2005a) – it is relatively simple to compute by hand. SPSS does not compute the Spearman–Brown formula but it can give the Guttman reliability. The Guttman reliability coefficient is much like the split-half reliability adjusted to the full-scale length using the Spearman–Brown formula – and is actually more generally applicable than the Spearman–Brown method.

Why is the internal reliability important? The better the internal reliability of a measure then the better the measure (all other things being equal). Furthermore, the better the measure then the higher will be the correlation between that measure and other variables. It is fairly intuitive that a bad measure of honesty, say, will correlate less well with, say, lying to get out of trouble than would a good measure of honesty. One reason why a measure is bad is because it has low internal reliability. The correlation of any variable with any other variable is limited by the internal reliability of the variable. So when interpreting any correlation coefficient then information on the reliability of the variables involved is clearly desirable. The maximum size that the correlation between variables A and B can be is the square root of product of the reliability of variable A and the reliability of variable B (e.g. $\sqrt{0.8 \times 0.9} = 0.85$). Without knowing this, the researcher who obtains a correlation of 0.61 between variable A and variable B might feel that the correlation is just a moderate one. So it is between the two measures, but actually the correlation between two variables could be only 0.85 at most. Hence the correlation of 0.61 is actually quite an impressive finding. There is a simple correction which allows one to adjust a correlation by the reliabilities of one or both of the variables. This is described in Chapter 3, p. 49. Given the difference that this adjustment can make to the interpretation of the obtained relationships, it is probably too often neglected by researchers.

Finally, a note of caution is appropriate. Many textbooks stress that internal reliability is an important and essential feature of a good test. This is true but only up to a point. If one is trying to measure a carefully defined psychological construct (intelligence, extraversion, need for achievement) then internal reliability should be as high as can be practically achieved. On the other hand, the measurement of such refined psychological concepts may not be the main objective of the test. Since much human behaviour is multiply determined (being the result of the influence of a number of variables though not necessarily any of them) then a measure that measures a lot of different variables may actually be better at predicting behaviour.

A good example of this is Hare's psychopathy checklist (Hare, 1991). Psychopaths are known to be especially common in criminal populations for example. The checklist is scored by simply adding up all of the features of psychopathy that an individual possesses. These features include glibness, pathological lying, manipulativeness and grandiose estimates of self-worth. The score is simply the number of different characteristics of psychopathy manifested by that individual. For a characteristic like psychopathy which is a syndrome of diagnostic features, internal reliability is less crucial than including all possible diagnostic features of the syndrome.

Stability over time or different measures

Psychologists also apply the consistency criterion to another aspect of measurement – how their tests and measures perform at a time interval or across similar versions of a test. There are several different types of this:

■ *Test–retest reliability*   This is simply the correlation between scores from a sample of participants on a test measured at one point in time with their scores on the same test given at a later time. The size of test–retest reliability is basically limited by the *internal reliability* of the test. Of course, the test–retest reliability is affected by any number of factors in addition. The longer the interval between the test and retest the more opportunity there is for the characteristics of individuals to simply change, thus affecting the test–retest reliability adversely. However, test–retest reliability may be affected by carry-over from the first administration of the test to the second. That is, participants may simply remember their answers to the first test when they complete the retest.

■ *Alternate-forms reliability*   A test may be affected by 'memory' contamination if it is used as a retest instrument. This may be a simple learning effect, for example. Consequently, many tests are available in two versions or two forms. Since these contain different items, some of the 'memory' contamination effects are cancelled out – though possibly not all. The relationship between these two alternate forms is known as the alternate-forms reliability. Once again, the maximum value of alternate-forms reliability is the product of the two internal reliabilities. If the alternate-forms reliability is similar to this value then it seems clear that the two forms of the test are assessing much the same things. If the alternate-forms reliability is much lower that the maximum possible, then the two forms are measuring rather different things. A correlation between two tests does not mean that they are measuring the same thing – it means that they are partially measuring the same thing. The bigger the correlation up to the maximum given the reliabilities of the tests, the more they are measuring substantially the same things. As with test–retest reliability, alternate-forms reliability is limited by the internal reliability of the tests.

The reason for the close relationship between internal reliability and other forms of reliability has already been explained. To repeat, the lower the internal reliability of a test then the lower the maximum correlation of that test with any other variable (including alternate forms of the test and retests on the same variable). The bigger the internal reliability value then, all other things being equal, the bigger the correlation of the test with any other variable it correlates with. In other words, there is a close relationship between different forms of reliability despite their superficial differences.

A measure should be reliable over time if the concept to which it refers is chronologically stable. We do not expect a thermometer to give the same readings day after day. However, we might expect that bathroom scales will give more or less stable readings of our weight over a short period of time. That is, we expect the temperature to vary constantly but our weight should be largely constant. In the same way, reliability over time (especially test–retest reliability) should only be high for psychological characteristics which are themselves stable over time. Psychological characteristics which are not stable over time (attention, happiness, alertness, etc.) should *not* necessarily give good levels of test–retest reliability. Characteristics which we can assume to be stable over time (intelligence, honesty, religious beliefs) should show strong test–retest reliability. In other words, reliability must be carefully assessed against how it is being measured and what is being measured. That accepted, psychologists tend to want to measure stable and enduring psychological characteristics, hence test–retest reliability is generally expected to be good for most psychological tests and measures.

13.2 Validity

Validity is usually defined as 'whether a test measures what it is intended to measure'. This fits well with the dictionary definition of the term *valid* as meaning whether something is well founded, sound or defensible. The following should be considered when examining the validity of a test:

■ Validity is not a property of a test itself but a complex matter of the test, the sample on which a test is used, the social context of its use, and other factors. A test which is good at measuring religious commitment in the general population may be hopelessly inadequate when applied to a sample of priests. A test which is a good measure in research may prove to be flawed as a part of job selection in which applicants will put their best face forward (i.e. maybe not tell the truth). Famously this issue is often put as a question 'Valid for what?'. The implication of this is that validity is not an inherent feature of a test or measure but something that should be expected to vary according to the purpose to which the test or measure is being put.

■ Reliability and validity are, conceptually, quite distinct and there need not be any necessary relationship between the two. So be very wary about statements which imply that a valid test or measure has to be reliable. We have already seen that in psychology the emphasis in measurement is generally on relatively stable and enduring characteristics of people (e.g. their creativity). Such a measure should be consistent over time (reliable). It also ought to distinguish between inventors and the rest of us if it is a valid measure of creativity. A measure of a characteristic which varies quite rapidly over time will not be reliable over time – if it is then we might doubt its validity. For example, a valid measure of suicide intention may not be particularly stable (reliable) over time though good at identifying those at risk of suicide. How reliable it is will depend on the interval between the test and retest.

■ Since validity is often expressed as a correlation between the test or measure and some other criterion, the validity coefficient (as it is called) will be limited by the reliability of the test or measure. Once again, the maximum correlation of the test or measure with any other variable has an upper limit determined by the internal reliability.

13.3 Types of validity

There are a number of generally recognised types of validity – face, content, criterion; i.e. concurrent and predictive validity, construct, known-group and convergent validity. (Other types of validity such as internal validity and external validity concern research design rather than measurement as such. These are dealt with in Chapter 10.) Over the years, the distinction between these different types of validity has become a little blurred in textbooks. We will try to reinstate the distinctive features of each.

Face validity

This form of validity can only be assessed informally. One inspects the test items in order to assess whether on the face of things (that is, in terms of the content of the items) the test would appear to be a measure of the psychological concept concerned. Generally speaking, the researcher inevitably applies this form of validity criterion whilst constructing the test since the measure will include items which the researcher considers to be viable. The problems with face validity are obvious given the need for item-analysis techniques. It would appear that the mere inspection of the items is no guarantee that the retained items form a valid measure. There are lots of reasons for this. For example, items which appear valid to the researcher may be understood very differently by the participants.

Face validity is a very minimum measure of validity which is subjective in that different researchers will come to different conclusions about the face validity of a test. Some tests and measures are constructed to measure what they measure without the researcher being concerned about what the test might correlate with or predict. In these circumstances face validity may be crucial. For example, if a researcher wished to measure opinions about the causes of crime, the content of the items on the measure would be important. Whether or not these opinions are associated with something else might not concern the researchers.

Content validity

In its classic formulation, good content validity follows from the careful creation of a broad range of items. These items are carefully collected together to reflect a wide variety of the facets of the concept being assessed. Using diverse means of eliciting potential items for inclusion is important. Such diversity would include the research literature, interviews with people similar to potential participants, established theory in the field and so forth. By seeking items from a wide domain, the content validity of the measure is enhanced.

Some authors present a rather different version of what constitutes content validity. They suggest that content validity is achieved by reference to experts on the topic being measured. The task of the expert is to offer insight into whether the items cover the range needed or whether significant aspects of the construct being measured have been omitted. This is a very limited view of what content validity is, although it is one aspect of it. By concentrating on such a limited aspect of content validity, authors such as Coolican (2004) misleadingly imply that content validity is merely a version of face validity – although it is a slightly more sophisticated version.

Concurrent validity

This is simply how well the test correlates with an appropriate criterion measured at the same time. One way of doing this is to correlate the test with another (possibly better established) test of the same thing applied to the same group of participants at the same time. So if one proposed to replace examinations with multiple-choice tests then the concurrent validity of the multiple-choice test would be assessed by correlating the multiple-choice test scores with the marks from an examination given at the same time. It stands to reason that a new test which purports to measure the same thing as the examination should correlate with examination marks. The better the correlation, the more confidence that can be placed in the new measure. Concurrent validity is assessed against a criterion, as we have seen. The next form of validity, predictive validity, is equally criterion based.

Predictive validity

This is the ability of the measure to predict future events. For example, does our measure of honesty predict whether a person will be in prison in five years' time? Predictive validity can be measured by the correlation between the test and the future event. Of course, the predictive validity will depend on the nature of the future event that is being predicted. Many psychological tests are not really intended for the prediction of future events so their lack of validity in this respect is of no consequence. It is a bonus if a test does predict future events when it is not intended to. A measure intended to predict future events does not always have to be rich in psychological detail in order to be effective – and there is good reason why it should show internal consistency. For example, if we wished to predict future offending then a measure consisting of variables such as number of previous convictions and gender may be the best way of predicting. Predicting from psychological traits may be relatively ineffective in these circumstances. Again, since this is a criterion-based assessment of validity, the researcher must have expectations that the test or measure will relate highly to future events and also know what these future events might be. In these circumstances, given that prediction is the prime concern, the content of the test as such probably does not matter. The important thing is that it does predict the future event.

Construct validity

For some researchers, life is not quite so simple as the criterion-based validity methods imply. Take a concept such as self-esteem, for example. If we develop what we see as being an effective measure of self-esteem, can we propose criteria against which to assess the concurrent and predictive validity? We might think that self-esteem is inversely related to future suicide attempts though probably very weakly. Alternatively, we might think that the measure of self-esteem should correlate with other measures of self-esteem as in concurrent validity. However, what if we developed a measure of self-esteem which utilised new theoretical conceptualisations of self-esteem. In these circumstances, relating our new measure of self-esteem to existing measures would not be sufficient. Since our new measure is regarded as an improvement then its lack of concurrent validity with older methods of measurement might be a good thing.

Construct validity is generally poorly understood and even more poorly explained in research methods textbooks. The reason is that it is presented as a technical measurement issue whereas, in its original conceptualisation, construct validity should be more about theory development and general progress of knowledge. So it is much more about being able to specify the nature of the psychological construct that underlies our measure than demonstrating that a test measures what it is supposed to measure. In one of the original classic papers on construct validity, Cronbach and Meehl (1955) put the essence of construct validity in the form of a graphic example very apposite for students:

> *Suppose measure* X *correlates 0.50 with* Y, *the amount of palmar sweating induced when we tell a student that he has failed a Psychology I exam. Predictive validity of* X *for* Y *is adequately described by the coefficient, and a statement of the experimental and sampling conditions. If someone were to ask, 'Isn't there perhaps another way to interpret this correlation?' or 'What other kinds of evidence can you bring to support your interpretation?', we would hardly understand what he* (sic) *was asking because no interpretation has been made. These questions become relevant when the correlation is advanced as evidence that 'test* X *measures anxiety proneness.' Alternative interpretations are possible; e.g., perhaps the test measures 'academic aspiration', in which case we will expect different results if we induce palmar sweating by economic threat. It is then reasonable to inquire about other* kinds *of evidence.* [p. 283]

Cronbach and Meehl then report a variety of 'findings' from other studies which help us understand the nature of test X better:

■ Test X has a correlation of 0.45 with the ratings of the students' 'tenseness' made by other students.

■ Test X correlates 0.55 with the amount of intellectual inefficiency which follows the administration of painful electric shocks.

■ Test X correlates 0.68 with the Taylor anxiety scale.

■ The order of means on test X is highest in those diagnosed as having an anxiety state, next highest in those diagnosed as reactive depression, next highest in 'normal' people, and lowest in those with a psychopathic personality.

■ There is a correlation of 0.60 between palmar sweat when threatened with failure in psychology and when threatened with failure in mathematics.

■ Test X does not correlate with social class, work aspirations and social values.

The reason Cronbach and Meehl include all of this extra information is that it seems to confirm that academic aspiration is not the explanation of the relationship between test X and palmar sweating. The above pattern of findings better supports the original interpretation that the relationship between test X and palmar sweating is due to anxiety. Cronbach and Meehl go on to suggest that, if the best available theory of anxiety predicts that anxiety should show the pattern of relationships manifested by test X, the idea that test X measures anxiety is even more strongly supported.

So delving into the origins of the concept of construct validity clearly demonstrate it to be a complex process. Test X is assessed in relation to a variety of information about that test, but also other variables associated with it. Put another way, construct validity is a method of developing psychological understanding that seeks to inform the researcher about the underlying psychological construct. In this sense, it is about theory building because we need constructs upon which to build theory. So when authors such as Bryman (2001) suggest that construct validity is about suggesting hypotheses about what a test will correlate with and Coolican (2004) says construct validity is about how a construct explains a network of findings, they are giving only partial accounts and not the totality of construct validity. It should also be clear that construct validity is much more an attitude of mind on the part of the researcher than it is a technical methodological tool. If one likes, construct validity is a methodological approach in the original sense of the term methodological – that is, strategies for enhancing and developing knowledge. In modern usage, methodological simply refers to means of collecting data. There is more to knowledge than just data. So it is possible for a construct to be refined and clarified during the progress of research in a field – the definition of a construct is not fixed for all time.

Construct validity may include a vast range of types of evidence, including some that we have already discussed – the correlations between items, the stability of the measure over time, concurrent and predictive validity findings, and so forth. What constitutes support for the construct depends on what we assume to be the nature of the construct. Finding that a test tends to be stable over time undermines the validity of a test which measures transitory mood, as we have already indicated.

Anyone struggling to understand how construct validity fits in with their work should note the following: 'The investigation of a test's construct validity is not essentially different from the general scientific procedures for developing and confirming theories' (Cronbach and Meehl, 1955, p. 300). This does not particularly help one apply construct validity to one's own research – it merely explains why the task is rather difficult. Construct validity is so important (and difficult) because it basically involves many aspects of the research process.

The following types of validity can be considered to be additional ways of tackling the complex issue of construct validity.

Known-groups validity

If we can establish that scores on a measure differ in predictable ways between two specified groups of individuals then this is evidence of the value of the test – and its known-groups validity. For example, a test of schizoid thought should give higher scores for a group of schizophrenics than a group of non-schizophrenic individuals. If it does, then the test can be deemed valid by this method. But we need to be careful. All that we have established is that the groups differ on this particular test. It does not, in itself, establish definitively that our test measures schizoid thought. Many factors may differentiate schizophrenics from others – our measure might be assessing one of these and not schizoid thought. For example, if schizophrenics are more likely to be men than women then the variable gender will differentiate the two groups. Gender is simply not schizoid thought.

A measure which has good known-groups validity is clearly capable of more-or-less accurately differentiating schizophrenics from other people. Being able to do this may add little to our scientific understanding of the construct of schizoid thought. It is only when it is part of a network of relationships that it is capable of adding to our confidence in the scientific worth of the construct – or not.

Triangulation

Triangulation uses multiple measures of a concept. If a relationship is established using several different types of tests or measures then this is evidence of the validity of the relationship, according to Campbell and Fiske (1959). Ideally, the measures should be quite different – for example, using interviewer ratings of extraversion compared to using a paper and pencil measure of the same concept. In some ways triangulation can be seen as a combination of concurrent and predictive validity. The basic assumption is that if two different measures of ostensibly the same construct both correlate with a variable which the construct might be expected to relate to, then this increases our confidence in the construct.

For triangulation to help establish the construct, all three components of the triangle ought to correlate with each other as in Figure 13.1. All of the arrows represent a relationship between the three aspects of the triangle. If test A and test B correlate then this is the basic requirement of demonstrating concurrent validity. If test A correlates with variable X, and test B also correlates with variable X then this is evidence of the predictive validity of tests

Figure 13.1   Triangulation compares several types of test of a concept

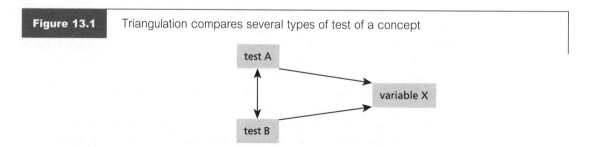

A and B. Notice that in effect this approach is building up the network of associations which Cronbach and Meehl regard as the essence of construct validation. As such, it is much more powerful evidence in favour of the construct than either the evidence of concurrent validity and predictive validity taken separately. Imagine test A and test B both predict variable *X*, but test A and test B do not correlate. The implication of this is that tests A and B are measuring very different things although they clearly predict different aspects of variable *X*.

Triangulation might be regarded as a rudimentary form of construct validation. It is clearly an important improvement over the crude empiricism of criterion validity (predictive and concurrent validity). Nevertheless it is *not* quite the same as construct validity. Its concerns about patterns of relationships are minimal. Similarly, triangulation has only weak allegiances with theory.

Convergent validity

This introduces a further dimension to the concept of validity – that is, a measures of, say, honesty should relate irrespective of the nature or mode of the measure. This means that:

- For example, a self-completion honesty scale should correlate with a behavioural measure of honesty (e.g. handing in to the police money found in the street) *and* assessments of lying on a polygraph (lie detector) test. All should correlate with each other well and be distinguishable from measures of different but partially related concepts such as religiousness.

- The *type* of measure should not unduly determine the relationships. If we find that our best correlations among measures of honesty and religiosity all use self-completion questionnaires then there may be a validity issue. The domain of measurement (self-completion) seems to be having greater bearing on the relationships than the construct being measured. If self-completion measures of religiousness and honesty have higher correlations with each other than self-completion measures of honesty have with behavioural measures of honesty there is clearly a validity problem. In other words, validity is enhanced by evidence that the concept may be measured by a multiplicity of measures from a wide variety of domain. This is a reasonable criterion of validity, but some of its underlying assumptions might be questioned. One of these assumptions is that there should be a strong relationship between different types of measure of a concept. This is a debatable assumption in some cases. For example, would we expect a strong relationship between racial attitudes as assessed by a self-completion attitude questionnaire and a behavioural measure of racial attitudes such as abusive racist behaviour in the street? Many people with racist attitudes are unlikely to express their attitudes in crude racist chants at a football match simply because 'they do not do that sort of thing' or they fear arrest by the police.

Discriminant validity

Convergent validities indicate that measures which are measuring the same thing ought to correlate with each other substantially. Discriminant validity is just the opposite. If measures are apparently measuring different things then they should not correlate strongly with each other. It should be obvious, then, that convergent and discriminant validity should be considered together when assessing the validity of a measure.

13.4 Conclusion

A crucial feature of the concepts of reliability and validity is that they are tools for thinking and questioning researchers. Employed to their fullest potential they constitute a desire to engage with the subject matter of the research in full. They should not be regarded as kite mark standards which, if exceeded, equate to evidence of the quality of the test or measure. Properly conceived, they invite researchers to explore both the theoretical and the empirical relationships of their subject matter. The value of a measure cannot be assessed simply in terms of possessing both high validity and high reliability. What is reasonable by way of reliability and validity is dependent on the nature of what is being measured as well as what ways are available to measure it.

Key points

■ All measures need to be assessed for objectivity, reliability and validity. There is no minimum criterion of acceptable standards of each of these since the nature of what is being measured is also crucial.

■ Information about the reliability and validity of some measures is readily available from standard databases, journal articles and the Internet. However, this is not always the case for every measure.

■ Reliability is about consistency within the measure or over time.

■ Cronbach's alpha, split-half reliability and odd–even reliability are all measures of internal reliability. Cronbach's alpha is readily computed and should probably be the measure of choice. Guttman's reliability is like split-half reliability but has been corrected for the length of the test.

■ Reliability is also assessed at correlating a measure given at different time points (test–retest reliability) and between different versions of the test (alternate-forms reliability).

■ Reliability over time should be high for measures of stable psychological characteristics but low for unstable psychological characteristics.

■ Validity is often described as assessing whether a test measures what it is supposed to measure. This implies different validities according to the purpose to which a measure is being put.

■ Face validity is an examination of the items to see if they appear to be measuring what the test is intended to measure.

■ Content validity refers to the processes by which items are developed – sampling from a wide variety of sources, using a wide variety of informants and using a variety of styles of item may all contribute to content validity.

■ Construct validity involves a thorough understanding of how the measure operates compared to other measures. Does the pattern of relationships between the measures appear meaningful for a variety of other constructs? Does the measure do what pertinent theory suggests that it should? Construct validity is an extensive and complex process which relates more to the process of the development of science than to a single index of validity.

■ Known-groups validity, triangulation and convergent validity can all be seen as partial aspects of construct validity. After all, they each examine the complex patterns of relationships between the measure, similar measures, different measures and expectations of what types of person are differentiated by the measure.

Activity

You ask your partner if they love you. Their reply is 'yes, very much so'. How would you assess the reliability and validity of this measure using the concepts discussed in this chapter?

14 Coding data

Overview

- Coding is the process of categorising the raw data, usually into descriptive categories.

- Coding is a basic process in both quantitative and qualitative research. Sometimes coding is a hidden process in quantitative research.

- In precoding, the participants are given a limited number of replies to choose from, much as in a multiple-choice test.

- Whenever data are collected qualitatively in an extensive, rich form, coding is essential. However, some researchers will choose to impose their own coding categories whereas others will endeavour to develop categories which match the data as supplied by the participants and which would be meaningful from the participants' perspectives.

- Coding schedules may be subjected to measures of inter-coder reliability and agreement when quantified.

This chapter is the dividing line between the quantitative and qualitative parts of this book. Perhaps a better way of regarding it is as a major point of intersection between quantitative and qualitative research. More than any other part of this book, coding brings together quantitative and qualitative research.

Coding in some form or another is central to all psychological research. This is true irrespective of the style of research involved – quantitative or qualitative. Inevitably when we research any complex aspect of human activity, we have to simplify this complexity or richness (note the very different ways of describing the same thing) in order to describe and even explain what is happening. No researcher simply videos people's activities and compiles these for publication, no matter how much they abhor quantification. There is always some form of analysis of what is occurring. In this way, all researchers impose structure on the social and psychological world. Coding is quintessentially how we develop understanding of the nature of the psychological world. Nevertheless, there are radical differences in the way that quantitative and qualitative researchers generally go about the categorisation process. It is important to recognise these differences and to appreciate their relative strengths. Then we may recognise the considerable overlap between the two.

Table 14.1   Relation between quantitative and qualitative data collection, and quantitative and qualitative data analysis

	Quantitative data collection	**Qualitative data collection**
Quantitative data analysis	Very common – often requires pre-coding in advance of data collection.	An attractive combination in that the data collected are often rich in detail allowing for detailed analysis. Researchers tend to impose coding categories in this style of research.
Qualitative data analysis	Not a realistic option as by collecting data quantitatively the point of qualitative analysis is defeated.	The basis of much modern qualitative research in fields such as discourse analysis and conversation analysis. In the ideal case, qualitative analysis seeks ethnographically developed categories which match the nuances of the data well.

Table 14.1 indicates the four possible combinations of quantitative and qualitative data collection and analysis methods. Three of the combinations are fairly common approaches. Only the qualitative analysis of quantitative data is rare or non-existent, although some researchers have suggested that it is feasible. The crucial thing about the table is that it differentiates between the data collection and the data analysis phases of research. The important consequence of this distinction is that it means that quantitative analysis may use exactly the same data collection methods as qualitative analysis. Thus, in-depth interviews, focus groups, biographies and so forth may be amenable to quantitative analysis just as they are amenable to qualitative analysis.

Coding has two different meanings in research:

■ The process by which observations, text, recordings and generally any sort of data are categorised according to a classificatory scheme. Indeed, categorisation is a better description of the process than is the word coding.

■ The process by which items of data are given a number for the purposes of computer analysis. For example, a variable like gender consists of the two categories: male and female. It simplifies computer applications if these are entered with a numerical code in which, say, 1 represents male and 2 represents female. This seems closer to the dictionary definition of code that suggests that coding is to represent one thing by another.

Often both of these occur in the same research. In highly structured materials such as multiple-choice questionnaires, the categorisation is actually done by the participant, leaving only the computer coding to the researcher. However, coding is a term that is not particularly associated with quantitative data any more than qualitative data. Coding reflects a major step between data collection and the findings of the research. It is really the first stage of the process by which the data are given structure.

Content analysis is a common term which refers to the coding of, especially, mass media content – books, television programmes and so forth. Television programmes provide a source of 'rich' and complex data. It is common for communications researchers to systematically classify or categorise media content. Frequently, they provide rates or frequencies of occurrence of different sorts of content. For example, the researcher might study sexism in television programmes. This would involve, for example, counting the number of times women are portrayed in domestic settings as opposed to work settings, or how often women are used as authoritative voice-overs in advertising. Content analysis typifies the categorisation process needed as part of the analysis of a variety of data.

14.1 Types of coding

There are at least three types of coding:

- pre-coding
- researcher-imposed coding
- coding emerging from the data.

The final form of coding is most characteristic of qualitative data analysis. Aspects of it are covered in Chapter 18 on grounded theory, for example. The other two are rather more characteristic of quantification. Pre-coding is characteristic of highly structured materials such as self-completion questionnaires. Researcher-imposed coding is more typical of circumstances in which the data have been collected in a fairly rich or qualitative form, but the researcher's intention is to carry out a quantitative or statistical analysis. Coding emerging from the data is probably much more typical of research that is not intended to be analysed numerically or statistically.

Pre-coding

This is very familiar since it is the basis of much quantitative research in psychology. So common is it that it has a taken for granted quality. It is also very familiar from magazine and other popular entertainment surveys, so widely has its influence spread. Typical examples of pre-coding are found in attitude and personality questionnaires. In these the participant replies to a series of statements relevant to a particular area of interest. However, typically the respondent only has a very limited predetermined list of alternative replies. In the simplest of cases, for example, participants may be asked to do no more than *agree* or *disagree* with statements like 'Unemployment is the most important issue facing the country today.'

The key feature of pre-coding is, of course, that it occurs prior to data collection. That is, the coding categories are predetermined and are not amenable to change or re-coding (other than the possibility of combining several categories together for the purposes of data analysis). Furthermore, it is participants who code their own 'responses' into one of the available coding categories. As a consequence the researcher is oblivious to how the coding is actually done. Let us examine the reasons for pre-coding by taking an example of a simple research study. A researcher asks a group of young people at a school to answer the following question:

Q 43: What is your favourite television programme? _____

A sample of a hundred young people might write down as many as 100 different television programmes. There may be overlaps, so the actual total may be lower. What can one do with these data which might include football, *Friends*, *The Simpsons* and *Big Brother*?

Given that a primary purpose of research is to give structure to data, simply listing all of the named programmes is not in itself the solution. The researcher must categorise (or code) the replies of the participants. There is no single and obvious way of doing this. It is important to understand the aims of the research. If the research is to investigate violent television programmes then the researcher could code the favourite programme as violent or not, or even code the level of violence characteristic of the programme. If the researcher is interested in whether children are watching programmes put on late at night for adults then it would be necessary to code the programme in terms of the time at which the programme was transmitted.

If the researcher has a clear conception as to the purpose of the question, coding categories may suggest themselves that are both simple and obvious. So in some circumstances, the researcher may choose to pre-code the range of answers that the respondent may give. Take the following question:

Q 52: Which one of the following is your favourite type of television programme?
(*a*) Sport
(*b*) Films
(*c*) Music
(*d*) Cartoons ☐
(*e*) Other c. 61

In Q 52 the favourite television programme has been pre-coded by asking the respondent to nominate their favourite from a few broad types of programme. Also notice the box c. 61 to the right of the question. This is so that the computer code for the participant's chosen answer may be entered – it also identifies which variable is being referred to on the computer spreadsheet. Apart from putting the respondent's replies in a form suitable for the computer, the researcher's input is minimal (but nevertheless crucial) with pre-coded material. Notice that the pre-coding has limited the information received from the participant quite considerably. That is, in this example nothing at all is known about the specific programmes which the participant likes. In other words, pre-coding of this sort produces very limited information that is of little value to the qualitative researcher. In fact, it misses the point of qualitative data analysis entirely. It is the sort of research that qualitative data analysts often rail against.

Pre-coding is not exclusively a feature of the analysis of self-completion questionnaires. A questionnaire may be used as part of an interview and administered by the researcher or some other interviewer. Furthermore, pre-coding may be employed in studies other than questionnaires. For example, the researcher may be intending to observe behaviour. Those observations may be taken in the form of notes, but there is no reason why the observation categories cannot be pre-coded. Leyens *et al.* (1975) used a pre-coded observational schedule in order to observe the aggressive behaviour of boys before and after they had seen violent or non-violent films. Such pre-coded observations will obviously greatly facilitate things like calculating the degree of agreement between different observers. That is, inter-observer or inter-rater reliability becomes easy to calculate using pre-coded observation schedules.

Pre-coding means that the data collected have largely been limited by the nature of the categories created by the researcher. Unless the participant adds something in the margin or qualifies what they choose, no one would be the wiser. If one is interviewing but only ticking the categories pre-coded on the questionnaire, then much of what the interviewee is saying is likely to simply be disregarded. Pre-coding reduces the richness of the data to a level manageable by the researcher and adequate to meet the purposes of the research. Inevitably, pre-coding means that nuances and subtleties are filtered out. This is neither a good nor a bad thing in any absolute sense. For some purposes, the researcher-imposed broad-brush categories may be perfect, for other purposes pre-coding is woefully inadequate.

So where do the pre-coded categories come from? There are a range of answers to this question as a perusal of the research literature will demonstrate:

■ *Conventional formats*   Some pre-coding formats are conventional in the sense that they have been commonly used by researchers over several decades. For example, the yes–no, agree–disagree pre-coded response formats are so established that we tend to take them for granted. However, even using such a simple format raises questions. For example, what if someone does not disagree and does not agree? In consideration of this, some response formats include a 'don't know' or '?' category. Similarly, the five-point Likert scale answer format (strongly agree, agree, ?, disagree and strongly disagree) is conventional and general works well for its purpose. But there is no reason why seven or nine point scales cannot be used instead. Actually, there is no absolutely compelling reason why the middle, neutral or '?' point cannot be left out to leave a four, six or eight-point scale. Some argue that the neutral point allows the participants to take the easy option of not making a choice between one end of the scale and the other.

■ *Piloting*   Many researchers will try out or pilot their materials on a group of individuals similar to the eventual sample. This is done in such a way as to encourage the participants to raise questions and problems which make it difficult to complete the questionnaire. In this way, difficulties with the response format may be raised. Of course, given the small number of gradations in this sort of answer format, inevitably there may be difficulties in finally making a choice. The danger is that participants may feel forced into making arbitrary and, to them, rather meaningless choices between limited answer categories. As a consequence, they may feel alienated from the research. They may feel that the researcher is not really interested in their opinions, that the researcher is incompetent by not getting at what they really think or feel, or that there is little point in putting any effort into thinking about the issues. On the other hand, they may feel very relieved that completing the questionnaire is so simple and straightforward.

■ *Focus groups, etc.*   By using focus groups or individual interviews (see Chapter 16), the researcher may develop an understanding of the major types of response to a question. Some themes may be very common and others so rare that they only apply to a few individuals. Some of the themes may appear crucial and others totally mundane. Some may seem irrelevant to the research. Knowing the dominant responses helps the researcher identify useful pre-coded answers.

■ Often the pre-coded categories are just the invention of the researchers themselves. What they create will be influenced by the particular set of priorities for the research. The purpose of the research, the consumers of the research and the insightfulness of the researchers are among the factors which will affect what pre-coding categories are selected. There is no reason to expect pre-coding to be inferior or superior to other forms of coding simply because of this reason. The value of research can never be assessed in terms of absolute standards. Fitness for purpose should be the main criterion. Of course, to the extent that the coding categories are created prior to collecting the data, they may match the data poorly for the simple reason that they were created without reference to the data.

Researcher-imposed coding

Sometimes researchers collect data in qualitative form because it is not possible to pre-structure the response categories. For example, the researcher may feel that they cannot anticipate the nature of the data or otherwise identify the likely major issues sufficiently well to allow the pre-structuring of their research instruments. As a consequence the data are collected in a richer, fuller format which can then be used to develop a coding scheme. While this material may be 'ethnographically' coded (see Chapters 15–21 for some of the possibilities), the researcher may prefer to quantify the data. Quantification is achieved through measuring features of the data – that is, imposing coding categories and counting frequencies in the categories.

There are any number of factors which influence the nature of the coding categories developed. The following are some of the possibilities:

- The researcher's interest in a theory which strongly suggests a system of analysis.
- The research may be guided by matters of public policy or may address a politically important topic. Hence the coding categories employed need to reflect those same issues.
- The researcher is interested only in strong trends in the data so simple, very broad categories may be appropriate.
- The research task may be so big that the researchers have to employ workers to do the coding. This tends to demand simpler coding categories.
- Many coding categories do not work (i.e. produce inconsistent or unreliable results across different coders) or are virtually unusable for other reasons.

The coding schedule is a very important document, as is the coding manual. The coding schedule is the list of coding categories applied to the data in question. It is used to categorise the data. The coder would normally have this list of coding categories – usually one schedule per set of data from a participant – and the data would be coded using the schedule. Often it is advantageous to use a coding schedule which is computer friendly. This is usually achieved by using numbered squares corresponding to the various variables on the computer data spreadsheet. In some respects the coding schedule is rather like a self-completion questionnaire but it consists of a list of implied questions (does the data fit this category?) about which categories fit the data best. Usually the coding schedule is a relatively brief document which lists very simple descriptions of the coding categories.

Sometimes the person drawing-up the coding schedule is not the same person as the coder. The person doing the coding needs to be informed in detail about the meaning of the various categories on the coding schedule. To this end, the coding manual is provided which gives detailed definitions of the coding categories, examples of material which would fit into each category and examples of problematic material. There are no rules about how detailed the manual needs to be, and it may be necessary for coders to get together to resolve difficulties. The basic idea, though, is to develop a coding process which can be delegated to a variety of individuals to enable them to code identical material identically. This is an ideal, of course, and may be only partially met.

Methodologically, another ideal is that each individual's data are coded independently by a minimum of *two* coders. In this way, the patterns of agreement between coders can be assessed. This is generally known as inter-rater or inter-coder reliability. It is probably more common that two coders are used on only a sample of the material rather than all of the data. There are obvious time and expense savings in doing so. There are also disadvantages in that coders may become sloppy if they believe nobody is checking their coding. Another risk is that over the research period the meaning of the coding categories is subtly altered by the coders, but evidence of inter-coder reliability is collected only in the initial stages of the research. Obviously, it might be best if the inter-rater reliability was assessed at various stages in the coding process. However, if the checking is done early on problems can be sorted out; problems identified later on are much more difficult to correct.

Inter-rater reliability is rarely perfect. This raises the question of how disagreements between coders should be handled. The possible solution varies according to circumstances:

■ If the second coding is intended just as a reliability check, then nothing needs to be done about the disagreements. The codings supplied by the main coder may be used for the further analysis. Inter-rater reliability assessments should nevertheless be given.

■ If coders disagree then they may be required to reach agreement or a compromise whenever this arises. This might involve a revision of the coding manual in serious cases. In minor cases, it may simply be that one of the coders had made an error and the coding schedule or manual need no amendment.

■ Reaching a compromise is a social process in which one coder may be more influential than the other. Consequently, some researchers prefer to resolve disagreements by an equitable procedure. For example, coding disagreements may be resolved by a random process such as the toss of a coin. Randomisation is discussed in Chapters 7 and 11.

■ If the coding category is a rating (that is a score variable), then disagreements between raters may be dealt with by averaging. For example, the coders may be required to rate the overall anxiety level of an interviewee. Since the ratings would be scores, then operations like averaging are appropriate. If the data are simply named categories, then averaging is impossible.

14.2 Reliability and validity

Like any other form of measurement, the issues of reliability and validity apply to coding categories. Validity is a particularly problematic concept in relation to coding categories. Quite what does validity mean in this context? One could apply many of the conceptualisations of validity which were discussed in the previous chapter. Face and content validity are probably the most frequent ways of assessing the validity of coding. It is more difficult to measure things like concurrent and predictive validity since it is often hard to think of criteria against which to validate the coding categories.

The assessment of the reliability of codings is much more common that the issue of validity. Reliability of codings is actually less straightforward than for scales and measurements. The following goes some way to explaining why this is the case:

■ Where ratings (scores) are involved, the reliability of the coding is easily calculated using the correlation coefficient between the two sets of ratings. However, it is harder to establish the degree of agreement between raters on their ratings since the correlation coefficient simply shows that the two sets of ratings correlate – not that they are identical. They may correlate perfectly but both coders' ratings can be entirely different. Correlation only establishes covariance not overlap or exact agreement.

■ The percentage agreement between the two coders in terms of which coding category they use might be considered. However, there is a difficulty. This is because agreement will tend to be high for codings which are very common. The overlap between coders may largely be a consequence of the coders choosing a particular coding category frequently. Rarely used coding categories may appear to have low levels of agreement simply because the categories are so rarely chosen. Suppose two raters, for example, code whether or not people arrested by the police are drunk or not. If they both always decide that the arrestees were drunk then the agreement between the coders is perfect. But this perfect agreement is not very impressive. Far more impressive is the circumstances in which both raters rate, say, half of the arrestees as being drunk and the other half as sober. If the two raters agree perfectly, then this would be impressive evidence of the inter-rater reliability or agreement between the raters.

■ For this reason, indices which are sensitive to the frequency with which a category is checked should be chosen as they are more appropriate. Coefficient kappa (see the companion statistics book, *Introduction to Statistics in Psychology*, Howitt and Cramer, 2005*a*, Chapter 33) is one such reliability formula. Coefficient kappa is sensitive to situations in which both raters are not varying the coding categories used much or using one coding to the exclusion of the others. Coefficient kappa is available on SPSS and is discussed in Chapter 30 of the companion computing text *Introduction to SPSS in Psychology* (Howitt and Cramer, 2005*b*).

What are the requirements of a good coding schedule and manual? We have seen that a coding schedule can be construed as a questionnaire – albeit one which is addressed to the researcher and not the participant. So all of the requirements of a good set of questions on a questionnaire would be desirable, such as clarity, which might be translated as the appropriateness of the category names and language for the coder, who may not be as familiar with the aims and objectives of the research as the researchers in charge of the research, and so forth. The following are some further considerations:

■ For any variable, the number of possible coding categories may be potentially large. All other things being equal it is probably best to err in the direction of using too many categories rather than too few. As computers are almost always used nowadays in research, the computer can be used to amalgamate (collapse) categories if it later proves to be appropriate.

■ It is usual, and probably essential, to have an 'other' category for every variable since even the best set of coding categories is unlikely to be able to cope with all of the data provided. Sometimes the 'other' category becomes a dominant category in terms of coding. This is clearly unsatisfactory as it basically means that there is little clarity about many participants' data. Generally, it is best to make a brief note of the essence of data being coded in the 'other' category when that category is used – that is, the sort of material that was being coded as 'other' needs to be recorded. Later on, the 'other' category may be reviewed in order to try to identify any pattern in the other category which might justify re-coding some or all of the data. That is, it becomes apparent that certain 'themes' are very common in the 'other' category. Where the 'other' category just consists of a variety of very different material nothing needs to be done. Unfortunately, if the other category gets large then it may swamp the actual coding categories used.

■ Serious consideration should be given to whether or not any variable may be multi-coded. That is, will the coder be confined to using just one of the coding categories for each case or will they be allowed to use more than one category. Generally speaking, we would recommend avoiding multi-coding wherever possible because of the complexity it adds to the statistical analysis. For example, multi-coding may well mean that dummy variables will have to be used. Their use is not too difficult, but is nevertheless probably best avoided by novices.

- Coding categories should be conceptually coherent in themselves. While it is possible to give examples of material which would be coded into a category, this does not, in itself, ensure the coherence of the category. This is because the examples may not be good examples of the category. Hence the coder may be coding into the category on the basis of a bad example rather than that the data actually fits the category.

- The process of developing a coding schedule and coding manual is often best regarded as a drafting and revision process rather than something achieved in a single stage – trial and error might be the best description. The reason is obvious – it is difficult to anticipate the richness of the data in advance of examining the data.

14.3 Qualitative coding

The final type of coding process is that adopted in qualitative data analysis. Characteristically this form of coding seeks to develop coding categories on the basis of an intimate and detailed knowledge of the data. This is an ideal which some qualitative analyses fail to reach. For example, one finds qualitative analyses which do no more than identify a few major themes in the data.

The next section contains a number of chapters on various aspects of qualitative data analysis. Anyone wishing to carry out a qualitative analysis needs to understand its historical roots as well as some of the practicalities of qualitative analysis. Qualitative analysis is *not* any analysis which does not include statistics. Qualitative analysis has its own theoretical orientation that is highly distinctive from the dominant psychological approaches that value quantification, hypothesis testing, numbers and objectivity.

14.4 Conclusion

The process of turning real-life into research involves a number of different stages. Among the most important of these is that of coding or categorisation. All research codes reality in some way or another, the ways in which the coding is achieved varies radically. For some research, the development of the coding categories is the main purpose of the research endeavour. In other research, coding is much more routine and standardised as in self-completion questionnaires with a closed answer format. Not only are there differences in the extent and degree of elaboration of the coding process, but there are differences in terms of who does the coding. The participant does the coding in self-completion questionnaires using codes (multiple choices, etc.) developed by the researcher.

Key points

- Through coding, in quantitative research, data are structured into categories which may be quantified in the sense that frequencies of occurrence of categories and the co-occurrence of categories may be studied. In qualitative research, often the endpoint is the creation of categories which fit the detail of the data.

■ Coding is a time-consuming activity which is sometimes economised on by pre-coding the data – that is, the participants in the research are required to choose from a list of response categories. In this way, the data collection and coding phases of research are combined. This is essentially a form of quantitative data collection.

■ Coding of data collected qualitatively (that is, through in-depth interview, focus groups, etc.) may be subject to researcher-imposed coding categories which have as their main objective quantification of characteristics judged important by the researcher for pragmatic or theoretical reasons, or because they recognise that certain themes emerge commonly in their data.

■ Coding requires a coding schedule which is a sort of questionnaire with which the researcher interrogates the data in order to decide in what categories the data fit. A coding manual details how coding decisions are to be made – what the categories are, how the categories are defined and perhaps examples of the sorts of data that fit into each category.

■ Such coding, which is almost always intended for quantitative and statistical analysis, may be subjected to reliability tests by comparing the codings of two or more independent coders. This may involve the use of coefficient kappa if exact correspondence of codings needs to be assessed.

■ If the analysis is intended to remain qualitative, then the qualitative analysis procedures discussed in the chapters on Jefferson coding, conversation analysis and discourse analysis, for example, should be consulted (Chapters 17, 19 and 20). The general principles of qualitative research are that the coding or categorisation process is central and that the fit of the categories to the data and additional data is paramount.

Activities

1. Create a list of the characteristics that people say make other people sexually attractive to them. You could interview a sample to get a list of ideas. Formulate a smaller number of coding categories which effectively categorise these characteristics. Try half the number of categories as characteristics first, then half this number, until you have two or three overriding categories. What problems did you have and how did you resolve them? Is there a gender difference in the categories into which the characteristics fall?

2. Obtain a pre-coded questionnaire, work through it yourself (or use a volunteer). What were the major problems in completing the questionnaire using the pre-coded categories? What sorts of things did you feel needed to be communicated but were not because of the format?

PART 4
Qualitative research methods

15 Why qualitative research?

Overview

■ This chapter presents the essential background to doing qualitative research. It is important to understand the underlying theoretical stance common to much qualitative research before looking in detail at methods of data collection, recording and analysis.

■ Qualitative research concentrates on describing and categorising the qualities of data. In contrast, quantitative research concentrates on quantifying (giving numbers to) variables.

■ Quantitative research is often described as being based on positivism, which is regarded as the basis of the hard sciences such as physics and chemistry.

■ The search for general 'laws' of psychology (universalism) is held to stem from positivism and is generally regarded as futile from the qualitative point of view.

■ Qualitative researchers attempt to avoid some of the characteristics of positivism by concentrating on data which are much more natural.

Superficially, at least, qualitative research is totally different from quantitative research. *Qualitative* research focuses on the description of the qualities (or characteristics) of data. Probably, historically, case studies of an individual person were the most common qualitative method in psychology. By individual case study we mean the detailed description of the psychological characteristics of, usually, one person (or perhaps a single organisation). Sigmund Freud's psychoanalyses of individual patients are early examples of the case study. Other classic examples of case studies would include *The Man Who Mistook His Wife for a Hat* by Oliver W. Sacks (1985). This book includes a detailed account of how a man with neurological problems dealt with his memory and perceptual problems. Such individual case studies utilising and developing psychological theory are very different from recent qualitative approaches in psychology. Modern qualitative research generally involves a detailed study of text, speech and conversation (which generically may be termed text) – and *not* the specific psychological characteristics of interesting individuals.

Qualitative research concentrates on conversational and similar exchanges between people in interviews, the media, counselling and so forth. It is rarely, if ever, concerned with analysis at the level of individual words, phrases and sentences. It analyses broader units of text – though what the minimum unit of analysis is depends on the theoretical orientation of the qualitative analysis.

One major problem facing anyone wishing to learn to do qualitative research is that it is not fully established as being at the core of psychological research and theory. That is, one can study psychology for years, and rarely if ever come across qualitative research and theory. This may be changing. In contrast to qualitative approaches, *quantitative* research is undeniably at the centre of psychology. Indeed, quantification characterises most psychology more effectively than the subject matter of the discipline. Take virtually any introductory psychology textbook off the shelf and it is likely to consist entirely of research and theory based on quantitative research methods. References to personality tests of many sorts, intelligence quotients, ability and aptitude measures, attitude scales and similar feature heavily as do physiological measures such as blood pressure, brain rhythms, PET scans and so forth. While all of these measure qualities ascribed to the data (usually called variables in this context), they are quantified in that they are assigned numerical values or scores. The magnitude of the numerical value indicates the extent to which each individual possesses the characteristic or quality.

Probably the most famous quantitative measure in psychology is the IQ (intelligence quotient) score which assigns a (usually) single number to represent such a complex thing as a person's mental abilities. Comparisons between individuals and groups of individuals are relatively straightforward. Sometimes quantitative data are gathered directly in the form of numbers (such as when age is measured by asking a participant's age in years). Sometimes the quantification is made easy by collecting data in a form which is rapidly and easily transformed into numbers. A good example of this is the Likert attitude scale in which participants are asked to rate their agreement with a statement such as 'University fees should be abolished'. They are asked to indicate their agreement on a scale of strongly agree, agree, neutral, disagree and strongly disagree. These different indicators are assigned the numbers 1 to 5. So common are self-completion questionnaires and scales in psychological research that there is a danger of assuming that such methods are synonymous with quantitative methods and not merely examples of them.

The growth of psychology into a major academic discipline and field of practice was possible because of the growth of quantification. It is also partly responsible for psychology's closeness to scientific disciplines such as biology, physiology and medicine. Historically, many decisive moments in psychology are associated with developments which enabled quantification of the previously unquantifiable:

■ Psychophysics was an early such development which found ways of quantifying subjective perceptual experiences.

■ The intelligence test developed in France by Alfred Binet at the start of 20th century provided a means of integrating a wide variety of 19th century ideas concerning the many qualities of intellectual functioning.

■ Louis Thurstone's methods of measuring attitudes in social psychology and the more familiar methods today of Likert were methodological breakthroughs which allowed the development of empirical social psychology.

The development of a good quantitative technique encourages the development of that field of research since it facilitates further research. Examples of research fields spurred on by quantification are topics like authoritarianism, psychopathy, suggestibility and many other psychological concepts as well as, for example, the MIR (millimetre-wave imaging radiometer) scan. All of this documents a great, collective achievement. Nevertheless, the consequence has been to squeeze out other, less quantifiable, subject matter. Consequently, the history of psychology is dotted with critiques of the focus of psychological knowledge (e.g. Hepburn, 2003). Often these critiques are portrayed as 'crises' though probably the term serves the interest of the complainants better than it reflects the view of the majority of researchers and practitioners.

There is a danger of presenting quantitative and qualitative research as almost separate fields of research. This is to neglect the numerous examples of apparently quantitative research which actually include a qualitative aspect which has tended to be overlooked. Examples of this are actually quite common in the history of psychology. Even archetypal laboratory studies sometimes collected significant amounts of qualitative material (e.g. Milgram, 1974). It has to be said, though, that recent developments in qualitative methods in psychology would probably eschew this. Whatever, it is evidence of an underlying view of many psychologists that quantification alone only provides partial answers.

15.1 What is qualitative research?

So is qualitative research that which is concerned with the nature or characteristics of things? One obvious problem with this is that does not *all* research, qualitative or quantitative, seek to understand the nature and characteristics of its subject matter? Perhaps this indicates that the dichotomy between qualitative and quantitative research is more apparent than real. If the distinction is of value then it should be apparent in the relationship between qualitative and quantitative research. Immediately we explore this question, we find that several different claims are made about the interrelationship:

■ Qualitative methods are a preliminary stage in the research process which contributes to the eventual development of adequate quantification. Quantification is, in this formulation, the ultimate goal of research. There is a parallel with the physical sciences. In many disciplines (such as physics, biology and chemistry) an early stage involves observation and classification. For example, botanists collected, described and organised plants into the 'families' – groups of plants. Members of a 'family' tended to be similar to each other in terms of their characteristics and features. In chemistry, exploration of the characteristics of different elements led to them being organised into the important analysis tool – the periodic table – which allowed their characteristics to be predicted and undiscovered elements to be characterised. This was done on the basis of features such as the chemical reactivity and the electrical conductivity of elements. In many disciplines, qualitative methods (which largely involve categorisation) have led to attempts to quantify the qualities so identified. The model for this is:

Qualitative analysis → Quantitative analysis

This process is not uncommon in psychology. If we return again to the common example of intelligence testing, we can illustrate the process. During the 19th century under the influence of an Austrian, Franz Joseph Gall, the idea that different parts of the brain had different mental functions developed. Unfortunately things went wrong in some ways as one of the immediate consequences was the emergence of phrenology as a 'science'. Phrenology holds that the different parts of the brain are different organs of the mind. Furthermore, the degree of development of different parts of the brain (assessed by the size of the 'bumps' on the skull at specific locations) was believed to indicate the degree of development of that mental faculty (or mental ability). Gall believed that the degree of development was innate in individuals. The range of mental faculties included things like firmness, cautiousness, spirituality and veneration, which are difficult to define, and others like constructiveness, self-esteem and destructiveness, which have their counterparts in 20th century psychology. The point is that these mental faculties could only be suggested as a result of attempts to describe the characteristics of the mind – that is a process of categorising what was observed. Phrenology's approach to quantification was immensely crude – that is the size of different bumps. But the idea that the mind is organised into various faculties was a powerful one, and attempts to identify what they were formed the basis of the conceptualisation of intelligence, which was so influential on Alfred Binet who developed the seminal measure of intelligence. For Binet, intelligence was a variety of abilities none of which in themselves defined the broader concept of intelligence but all of which were aspects of intelligence. The idea that qualitative research is a first step to quantification is valuable but neglects the fact that the process is not entirely one way. There are many quantitative techniques (e.g. factor analysis and cluster analysis) which identify empirical patterns of interrelationships which may help develop theoretical categorisation or classification systems.

■ Qualitative methods provide a more complete understanding of the subject matter of the research. Some qualitative researchers argue that quantification fails to come to terms with or misses crucial aspects of what is being studied. Quantification encourages premature abstraction from the subject matter of research and a concentration on numbers and statistics rather than concepts. Because quantification ignores a great deal of the richness of the data, the research instruments often appear to be crude and, possibly, alienating. That is, participants in quantitative research feel that the research is not about them and may even think that the questions being asked them or tasks being set are simply stupid. Some research is frustrating since, try as the participant may, the questionnaires or other materials cannot be responded to accurately enough. They simply are not convinced that they have provided anything of value to the researcher. Of course, the phrase 'richness of data' might be regarded as a euphemism for unfocused, unstructured, unsystematic, anecdotal twaddle by the critical quantitative researcher. We will return to the issue of richness of data in subsequent chapters.

■ A more humanistic view of qualitative data is that human experience and interaction are far too complex to be reduced to a few variables as is typical in quantitative research. This sometimes is clearly the case especially when the research involves the study of topics involving interactive processes. A good example of this is when one wishes to study the detailed processes involved in conversation – there are simply no available methods for turning many of the complex processes of conversation into numbers or scores. To be sure, one could time the pauses in conversation and similar measures – but selecting a variable simply because it is easy to quantify is unsatisfactory. Choosing a measure simply because it is easy and available merely results in the researcher addressing questions other than the one they want to address. What, for example, if the researcher wants to identify the rules which govern turn taking in conversation. The subtlety of the measurements needed may mean that the researcher has no choice but to choose a qualitative approach.

As we have seen, qualitative and quantitative methods are not necessarily stark alternatives. The choice between the two is not simple nor is it always the case that one is to be preferred over the other. Often a similar topic may be tackled qualitatively or quantitatively but with rather different objectives and consequently outcomes. Some research successfully mixes the two. Many of the classic studies in some fields of psychology actually took the mixed approach though often it would not be apparent from modern descriptions of this research. Examples include Stanley Milgram's electric shock/obedience experiments (Milgram, 1974). In these cases, the two approaches are complementary and supplementary. There are certain researchers who invariably choose quantification irrespective of their research question. Equally there are other researchers who avoid quantification when it would be straightforward and appropriate. There are a number of reasons for this diversity:

■ Quantification requires a degree of understanding of the subject matter. That is, it is not wise to prematurely quantify that which one cannot describe with any accuracy.

■ Quantification may make the collection of naturalistic data difficult or impossible. Quantification (such as the use of questionnaires or the use of laboratory apparatus) by definition implies that the data are 'unnatural'. Quantified data are collected in ways which the researcher has highly structured.

■ Some researchers see flaws in quantification or qualitative research and so are attracted to the other approach.

■ Some research areas have had a long tradition of quantification which encourages the further use of quantification. Research in new areas often encourages qualitative methods because measurement techniques have not been developed or because little is known about the topic.

Apart from career quantifiers and career non-quantifiers who won't or can't employ the other method, many researchers tailor their choice of methods to the situation and, in particular, the research question involved. All researchers should have some appreciation of the strengths and weaknesses of each approach. Probably the healthiest situation is where researchers from both perspectives address similar research questions.

15.2 History of the qualitative/quantitative divide in psychology

Laboratory experiments and statistical analyses dominate the contents of most introductory textbooks in psychology. One short explanation of this is that skills in experimentation and quantitative analysis are very marketable commodities in and out of academia. Few disciplines adopted such an approach, though it had the advantage that it suggested that psychologists were detached and objective. These characteristics also tended to position psychology closely to the physical sciences. The setting-up of the psychology laboratory at Leipzig University by Wilhelm Wundt in 1879 was a crucial moment for psychologists according to psychology's historians (Howitt, 1992a). A number of famous American psychologists trained at that laboratory. Wundt, however, did not believe that the laboratory was the place for all psychological research. He regarded the laboratory as a hapless context to study matters related to culture. Nevertheless, the psychological laboratory was regarded as the dominant icon of psychology.

The term *positivism* dominates the quantitative–qualitative debate. Some use it as a pejorative term though it is a word which, seemingly, is often misunderstood. For example, some writers appear to imply that positivism equals statistics. It does not. Positivism is a particular epistemological position. Epistemology is the study of, or theory of, knowledge. It is concerned with the methodology of knowledge (how we go about knowing things) and the validation of knowledge (the value of what we learn). Prior to the emergence of positivism during the 19th century, two methods of obtaining knowledge dominated:

■ *Theism*, which held that knowledge was grounded in religion which enabled us to know because truth and knowledge were revealed spiritually. Most religious texts contain explanations and descriptions of the nature of the universe, morality and social order. While these are matters studied by psychologists, there is little in modern psychology which could be conceived as being based on theism.

■ *Metaphysics*, which held that knowledge was about the nature of our being in the world and was revealed through theoretical philosophising. Relatively little psychology is based on this.

Neither theism nor metaphysics have retained their historical importance. Religious knowledge was central throughout the history of civilisation. Only recently has its pre-eminence faltered. Metaphysics had only a brief period of ascendancy during the period of the Enlightenment (18th century) when reason and individualism were emphasised. Positivism is the third major method of epistemology and directly confronts theism and metaphysics as methods of achieving knowledge. Positivism was first articulated in the philosophy of Auguste Comte in the 19th century in France. He stressed the importance of observable (and observed) facts in the valid accumulation of knowledge. It is a small step from this to appreciating how positivism is the basis of the scientific method in general. More importantly in this context, positivism is at the root of so-called scientific psychology.

It should be stressed that positivism applies equally to quantitative methods and to qualitative research methods. It is *not* the province of quantitative psychology alone. There is very little work in either quantitative or qualitative psychology which does not rely on the collection of observed information in some way. Possibly just as a fish probably does not realise that it is swimming in water, qualitative researchers often fail to recognise positivism as the epistemological basis of their work. Silverman (1997) makes a number of points which contradict the orthodox qualitative research view of positivism:

> *Unfortunately, 'positivism' is a very slippery and emotive term. Not only is it difficult to define but there are very few quantitative researchers who would accept the label . . . Instead, most quantitative researchers would argue that they do not aim to produce a science of laws (like physics) but simply to produce a set of cumulative, theoretically defined generalizations deriving from the critical sifting of data. So, it became increasingly clear that 'positivists' were made of straw since very few researchers could be found who equated the social and natural worlds or who believed that research was properly theory-free.* [pp. 12–13]

The final sentence is very important. It highlights the difficulty which is that, although positivism stresses the crucial nature of observation, it is the end point or purpose of the observation which is contentious. The real complaint about positivism is that it operates as if there were permanent, unchanging truths to be found. That is, underlying our experiences of the world are consistent, lawful and unchanging principles. The phrase 'the laws of psychology' reflects this universality. The equivalent phrases in the natural sciences are ones like 'the laws of planetary motion', 'the laws of thermodynamics, 'the inverse square law of light', that $e = mc^2$ and so forth. These physical laws are believed to be universally applicable and apply no matter where in the universe. The trouble is that universalism encourages psychologists to seek principles of human nature in, say, New York which they would then apply unchanged in Addis Ababa, Beijing or Cairo – and equally in 1850 as in 2050.

There were psychologists who were very important in their time who operated more or less according to the positivist maxims and the quest for the laws of human activity in particular. These were members of the Behaviourist School of Psychology which dominated much psychology between the 1920s and the 1960s and beyond. Virtually everything they did reeked of the quest for general laws of psychology. First of all, they argued the basic positivistic position that knowledge comes from observation. So they stressed that psychology should study the links between the incoming stimulus and the outgoing response. There was no point in studying what could not be tested directly through observation. They were primarily interested in the experimental method. If one is seeking universal principles of human behaviour then these should apply in the psychology laboratory just as much as anywhere else. Since the laboratory had other advantages, then why not study human psychology exclusively in such laboratories? They went so far as to wear white coats in the laboratory to emulate scientists from the physical sciences – probably more to enhance their stature by association than because of any direct practical advantage. Famous names in behavioural psychology are B. F. Skinner, Clark Hull and John Watson, the founder of behaviourism.

Realism would be a term applied to positivism of this sort (i.e. there is a reality which research is trying to tap into). *Subjectivism* would take the view that there is no reality to be grasped and in Trochim's (2002) phrase 'we're each making this all up'. Since most psychologists nowadays would not accept the view that universal laws of human psychology are possible or desirable, some would argue that psychology is currently in a *post-positivist* stage. Post-modernism has virtually the same meaning in this context. Psychology's allegiance is still to the importance of observation. However, its aspirations of what knowledge is possible have changed. Probably the failure of the out-and-out positivists to come up with anything which constitutes a worthwhile general law of psychology has led to the present situation. Silverman (1997), in the above quotation, characterises the quest of many modern researchers as being for 'cumulative, theoretically defined generalisations deriving from the critical sifting of data'. Perhaps psychologists, more than some other disciplines, remain inclined towards gross, decontextualised generalisations. They write as if the statements they make concerning their research findings apply way beyond the context in which they were studied. Owusu-Bempah and Howitt (2000) are among a number of writers who point out that such a tendency makes psychology practically unworkable beyond limited Western populations, incapable of working with the cultural diversity to be found within modern Western communities.

Qualitative researchers tend to regard the search for the nature of reality as a futile quest. *Critical realism* is the philosophy that can be summed up as accepting that there is a 'reality' out there but we can at best view it through an infinite regress of windows. That is, there is always yet another window that we are looking through and that each window distorts reality in some way. While this implies that there will always be different views of reality depending on which particular window we are looking through, the major problem is the degree of distortion that we are experiencing. Some qualitative analysts will point to the fact that much research in psychology and the social sciences relies on data in the form of language. Language, however, they say, is not reality but just a window on reality. Furthermore, different speakers will give a different view of reality. They conclude that the search for reality is a hopeless task and – to push the metaphor beyond the bounds of endurance – that we should just study the diversity of what is seen through the different windows. Well, that is one approach but not the only one based on critical realism (which only demands that researchers try to get close to reality while realising that they can never achieve that goal). Every method of measuring reality is fallible, but if we use many different measures and they concur, then maybe we are getting towards our goal. One of the reasons why our data are problematic is that our observations are theory laden. That is, the observer comes to the observation with baggage and expectations. That baggage will include our culture, our vested interests and our general perspective on life, for example. Psychologists are not born with the ability to see the world without the windows. One strategy to overcome our preconceptions is to throw our observations before others for their critical response as part of the process of analysing our observations.

As we have seen, there is no justification for some of the characteristics attributed to positivism. As we explained, some critiques of mainstream psychology labour under the impression that positivism equates to statistical analysis. Yet some of the most important figures in positivistic psychology such as Skinner had little or no time for statistics and did not use them in their work. The use, or not, of statistics does not make for positivism. Similarly, atheoretical empiricism – virtually the collection and analysis of data for their own sake – has nothing to do with positivism which is about knowing the world rather than accumulating data as such.

15.3 The quantification–qualitative methods continuum

The conventional rigid dichotomy of quantitative–qualitative methodologies is inadequate to differentiate different types of research. It implies that research inevitably falls into one or other of these apparently neat boxes. This is not necessarily the case. There is some research which is purely quantitative and other research which is purely qualitative. However, this is to neglect much research that draws on both. Conceptually, research may be differentiated into two major stages:

■ data collection
■ data analysis.

Of course there are other stages but these are the important ones for now.

At the *data collection stage*, there is a range of possibilities. The degree of quantification (assigning of numbers or scores) and qualification (collecting data in terms of rich detail) may vary:

■ *Pure quantitative* The data are collected using highly structured materials (such as multiple-choice questionnaires or physiological indexes such as blood pressure levels) in relatively highly structured settings (such as the psychological laboratory). A good example of such a study would one in which the levels of psychoticism (measured using a self-completion question) in sex offenders versus violent offenders (as assessed by their current conviction).

■ *Pure qualitative*   The data are collected to be as full and complete a picture as the researcher can possibly make it. This is done, for example, by video or tape recording extensive amounts of conversation (say between a counsellor and client). There may be no structuring to the data gathered than that, though sometimes the researcher might choose to interview participants in an open-ended manner. Many qualitative researchers try to use as much naturalistic material as possible.

■ *Mixed data collection*   Between these extremes of quantification and qualitative data gathering are many intermediary possibilities. Some researchers choose to collect data in a quantitative form where there are good means of quantifying variables and concepts but use open-ended and less structured material where the concepts and variables cannot be measured satisfactorily for some reason. Sometimes the researcher will use a mixture of multiple-choice type questions with open-ended questions which may help paint a fuller picture of the data.

However, we ought also to consider the *data analysis stage* of research in terms of the qualitative–quantitative distinction. The same options are available to us:

■ *Pure quantification*   If data have been collected solely in quantitative form, then there is little option but to analyse the data quantitatively. However, data may have been collected in qualitative form but the researcher wishes to quantify a number of variables or create scores based on the qualitative data. The commonest method of doing this is through a process known as coding (see Chapter 14). In this the researcher develops a categorisation (coding) scheme either based on pre-existing theoretical and conceptual considerations, or develops a categorisation system based on examining the data. This can involve the researcher rating the material on certain characteristics. For example, a global assessment of a participant's hostility to global environmental issues may be obtained by having the researcher rate each participant on a scale. Usually another rater will also independently rate the participant on the same rating scale and the correspondence between the ratings assessed (inter-rater reliability).

■ *Pure qualitative*   This option is generally only available if the data have been collected in qualitative form (quantitative data are rarely suitable for qualitative analysis, for obvious reasons). Quite what the qualitative analysis should be depends to a degree on the purpose of the research. As conversation (interviews or otherwise) are a common source of qualitative data, then discourse analysis and/or conversation analysis may be helpful. But this is a complex issue, which may best be left until qualitative methods have been studied in a little more depth.

■ *Mixed data analysis*   This may follow from mixed data collection but equally may be the result of applying qualitative and quantitative methods to qualitative data. This is quite a common approach though it is often fairly informally applied. That is, the researcher often has a primarily quantitative approach which is extended, illustrated or explicated using simple qualitative methods. For example, the researcher may give illustrative quotations from the open-ended material that is collected in addition to the more quantitative main body of the data. Such approaches are unlikely to satisfy the more demanding qualitative researcher.

The main points to emerge out of this is that we should distinguish data collection from data analysis and appreciate that quantitative and qualitative methods may be applied at either stage – this is summarised in Table 15.1.

Table 15.1 Varieties of data collection and analysis

	Quantitative data collection		Quantitative data collection	
quantitative data analysis	generally qualitative analysis not possible but some qualitative researchers suggest it sometimes is		quantitative data analysis	qualitative data analysis

15.4 Evaluation of qualitative versus quantitative methods

Denzin and Lincoln (2000) claim that there are five major features distinguishing quantitative from qualitative research *styles*. Some of these have already been touched on already in this chapter but they are worth reiterating systematically:

■ *Use of positivism and post-positivism*   Quantitative and qualitative methods are both based on positivism and many qualitative researchers have applied 'positivist ideals' to messy data. However, qualitative researchers are much more willing to accept the *post-positivist* position that whatever reality there is that might be studied, our knowledge of it can only ever be approximate and never exact. In their actions, quantitative researchers tend to reflect the view that there is a reality that can be captured despite all of the problems. Language data would be regarded by them as reflecting reality whereas the qualitative researcher would take the view that language is incapable of representing reality. Quantitative researchers often treat reality as a system of causes and effects and often appear to regard the quest of research as being generalisable knowledge.

■ *Qualitative researchers accept other features of the postmodern sensibility*   This really refers to a whole range of matters which the traditional quantitative researcher largely eschewed. Examples of this include verisimilitude, in that the researcher studies things which appear to be real rather than the synthetic product of psychology laboratories for example. The qualitative researcher is represented as having an ethic of caring as well as political action and dialogue with participants in the research. The qualitative researcher has a sense of personal responsibility for their actions and activities.

■ *Capturing the individual's point of view*   Through the use of in-depth observation and interviewing the qualitative researcher believes that the remoteness of the research from its subject matter (people) as found in some quantitative research may be overcome.

■ *Concern with the richness of description*   Quite simply qualitative researchers value rich description almost for its own sake, whereas quantitative researchers find that such a level of detail actually makes generalisation much more difficult.

■ *Examination of the constraints of everyday life*   It is argued that quantitative researchers may fail to appreciate the characteristics of the day-to-day social world which then become irrelevant to their findings. On the other hand, being much more wedded in society through their style of research, qualitative researchers tend to have their 'feet on the ground' more.

Probably the majority of these claims would be disputed by most quantitative researchers. For example, the belief that qualitative research is subjective and impressionistic would suggest the lack of grounding of qualitative research in society, not higher levels of it.

The choice between quantitative and qualitative methods when carrying out psychological research is not an easy one to make. The range of considerations is enormous. Sometimes the decision will depend as much on the particular circumstances of the research, such as the resources available, as on profound philosophical debates about the nature of psychological research.

When to use quantification

The circumstances in which quantification is most appropriate include the following:

- When addressing very clearly specified research questions.
- When there is a substantial body of good quality theory from which hypotheses can be derived and tested.
- In addressing research questions for which there is high quality research which has typically employed quantification.
- When it can be shown that there are very satisfactory means of collecting information using measures.
- When the researcher has good understanding of quantitative methods combined with a lack of interest or knowledge concerning qualitative methods.

When to use qualitative research methods

A researcher might consider using qualitative research methods in the following circumstances:

- When the researcher wishes to study the complexity of something in its natural setting.
- When there is a lack of clarity about what research questions should be asked and what the key theoretical issues are.
- When there is generally little or no research into the topic.
- When the research question relates to the complex use of language, such as in extended conversation or other textual material.
- When the researcher has read qualitative research in some depth.
- Where the use of structured materials, such as multiple-choice questionnaires, may discourage individuals from participating in the research.

15.5 Conclusion

The divide between quantitative and qualitative research is not easy to cross. In many ways there are two cultures in psychology and often they are seeking answers to radically different sorts of questions. However, there is more to it than that since if there were simply two camps of psychologists – quantitative and qualitative – who just do totally different things then that would be fine. After all, specialities within psychology are very common. It is virtually unknown to come across psychologists who are well versed in more than a couple of sub-disciplines of psychology. Where it seems an unsatisfactory situation to have quantitative and qualitative camps is in so far as psychologists should be interested in the topic of research and not be straitjacketed within methods. So our preference is for *all* psychologists to have the choice of approaches from which to select when planning their research. This is a convoluted way of saying that the research problem should have primacy. The best possible answer to the question that the researcher is raising cannot lie in any particular method.

This and the next few chapters are our modest answer to uniting the quantitative and qualitative camps in a joint enterprise, not a battle.

Key points

- Qualitative research, especially in the form of case studies, has been a significant but relatively minor aspect in the history of psychological methods. Nowadays, interest in qualitative methods has increased especially in terms of the analysis of language based data such as conversations, media content and interviews.

- Advances in quantification, nevertheless, have often been significant foci of new psychological research.

- Qualitative research can be regarded as a prior stage to quantitative research. However, there are research questions which are difficult to quantify especially with complex processes such as conversation.

- Positivism is a philosophical position on how knowledge can be obtained which is different from theism (religious basis of knowledge) and metaphysics (knowledge comes from reflecting on issues). Positivism required an empiricist (observational) grounding for knowledge. However, it became equated with relatively crude and quantified methods. Qualitative researchers often overlook their allegiance to positivism.

- Quantification may be applied to data collection or data analysis. Research data collected through the 'rich' methods may be quantified for analysis purposes. Whether or not this is appropriate depends on circumstances.

Activity

Many psychology students are unfamiliar with examples of qualitative research. Qualitative research needs a positive orientation and a great deal of reading. So now is the time to start. Spend half an hour in the library looking through likely psychology journals for examples to study. Failing that,

MacMartin, C. and Yarmey, A. D. (1998). 'Repression, dissociation, and the recovered memory debate: Constructing scientific evidence and expertise', *Expert Evidence*, 6, 203–26

is an excellent example which crosses a range of issues relevant to the work of many psychologists.

16 Qualitative data collection

Overview

■ The commonest qualitative data collection methods are probably the in-depth interview, participant observation and focus groups. These are discussed in this chapter to illustrate the range of concerns of qualitative analysts.

■ Virtually all qualitative approaches to data collection have an equivalent structured approach. For example, in-depth or semi-structured interviews may be compared with the structured interview common in market research.

■ Qualitative data may, in appropriate circumstances, be analysed quantitatively or qualitatively depending on the objectives of the researcher and the characteristics of the data. Qualitative data collection should not be confused with qualitative data analysis.

■ Aspects of observation, focus groups and interviewing as means of collecting qualitative data are presented.

Qualitative data collection is not necessarily followed by qualitative data analysis. Qualitatively collected data may be analysed, sometimes, quantitatively. Qualitative data collection methods essentially provide extensive, detailed and 'rich' data for later analysis. Nevertheless, the primary purpose of the analysis is to turn the complexity of the data into relatively structured numerical analyses. At first sight this may seem a little pointless since we know that researchers often collect data in quantitative form so why bother with qualitative data collection if the analysis is to be quantitative? However, there are circumstances in which it is simply impossible, or undesirable, to collect data quantitatively prior to quantitative analysis:

■ It is difficult to design, for example, a self-completion questionnaire which will effectively collect a biographical record of an individual or capture the detail of a complex sequence of events.

■ There may be factors that militate against some individuals supplying quantitative data. For example, a researcher wishing to collect accounts of the experience of depression from seriously depressed individuals may find greater success through giving the participants attention by interviewing them than by sending them a questionnaire though the post. Some individuals may not have the intellectual resources or even the writing and reading skills to complete a self-completion question. It would be silly, for example, to carry out research into illiteracy through a questionnaire.

■ The researchers may not have sufficient familiarity with the research topic to enable effective structuring of quantitative materials. They may have chosen an entirely novel area of research, for example, so they cannot draw ideas from previous researchers. Some researchers will collect data qualitatively since this allows a degree of exploration of the topic with the participants. Interviews and similar techniques may be part of an exploration process.

The range of methods by which appropriate data for qualitative studies may be obtained is wide. Indeed, any data that are 'rich and detailed' rather than 'abstracted and highly structured' may be candidates for qualitative analysis. Some of the more familiar data collection methods for qualitative analysis include:

■ Observation: relatively unstructured observation and participation would be typical examples. Observation that involves just a few restricted ratings would probably not be appropriate.

■ Biographies (or narratives) which are accounts of people's lives or aspects of the lives.

■ Focus groups.

■ In-depth interviews.

■ Recordings of conversations.

■ Mass media output.

■ Documentary and historical records.

Often qualitative analysis uses material from a range of different types of methods. The material, in general, is overwhelmingly textual. Observations, for example, will be recorded in words. This does not mean that other forms of material (including the visual) cannot be used, but as, in effect, these are transformed into words, then the dominance of words or text is obvious. It is not the broad method by which the data are collected which determines whether the data collected are suitable for qualitative analysis. For example, interviews may be used to collect quantitative data only or they may be used to collect qualitative data. It is the detail, expansiveness and richness of the data that determine their suitability for qualitative analysis. Imagine that researchers wish to study violence in television programmes. They might consider two alternatives:

■ They could count the number of acts of violence which occur in a sample of television programmes. The relative frequency of such violence in different types of television programmes (e.g. children's programmes or imported programmes) could be assessed as part of this.

■ Episodes of violence on television could be videotaped, transcribed and described in prolific detail.

The first version of the research is clearly quantitative as all that has happened is that a total of a certain category of content has been obtained. The second version of the research appears to be much more amenable to qualitative analysis strategies. It is the richness of the detail which makes the difference. The researchers may be studying exactly the same television programmes in both cases, but the nature of the data obtained is radically different. The qualitative research approach might allow the researcher to say much more about the context of the violence. However, without counting, the number of violent episodes cannot be assessed.

Generally speaking, although the quality of the research data is of paramount importance, what the best data are depends on a range of factors. These include, for example, the precise nature of the research questions, the nature of participants, the stage of the development of that particular field, the researcher' personal preferences and the resources available, among many other considerations.

16.1   Major qualitative data collection approaches

The key feature of qualitative data is encapsulated in the phrase 'richness of data'. But, as we have seen, there are many associated characteristics, such as unstructured data collection, extensive and interactive textual material, such as that collected in some interviews, the talk of politicians and so forth. Richness does not necessarily relate to interesting or similar ideas. Some qualitative researchers actually like dull, mundane material as this challenges their analytic skills greatly. The range of qualitative data collection methods (and sources of qualitative data) is remarkable. Consequently, it is only possible to give a few examples of the dominant approaches taken to qualitative data collection. We will concentrate on participant observation, focus groups and interviews.

Method 1: Participant observation

Participant observation would seem to offer the opportunity to gather the richly detailed data that qualitative researchers seek. Its origins are usually attributed to the work of the so-called Chicago School of Sociology, starting in the 1920s. The key aim of participant observation is to describe and explain the social world from the point of view of the actors or participants in that world. By being a participant and not just an observer, access to the point of view of the participant is assured. According to Bryman (2001), the major characteristics of participant observation are:

■ The researcher is 'immersed in a social setting' (p. 163) for a considerable period of time. The social setting could be, for example, an informal social group, an organisation or a community.

■ The researcher observes the behaviours of members in that social setting.

■ The researcher attempts to accurately record activity within that setting.

■ The researcher seeks to identify the 'meanings' that members of that setting give to the social environment within which they operate and the behaviour of people within that setting.

In some disciplines, participant observation has been the most central research tool. Observational research into human social activity is an evident feature of several centuries of cultural or social anthropology. Eventually the method was extended to include the researcher's own culture (especially by sociologists).

Stereotypically, the cultural anthropologist is a committed researcher who spends years living and working among an aboriginal group isolated from Western culture. The researcher is, therefore, most definitely an alien to the aboriginal culture – a fact which is regarded as part of the strength of the method. After all, it is hard to recognise the distinctive characteristics of routine parts of our lives. This anthropological approach has occasionally found some resonance with psychology. For example, Margaret Mead's *Coming of Age in Samoa* (1944) argued that adolescence is not always a period of upset, rebellion and conflict as it is characterised in Western cultures. It would appear that societies which do not have the West's rigid separation of childhood and adulthood may avoid the typical Western pattern of the adolescent in turmoil; though the adequacy of Mead's study has been questioned.

The term *participant observation* is a blanket term for a variety of related approaches. There are a number of important dimensions which identify the different forms of participant observation (M. Dereshiwsky, 1999 web pages; also based on Patton, 1986):

■ *The observer's role in the setting* Some observers are best described as outsiders with little involvement in the group dynamics whereas others are full members of the group.

■ *The group's knowledge of observation process* Overt observation is when the participants know that they are being observed and by whom. Covert observation is when the participants in the study do *not* know that they are being observed and, obviously, cannot know by whom they are being observed.

■ *Explication of the study's purpose* This is more than a single dimension and may fall into at least one of the following categories:

   – There is a full explanation given as to the purpose of the research prior to starting the research.
   – Partial explanation means that the participants have some idea of the purpose of the study but this is less than complete for some reason.
   – There is no explanation of the study's purpose because the observation is covert.
   – There is a misleading or false explanation as to the purpose of the study.

■ *Length* The observation may be a single session of a very limited length (e.g. a single session of one hour) or there may be multiple observation sessions of considerable length which may continue for weeks or years.

■ *Focus* The researcher may focus very narrowly on a single aspect of the situation; there may be an 'expanded' focus on a lengthy but nevertheless predetermined list of variables; there may be a holistic or 'rich data' approach which involves the observation of a wide variety of aspects in depth.

It is very difficult to set out the minimum requirements for a participant observation study. For example, what is required to justify the observation being described as a *participant* observation? Participant observation is uncommon in psychological research though it is frequently a topic for research methods modules – and textbooks. One of its major difficulties as a means of psychological research lies in its frequent dependency on the observations of a single individual. That is, participant observation may be accused of subjectivity because it is dependent on uncorroborated observations. It would be regarded as more objective if the strength of the agreement between different participant observers could be established, which is rarely the case.

Method 2: Focus groups

In some respects, focus groups are like the daytime television discussion shows in which the presenter throws in a few issues and questions, and the audience debates them amongst themselves. It is the dynamic quality of the focus group situation which differentiates it from interviews and is the main advantage of the method. Focus groups generate data which are patently the product of a group situation and so may, to some extent, generate different findings from individual interviews. Focus groups originated in the work of the famous sociologist Robert Merton when he researched the effectiveness of propaganda using a method he termed *focused interviewing* (Merton and Kendall, 1946). In subsequent decades it was taken up by advertising and market researchers. Focus groups allowed the researcher to concentrate on matters which market research interviews fail to assess adequately. In recent years, researchers have increasingly regarded focus groups as a means of generating ideas and understanding, especially for new research topics, perhaps prior to another more quantitative approach. In effect, the members of the focus group are given the task of making sense of the issue. This is achieved through the group dynamics – that is, through the relatively normal processes of discussion and debate among ordinary people. This is very difficult to achieve through conventional interviewing techniques involving a single interviewee.

Focus groups may be used in at least three different ways:

■ As an early stage of research in order to explore and identify what the significant issues are.

■ To generate broadly conversational data on a topic to be analysed in its own right.

■ To evaluate the findings of research in the eyes of the people that the research is about. That is, discussion of research conclusions.

For the researcher, the focus group has other advantages; that is, most of the resources come from the participants. The researcher generally 'facilitates' the group processes in order to ensure that a pre-planned range of issues is covered but at the same time allowing unexpected material to enter the discussion. So, ideally, the researcher does not dominate the proceedings. If necessary, the researcher steers the discussion along more productive lines if the group seems to be 'running out of steam'. The researcher running the focus group is known as the moderator or the facilitator.

In order to organise focus group research effectively, the following need some consideration:

■ Allow up to about two hours running time for a focus group. Short running times may indicate an unsatisfactory methodology.

■ A single focus group is rarely if ever sufficient even if the group seems very product-ive in terms of ideas and discussion. The researcher will need to run several groups in order to ensure that a good range of viewpoints has been covered. It is difficult to say just how many groups without some knowledge of the purpose of the research. Indeed, the researcher may consider running groups until it appears that nothing new is emerging. In a sense this is subjective, but it is also practical within the ethos of qualitative methodology.

■ The size of a focus group is important. If there are too many participants some will be inhibited from talking or unable to find the opportunity to participate; too few and the stimulation of a limited range of viewpoints will risk stultifying the proceedings. Generally it appears that the ideal is six to ten individuals, though this is not a rule.

■ Participants in focus groups are not intended to be representative of anything other than variety. They should be chosen in order to maximise the productivity of the discussion. This is, of course, a matter of judgement which will get better with experience in focus group methodology. However, Gibbs (1997) offers the following practical advice, which is worthwhile considering:

 – Don't tell focus group members too much in advance of the meeting. If you do then the risk is that they will figure out their own particular thoughts and attitudes on the topic of the focus group – and consequently they may be unresponsive to the input of others in the group.
 – Unless there is a very good reason for doing otherwise, ensure that the focus group members are strangers to each other prior to the meeting.
 – Focus group members should generally be varied (heterogeneous) in terms of obvious factors. That is, they should vary in educational level, race and ethnicity, gender and social economic status. However, it should be appreciated that some of these factors in some circumstances may be inhibitory. For example, a discussion of race may be affected by having different races present.

The tasks of the focus group moderator include (Gibbs, 1997):

■ Explaining the purpose and objectives of the focus group session.
■ Creating a positive experience for the group members and making them feel comfortable in the situation.
■ Prompting discussion by posing questions that may open up the debate or by focusing on an issue.
■ Enabling participation by all members of the group.
■ Highlighting differences in perspective between people so that they are encouraged to engage in the nature of this difference in the discussion.
■ Stopping conversational drifts from the point of the topic of the focus group.

Amongst the characteristics required of the focus group moderator are:

■ The ability *not* to appear judgemental.
■ *Not* expressing personal opinions.

It is nonsensical to evaluate a focus group in the same terms as, say, an individual interview. A focus group is not intended to be a convenient substitute for the individual interview and cannot compete with it in all respects. In particular, focus groups cannot be used to estimate population characteristics. Any attempt to use focus group data as indicative of the typical attitudes, beliefs or opinions of people in general is mistaken. Focus groups do not involve, say, random sampling from the population so they are not indicative of population characteristics. Focus groups have a number of disadvantages which mean that they should not be undertaken without clear reasons:

■ They take a great deal of time and effort to organise, run and transcribe. For example, bringing a group of strangers together is logistically not always straightforward.

■ The focus group takes away power from the researcher to direct the research process and the sorts of data collected. Consequently, it is difficult to imagine a profitable use of the focus group as a method of collecting data for the typical laboratory experiment.

Among the advantages of the focus group is the motivation aroused in the participants simply through being in a group situation. The participant is not a somewhat alienated individual filling in a rather tedious questionnaire in isolation. Instead the participant is a member of a group being stimulated by other members of the group. So the experience is social, interesting and to a degree fun. Furthermore, membership of a focus group can be, in itself, empowering. Members of a focus group are given a voice to, perhaps, communicate to the management of their organisation via the focus group and the researcher.

The analysis of focus group data may follow a number of routes. The route chosen will largely be dependent on why the focus group approach was selected for data collection. If the focus group is largely to generate ideas for further research or as a preliminary to more structured research, the researcher may be satisfied simply by listing the major and significant themes emerging in the focus group discussions. On the other hand, the focus group may have served as a means of generating verbal data for detailed textual analysis of some sort. Detailed data analysis of this sort requires transcriptions to be made of the group discussion from the audio or video tape. The Jefferson transcription system (Chapter 17), for example, may be appropriate in many cases. However, the level of detail recorded in Jefferson transcription may be too much for some research purposes. Appropriately transcribed data may be analysed using the broad principles of grounded theory, conversation analysis or discourse analysis in particular (see Chapters 18–20). Of these, grounded theory analysis may suit more researchers than the other more specific approaches. In other words, the analysis, as ever, needs to be tailored to the purpose of the research.

Method 3: Interviews

The interview is a very diverse situation with very little evidence of a common strategy being used by the majority of researchers. Our short coverage can only give some indication of the range of activities that constitute the interview. Interviews can be highly structured (little different in many ways from a self-completion questionnaire). These would be known as structured interviews. Alternatively, interviews may be unstructured such that emerging issues can be explored rather than questions asked and answers recorded. These are qualitative interviews.

Structured interviews

Market research interviewers are everywhere – in the streets, on our phones, etc. Few of us have not been subjected to their questions. Characteristically the questions are highly structured and a range of response alternatives provided from which we choose. The interviewer mostly tries to stick to the 'script' of the questionnaire. Such interviews have a number of advantages so far as the researcher is concerned:

■ Since the interviewers have quotas of persons to interview, the approach ensures satisfactory numbers of completed questionnaires are obtained. There is usually little or nothing in the interview that could not have been achieved by the questionnaire being completed by the interviewee alone.

■ Probably the main reason why interviews are used is that the participants are recruited on the spot. Mailing questionnaires to a sample of people is likely to result in derisory return rates and derisory sample sizes as a consequences.

■ The pre-coded, multiple choice format allows quick computer analyses of the data.

■ The process is quick and it is perfectly feasible to plan research and have some sort of report ready for clients in a very short period of time – even just a few days.

Variants on structured interviewing are employed by academic researchers, and the strengths and weaknesses remain much the same. Nevertheless, if the structured approach is adequate for the purposes of one's research, then it should be considered if only for reasons of economy.

In-depth interviews

Sometimes also referred to as semi-structured interviews, these reverse the principles of the structured interview. Consequently, the qualitative ethos pervades research using such interviews. Some researchers are attracted to in-depth interviews because of their conversational characteristics. However, it is very misguided to regard them in normal conversational terms. They are a highly specialised form of conversation which occur in a very different context from normal conversation. For one thing, they are intended to be much more one sided in terms of input. That is, the rule is that the interviewee is talking about themselves whereas the interviewer will spend little or no time doing this. Most conversation taxes neither of the participants. In-depth interviews are likely to be difficult for interviewee and interviewer. The interviewee will be pressed on detail about matters beyond what is normal in everyday conversation. The interviewer will have prepared extensively for the interview – in addition the interviewer of necessity must absorb a lot of information during the course of the interview in order to effectively question and probe. Having a tape recorder does not do away with this demand since the recording cannot be referred to during the course of the interview. In other words, one should expect in-depth interview to be taxing. Table 16.1 extends the comparison of structured interviewing and qualitative interviewing (drawing on Bryman and Bell, 2003).

Almost invariably, the interviewer in qualitative interviewing will have at the minimum the skeleton of the interview in the form of a list of topics or questions to be covered. This is known as the *interview guide*. The guide may be added to as the researcher interviews more participants and becomes aware of issues which could not or had not been anticipated at the start of the research. The guide is often little more than a memory aid which gives the basics of what the researcher intends to cover and probably is a poor reflection of the contents of the interviews themselves. This is only to be expected if the ideals of qualitative research are met by the researcher. That is, the topics are partially formulated by the participant, the enterprise is very exploratory, and rich detail (which by definition is not routine) is the aim. Experienced researchers will probably refer very little to the interview guide – perhaps only using it as a check at the end of the interview in order to ensure that the major issues have been covered.

Certain considerations need to be addressed in preparing the interview guide:

■ The researcher may wish to record some routine, basic information in a simple structured form. Matters such as the participant's age, gender, qualifications, job and so forth may be dealt with by using a simple standardised list of answer categories – e.g. the highest level of academic qualification obtained.

■ The formulation of questions and topics should not simply be a list of obvious questions or questions included because the replies *just might* be interesting. The questions need to be developed in terms of the requirements of the research. Just what sorts of information would help the researcher address what they regard as the important things about the research topic? The interview guide may need modifying part-way through the research to take account of things learnt during the earlier interviews.

Table 16.1 Structured and qualitative interviewing contrasted

Structured interview	Qualitative interview
Researcher has highly specific and well formulated questions that require answers.	The researcher has a less clear agenda in terms of content and the agenda is less clearly researcher led.
The format allows ready assessment of reliability and validity.	Reliability and validity are rather problematic or complex concepts in this context.
The research addresses concerns that emerge from the status of the researcher – which has research based knowledge and theory as part of the components.	The research normally is led in part by the agenda of concerns as felt by the participant. The researcher has a broader agenda which accommodates this.
Participants are 'forced' to stick to the point and there is little or no scope for them to express idiosyncratic points of view. Sometimes token questions such as 'Is there anything that you think should be mentioned but has not been?' are appended.	According to some, rambling accounts are to be encouraged in qualitative interviewing as this pushes the data far wider than the researcher may have anticipated.
Structured interviews allow little or no departure of the interviewer from the questionnaire in the interests of standardisation.	Qualitative interviewers expect to rephrase questions appropriately, formulate new questions and probes in response to what occurs in the interview, and generally to engage in a relatively relaxed approach to standardisation.
Inflexible	Flexible
Answers generated are supposed to be readily and quickly coded with the minimum of labour.	The researcher is looking for rich and detailed answers which result in extensive and labour intensive coding processes (e.g. see Chapter 18 on grounded theory).
Repeat interviewing is rare except in longitudinal studies in which participants may be interviewed on a number of separate occasions.	Repeat interviewing is not uncommon since it allows the researcher to 'regroup' – to reformulate their ideas during the course of the research. Checking and gathering data that had previously been omitted from the first interview, etc. are among these characteristics.

■ The questions or topics should be structured in a sensible and helpful order. This makes them easier for the interviewer and interviewee to deal with. There is a lot of memory work or other thinking for both participants so a logical structure is important.

■ Frame the interview schedule using the appropriate language for the participant group. Children will require different language from adults, for example. However, this is also true for adult groups. What is appropriate may not be known to the researcher without talking to members of that group or without piloting the methodology.

If in-depth interviewing sounds easy then the point has been missed. This is probably best illustrated by asking what the researcher is actually doing when conducting the interview. We can begin by suggesting what they do *not* do:

■ The researcher is *not* taking detailed notes. A high quality tape recording or video recording of the interview is the main record. Some researchers may make simple notes but this is not a requisite of the sort that the recording is. These notes are more useful as a memory aid during the course of the interview rather than as data for future analysis. It is very easy to be overawed by the interview situation and forget one's place in the schedule or forget what has been said.

So what is the interviewer doing? The following are the ideal from the perspective of qualitative methods though difficult to achieve:

■ The interviewer is actively building as best they can an understanding of what they are being told. In contrast, it hardly matters in a structured interview whether the interviewer gets an overview of this sort since they merely write down the answers to individual questions. However, without concentrating intensely on the content of the interview, the qualitative researcher simply cannot function effectively.

■ The interviewer formulates questions and probes in a way which clarifies and extends the detail of the account being provided by the participant. Why did they say this? Who is the person being described by the participant? Does what is being said make sense in terms of what has been said before? Is what is being communicated unclear? The list of questions is of course virtually endless. But this aspect of the task is very demanding on the cognitive and memory resources of the interviewer as it may also be for the participant.

■ The interviewer is cognisant of other interviews which they (and possibly co-workers) have conducted with other participants. Issues may have emerged in those which appear missing in the current interview. Why is that? How does the participant respond when specifically asked about these issues?

■ The objective of the interviewer's activity is to expand the detail and to interrogate the information as it is being collected. This is very much in keeping with the view that qualitative data *analysis starts* at the stage of data collection. It also reflects the qualitative ideal that progress in research depends on the early and repeated processing of the data.

In addition to all of this, there are practical issues which are too easily overlooked by the researcher but may have a significant impact on the quality of the research generated by the in-depth interview:

■ Just how many different researchers will be conducting the interviews? Using two or more different interviewers produces problems in terms of ensuring similarity and evenness of coverage across interviews.

■ How are developments communicated between the interviewers? It is probably worth considering the use of semi-structured interviews if the logistics of using several interviewers become too complex.

■ The data are usually no more than whatever is on the recording. As a consequence, it is important to obtain the best possible recording as this greatly facilitates the speed and quality of the final transcription (e.g. see Chapter 17). Beginners tend to assume that a tape recorder that functions well enough when spoken into by the researcher will be adequate to pick-up an interview between two people, physically set apart, in perhaps a noisy environment. Consider the best equipment available as an investment in terms of the quality of recording commensurate with the saving in transcription time. A recorder which allows the recording to be monitored through an earphone as it is being made will help ensure that the recording quality may be optimised.

■ The physical setting of the interview needs to be considered. Sometimes privacy will be regarded as essential for the material in question. In other circumstances privacy may not be so important (that is, if the topic is in no way sensitive). Taking the research to the home or workplace of the participants may be the preferred option over inviting the participants along to the researcher's office, for example. Interviews at home may unexpectedly turn into family interviews if one does not take care to ensure that it is understood that this is an individual interview. Many homes will have just a couple of places in which the interview may take place so be prepared to improvise.

Much of the available advice to assist planning an interview is somewhat over general. What is appropriate in one sort of interview may be inappropriate in another. What may be appropriate with adults may not work with youngsters with learning difficulty. If one gets the impression that good interviewing requires social skills, quickness of thought or a great deal of concentration, and resourcefulness, then that is just about right. For example, *Child Abuse Errors* (Howitt, 1992*b*) contains psychological research based on in-depth qualitative interview methods. The research essentially addresses the question of the processes by which parents become falsely accused of child abuse. This was partly stimulated by the cases in Cleveland in England where a number of parents were accused of child sexual abuse against their own children. The children were given a simple medical test which was erroneously believed by some doctors to be indicative of anal abuse. But these are not the only circumstances in which parents are accused, apparently falsely, of child abuse. The problems of this research in many ways are the ones which stimulate in-depth interviewing in general. That is, at the time there was virtually no research on the topic, indeed there was virtually nothing known about such cases. So inevitably the task was to collect a wide variety of accounts of the parents' experiences from a wide variety of circumstances. The initial interviews were, consequently, 'stabs in the dark'. The parents taking part in the study were participants with much, in general, to say about their experiences. Consequently, there was a complex account to absorb very quickly as the participants spoke. Furthermore, these were, of course, emotional matters for the parents who had essentially had their identity as good parents and their role of parent removed. The complexity and demanding nature of the in-depth interviewer's task in such circumstances are obvious.

16.2 Conclusion

The main criterion for an effective qualitative data collection method is the richness of the data it provides. Richness is difficult to define but it refers to the lack of constraint on the data which would come from a highly structured data collection method. Part of the richness of data is a consequence of qualitative data collection methods being suitable for exploring unknown or previously unresearched research topics. In these circumstances the researcher needs to explore a wide variety of aspects of the topic, not selected features. Some of the qualitative data collected by researchers using methods like those described in this chapter will be analysed in a traditional positivist analytic tradition with the participants' contributions being used as something akin to representing reality. Other data collected using these self-same methods might be subjected to discourse analysis, for example, which would eschew the representational nature of the material in favour of the language acts that are to be seen in the text.

Key points

- Qualitative data analysis is *not* the same thing as qualitative data collection. Qualitative data collection may in some cases become a quantitative analysis if quantifiable coding techniques are developed for the data.

- All qualitative data collection methods vary in terms of their degrees of structuring across different research studies. That is, there is no agreed standard of structuring which is applied in every case.

- Participant observation essentially has the researcher immersed as a member of a social environment. It has its origins in anthropology as a means of studying cultures. There is not a strong research tradition using it in psychology.

- Focus groups are increasingly popular in psychology and other disciplines as a means of collecting rich, textual material. It is a rather social research method in which the participants actively interact with others, under the gentle steering of the researcher. Because it highlights similarities and differences between group members, it is very useful for generating ideas about the topic under research as part of the pilot work, though it is equally suitable for addressing more developed research questions.

- Interviewing may be structured or unstructured. Generally, somewhat unstructured interviews are most likely to be the foundation of qualitative research simply because the lack of structure provides 'richer' unconstrained textual data. In-depth interviewing places a lot of responsibility on the interviewer in terms of the questioning process, coping with the emotions of the interviewee, and ensuring that the issues have been covered exhaustively.

Activities

1. Write a schedule for a structured interview on text messaging. Interview a volunteer using the schedule. Re-interview them using the schedule as a guide for a qualitative interview. What additional useful information did the structured interview uncover?

2. Get a group of volunteers together for a focus group on text messaging. What did you learn from the focus group compared to the interviews above?

17 Transcribing language data
The Jefferson system

Overview

■ Transcription is the process by which recordings are transformed into written text.

■ The transcription of audio and visual recordings is a vital stage in analysing much qualitative data.

■ Transcription techniques are much better developed for auditory than for visual recordings.

■ Transcription inevitably loses information from the original recording. Methods and transcribers differ in the extent that they can deal with the nuances of the material on the original recording.

■ The detail required of the transcription is dependent on the purposes of the research and the resources available.

■ The Jefferson transcription method places some emphasis on pauses, errors of speech, and people talking over each other or at the same time.

■ It is evident from research that 'errors' are not uncommon in transcriptions.

Research imposes structure on its subject matter. The structuring occurs at all stages of the research process. For example, the way the researcher decides to collect research data affects the nature of the research's outcome. If the researcher takes notes during an interview, what is recorded depends on a complex process of questioning, listening, interpreting and summarising. It could not be otherwise. Research is the activity of humans, *not* superhumans. If a researcher audiotapes conversation then all that is available on permanent record is the tape-recording. Visual information such as body posture and facial expression are not recorded. Once the tape-recording is transcribed as text, further aspects of the original events are lost. The intonation of the speaker, errors of speech and other features cannot be retained if the recording is merely transcribed from the spoken word to the written word. This does not make the transcription bad, it just means that it may be useless for certain purposes. If the researcher wishes to obtain 'factual' accounts of a typical day in the life of a police officer, the literal transcription may be adequate. (That is, the researcher is using language as a representation of reality and would have no problems with such a transcription. Qualitative researchers who argue that this view is wrong would regard such a transcription as useless.)

Research may have a vast range of valid purposes. Take, for example, the needs of a researcher who is interested in the process of conversation. The literal words used are inadequate to understand the nuances of conversation. On the other hand, a speech therapist might well be interested in transcribing particular features of speech which are most pertinent to a speech therapist's professional activities. Thus pronunciation of words may be critical as may be recording speech impediments such as stuttering. In other words, the speech therapist may be disinclined to record information which helps to understand the structuring of conversation as opposed to the speech of a single individual (Potter, 1997). So there is a test of 'fitness for purpose' which should be applied when planning transcription.

An example may be helpful. Take the following sentence as an example of 'literal' text:

Dave has gone on his holidays.

Strictly grammatically and literally, this sentence may mean something quite different in the context of a real-life conversation. Perhaps the researcher has actually transcribed the sentence as:

Dave has gone on errrrr (pause) his holidays.

This second version could be understood to mean that Dave is in prison. The 'errrrr' is not a word and the pause is not a word. They are paralinguistic features which help us to revise what the meaning of the sentence is. Given this, researchers studying language in its social context need to incorporate paralinguistic elements since they provide evidence of how the words are interpreted by participants in conversation. The paralinguistic features of language often have subtle implications. For example, 'errrr', which is a longer version of 'er', may often imply different things. 'Errrr' implies a deliberate search for an appropriate meaning, whereas 'Er' may often simply signal that one has forgotten the word. The experts on the subtle use of language are ordinary, native speakers of the language. One may describe this as an ethnographic approach to social interaction since we need to understand the conversation much as the participants in the conversation would. Of course, there is no *fixed* link between paralinguistic features of language and the meaning they add. So the presence of a particular feature should be regarded as informative rather than indicative.

17.1 Jefferson transcription

One popular system for transcribing speech is the system developed by Gail Jefferson. This has its origins in her work with Harvey Sacks – the 'founding-parent' of conversation analysis (see Chapter 20). The Jefferson system can appear a little confusing to novices – and not so easy for those familiar with it – but it is a skill which will improve with practice.

Jefferson's system has *no* special characters so it can be used by anyone using a standard computer or typewriter keyboard. Consequently, some familiar keystrokes have a distinctive meaning in Jefferson transcription. These keystrokes are used as symbols to indicate the way in which the words are delivered in the recording. This means, for example, that conventional punctuation may have its conventional meaning or may have a distinctive Jefferson meaning. Thus *capital* letters may indicate the start of a sentence or a proper noun – but they may indicate that the speaker has said a word with considerable emphasis using greater emphasis than the surrounding words. The main Jefferson conventions are given in Table 17.1. There are symbols which are used to indicate pauses, elongations of

Table 17.1 Main features of the Jefferson transcription system

Jefferson symbol	Meaning
CAPITALS	Indicate that the word(s) is louder than the surrounding words.
Under<u>lining</u>	Indicates emphasis such as on a particular syllable.
Aster*isk	The speaker's voice becomes squeaky.
Numbers in brackets (1.2)	Placed in text to indicate the length of a pause between words.
A dot (.) in brackets	This is a micropause – a noticeable but very short pause in the speech.
[ ]	Square brackets are used when two (or more) speakers are talking together. The speakers are given different lines and the brackets should be in line where the speech overlaps.
//	Another way of indicating the start of the second overlapping speaker's utterance.
; or :	Used to separate the speaker's name from their utterances.
?;	Indicates that the speaker is not recognisable to the analyst of the transcript.
?Janet;	Indicates a strong likelihood that Janet is the speaker.
. . .	Three dots are used to indicate a pause of untimed length.
??;	Two or more ? marks indicates that this is a new unidentified speaker from the last unidentified speaker.
[. . .]	Indicates material has been omitted at that point.
°I agree°	Words between signs ° are spoken more quietly by the speaker.
→	This is *not* part of the transcription. It is placed next to lines which the analyst wishes to bring to the reader's attention.
↑ ↓	Used to indicate substantial movements in pitch. They indicate out of the ordinary changes, not those characteristic of a particular dialect, for instance.
Heh heh	Indicates laughter which is voiced rather almost as if it were a spoken word rather than the uncontrolled noises that may constitute laughter in some circumstances.
I've wai::ted	The preceded sound is extended proportionate to the number of colons.
hhh	Expiration – breathing out sounds such as when signalling annoyance.
(what about)	Words in brackets are the analyst's best guess as to somewhat inaudible passages.
((smiles))	Material in double brackets refers to non-linguistic aspects of the exchange.
(? ?)	Inaudible passage approximately the length between the brackets.
I don't accept your argument = and another thing I don't think you are talking sense	Placed between two utterances to indicate that there is no identifiable pause between the two. Also known as latching.
= signs placed vertically on successive lines by different speakers	In this context, the = sign is an indication that two (or more) speakers are overlapping on the text between the = signs.
[ ] placed vertically on successive lines by different speakers	As above, but instead the [ ] brackets are used to indicate that two (or more) speakers are overlapping on the text between the brackets.
>that's all I'm saying<	Talk between > and < signs is speeded up.
< that's it>	Talk between < and > signs is slowed down.

For more details of Jefferson coding see Hutchby and Woolfit (1998).

word sounds, where two speakers are overlapping and so forth. Refer back to this table whenever necessary to understand what is happening in a transcript. You may also spot that there are slight differences between transcribers on certain matters of detail.

Jefferson transcription is not unproblematic in every instance. To illustrate this, take the following

For:::get it

The ::: indicates that the For should be extended in length. However, just what is the standard length of 'for' in 'forget'? In some dialects, the For will be longer than in others. And just what is the difference between for:::get and for::get?

Example of Jefferson transcription

The following excerpt is from a study of police interviews with paedophile suspects (Benneworth, 2004). The researcher had access to police recordings of such interviews. As a consequence, the data consist solely of audiotaped text without any visual information. Of course the researcher might have wanted to video-record the interviews in order to get evidence of facial expression, etc., but this was not an available option. Sound recordings are routine for British police interviews so the transcription may be regarded as being of a naturally produced conversation – a tape-recorded police interview – not an artefact of the research process. The people involved in the transcribed material below are a Detective Constable (DC) and the suspect being interviewed (susp). The issue is about the suspect's use of pornography in his dealings with a young girl:

```
363 DC:     What made you feel okay about showing them to a
364         [eleven year old girl]
365 Susp:   [accidentally          ] she first saw them when
366         I opened my boot one day I forgot they were
367         there and then she (1.8) °expressed an interest
368         in them and like looking at them and that's how
369         it developed.°
370 DC:     So you felt confident about showing them to (.)
371         Lucy whereas you wouldn't have shown them to
372         [your wife].
373 Susp:   [yeah I was] I was (3.8) s::::exually (0.8) umm
374         (4.0) unconfident anymore about sex and Lucy
375         showing an interest in me and that was
376         flattering in itself and .hhh cos there was no
377         sexual relationships with my wife.
378 DC:     Was it easier to feel confident with Lucy
379         because she was so young? <And you were an
380         adult and [more in control.>]
381 Susp:               [no it's just that] >it was the first
382         .hhh first young lady that's ever expressed an
383         interest in me during my troubled (.) marriage
384         over the past three years< (.) °I said°.
```

You will probably have noted a number of features of the transcript:

■ Each line is numbered 363, 364, etc., so it is clear that this is just an excerpt from a much longer transcript. The numbering is fairly arbitrary in the sense that another researcher may have produced lines of a different length and hence different numbers would be applied in their transcriptions. Notice that the lines do not correspond to sentences or any other linguistic unit.

■ Look at lines 364 and 365. The words enclosed in square brackets [ ] are parts of the conversation where the two participants overlap. This would not be possible to transcribe this if the system did not utilise arbitrary line lengths.

■ The use of Jefferson notation is not only time-consuming for the researcher, but it makes it difficult for readers unskilled in the Jefferson system. Simply attempting to read the literal text ignoring the transcription conventions is not easy.

■ Jefferson transcription cannot be done by untrained personnel such as secretaries.

■ The researcher would almost certainly have used a transcription machine which allows rapid replays of short sections of the recording. In other words, transcription is a slow, detailed process that should only be undertaken if the aims and objectives of the research study require it.

It is also worthwhile noting that Jefferson's transcriptions of the identical material will vary from researcher to researcher. It is probably fair to say that this transcription is at an intermediate level of transcription detail. In other words, by this stage the researcher has made a contribution to the nature of the data available for further analysis. Anyone carrying out Jefferson transcription will experience a degree of uncertainty as to whether they have achieved an appropriate level of transcription detail. It should be remembered that qualitative researchers tend to be very familiar with their texts before the transcription is complete. This familiarity will help them set the level of detail that is appropriate for their purposes.

An important question is what the Jefferson transcription enables which a secretary's word-by-word transcription might miss out. The following gives the above transcription with notation omitted. Often a secretary would fail to give the overlapping talk so the dominant voice at the time of the overlap would be transcribed and the other voice perhaps noted as inaudible. This is possibly because a secretary would regard text as linear much as when taking dictation from the secretary's boss. The following is a guess as to what a typical secretary's transcription of the same type might be. Two people talking together would probably be regarded as inaudible:

DC: What made you feel okay about showing them to a eleven year old girl?

Susp: (inaudible) she first saw them when I opened my boot one day I forgot they were there and then she expressed an interest in them and like looking at them and that's how it developed.

DC: So you felt confident about showing them to Lucy whereas you wouldn't have shown them to your wife.

Susp: (inaudible) I was sexually unconfident anymore about sex and Lucy showing an interest in me and that was flattering in itself and cos there was no sexual relationships with my wife.

DC: Was it easier to feel confident with Lucy because she was so young? And you were an adult and more in control?

Susp: (inaudible) it was the first first young lady that's ever expressed an interest in me during my troubled marriage over the past three years I said.

It has to be said that even in this version of the text there is a great deal that strikes one as important. For example, the following:

■ The way in which the suspect presents the pornography as something that the girl happened on by chance and as a result of her actions. There is no indication that the suspect actively created a situation in which she was exposed to the pornography.

■ The way in which the suspect excuses his offending by blaming his troubled marriage and his wife.

■ The way in which the offender represents his non-normative relationship (an adult man with a 11-year-old girl) as if two adults were involved. So the 11-year-old girl is represented as a 'young lady' indicating maturity rather than a 'young girl' which represents an immature person.

Researchers and practitioners with knowledge and experience of paedophiles and other sex offenders have themselves noted such 'denial' and 'cognitive distortion' strategies (Howitt, 1995). Indeed, much of the therapy for sex offenders involves group therapy methods of modifying such cognitions. The above excerpt is perhaps not altogether typical of the sort of text used by qualitative researchers. For one thing, it is the sort of text which is unfamiliar to many and so is quite different from the everyday, routine conversation studied by many qualitative researchers. The implication being that unfamiliar subject matter is likely to reveal a lot because it contrasts markedly with more familiar sorts of conversation from everyday life. It is likely that at least some researchers would find in this simple transcriptions all that they require for their research purposes. For example, if a researcher was interested in the types of denial and cognitive distortions demonstrated by offenders, the transcription process may not need the Jefferson-style of elaboration.

So what does the Jefferson transcription system add which a secretary's transcription omits? There are a few obvious things:

■ The Jefferson transcription gives a lot more information about what happened in the conversation. The secretary's version gives the impression of a smooth, unproblematic conversational flow. The Jefferson transcription demonstrates a variety of turn-taking errors, quite lengthy pauses in utterances, and dynamic qualities of the way that the conversation is structured – for example, the very quiet passages.

■ The Jefferson transcription allows parts of the conversation to be rapidly referred to.

■ Even by carefully reading the transcription, let alone doing the transcription, a reader has a more intimate knowledge of the text. Consequently, the extra detailed work done in order to produce a Jefferson transcript means that the researcher becomes very familiar with the material. They may begin to conceptualise what is happening in the text sooner. This early and detailed familiarity with the data is claimed to be one of the analytic virtues of qualitative research – though this is greatly undermined if researchers do not do their own transcription.

What else does the researcher gain by using the Jefferson transcription system? After all, some may regard the Jefferson system as merely providing irrelevant and obscuring detail. Suggestions include:

■ If we look carefully for what the Jefferson transcription adds to the information available to the researcher, we find in line 373/4 the following: Susp:[yeah I was] I was (3.8) s::::exually (0.8) umm (4.0) unconfident anymore about sex. Not only is the word sexually highlighted in speech by the elongation into s::::exually but it is also isolated by lengthy gaps of four or so seconds on each side. Benneworth (2004) refers to this as a 'conversational difficulty' which takes the form of 'hesitant speech' and 'prolonged pauses'. This may have led her to pointing out that the term 'sexually' is part of a particular language repertoire which the suspect only applies to relationships with an adult. When speaking of the child, he employs what Benneworth (2004) describes as 'relationship discourse and euphemism'. *'Lucy showing an interest in me . . . that was flattering in itself'*. The offender does not use the term 'victim' of the child, though it is a term that most of us would use. That is, the offender is not using language repertoire that would indicate the child has been abused sexually as opposed to the language repertoire used to indicate a mutual relationship.

■ The use of Jefferson transcription clearly encourages the researcher to concentrate closely on the text as a matter of a social exchange rather than information requested and supplied. For example, Benneworth notes how the Detective Constable constantly brings the youth of the girl into the conversation which contrasts with the offender's representation of the girl as if she were a mature female rather than a child. Furthermore, by taking this excerpt and contrasting it with other excerpts from other interviews, the researcher was able to explore different interview styles – one is more confrontational and challenging of the suspect, whereas the other almost colludes with the offender's 'distorted' cognitions.

■ Similarly, the use of the Jefferson transcription facilitates the linking of the text under consideration with established theory in the field. So Benneworth argues that the words 'I opened my boot one day' in line 366 grounds the offender's account in common day-to-day experience rather than the more extraordinary abuse of a child. Such a device may be seen as a discursive device for creating a sense of ordinariness (Jefferson, 1984) and essentially creates a distance from the suspect's actions and the criminal consequences ensuing from them.

17.2 Advice for transcribers

It should be emphasised that the Jefferson system is only one of a number of systems of transcription that can be employed. Indeed, there is no reason why a researcher should not contemplate developing their own system if circumstances require it. O'Connell and Kowal (1995) evaluated a number of text transcription systems employed by researchers, including that of Jefferson. They suggest that transcription is not and cannot be 'a genuine photograph of the spoken word' (p. 105). Generally all transcription systems attempt to record the exact verbal words said. Nevertheless, transcription systems vary considerably in terms of transcribing other features of speech, indeed in some cases other features are not included. So some systems include prosodic features such as how a word was spoken (loudly, softly, part emphasised, etc.), paralinguistic features (such as words said with a laugh or sigh) and extralinguistic features (facial expressions, gestures, etc.) – some systems exclude some or all of them.

The following is some of the generic advice offered to transcribers by O'Connell and Kowal:

■ The principle of parsimony: only those features of speech which are to be analysed should be transcribed. That is, there is little point in including extralinguistic features such as gestures in the transcription if they will not be part of the analysis.

■ Similarly, the transcriptions provided in reports should only include whatever is necessary to make the analysis intelligible to the reader.

■ Subjectively assessed aspects of conversation should not be included in the transcription as if they are objective measurements. For example, transcribers may subjectively estimate the lengths of short pauses (0.2) but enter them as if they are precise measures. O'Connell and Kowal report that that transcribers omitted almost four out of five of such pauses in radio interviews. This begs the question why the other pauses were included.

■ Transcribers make frequent, uncorrected errors. For example, verbal additions, deletions, relocations and substitutions are commonly found when a transcript is compared with the original tape. Qualitative researchers often stress the importance of checking the transcription against the original source to minimise this problem.

There is other, perhaps more routine, advice available to transcribers. For example, Potter (2004) suggests that technological advances have made transcription easier. Transcription is labour intensive and twenty hours of transcription may be necessary for one hour of recording. It is obvious that high quality digital recordings using, say, a mini-disc player will be enormously beneficial – and result in fewer errors. Furthermore, there are digital editing programs (e.g. Cool Edit) which allow the transcription of recordings on screen. As the recording is held as a file on the computer, the system allows frequent checking against the original. Since the recording may be displayed as a visual waveform, it becomes easier to measure precisely gaps and pauses in conversation and speech.

17.3 Conclusion

Although normally described as a *transcription* system, Jefferson's approach is also a low-level coding or categorisation system. If researchers want a perfect transcription of the recording then what better than their original tape recording? Of course, what they want is a simplified or more manageable version of the recording. Inevitably this means coding or categorising the material and one can only capture what the system of coding can capture. Conversational difficulties, for example, are highlighted by the Jefferson system so these are likely to receive analytic consideration. Facial expression is not usually included so facial expressions (which may totally negate the impression created in a conversation) are overlooked.

Transcription is a very time consuming process – the Jefferson system is more detailed than most and takes up even more time. So there is little point in using any system of transcription unless it adds something to achieving the sort of analysis the researcher requires. Transcription is generally regarded by qualitative researchers as a task for the researcher themselves. Ideally it is not something farmed out to junior assistants or clerical workers. Qualitative researchers need intimate familiarity with their material – this is facilitated by doing one's own transcriptions.

Key points

- Transcription is the stage between the collection of data in verbal form and analysis. Usually it is producing a written version of audio-recordings, but video material may also be transcribed.

- In qualitative data analysis, transcription may take into account more than the words spoken by indicating how the words are spoken. That is, errors of speech are included, pauses are indexed, and times when people are speaking at the same time are noted.

- Transcription is not regarded as a necessary chore but one of the ways in which the researcher becomes increasingly familiar with their data and is not usually passed over to others.

- Inevitably transcription omits aspects of the original and there is the risk that the transcription is inadequate. It is normally recommended that the researcher refers back to the original tape when the transcription appears complete or consider asking another researcher to assess the veracity of it.

The commonest form of transcription is the Jefferson method which has its roots in conversation analysis. It is very commonly used by qualitative researchers but can be unnecessarily time consuming if the analysis is only of the words.

Activities

1. In pairs, act out the conversation which was subject to Jefferson transcription in the main body of the chapter between the police and the suspect. Record the conversation if you can and compare the product of the attempts of different pairs of actors.

2. Tape-record a conversation, select an interesting part, transcribe it and annotate it with Jefferson transcription symbols. List the difficulties you experience for discussion.

18 Data analysis
Grounded theory

Overview

- Grounded theory basically involves a number of techniques which enable researchers to effectively analyse 'rich' (detailed) qualitative data effectively.

- It reverses the classic hypothesis-testing approach to theory development (favoured by some quantitative researchers) by defining data collection as the primary stage and requiring that theory is closely linked to the entirety of the data.

- The researcher keeps close to the data when developing theoretical analyses – in this way the analysis is 'grounded' in the data rather than being based on speculative theory which is then tested using hypotheses derived from the theory.

- Grounded theory does not mean that there are theoretical concepts just waiting in the data to be discovered. It means that the theory is anchored in the data.

- In grounded theory, categories are developed and refined by the researcher in order to explain whatever the researcher regards as the significant features of the data.

Sometimes qualitative data analysis is regarded as being an easy route to doing research. After all, it does not involve writing questionnaire items, planning experimental designs or even doing statistics. All of these tasks are difficult and, if they can be avoided, are best avoided. Or so the argument goes. Superficially, qualitative data analysis does seem to avoid most of the problems of quantification and statistical analysis. Carry out an unstructured interview or conduct of focus group or get a politician's speech off the Internet or something of the sort. Then record it using an audio recorder or video recorder, or just use the written text grabbed from the Web. Sounds like a piece of cake. You are probably familiar with the caricature of quantitative researchers as boffins in white coats in laboratories. The qualitative researcher may similarly be caricatured. The qualitative researcher is more like a manic newspaper reporter or television reporter who asks a few questions or takes a bit of video and then writes an article about it.

What is the difference between the qualitative researcher and the TV reporter with the tape-recorder or camera crew? The answer to this question will take most of this chapter.

The book, *Discovery of Grounded Theory* (Glaser and Strauss, 1967), is still regarded as a major source on the topic of grounded theory. Historically, it was the first and most influential major publication arguing for this new conceptualisation of data analysis. Glaser and Strauss' approach was as much a reaction to the dominant sociology of the time as it was radically innovative. Basically, the book takes objection to the largely abstract socio-logical theory of the time which seemed divorced from any social or empirical reality. Indeed, empirical research was as atheoretical as the theoretical research was unempirical at the time. Grounded theory reversed many of the axioms of conventional research in an attempt to systematise many aspects of qualitative research. As such, it should be of interest to quantitative researchers since it highlights the characteristics of their methods.

However, many readers of this chapter will not yet have read any research that involves the use of grounded theory. So what are the characteristics of a grounded theory analysis? Ultimately the aim is to produce a set of categories into which the data fit closely and which amounts to a theoretical description of the data. Since the data are almost certain to be textual or spoken language then major features of most analyses can be anticipated. Like all forms of research, there are excellent grounded-theory analyses, but also inadequate or mundane ones. A word of warning: to carry out a grounded-theory analysis are a some-what exacting task. Sometimes authors claim to have used grounded theory though perusal of their work reveals no signs of the rigours of the method. Sometimes the categories developed fit the data because they are so broad that anything in the data is bound to fit into one or other of the coding categories.

Like properly done qualitative data analyses in general, grounded-theory approaches are time consuming, arguably because of the need for great familiarity with the data. Grounded theory employs a variety of techniques designed to ensure that researchers enter into the required intimate contact with their data as well as bringing into juxtaposition different aspects of the data. The approach has a lot of aficionados amongst the wide cross-section of qualitative research – though its use is far from universal.

Just to stress, grounded-theory methods result in categories which encompass the data (text or speech almost invariably) as completely and unproblematically as the researcher can manage. In this context, theory and effective categorisation are virtually synonymous. This causes some confusion among those better versed in quantitative methods who tend to assume that theory means an elaborate conjecture system from which hypotheses are derived for testing. That is not what grounded theory provides – the categorisation system is basically the theory. Furthermore, researchers seeking a theory that yields precise pre-dictions will be disappointed. While grounded theory may generalise to new sets of data, it is normally *incapable* of making predictions of a more precise sort. Charmaz (2000) explains:

> . . . *grounded theory methods consist of* systematic inductive guidelines *for collecting and analyzing data to build* middle-range theoretical frameworks that explain the collected data. *Throughout the research process,* grounded theorists develop analytic interpretations of their data *to focus further data collection, which they use in turn to inform and refine their developing theoretical analyses.* [Charmaz, 2000, p. 509, emphases added]

Several elements of this description of grounded theory warrant highlighting:

■ Grounded theory consists of *guidelines* for conducting data collection, data analysis and theory building, which may lead to research which is closely integrated to social reality as represented in the data.

- Grounded theory is *systematic*. In other words, the analysis of data to generate theory is not dependent on a stroke of genius or divine inspiration, but on perspiration and application of general principles or methods.

- Grounded theory involves *inductive* guidelines rather than deductive processes. This is very different from what is often regarded as conventional theory building (sometimes described as the 'hypothetico-deductive method'). In the hypothetico-deductive method, theory is developed from which hypotheses are derived. In turn, these hypotheses may be put to an empirical test. Research is important because it allows researchers to test these hypotheses. The hypothetico-deductive method characterised psychology for much of its modern history. Without the link between theory building and hypothesis testing, quantitative research in psychology probably deserves the epithet of 'empiricism gone mad.' Particularly good examples of the hypothetico-deductive approach are to be found in the writings of psychologists such as Hans Eysenck (e.g. Eysenck, 1980). However, grounded theory, itself, was not really a reaction against the hypothetico-deductive method but one against overly abstracted and untestable social theory.

- Grounded theory requires that theory should develop out of an understanding of the complexity of the subject matter. Theories (i.e. coding schemes) knit the complexity of the data into a coherent whole. Such theories may only be tested effectively in terms of the fit between the categories and the data, and by applying the categories to new data. In many ways this contrasts markedly with mainstream quantitative psychology. There is no requirement that the analysis fits all of the data closely – merely that there are statistically significant trends, irrespective of magnitude, which confirm the hypothesis derived from the theory.

- The theory building process is a continuous one rather than a sequence of critical tests of the theory through testing hypotheses. In many ways, it is impossible to separate the different phases of the research into discrete components such as theory development, hypothesis testing, followed by refining the theory. The data collection phase, the transcription phase and the analysis phase all share the common intent of building theory by matching the analysis closely to the complexity of the topic of interest.

18.1 Development of grounded theory

Grounded theory is usually described as being a reaction against the dominant sociology of the 20th century – specifically the Chicago School of Sociology. Some of the founders of this school specifically argued that human communities were made up of subpopulations, each of which operated almost on a natural science model – they were like ecological populations. For example, subpopulations showed a pattern whereby they began to invade a territory, eventually reaching dominance, and finally receding as another subpopulation became dominant. This was used to explain population changes in major and developing cities such as Chicago. Large scale social processes and not the experiences of individuals came to be the subject of study. The characteristics which are attributed to the Chicago are redolent of a lot of psychology. In particular, the Chicago School sought to develop exact and standard measuring instruments to measure a small number of key variables that were readily quantified. In sociology, research in natural contexts began to be unimportant in the first half of 20th century – the corresponding change in psychology was the increased importance of the psychological laboratory as a research base. In sociology, researchers undertook field research mainly in order to develop their measuring instruments. Once developed, they became the focus of interest themselves. So social processes are ignored in favour of broad measures such as social class and alienation, which are abstractions. The theorist and the researcher were often different people, so much so that much research became alienated from theory – that is atheoretical (Charmaz, 1995).

Grounded-theory methodology basically mirror-imaged or reversed features of the dominant sociology of the 1960s in a number of ways:

■ Qualitative research became seen as a legitimate domain in its own right. It was not a preliminary or preparatory stage for refining one's research instruments prior to quantitative research.

■ The division between research and theory was undermined by requiring that theory comes after or as part of the data collection and is tied to the data collected. Furthermore, data collection and their analysis were reconstrued as being virtually inseparable. That is, analysis of the data was encouraged early in the collection of data and this early analysis could be used to guide the later collection of data.

In order to achieve these ends, grounded theory had to demonstrate that quantitative research could be made rigorous, systematic and structured. The idea that quantitative data analysis is no more than a few superficial impressions of the researcher was no part of grounded theory. Equally, case studies are considered in themselves *not* to achieve the full potential of qualitative research.

Despite being the mirror image of mainstream research, grounded-theory analysis does not share all of the features of other qualitative methods such as discourse analysis and ethnomethodology. In particular, some users of grounded theory reject *realism* (the idea that out there somewhere is a social reality which researchers will eventually uncover) whereas others accept it. Similarly, some grounded theories aim for objective measures and theory development that does not depend on the researcher's subjectivity. Others regard this as a futile and inappropriate aim.

18.2 Data in grounded theory

Grounded theory is not primarily a means of collecting data but the means of data analysis. Consequently, grounded theory does not require any particular type of data although some types of data are better for it than others. So, for example, grounded theory can be applied to interviews, biographical data, media content, observations, conversations and so forth. All of these sources potentially may be introduced into any study. The key thing is, of course, that the data should be as richly detailed as possible – that is not simple or simplified. Charmaz (1995, p. 33) suggests that richly detailed data involve 'full' or 'thick' written descriptions. So, by this criterion, much of the data collected by quantitative researchers in the so-called quantitative approach would be unsuitable. There is little that a grounded-theory researcher could do with answers to a multiple-choice questionnaire or personality scale. Yes–no and similar response formats do not provide detailed data. The data for grounded-theory analysis mostly consist of words, but this is typical of much data in psychology and related disciplines. As such, usually data are initially transcribed using a notation system such as Jefferson's (Chapter 17). Some lessons from grounded theory could be useful to all sorts of researchers. In particular, the need for richness of data, knowing one's data intimately and developing theory closely in line with the data would benefit a great deal of research.

18.3 How to do grounded-theory analysis

Potter (1998) likens grounded theory to a sophisticated filing system. This filing system does not merely put things under headings but there is cross-referencing to a range of other categories. It is a bit like a library book that may be classified as a biography, but it may also be a political book. Keep this analogy in mind as otherwise the temptation is to believe that the data are only filed under one category in grounded-theory analysis. There seems to be a general acceptance that grounded-theory analysis has a number of key components. These are outlined below.

Comparison

Crucially, grounded-theory development involves constant comparisons at all stages of the data collection and analysis process – without comparing categories with each other and with the data, categories cannot evolve and become more refined:

■ People may be compared in terms of what they have said or done or how they have accounted for their actions or events, for example.
■ Comparisons are made of what a person does or says in one context with what they do and say in another context.
■ Comparisons are made of what someone has said or done at a particular time with a similar situation at a different time.
■ Comparisons of the data with the category which the researcher suggests may account for the data.
■ Comparisons are made of categories used in the analysis with other categories used in the analysis.

So, for example, it is a common criticism of quantitative research that the researcher forces observations into ill-fitting categories for the purpose of analysis; in grounded theory the categories are changed and adjusted to fit the data better. This is often referred to as the method of *constant comparisons*. Much of the following is based on Charmaz's (1995, 2000) recommendations about how to proceed.

Coding/naming

Grounded-theory principles require that the researcher repeatedly examines the data closely. The lines of data will be numbered at some stage to aid comparison and reference. In the initial stage of the analysis, the day-to-day work involves coding or describing the data line-by-line. It is as straightforward as that – and as difficult. (Actually, there is no requirement that a line be the unit of analysis and a researcher may choose to operate at the level of the sentence or the paragraph, for example.) The line is examined and a description (it could be more than one) is provided by the researcher to describe what is happening in that line or what is 'represented' by that line. In other words, a name is being given to each line of data. These names or codings should be generated out of what is in that particular line of data. In many ways, describing this as coding is a little misleading, because it implies a pre-existing system which is not the case. Others describe the process in slightly different terms. For example, Potter (1997) describes the process as being one of giving labels to the key concepts that appear in the line or paragraph.

The point of the coding is that it keeps the researcher's feet firmly in the grounds of the data. Without coding, the researcher may be tempted to over-interpret the data by inappropriately attributing 'motives, fears or unresolved personal issues' (Charmaz, 1995, p. 37) to the participants. At the end of this stage, we are left with numerous codings or descriptions of the contents of many lines of text.

Categorisation

Quite clearly, the analyst has to try to organise these codings. Remember that codings are part of the analysis process and the first tentative steps in developing theory. These are the smallest formal units in the grounded-theory analysis. While they may describe the data more-or-less well, by organising them we may increase the likelihood that we will be able to effectively revise them. This is a sort of reverse filtering process: we are starting with the smallest units of analysis and working back to the larger theoretical descriptions. So the next stage is to build the codings or namings of lines of data into categories. This is a basic strategy in many sorts of research. In quantitative research, there are statistical methods which are commonly used in categorising variables into groupings of variables (e.g. factor analysis and cluster analysis). These statistical methods are not generally available to the grounded theorist, so the categorisation process relies on other methods. Once again, the process of constant comparison is crucial, of course. The analyst essentially has to compare as many of the codings with the other codings as possible. That is, is the coding for line 62 really the same as that for line 30 since both lines are described in very similar words? Is it possible to justify coding lines 88 and 109 in identical fashion since when these data lines are examined they appear to be very different?

The constant comparing goes beyond this. For example, does there seem to be a different pattern of codings for Mr X than for Mrs Y? That is, does the way that they talk about things seem to be different? We might not be surprised to find different patterns for Mr X and Mrs Y when we know that this is a couple attending relationship counselling or that one is the boss of a company and the other an employee. The data from a person at a particular point in time or in a particular context may be compared with data from the same person at a later point in time or in different contexts.

It need not stop there. Since the process is one of generating categories for the codings of the data which fit the data well and are coherent, one must also compare the categories with each other as they emerge or are developed. After all, it may become evident, for example, that two of the categories cannot be differentiated – or you may have given identical titles to categories which actually are radically different. The process of categorisation may be facilitated by putting the data or codings or both onto index cards which can be physically moved around on a desk or table in order to place similar items close together and dissimilar items further apart. In this way, relationships can begin to be identified in a more active visual way.

Table 18.1   A modified extract of grounded-theory coding based on Charmaz (1995, p. 39)

Interview transcript	Coding by researcher
If you have lupus, I mean one day it's my liver	Shifting symptoms
One day it's in my joints; one day it's in my head, and	Inconsistent days
It's like people really think you're a hypochondriac if you keep	Interpreting images of self
. . . It's like you don't want to say anything because people are going to start thinking	Avoiding disclosure

It is difficult to give a brief representative extract of grounded-theory style codings. Table 18.1 reproduces a part of such codings from Charmaz (1995) which illustrates aspects of the process reasonably well. Take care though since Table 18.1 contains a very short extract from just one out of nearly two hundred interviews conducted by her. It can be seen that the codings/categories are fairly close to the data in this example. It should be noted that her's are not the only codings which would work with the data.

Memo-writing

None of the stages in grounded-theory analysis are as distinct as they first appear. The process of analysis is not sequential, although explaining grounded-theory analysis makes it appear so. It is a back-and-forward process. Memo-writing describes the aspect of the research in which the data are explored rather than described and categorised. The memo may be just as one imagines – a notebook – in which the researcher notes suggestions as to how the categories may be linked together in the sense that they have relationships and interdependencies. But the memo does not have to be a purely textual thing. A diagram – perhaps a flow diagram – could be used in which the key concepts are placed in boxes and the links between them identified by annotated arrows. What do we mean by relationships and interdependencies? Imagine the case of male and female. They are conceptually distinct categories but they have interdependencies and relationships. One cannot understand the concept of male without the concept of female.

The memo should not be totally separated from the data. Within the memo one should include the most crucial and significant examples from the data which are indicative and typical of the more general examples. So the memo should be replete with illustrative instances as well as potentially ill-fitting or problematic instances of ideas, conceptualisations and relationships that are under development as part of the eventual grounded theory:

> *If you are at a loss about what to write about, look for the codes that you have used repeatedly in your data collection. Then start elaborating on these codes. Keep collecting data, keep coding and keep refining your ideas through writing more and further developed memos.* [Charmaz, 1995, p. 43]

In a sense, this advice should not be necessary with grounded theory since the processes of data collection, coding and categorisation of the codes are designed to make the researcher so familiar with their data that it is very obvious what the frequently occurring codings are. However, it is inevitable that those unaccustomed to qualitative analysis will having writing and thinking blocks much the same as a quantitative researcher may have problems writing questionnaire items or formulating hypotheses.

Sometimes the memo is regarded as an intermediary step between the data and the final written report. Though, as ever in grounded theory, in practice the distinction between the different stages is not rigid. Often the advice is to start memo writing just as soon as anything strikes one as interesting in the data, the coding or categorisation. The sooner the better would seem to be the general consensus. This is very different from the approach taken by quantitative researchers. Also bear in mind that the process of theory development in grounded theory is not conventional in that the use of a small number of parsimonious concepts is not a major aim. (This is essentially Occam's razor which is the logical principle that no more than the minimum number of concepts or assumptions are necessary. This is also refered to as the principle of parsimony.) Strauss and Corbin (1999) write of conceptual density which they describe as a richness of concept development and relationship identification. This is clearly intended to be very different from reducing the analysis to the very minimum number of concepts as is characteristic of much quantitative research.

Theoretical sampling

Theoretical sampling is about how to validate the ideas developed within the memo. If the ideas in the memo have validity then they should apply to some samples of data but not to others. The task of the researcher is partly to suggest which samples that categories apply to and which they should not apply to. This will help the researcher identify new sources of data which may be used to validate the analysis to that point. As a consequence of the analysis of such additional data, subsequent memo writing may be more closely grounded in the data which it is intended to explain.

Literature review

In conventional methodological terms, the literature review is largely carried out in advance of planning the detailed research. That is, the new research builds on the accumulated previous knowledge. In grounded theory, the literature review should be carried out after the memo-writing process is over – signed, sealed and delivered. In this way, the grounded theory has its origins in the data collected *not* the previous research and theoretical studies. So why bother with the literature review? The best answer is that the literature review should be seen as part of the process of assessing the adequacy of the grounded-theory analysis. If the new analysis fails to deal adequately with the older research then a reformulation may be necessary. On the other hand, it is feasible that the new analysis helps integrate past grounded-theory analyses. In some respects this can be regarded as an extension of the grounded theory to other domains of applicability.

That is what some grounded theorists claim. Strauss and Corbin (1999) add that the grounded-theory methodology may begin in existing grounded theory so long as they 'seem appropriate to the area of investigation' and then these grounded theories 'may be elaborated and modified as incoming data are meticulously played against them' (pp. 72–3).

18.4   Computer grounded-theory analysis

A number of commercially available grounded-theory analysis programs are available. Generically they are known as CAQDAS (computer assisted qualitative data analysis software). NUDIST was the market leader but it has been replaced by NVIVO, which is very similar, and there are others. These programs may help with the following aspects of a grounded theory:

■ There is a lot of paper work with grounded-theory analysis. Line-numbered transcripts are produced, coding categories are developed, and there is much cutting and pasting of parts of the analysis in order to finely tune the categories to the data. There is almost inevitably large amounts of textual material to deal with – a single focus group, for example, might generate ten or twenty transcribed pages. Computers, as everyone knows, are excellent for cutting down on paper when drafting and shifting text around. That is, the computer may act as a sort of electronic office for grounded analyses.

■ One key method in grounded theory is searching for linkages between different aspects of the data. A computer program is eminently suitable for making, maintaining and changing linkages between parts of a document and between different documents.

■ Coding categories are developed but frequently need regular change, refinement and redefinition in order for them to fit the data better and further data that may be introduced perhaps to test the categories. Using computer programs, it is possible to recode the data more quickly, combine categories and the like.

18.5   Evaluation of grounded theory

Potter (1998) points out that central to its virtues is that grounded theory:

> . . . *encourages a slow-motion reading of texts and transcripts that should avoid the common qualitative research trap of trawling a set of transcripts for quotes to illustrate preconceived ideas.* [p. 127]

This is probably as much as a weakness as a strength since the size of the task may well defeat the resources of novice and others. Certainly it is not always possible to be convinced that preconceived ideas do not dominate the analysis rather than the data leading the analysis.

There are a number of criticisms which seem to apply to grounded theory:

■ It encourage a pointless collection of data – that is, virtually anything textual or spoken could be subject to a grounded-theory analysis. There are no clear criteria for deciding, in advance, what topics to research on the basis of their theoretical or practical relevance. Indeed, the procedures tend to encourage the delay of theoretical and other considerations until after the research has been initiated.

■ Potter (1998) suggests that 'The method is at its best where there is an issue that is tractable from a relatively common sense actor's perspective . . . the theoretical notions developed are close to the everyday notions of the participants' (p. 127). This means that commonsensical explanations are at a premium – explanations which go beyond common sense may be squeezed out. Potter puts it another way elsewhere '. . . how far is the grounding derived not from theorizing but from reproducing common sense theories as if they were analytic conclusions?' (Potter, 1998, p. 127). This may be fair criticism. The difficulty is that it applies to any form of research which gives voice to its participants. Ultimately, this tendency means that grounded theory may simply codify how ordinary people ordinarily understand the activities in which they engage.

■ There is a risk that grounded theory, which is generally founded on admirable ideals, is used to excuse inadequate qualitative analyses. It is a matter of faith that grounded theory will generate anything of significant value – yet at the same time, done properly, a grounded-theory analysis may have involved a great deal of labour. Consequently, it is hard to put aside a research endeavour which may have generated little but cost a lot of time and effort. There are similar risks that grounded-theory methods will be employed simply because the researcher has failed to focus on appropriate research questions so leaving them with few available analysis options. These risks are particularly high for student work.

■ Since talk and text are analysed line by line (and these are arbitrarily divided – they are not sentences for example) then the researcher may be encouraged to focus on small units rather than the larger units of conversation as, for example, favoured by discourse analysts (Potter, 1998). Nevertheless, grounded theory is often mentioned by such analysts as part of their strategy or orientation.

So it is likely that grounded theory works best when dealing with issues that are amenable to common sense insights from participants. Medical illness and interpersonal relationships are such topics where the theoretical ideas that grounded theory may develop are close to the ways in which the participants think about these issues. This may enhance the practicality of grounded theory in terms of policy implementation. The categories used and the theoretical contribution are likely to be in terms relatively easy for the practitioner or policymaker to access.

18.6 Conclusion

Especially pertinent to psychologists is the question of whether grounded theory is really a sort of Trojan horse which has been cunningly brought into psychology, but is really the enemy of advancement in psychology. Particularly troubling is the following from Strauss and Corbin (1999):

> . . . grounded theory researchers are interested in patterns of action and interaction between and among various types of social units (i.e., 'actors'). So they are not especially interested in creating theory about individual actors as such (unless perhaps they are psychologists or psychiatrists). [p. 81]

Researchers like Strauss and Corbin are actually willing to allow a place for quantitative data in grounded theory. So the question may be one of how closely psychological concepts could ever fit with grounded-theory analysis which is much more about the social (interactive) than the psychological.

Key points

- Grounded theory is an approach to analysing (usually textual) data designed to maximise the fit of emerging theory (categories) to the data and additional data of relevance.

- The aim is to produce 'middle range' theories which are closely fitting qualitative descriptions (categories) rather than, say, cause-and-effect or predictive theories.

- Grounded theory is 'inductive' (that is, does not deduce outcomes from theoretical postulates). It is systematic in that an analysis of some sort will almost result from adopting the system. It is a continuous process of development of ideas – it does not depend on a critical test as in the case of classic psychological theory.

- Comparison is the key to the approach – all elements of the research and the analysis are constantly compared and contrasted.

- Coding (or naming or describing) is the process by which lines of the data are given a short description (or descriptions) to identify the nature of their content.

- Categorisation is the process by which the codings are amalgamated into categories. The process helps find categories which fit the codings in their entirety, not simply a few pragmatic ideas which only partially represent the codings.

- Memo writing is the process by which the researcher records their ideas about the analysis throughout the research process. The memo may include ideas about categorisation but it may extend to embrace the main themes of the final report.

- Computer programs are available which help the researcher organise the materials for the analysis and effectively alter the codings and categories.

- A grounded-theory analysis may be extended to further critical samples of data which should be pertinent to the categories developed in the analysis. This is known as theoretical sampling.

- The theoretical product of grounded-theory analysis is not intended to be the same as conventional psychological theorisation and so should not be judged on those terms.

Activity

Grounded theory involves the bringing of elements together to try to forge categories which unite them. So choose a favourite poem, song or any textual material, and write each sentence on a separate sheet of paper. Choose two at random. What unites these two sentences? Then choose another sentence. Can this be united with the previous two sentences? Continue the exercise until you cease coming up with new ideas. Then start again.

19   Discourse analysis

Overview

- Discourse analysis refers to a variety of ways of studying and understanding talk (or text) as social action.

- The intellectual roots of discourse analysis are largely in the linguistic philosophy of the 1960s. Most significant in this regard is the conceptualisation that discourse is designed to do things linguistically and that the role of the discourse analysts is to understand what is being done and how it is done through speech and text.

- At one level, discourse analysis may be regarded as a body of ideas about the nature of talk and text which can be applied to the great mass of data collected by psychologists in the form of language.

- A number of themes are common in discourse analysis – these include rhetoric, voice, footing, discursive repertoires and the dialogical nature of talk.

- The practice of discourse analysis involves a variety of procedures designed to encourage the researcher to process and reprocess their material. These include transcription, coding and re-coding.

Discourse analysis has its roots outside of psychology. According to *The Oxford Companion to the English Language* (McArthur, 1992) its early origins lie in the work which extended linguistics into the study of language beyond the individual sentence. Perhaps the earliest of these was Zellig Harris who worked in the USA in the 1950s on issues such as how text is related to the social situation within which it was created. A little later, a linguistic anthropologist, Dell Hymes, investigated forms of address between people – that is speech as it relates to the social setting. In the 1960s, a group of British linguistic philosophers (J. L. Austin, J. R. Searle and H. P. Grice) began to regard language as social *action* – a key idea in discourse analysis. Potter (2001) takes the roots back earlier to the first half of the 20th century by adding the philosopher Ludwig Wittgenstein into the melting pot of influences on discourse analysis theory. Particularly important is Wittgenstein's idea that language is a toolkit for *doing* things rather than a means of merely representing things.

It is a largely wasted effort to search for publications on discourse analysis by psychologists before the 1980s. The term first appears in a psychology journal in 1954 but applied to ideas very different from its current meaning. However, despite its late appearance in psychology, the study of discourse began to grow rapidly in the 1960s in other disciplines. Consequently, discourse analysis draws from a variety of disciplines, each of which has a different take or perspective on what discourse analysis is. Because of the pan-disciplinary base for discourse analysis, a psychologist, no matter how well versed in other aspects of psychology, may feel overawed when first exploring the approach. Not all psychologists have, say, the detailed knowledge of linguistics, sociology and other disciplines that contribute to the field. Furthermore the distinctive contribution made by psychologists to discourse analysis is not always clear.

So discourse analysis studies language in ways very different from traditional linguistics. The latter is largely concerned with:

■ word sounds (phonetics and phonology)
■ units which make up words (morphology)
■ meaning (semantics)
■ word order within sentences (syntax)

Beaugrande (1996) refers to this traditional style of linguistics, in a somewhat derogatory fashion, as 'language science'. For him, traditional linguistics was at fault for profoundly disconnecting language from real-life communications – to just study sounds, words and sentences. In discourse analysis, language is regarded as being much more complex. Discourse is how language operates in real-life communicative events. Discourse analysis involves the analysis of speech, text and conversation so its concerns are with analyses beyond the level of the sentence. Hence, Stubbs (1983, p. 1) defines discourse analysis as being about the way in which language is used at the broader level than the sentence and other immediate utterances. A good illustration of this (Tannen, 2004) are the two signs at a swimming pool:

Please use the toilet, not the pool.
Pool for members only.

Considered separately, just as sentences, the signs convey clear messages. However, if they are read as a unit of two sentences, then they either constitute a request for non-members to swim in the toilet or an indication that members have exclusive rights to urinate in the swimming pool! Analysing just two sentences at a time as in this example causes us to re-write the meaning of both sentences.

Discourse analysis emphasises the ways in which language interacts with society especially in the nature of dialogue in ordinary conversation. Above all, then, discourse analysis is a perspective on the nature of language. Discourse analysis does *not* treat language as if it were essentially representational – language is not simply the means of articulating internal mental reality. Quite the reverse – discourse analysis is built on the idea that truth and reality are *not* identifiable or reachable through language.

Language for the discourse analyst is socially situated and it matters little whether the text under consideration is natural conversation or written text in the form, say, of newspaper headlines. Each of these provides suitable material for analysis. Since discourse analysis is a shift in the way language is conceptualised, what language does becomes more important than what is represented by language. Researchers in this field have different emphases, but it is typically the case that language is regarded as doing things and especially it is regarded as doing things in relation to other people in a conversation. As such, discourse analysis employs 'speech act theory' (Austin, 1975) which regards language as part of a social performance. In the course of this performance, social identities are formed and maintained, power relations are created, exercised and maintained, and generally a lot of social work is done. None of these can be effectively construed as language simply and directly communicating internal thought. Language in this context becomes a practice not a matter of informal or formal structures.

The phrase discourse analysis may arouse pictures of a well established empirical method of analysing people talking, interviews and so forth. In a sense it is. However, discourse analysis is *not* merely a number of relatively simple analytical skills that can quickly be learnt and easily applied. Some aspects are relatively simple. For example, transcription methods such as Jefferson's (Chapter 17) are relatively easily assimilated. In contrast, discourse analysts have frequently presented the definition and practice of discourse analysis as problematic. For example, Edley (2001) wrote:

> ... *there is no simple way of defining discourse analysis. It has become an ever-broadening church, an umbrella term for a wide variety of different analytic principles and practices.* [p. 189]

and Potter (2004) adds to the sense of incoherence:

> ... *in mid 80s it was possible to find different books called* Discourse Analysis *with almost no overlap in subject matter; the situation at the start of the 00s is, if anything, even more fragmented.* [p. 607]

and Taylor (2001) reinforces the view that discourse analysis should not be regarded as merely another variant or sub-discipline of methods:

> ... *to understand what kind of research discourse analysis is, it is not enough to study what the researcher does (like following a recipe!). We also need to refer back to these epistemological debates and their wider implications.* [p. 12]

Even discourse analysts with backgrounds in psychology do not offer a united front on its nature. Different viewpoints exist partly because they draw on different intellectual roots. Consequently, one needs to be aware that there is no consensus position which can be identified as the core of discourse analysis. This would help heighten and facilitate the theoretical debate, it is not a criticism.

19.1 Important characteristics of discourse

Within discourse analysis, there is a variety of ideas, observations and concepts that broadly suggest ways in which language and text should be analysed. These are discussed in this section.

Speech acts

Of particular importance to psychologists working in discourse analysis is the theory of *speech acts*. This originated in the work of Austin (1975). Performatives was his term for utterances which have a particular social effect. For Austin, all words perform social acts:

- *Locution*   This is simply the act of speaking.
- *Illocution*   This is what is done by saying these words.
- *Perlocution*   This is the effect or consequence on the hearer who hears the words.

To speak the words is essentially to do the act (speech act). For the words to have an effect certain conditions have to be met. These were illustrated in Searle (1969) using the following utterances:

> Sam smokes habitually
> Does Sam smoke habitually?
> Sam. Smoke habitually!
> Would that Sam smoked habitually.

Saying the words constitutes an *utterance act* or *locutory act*. They constitute the act of uttering something. At the same time, they are also propositional acts because they refer to something and predicate something. Try introducing any of them into a conversation with a friend. It is unlikely that the sentence could be said without some sort of response from the other person on the topic of Sam, smoking or both. Each of the sentences also constitutes an *illocutory act* because they do things like state, question, command, promise, warn, etc.

For example, in some contexts each of these sentences may contain an unstated indication that the speaker wishes to do something about Sam's smoking. 'Would that Sam smoked habitually' may be a slightly sardonic way of suggesting that it would be great if Sam could be persuaded to smoke as infrequently as habitually! Equally, if they were uttered by a shopkeeper about his customer Sam who spends large amounts on chocolates for his wife every time he calls in for a packet of cigarettes, the same words would constitute a different *illocutory act*. The sentences are also *perlocutionary* acts in that they have an effect or consequence on the hearer though what this effect is depends on circumstances. For example, the locution 'Sam smokes habitually' might be taken as a warning that the landlord is unhappy about Sam smoking in violation of his tenancy contract if said by Sam's landlord to Sam's wife. In speech act theory, the indirect nature of speech is inevitably emphasised since the interaction between language and the social context which is partially responsible for meaning.

Grice's maxims of cooperative speech

Another contribution which comes from the philosophy of language are Grice's (1975) maxims. These indicate something of the rule-based nature of exchanges between people. The overriding principle is conversational cooperativeness over what is being communicated at the time. Cooperativeness is achieved by obeying four maxims:

- Quality, which involves making truthful and sincere contributions.
- Quantity, which involves the provision of sufficient information.
- Manner, which involves making one's contributions brief, clear and orderly.
- Relation, which involves making relevant contributions.

These maxims contribute to effective communications. They are not the only principles underlying social exchanges. For example, unrestrained truthfulness may offend when it breeches politeness standards in conversation.

Face

Similarly, language often includes strategies for protecting the status of the various participants in the exchange. The notion of 'face' is taken from the work of Goffman (1959) to indicate the valued persona that individuals have. We speak of saving face in everyday conversation. Saving face is a collective phenomenon in which all members of the conversation may contribute, not simply the person at risk of losing face.

Register

The concept of register highlights the fact that when we speak the language style that we use varies according to the activity being carried out. The language used in a lecture is not the same as that used when a sermon is being given. This may be considered a matter of style but it is described as register. Register has a number of components including:

- field of activity (e.g. police interview, radio interview)
- medium used (e.g. spoken language, written language, dictated language)
- tenor of the role relationship in a particular situation (e.g. parent–child, police officer–witness)

19.2 The agenda of discourse analysis

It should be clear by now that discourse analysis is not a simple to learn, readily applied technique. Discourse analysis is a body of theory and knowledge accumulated over a period of 50 years or more. It is not even a single, integrated theory. Instead it provides an analytical focus for a range of theories contributed by a variety of disciplines such as philosophy, linguistics, sociology and anthropology. Psychology as somewhat a latecomer to the field is in the process of setting its own distinctive stamp on discourse analysis. What is the agenda for a discourse analysis-based approach to psychology? To re-stress the point, there are no short cuts to successful discourse analysis. Intellectual and theoretical roots are more apparent in the writings of discourse analysts than practically any other field of psychology. In other words, the most important *practical* step in using discourse analysis is to immerse oneself in its theoretical and research literature. One cannot just get on with doing discourse analysis. Without understanding in some depth the constituent parts of the discourse analytic tradition, the objectives of discourse analysis cannot be appreciated fully. This would be equally true of designing an experiment – we need to understand what it does, how it does it, why it does it, and when it is inappropriate.

The agenda of psychological discourse analysis according to Potter and Wetherell (1995) includes:

- *Practices and resources* Discourse analysis is not simply an approach to the social use of language. It focuses on discourse practices – the things that people do in talk and writings. But it also focuses on the resources that people employ when achieving these ends. For example, the strategies employed in their discourse, the systems of categorisation they use, and the interpretative repertoires that are used. Interpretative repertoires are the '. . . broadly discernible clusters of terms, descriptions, and figures of speech often assembled around metaphors or vivid images' (Potter and Wetherell, 1995, p. 89). So, for example, when newspapers and politicians write and talk about drugs they often use the language repertoire of war and battle. Hence the 'war on drugs', 'the enemy drugs' and so forth. Discourse analysis seeks also to provide greater understanding of traditional (socio-)psychological topics such as the nature of individual and collective identity, how to conceive social action and interaction, the nature of the human mind, and constructions of the self, others and the world.

■ *Construction and description*   During conversation and other forms of text, people create and construct 'versions' of the world. Discourse analysis attempts to understand and describe this constructive process.

■ *Content*   Talk and other forms of discourse are regarded as the important site of psychological phenomena. No attempt is made to postulate 'underlying' psychological mechanism to explain that talk. So racist talk is regarded as the means by which discrimination is put into practice. There is no interest in 'psychological mechanisms' such as authoritarian personalities or racist attitudes.

■ *Rhetoric*   Discourse analysis is concerned with how talk can be organised so as to be argumentatively successful or persuasive.

■ *Stake and accountability*   People regard others as having a vested interest (stake) in what they do. Hence they impute motives to the actions of others which may justify dismissing what these others say. Discourse analysis studies these processes.

■ *Cognition in action*   Discourse analysis actively rejects the use of cognitive concepts such as traits, motives, attitudes and memory stores. Instead it concentrates on the text by emphasising, for example, how memory is socially constructed by people, such as when reminiscing over old photographs.

This agenda might be considered a broad framework for psychological discourse analysis. It points to aspects of text which the analyst may take into account. At the same time, the hostility of discourse analysis to traditional forms of psychology is apparent.

BOX 19.1   CRITICAL DISCOURSE ANALYSIS

The term 'critical discourse analysis' has a rather narrower focus than the words might imply. Critical does *not* mean crucial in this context and neither does it imply a generally radical stance within the field of discourse analysis. Critical discourse analysis is simply a school of thought which emphasises *power and social inequality* in the interpretation of discourse. Critical discourse analysis studies the way in which power is attained and maintained through language. According to van Dijk (2001), *dominance* is the exercise of social power by elites, institutions and social groups. Consequences of the exercise of power include varieties of social inequality – ethnic, racial and gender inequality, for example. Equally, language has the potential to serve the interests of disadvantaged groups in order to redress and change the situation. The phrase 'black is beautiful', for example, was used to counter destructive effects on the self-image of black children of racist views of themselves.

→

Box 19.1 continued

Dominance is achieved using language in a variety of ways. For example, the way a group is represented in language, how language is used to reinforce dominance, and the means by which language is used to deny and conceal dominance:

> . . . *critical discourse analysts want to know what structures, strategies or other properties of text, talk, verbal interaction or communicative events play a role in these modes of reproduction.* [van Dijk, 2001, p. 300]

Brute force is an unacceptable means of achieving power in modern society. Persuasion and manipulation through language provide a substitute for violence, and so power is achieved and maintained through language.

Others extend the notion of 'critical' to include a wider set of concerns than van Dijk (2001). Hepburn (2003) suggests that it also includes issues of politics, morality and social change. These are all components or facets of van Dijk's notion of power. Concerns like these link to a long tradition of concerned psychology in which power, politics, morality and social change are staple ingredients (e.g. Howitt, 1992*a*).

19.3 Doing discourse analysis

It cannot be stressed too much that the objectives of discourse analysis are limited in a number of ways – especially the focus on the socially interactive use of language. In a nutshell, there is little point in doing a discourse analysis to achieve ends not shared by discourse analysis. Potter put the issue as follows:

> *To attempt to ask a question formulated in more traditional terms ('what are the factors that lead to condom use amongst HIV+ gay males') and then use discourse analytic methods to answer it is a recipe for incoherence.* [Potter, 2004, p. 607]

Only when the researcher is interested in language as social action is discourse analysis appropriate. Some discourse analysts have contributed to the confusion by offering it as a radical and new way of understanding psychological phenomena; for example, when they suggest that discourse analysis is anti cognitive psychology. This, taken superficially, may imply that discourse analysis supersedes other forms of psychology. It is more accurate to suggest that discourse analysis performs a different task. A discourse analysis would be useless for biological research on genetic engineering but an excellent choice to look at the ways in which the moral and ethical issues associated with genetic engineering are dealt with in speech and conversation.

Although a total novice can easily learn some of the skills of discourse analysis (e.g. Jefferson transcription), doing a good discourse analysis is far harder. Reading is crucial but experience and practice also play their parts. The best way to get a feel of what a discourse analysis is, is to read the work of the best discourse analysts. That would apply to all forms of research. A report of a discourse analysis makes frequent reference to research and theory in the field. We have outlined some of this but ideas are developing continually.

There is a degree of smog surrounding the steps by which a discourse analysis is done. It is not like calculating a *t*-test or chi-square in a step-by-step fashion. No set of procedures exists which, if applied, guarantee a successful discourse analysis. Potter puts it as follows:

> *There is no single recipe for doing discourse analysis. Different kinds of studies involve different procedures, sometimes working intensively with a single transcript, other times drawing on a large corpus. Analysis is a craft that can be developed with different degrees of skill. It can be thought of as the development of sensitivity to the occasioned and action-oriented, situated, and constructed nature of discourse. Nevertheless, there are a number of ingredients which, when combined together are likely to produce something satisfying.* [Potter, 2004, p. 611]

The use of the word 'craft' suggests the carpenter's workshop in which nothing of worth can be produced until the novice has learnt to sharpen tools, select wood, mark out joints, saw straight, and so forth. Likewise in discourse analysis, the tools are slowly mastered. Actually, Potter (1997) puts it even more graphically when he wrote that for the most part:

> *. . . doing discourse analysis is a craft skill, more like bike riding or chicken sexing than following the recipe for a mild chicken rogan josh.* [p. 95]

Publications which seek to explain the process of discourse analysis often resort to a simple strategy: students are encouraged to apply the concepts developed by major contributors to discourse theory. In other words, tacitly the approach encourages the novice discourse analyst to find instances in their data of key discourse analytic concepts. For example, they are encouraged to identify what register is being employed, what awkwardness is shown in the conversation, what rhetorical devices are being used, what discourse repertoires are being employed and so forth. Some of this is redolent of the work of expert discourse analysts. If one initially attempts to understand the text under consideration using standard discourse analytic concepts, the later refinement and extension of these concepts will be facilitated. Areas which are problematic in terms of the application of standard concepts will encourage the revision of those concepts. At this stage, the analysis may begin to take a novel turn.

The features of language which need to be examined in a discourse analysis can be listed. This may be described as an itinerary for discourse analysis (Wetherell and Taylor, 2001). Where to go and what to look for, as well as the dead-ends that should be ignored, are part of this. So one may interrogate one's data to find out which of the following are recognisable or applicable to the particular text in question:

■ Language is an inappropriate way of accessing reality. Instead language should be regarded as constructive or constitutive of social life. Through discourse, individuals and groups of individuals build social relations, objects and worlds.

■ Since discourse constructs versions of social reality, an important question of any text is why a particular version of reality is being constructed through language and what does this particular version accomplish?

■ Meaning is produced in the context of speech and does not solely reside in a cultural storehouse of agreed definitions. Discourse analysts refer to the co-production of meaning. The analysis partly seeks to understand the processes by which meaning is created. Meaning, for example, is a 'joint production' of two or more individuals in conversation.

■ Discursive practice refers to the things which happen in language to achieve particular outcomes.

■ Discursive genres are the type of language extract under consideration. So the discourse analyst may study the particular features of news and how it differs from other types of language. There are cues in news speech which provide indicators that it is news speech rather than, say, a sermon (contextualisation cues).

■ Footing (a concept taken from the sociologist Goffman) refers to whether the speaker talks as if they are the author of what is being said, the subject of the words that are being said, or whether they are presenting or animating the words of someone else. These different footings are not mutually exclusive and all may be present in any text.

■ Speech is dialogical. That is, when we talk we combine or incorporate things from other conversations. Sometimes this is in the form of reporting what 'he said' or what 'she replied'. More often, however, the dialogical elements are indirect and not highlighted directly as such. For example, children who say something like 'I mustn't go out on my own' reflect previous conversations with their parents and teachers.

Taylor (2001) characterises discourse analysis as an 'open-ended' and circular (or iterative) process. The task of the researcher is to find patterns without a clear idea of what the patterns will be like. She writes of the 'blind faith' that there must be something there worthy of the considerable effort of analysis. The researcher will need to go through the data repeatedly 'working up' the analysis on the basis of what fits and does not fit tentative patterns. 'Data analysis is not accomplished in one or two sessions' (pp. 38–9). Taylor indicates that the process of examination and re-examination may not fit comfortably with conventional research time scales. The direction or end point of the analysis is also difficult to anticipate. She feels that qualitative data are so 'rich' (that is detailed) that there may be more worth studying in the data even when the possibilities seem to be exhausted.

Example

In research on menstruation, Lovering (1995) talked with 11 and 12-year-old boys and girls in discussion groups. Among a range of topics included on her guide for conducting the discussions were issues to do with menstruation. These included questions such as: 'Have you heard of menstruation?'; 'What have you been told about it?'; 'What do you think happens when a woman menstruates?'; 'Why does it happen?'; and 'Who has told you?' (Lovering, 1995, p. 17). In this way relatively systematic material could be gathered in ways closer to ordinary conversation than would be generated by one-on-one interviews. She took detailed notes of her experiences as soon as possible after the discussion groups using a number of headings (p. 17):

■ How she felt
■ General emotional tone and reactions
■ Non-verbal behaviour
■ Content recalled
■ Implications and thoughts.

This is a form of diary writing of the sort discussed already in relation to grounded theory. The difference perhaps is that she applied it to the data collection phase rather than the transcription phase. Lovering transcribed the tape-recording herself – eventually using the Jefferson system described in Chapter 17. She also employed a computer based analysis program (of the sort that N-vivo is the modern equivalent). Such a program does not do the analysis for you – it allows you to store and work with a lot of text, highlight or mark particular parts of the text, sort the text and print it out. All of these things can be achieved just using pencil and paper, but a computer is more convenient.

The next stage was to sort the text into a number of categories – she had initially more than 50. She developed an analysis of the transcribed material partly based on her aware-ness of a debate about the ways in which male and female bodies are socially construed quite differently. Boys' physical development is regarded as a gradual and unproblematic process, whereas in girls the process is much more problematic. The following excerpts from a transcript illustrate this:

A: They [school teachers] don't talk about the boys very much only the girls = yes = yes.
A: It doesn't seem fair. They are laughing at us. Not much seems to happen to boys.
A: Girl all go funny shapes = yes = like that = yes.
A: Because the boys, they don't really . . . change very much. They just get a little bit bigger.
A: It feels like the girls go through all the changes because we are not taught anything about the boys REALLY. [Lovering, 1995, pp. 23–4]

Menstruation was learnt about from other people – predominantly female teachers or mothers. Embarrassment dominated, and the impression created was that menstruation was not to be discussed or even mentioned as a consequence. Talk of female bodies and bodily functions by the youngsters features a great deal of sniggering. In contrast, when discussing male bodies things become more ordinary and more matter of fact. Further-more, boys are also likely to use menstruation as a psychological weapon against girls. That is, menstruation is used to make jokes about and ridicule girls. In Lovering's analysis, this is part of male oppression of females – even in sex education lessons learning about menstruation is associated in girls minds as being 'laughing at girls'.

Of course, many more findings emerged in this study. Perhaps what is important is the complexity of the process by which the analysis proceeds. It is not possible to say that if the researcher does this and then does that, a good analysis will follow. Nevertheless, it is easy to see how the researcher's ideas relate to key aspects of discourse analytic thinking. For example, the idea that menstruation is used as a weapon of oppression of females clearly has its roots in feminist sexual politics which suggests that males attempt to con-trol females in many ways from domestic violence through rape to, in this example, sex education lessons. One could equally construe this as part of Edwards and Potter's (1993) discursive action model. This suggests, amongst other things, that in talk, conversation or text, one can see social action unfolding before one's eyes. One does not have to regard talk, text or conversation as the external manifestation or symptom of an underlying mental state such as an attitude. A topic like menstruation may be seen to generate not merely hostility in the form of laughter towards the female body, but also as a means of accessing concepts of femininity in which the female body is construed as mysterious, to be embarrassed about, and sniggered over by both sexes. Horton-Salway (2001) uses the same sort of model to analyse how the medical profession went about presenting the medical condition ME in a variety of ways through language.

Discourse analysis, like other forms of qualitative analyses, is not amenable to short summaries. This might be expected given that a discourse analysis seeks to provide appropriate analytic categories for a wide range of texts. The consequence is that anyone wishing to understand discourse analytic approaches will need to read original analyses in detail.

19.4 Conclusion

One of the significant achievements of discourse analysis is that of bringing to psychology a theoretically fairly coherent set of procedures for the analysis of the very significant amounts of textual material which forms the basis of much psychological data. It has to be understood that discourse analysis has a limited perspective on the nature of this data. In particular, discourse analysts reject the idea that language is representational – that is, in language there is a representation of, say, the individual's internal psychological state. Instead they replace it with the idea that language is action and is designed to do something, not represent something. As a consequence, discourse analysis is primarily of use to researchers who wish to study language as an active thing. In this way, discourse analysis may contribute a different perspective on many psychological processes, but it does not replace or supersede the more traditional viewpoints within psychology.

Key points

- Discourse analysis is based on early work carried out by linguists, especially during the 1950s and 1960s which reconstrued language much as a working set of resources to allow things to be done rather than regarding language as merely being a representation of something else.

- The analysis uses larger units of speech than words or sentences such as a sequence of conversational exchanges.

- Precisely how discourse analysis is defined is somewhat uncertain as it encompasses a wide range of practices as well as theoretical orientations.

- Central to most discourse analysis is the idea of speech as doing things – such as constructing and construing meaning.

- Discourse analysis has its own roadmap which should be considered when planning an analysis. Discourse practices and resources, for example, are the things that people do in constructing conversations, texts and writings. Rhetoric is about the wider organisation of language in ways that facilitate its effectiveness. Content is regarded for what it is rather than what underlying psychological states it represents.

- Critical discourse analysis has as its central focus the concept of power. It primarily concerns how social power is created, reaffirmed and challenged through language.

Activities

1. When having a coffee with friends, note occasions when the conversation might be better seen as speech acts rather than taken literally. Better still, if you can tape record such a conversation, transcribe a few minutes' worth and highlight in red where literal interpretations would be appropriate and in yellow where the concept of speech act might be more appropriate.

2. Study day-to-day conversations of which you are part. Is there any evidence that participants spare other participants in the conversation embarrassment over errors? That is, to what extent does face-saving occur in your day-to-day experience?

3. Choose a chapter of your favourite novel: does discourse analysis have more implications for its contents than more traditional psychology?

20 Conversation analysis

Overview

■ Conversation analysis studies the structure of conversation by detailed examination of successive turns or contributions to a conversation.

■ It is based on ethnographic approaches derived from sociology that stress the importance of participants' understandings of the nature of the world.

■ Many of the conventions of psychological research are turned on their head in conversation analysis. The primacy of theory in developing research questions and hypotheses is replaced by a stress on the importance of the data in generating explanations.

■ Because of its reversal of conventional psychological research methodology, conversation analysis warrants the careful attention of all psychologists since it helps define the nature of psychological research.

Conversation analysis has its intellectual roots in ethnomethodology championed in the 1960s by the American sociologist Howard Garfinkel (1967). He wanted to understand the way in which interactions in everyday life are conducted. In particular, ethnomethodologists were concerned with ordinary everyday conversation. The term 'ethnomethodology' signifies his method of studying the common sense 'methodology' used by ordinary conversationalists to conduct social interactions. Just how is interaction constructed and managed into largely unproblematic sequences?

One of Garfinkel's major contributions was to show that everyday interaction between people involves a *search for meaning*. Care is needed because Garfinkel was *not* saying that everyday interaction is meaningful as such – only that participants in that interaction regard it as meaningful. To demonstrate this he relied on a form of experimental research. In one example of this, students attended a 'counselling' session in a university's psychiatry department (McHugh, 1968). The situation was such that participants only communicated indirectly with the 'counsellor' who, totally at random, replied to the client with either 'yes' or 'no'. In this instance, essentially the real-world was chaotic and meaningless (unless, of course, one is aware of the random process and the purpose of the study). Nevertheless the participants in the research dealt with this chaotic situation of random responses by imposing a meaningful and organised view of the situation. The concern of ethnomethodologists such as Garfinkel and Cicourel with the fine detail of this sense-making process influenced others – the most important of whom was Harvey Sacks, who is regarded as the founder of conversation analysis.

During the 1960s, Sacks became interested in the telephone calls made to hospital emergency departments (Sacks, 1992). While some researchers might have sought to classify the types of calls made, for example, Sacks had a much more profound approach to his chosen subject matter. Substantial numbers of callers to the emergency department would wind up not providing their name. Obviously, this limited the possible response of the hospital once the conversation ceased – in those days, without a name it would be virtually impossible to track down the caller. Sacks wanted to know by what point in a telephone conversation one could know that the caller would be unlikely to give their name. That is, what features of the telephone conversation were associated with withheld names?

His research strategy involved an intense examination of the detail of such conversations. In conversation analysis, emphasis is placed on the analysis of turn taking – members of conversations take turns to speak. Look at the following opening turns in a telephone conversation:

Member of staff: Hello, this is Mr Smith. May I help you?
Caller: Yes this is Mr Brown.

The first turn is the member of staff's 'Hello, this is Mr Smith. May I help you?' In this case, by the second turn in the conversation (the contribution of the caller), the caller's name is known. However, if the *second* turn in the conversation was something like:

Caller: Speak up please – I can't hear you.

or

Caller: Spell your name please.

there would be the greatest difficulty in getting the caller's name. Often the name would not be obtained at all. One reason for this is that the phrase 'May I help you?' may be interpreted by the caller as indicative of a member of staff who is just following the procedures laid down by the training scheme for staff at the hospital. In other words, if the caller believes that they have special needs or that their circumstances are special, 'May I help you?' merely serves to indicate that the they are being treated as another routine case.

Two conversation turns (e.g. as in the above examples) in sequence are known as 'adjacency pairs' and essentially constitute the major unit of analysis in conversation analysis. Without the emphasis on adjacency pairs, the structured, turn-taking nature of conversation would be obscured. A prime objective of conversation analysis is to understand how an utterance is 'designed' to fit in with the previous utterances – and the likely nature of subsequent turns in the conversation. In other words, conversation analysis explores the coherence of patterns in turns. By concentrating on adjacent pairs of turns, the researcher works with much the same building blocks as the participants in the conversation themselves in their task of giving coherence to the conversation.

Telephone conversations illustrate conversation analysis principles well in that they indicate something of the organised nature of even the simplest of conversational acts:

a: Hello
b: Hello its me
a: Hi Jenny
b: You took a long time to answer the phone

It is quite easy to see in this the use of greetings such as *Hello* to allow for the voice identification of the speaker. There is also an assumption that the hearer should be able to recognise the voice. Finally there is an expectation that the ring of a telephone should initiate the response fairly rapidly in normal circumstances. It does not take a great deal to figure out that this is likely to be a call between close friends rather than, say, a business call. This interpretation may not be sophisticated in terms of the principles of conversation analysis, but it does say a good deal about the nature of turn taking in general and especially in telephone calls.

For anyone grounded in the mainstream methods of psychology, there is a major 'culture shock' when confronted with a research paper on conversation analysis. It is almost as if one is faced with a research paper stripped bare. The typical features of a psychology report may well be missing. For example, the literature review may be absent or minimal, details of sampling, or participant or interaction selection are often sparse, and generally detail of the social context in which the conversation took place is largely missing. Some of the reasons for this are the traditions of conversation analysis. More important is the realisation that what is crucial in terms of understanding everyday conversation is the way in which the conversation is understood structurally by the participants. As such, theoretical discussions would obstruct ethnomethodological understanding since the theory is not being used by the participants in the conversation. Similarly, details of the social context of the conversation, while important from some perspectives, for a conversation analyst they miss the point. The key point is that in conversation analysis the principles of conversation are regarded as directly governing the conversation. The consideration of factors extraneous to the conversation merely diverts attention away from this.

In conversation analysis the study of how ordinary life is conducted involves:

■ The *recording* stage in which conversation is put on video tape or audio-only recording equipment.

■ *Transcription* in which the recording or parts of the recording are transcribed using minutely detailed transcription conventions of the sort primarily associated with Gail Jefferson (see Chapter 17). These conventions do not merely include what has been said but, crucially, detail of the *way* in which it has been said.

■ *Analysis* consists of the researcher identifying aspects of the transcription of note for some reason, then offering suggestions as to the nature of the conversational device which may be responsible for the significant features.

Conversation analysis essentially eschews the postulate that there are key psychological mechanisms which underlie conversation. Interaction through talk is not regarded as the external manifestation of inner cognitive processes. In this sense, whether or not participants in conversation have intentions, motives or interests, personality and character is irrelevant. The domain of interest in conversation analysis is the structure of conversation (Woolfit, 2001). This, of course, refers to the psychological theorising of the researcher – the participants in the conversation may well incorporate psychological factors into their understanding of the conversation and, more importantly, refer to them in the conversation.

20.1 Precepts of conversation analysis

A major objective of conversation analysis is the identification of repeated patterns in conversation that arise from the joint endeavour of the speakers to produce conversation. One example of such a pattern is the preference of members of a conversation to allow conversational errors to be self-corrected (as opposed to being corrected by other participants in the conversation). The next person to speak after the error may offer some device to prompt or initiate the 'repair' without actually making the repair. For example, a brief silence may provide the opportunity for the person who has said the wrong thing to correct themselves.

Drew (1995) provided a list of methodological precepts or principles for doing a conversation analysis:

- A participant's contribution (turn) is regarded as the product of the sequence of turns preceding it in the conversation. Turns are basically subject to a requirement that they fit appropriately and coherently to the prior turn. That is, adjacency pairs fit together effectively and meaningfully.

- Participants develop analyses of each other's verbal conduct. The nature of these analyses is to be found in the detail of each participant's utterances. Contributors to a conversation interpret one another's intentions and attribute intention and meaning to each other's turns as talk. (Notice that intention and meaning are *not* being provided by the researcher but by the participants in the conversation.)

- Conversation analysts study the design of each turn in the conversation. That is, they seek to understand the activity that a turn is designed to perform in terms of the details of its verbal construction.

- The principal objective of conversational analysis is to identify the sequential organisation or patterns in conversation.

- The recurrence and systematic nature of patterns in conversation are demonstrated and tested by the researcher. This is done by reference to collections of cases of the conversational feature under examination.

- Data extracts are presented in such a way as to enable others to assess or challenge the researcher's analysis. That is, detailed transcriptions are made available in a conventional transcription format (Jefferson transcription).

To make things more concrete, conversation analysts have a special interest in:

- How turn-taking is achieved in conversation.
- How the utterances within a person's turn in the conversation are constructed.
- How difficulties in the flow of a conversation are identified and sorted-out.

Having addressed these basic questions or issues, conversation analysts then attempt to apply them to other domains of conversation. So they might study what happens in hearings in courts of law, telephone conversations, when playing games or during interviews. In this way, the structure of conversation can be explored more deeply and more comparatively.

20.2 Stages in conversation analysis

Unlike most other approaches to research, conversation analysis rejects theoretical speculation about the significant aspects of conversation. A conversation analyst does *not* start with theory which is explored or tested against conversation. The conversation analyst's way of studying conversation is to understand the rules that ordinary people are using in conversation. So the ethnomethodological orientation of conversation-analysis strategy stresses the importance of the participant's interpretations of the interaction – the priorities are not to be laid down by the researcher in this sense. The participants' interpretations as revealed in the conversation are assumed to be much more salient than any arbitrary, theory-led speculative set of priorities established by researchers (Woolfit, 2001). That is, conversation analysis does *not* involve hypothesis testing based on cumulative and all-embracing theory.

The conversation analyst's fundamental strategy is to work through the fragments of conversation, making notes of anything that seems interesting or significant. There is no limit to the number of observations that may be written down as part of the analysis process. However, it is crucial that the conversation analyst confines themselves solely to the data in question. They must not move beyond the data to speculate whether, for example, the participant has made a revealing Freudian slip or that in reality they meant to say something quite different. If you like, this is the conversation analysis mindset – a single-minded focus on seemingly irrelevant, trivial detail. Nothing in the interaction being studied can be discarded or disregarded as inconsequential. Consequently, the transcripts used in conversation analysis are messy in that they contain many non-linguistic features. In order to ensure the transcript's fidelity to the original tape, transcripts contain such things as false starts to words and the gaps between words and participants' turns. In conversation analysis, tidying up transcripts is a cardinal sin.

Paul ten Have (2003) has provided a seven-step model of conversation analysis' research practices. Practice implies the way things are done rather than some idealised concept of a research method. Conversation analysts frequently claim that there are no set ways of proceeding. Nevertheless, analysis is confined by fairly strict parameters, knowledge of which should help the novice to avoid straying too far beyond the purview of conversation analysis. Have's steps are best regarded as an ideal for researchers in the field. They are not necessarily characteristic of any particular analyst's work in their entirety.

Step 1: *Mechanical production of the primary database (materials to be analysed)*

Data recording is done by a machine. A human decides what and when to record, but the recording is basically unselective, so that what is recorded is not filtered through human thinking systems, tidied up and the like. This original recording may be returned to at any point. For that reason, the recording remains available continually throughout the analysis for checking purposes by the researcher or even by others (Drew, 1995).

Step 2: *Transcription*

The production of the transcript is ideally free from considerations of the expectations of the researcher. That is, the transcription should be as unsullied by the transcriber as possible. To this end, the transcript may be checked against the mechanical recording by the transcriber or other researchers. There are, of course, several possible 'hearings' for any mechanical recording. Each transcriber needs to be alert to this possibility. Many regard it as essential that the researcher themselves transcribes the recording. This ensures the close familiarity that is needed for effective analysis. However, no matter how good the transcription is, it cannot be complete and something must be lost in the process. Nevertheless, the transcription forces the researcher to confront a rich detail of the conversation. The presence of the transcript in the research report means that the analyst and others must be precise in their analysis of the detail of the conversation. This direct link with the data is not possible in some other styles of research. The summary tables of statistics, for example, found in much psychological research cannot be related directly back to the data that were collected. The links are too deeply buried for this. Few researchers present their data in such a raw form as is conventional in conversational analysis.

Step 3: *Selection of the aspects of the transcript to be analysed*

There are no formal rules for this and it can simply be a case of the analyst being intrigued by certain aspects of the conversation. Others may be interested in particular aspects of an interaction – as Sacks was when he investigated name-giving in telephone conversations to hospitals. Others may wish to concentrate on the contributions of particularly skilled contributors to a conversation such as where a major shift in the conversation is achieved. Just the one adjacency pair (the minimum unit that makes up a conversation) may be sufficient to proceed.

Step 4: *Making sense of/interpreting the conversational episode*

Researchers are part of the culture that produced the conversational episode. Hence, they can use their own common sense knowledge of language to make sense of the episode. This is appropriate since it reflects what participants in the interaction do when producing and responding in the conversation (constructing adjacency pairs). Typically the analyst may ask what aspects of the conversation do or achieve during exchanges. The relation between different aspects of conversation can then be assessed.

Step 5: *Explication of the interpretation*

Because the conversation analyst is a member of the broad community whose conversations he or she studies, the researcher's native or common sense understanding of what happens in an episode is clearly a useful resource. Nevertheless, this is insufficient as an explication without bringing the links between this resource and the detail of the conversational episode together. That is, the analyst may feel they know what is happening in the conversation, but they need to demonstrate how their understanding links to the detail of the conversation.

Step 6: *Elaboration of the analysis*

Once a particular episode has been analysed, the rest of the transcription can be used to elaborate on it. Later sequences in the conversation may in some way, directly or indirectly, relate back to the analyst's central conversational episode. The conversationalists may hark back to the earlier episode and reveal ways in which they understood it. As a consequence, the analyst may need to reformulate the analysis in some way or even substitute a completely different analysis.

Step 7: *Comparison with episodes from other conversations*

The analysis process does not end with a particular transcription and its analysis. It continues to other instances of conversation which are apparently similar. This is vital since a particularly conversational episode is *not* considered to be unique since the devices or means by which a conversational episode is both recognised and produced by the conversationalists are the same for other conversationalists and conversations. Some studies specifically aim to collect together different 'samples' of conversation in order that these different samples may be compared one with the other. In this way, similarities and dissimilarities enforce refinement of the analysis.

Steps 4 to 7 may seem less distinct in the analysis process itself than is warranted by describing them as separate steps. Have's steps are schematic. They do not always constitute a precise and invariant sequence of steps which analysts must follow invariably and rigidly. Ultimately the aim of conversational analysis is not the interpretation of any particular episode of conversation. Conversation analysis adopts the basic ethno-methodological aim of understanding the structure of everyday social activity as its fundamental quest.

20.3 Examples

There are a number of good examples of conversation analysis in the work of psychologists – even though it is difficult to specify how the work of a sociologist, for example, analysing the same conversation would be different. The following are particularly useful in that they clearly adopt some of the sensibilities of mainstream psychology.

Cold reading

Psychic phenomena are controversial. Woolfit (2001) studied 'cold reading'. That is, the situation when on the basis of very little conversation with a client, the medium seems to have gathered a great deal of information from beyond the grave. Some commentators suggest that the medium simply uses the limited interaction with the client to gather information about the client. This information is then fed back to the client as evidence of the medium's psychic powers.

Conversation analysts might be expected to have something to say about these 'conversations' between a medium and a client. The following excerpt from such a conversation is typical of what goes on between a psychic (P) and a client (S) (Woolfitt, 2001):

Extract 31
P: .h Ty'ever though(t) o(f) .h did you want to go into a caring profession early <u>on</u>,
     when you were choosing which way you were gonna go.
(.)
S: yeah I wanted to: go into child care actually when I
P: MMMmmm. . . .
S: =when I left school
P: That's right yeah >well< h (.) 'm being shown that>but (t)-< h it's (0.2) it's not
     your way ye(t) actually but i(t) y'y may be caring for (t-)ch- children or whatever
     later on okay?

Although this excerpt is written using Jefferson transcription methods (Chapter 17 will help you decode this), in this case the importance of the excerpt can be understood simply on the basis of the sequence of words.

What happens? Well first of all the psychic asks a question about caring professions. Then the client replies but the reply is fairly extended as the client explains that they wanted to go into child care. The psychic then interrupts with 'MMMmmm'. The client carries on talking but quickly at the first appropriate stage the psychic takes over the conversation again with 'That's right yeah'. The information is then characterised by the psychic as emanating from the spiritual world. In terms of the conventional explanation of cold reading phenomena, this is a little surprising. One would expect that the psychic would allow the client to reveal more about themselves if the purpose of the conversation is to extract information which is then fed back to the client as if coming from the spiritual world.

In contrast, what appears to be happening is that the psychic rapidly moves to close down the turn by the client. Woolfit (2001) argues that the first turn in the sequence (when the medium asks the question) is constructed so as to elicit a relatively short turn by the client (otherwise the psychic might just as well have asked the client to tell the story of their life). So ideally the client will simply agree with what the psychic says in the second turn of the sequence. This does not happen in the above example. If it had, then the floor (turn to speak) would have returned quickly to the psychic. As it happens, the psychic has to interrupt the client's turn as quickly as possible.

By analysing many such excerpts from psychic–client conversations, it was possible to show that if the client gives more than a minimal acceptance of what the psychic says, then the psychic will begin to overlap the client's turn, eventually forcing the client's turn to come to an end. Once this is done, the psychic can attribute their first statement (question) to paranormal sources. Woolfit describes this as a three-turn series of utterances: a proposal is made about the sitter, this is accepted by the sitter, and then it is portrayed in terms of being supernatural in origin. Without the emphasis on the structure of turns which comes from conversation analysis, Woolfit may well have overlooked this significant pattern.

Date rape

One notable feature of conversation analysis is that it dwells on the everyday and mundane. Much of the data for conversation analysis lack any lustre or intrinsic interest. This is another way of saying that conversation analysis has explored ordinary conversation as a legitimate research goal. However, it is intriguing to find that the principles originating out of everyday conversation can find resonance in the context of more extraordinary situations – date rape for example. Training courses to help young women prevent date rape often include sessions teaching participants how to say 'no' – that is, refusal skills in this case for unwanted sexual intercourse (Kitzinger and Frith, 2001).

Research by conversation analysts about refusals following invitations has revealed the problematic nature of saying 'no' irrespective of the type of invitation. That is, saying 'yes' to an invitation tends to be an extremely smooth sequence without gaps or any other indication of conversational hiccups. Refusing an invitation, on the other hand, produces problems in the conversation. For example, there is likely to be a measurable delay of half a second between invitation and refusal. Similarly, 'umm' or 'well' is likely to come before the refusal. Palliatives phrases such as 'That's really kind of you but . . .' may be used. Finally, refusal is likely to be followed by justifications or excuses for the refusal whereas acceptance requires no justification. Kitzinger and Frith (2001) argue that date-rape prevention programmes fail by not recognising the everyday difficulties inherent in refusing an invitation. That it is problematic (even when refusing sexual intercourse) can be seen in the following exchange between two young women:

> *Liz*: It just doesn't seem right to say no when you're up there in the situation.
> *Sara*: It's not rude, it's not rude – just sounds awful to say this, doesn't it.
> *Liz*: I know.
> *Sara*: It's not rude, but it's the same sort of feeling. It's like, 'oh my god, I can't say no now, can I?' [Kitzinger and Frith, 2001, p. 175]

Using a focus group methodology, Kitzinger and Frith (2001) found that young women who participated in these groups deal with the problem of refusing sexual intercourse on dates by 'softening the blow' with a 'more acceptable excuse':

> *. . . young women talk about good excuses as being those which assert their inability (rather than their unwillingness) to comply with the demand that they engage in sexual intercourse: from the vague (and perhaps, for that reason, irrefutable) statement that they are 'not ready', through to sickness and menstruation.* [p. 176]

20.4 Conclusion

Conversation analysis provides psychology with an array of analytical tools and methods that may benefit a range of fields of application. Nevertheless, essentially conversation analysis springs from rather different intellectual roots from the bulk of mainstream psychology and specifically excludes from consideration many quintessential psychological approaches. Furthermore, in terms of detailed methodological considerations, conversation analysis reverses many of the conventional principles of mainstream research methods. For example, the context of the conversation studied is not a particular concern of conversation analysts so detail about sampling and so forth may appear inadequate. This reversal of many of the assumptions of conventional psychological research methods warrants the attention of all researchers as it helps define the assumptions of conventional research.

Like other areas of qualitative research, some practitioners are gradually beginning to advocate the use of quantification in the analysis of data. This is obviously not popular with all qualitative researchers. However, if a conversation analyst makes claims that imply that there are certain relationships between one feature of conversation and another, it would seem perverse not to examine the likelihood that one feature of conversation will follow another.

Key points

- Conversation analysis emerged in the 1960s in the context of developments in sociological theory.

- Ethnomethodology was developed by Garfinkel almost as the reversal of the grand-scale sociological theories of the time. Ethnomethodology concerned itself with everyday understandings of ordinary events constructed by ordinary people.

■ Harvey Sacks is considered to be the founder of conversation analysis. His interest was in the way conversation is structured around turns and how one turn melds with the earlier and later turns.

■ Conversation analysis requires a detailed analysis and comparison of the minutiae of conversation as conversation. It draws little on resources outside of the conversation (such as the social context, psychological characteristics of the individuals and so forth).

■ Superficially, some of the features characteristic of conversation analysis may seem extremely sloppy. For example, the downplaying of the established research literature in the field prior to the study of data, the lack of contextual material on the conversation, and the apparent lack of concern over matters like sampling are reversals of the usual standards of psychological research.

■ Carrying out conversation analysis involves the researcher in close analysis of the data in a number of ways. In particular, the Jefferson conversation transcription system encourages the researcher to examine the detail rather than the broad thrust of conversation. The transcription is interpreted, reinterpreted, checked and compared with other transcriptions of similar material in the belief that there is something 'there' for the analyst.

■ Conversation analysis is commonly applied to the most mundane of material. Its primary concern, after all, is understanding the structure of ordinary or routine conversation. However, the insights concerning ordinary conversation highlight issues for researchers attempting to understand less ordinary situations.

Activities

1. Collect samples of conversation by tape recording 'natural' conversations. Does turn-taking differ between genders? Does turn-taking differ cross-gender? Is there any evidence that 'repairs' to 'errors' in the conversation tend to be left to the 'error-maker'?

2. Make a list of points which explain what is going on in an episode of conversation. Which of your points would be acceptable to a conversation analyst? Which of your points involve considerations beyond the episode such as psychological motives or intentions, or sociological factors such as social class?

21 Evaluating qualitative research

Overview

- The evaluation of qualitative research emphasises the value of the analysis – that is the coding process.

- Evaluating qualitative research requires a clear understanding of the intellectual roots and origins of qualitative research in psychology. Hence you need to study Chapters 15 to 20 before this chapter.

- Many criteria are similar in some ways to those applied to quantitative analysis. However, great emphasis is placed on ensuring that the analysis corresponds closely to qualitative ideals.

- Suggestions are made as to how a newcomer to qualitative research should tackle self-evaluation of their work.

Surely qualitative research is evaluated in much the same ways as quantitative research? This is not so. Qualitative research may be evaluated in a number of ways, none of which in themselves can be regarded as seals of approval. Some of the criteria are quite close to the positivistic position (reliability and validity) but, as we saw in Chapter 15, this is eschewed by at least some qualitative researchers. Some of these prefer to emphasise the radically different philosophies which straddle the quantitative–qualitative divide. For example, quantitative researchers take it for granted that observations should be reliable in the sense that different researchers' observations of the same events are expected to be similar. That is, different observers should observe the same thing if the data are of value. In contrast, some qualitative researchers argue that this is an inappropriate criterion for evaluating data. They point out that different readers of any text will have a different interpretation (reading) of the text. The diversity of interpretations, they argue, is the nature of textual material and should be welcomed by qualitative analysts and so different 'readings' of the data should not be regarded as methodological flaws. The underlying difference between quantitative and qualitative researchers is not a matter of numbers and statistics. It is much more fundamental. At its most extreme, quantitative and qualitative research are alternative ways of seeing the world, not just different ways of carrying out research.

According to Denscombe (2002) there are a number of features that distinguish good research *of all types* from not so good research. Among the features that he lists are the following:

■ The contribution of new knowledge.
■ The use of precise and valid data.
■ The data are collected and used in a justifiable way.
■ The production of findings from which generalisations can be made.

These are tantalisingly simple criteria which are hard to question. Perhaps the difficulty is that they are so readily accepted. Some might suggest that we are all so imbued with positivist ideas that we no longer recognise them in our thinking. Phrases such as 'new knowledge', 'precise/valid data', 'justifiable' and 'generalisation' may be more problematic than at first appears. What is new knowledge for example? By what criteria do we decide that research has contributed new knowledge? What is precise and valid data? How precise need data be to make them acceptable in research? For what purposes do the data need to be valid to make them worthwhile? Why should worthwhile knowledge be generalisable? Should knowledge that works for New York City be generalisable to a village in Mali?

This boils down to the problematic nature of evaluation criteria. If it is difficult to suggest workable criteria for quantitative research, just what criteria should be applied to qualitative research? One approach is to recognise that much qualitative research has its intellectual roots in post-modernist ideas which, in themselves, are a reaction against the modernist ideas of traditional science and positivism. That is, it would seem that the criteria should be different for qualitative and quantitative research. It would seem better to seek criteria which are equally applicable to post-modernist and modernist work. One such set of criteria are those which determine high standards of scholarship in any field. What are these criteria? Careful analysis, detachment, accuracy, questioning and insight are among the suggestions. But there is nothing in such criteria which clarifies what is good psychology and what is bad. As we saw in Chapter 15, the intellectual roots of qualitative analysis are outside psychology. And why is detachment a useful criterion – it hints that the researcher ideally is an almost alienated figure. Indeed, criteria such as detachment have been criticised for encouraging research to be anodyne (e.g. Howitt, 1992*a*).

Universal criteria for evaluating what is good psychology may be a futile quest and possibly an undesirable one. Such an endeavour would seem to miss the point since epistemological bases of qualitative and quantitative research are in many ways incompatible. Many of the precepts of quantitative research are systematically reversed by coteries of qualitative researchers. For example, when qualitative researchers reject psychological states as explanatory principles, they reject much psychology. The alternative to finding universal evaluation criteria is to evaluate qualitative and quantitative methods by their own criteria – that is, in many respects differently.

21.1 Evaluating qualitative research

The distinction between qualitative data collection and qualitative data analysis is paramount (Chapter 16). If the research seeks to quantify 'rich' data collected through in-depth methods such as open-ended interviewing then criteria appropriate to qualitative analyses may not always apply. It is fair to say that qualitative researchers do not speak with one voice about what the evaluative criteria should be. Qualitative research is an umbrella term covering a multitude of viewpoints, just as quantitative research is.

Taylor (2001) discusses a number of evaluative criteria for qualitative research. Some of them apply to research in general but often they take on a special significance in qualitative research. Others are criteria which best make sense only when considering qualitative research. The following are some of Taylor's more general criteria for evaluating qualitative research. We will discuss her more specific criteria and those of others later:

■ *How the research is located in the light of previously published research* Traditionally in psychological research, knowledge grows cumulatively through a process which begins with a literature search, through development of an idea based on this search and data collection, to finally reporting one's findings and conclusions. This is not the case in all forms of qualitative research. Some qualitative researchers begin with textual material that they wish to analyse, and delay referring back to previous research until after their analysis is completed. The idea is that the previous literature is an additional resource, more text if one likes, with which to explore the adequacy of the current analysis and its fit with other circumstances. The delay also means that the researcher is not so tempted to take categories off the peg and apply them to their data. In some forms of qualitative analysis – especially conversation analysis – reference to the published research is notably sparse. So the research literature in qualitative research is used very differently from its role in quantitative research. In quantitative research, knowledge is regarded as building out of previous knowledge, so one reviews the state of one's chosen research and uses it as a base from which to build further research. Traditionally, quantitative research demands the support of previous research in order to demonstrate the robustness and replicability of findings across samples and circumstances. Often, in the quantitative tradition, researchers resort to methodological considerations as an explanation of the variability in past and current findings. In the qualitative tradition, any disparity between studies is regarded much more positively and as less of a problem. Disparity is seen as a stimulus to refining the analytic categories used, which is the central activity of qualitative research anyway.

■ *How coherent and persuasive the argument is rather than emotional* Argumentation and conclusion drawing in psychology are typically regarded as dependent on precise logical sequences. It is generally not considered appropriate to express oneself emotionally or to engage in rhetorical devices in psychological report writing. This is quite a different matter from being dispassionate or uninvolved in one's subject matter. A great deal of fine psychological writing has been built on the commitment of the researcher to the outcomes of the research. Nevertheless, the expectation is that the researcher is restrained by the data and logic. In this way, the researcher is less likely to be dismissed as merely expressing personal opinions. This is the case no matter what research tradition is being considered.

■ *Data should not be 'left to speak for themselves' and the analysis should involve systematic investigation* The meaning of data does not reside entirely in the data themselves. Data needs to be interpreted in the light of a variety of considerations of both a methodological and a theoretical nature. Little if any data has an intrinsic, indisputable and unambiguous meaning. Hence the role of the researcher as interpreter of the data has to be part of the process. This interpretation has to be done with subtlety. There is a temptation among newcomers to qualitative analysis to feel that the data should speak for itself. So large amounts of text are reproduced and little by way of analysis or interpretation offered. But to do so is to ignore a central requirement of research which is to draw together the data to tell a story in detail. In qualitative research this is through the development of closely fitting coding categories in which the data fit precisely but in a way which synthesises aspects of the data. Qualitative research may cause problems for novice researchers because they substitute the data for analysis of the data. Of course, ethnographically meaningful data should carry its meaning for all members of that community. Unfortunately, to push this version of the ethnographic viewpoint too far leaves no scope for the input of the psychologist. If total fidelity to the data is more important than the analysis of the data, then researchers may just as well publish videos of their interviews, for example. Indeed, there would be no role for the researcher as anyone could generate a psychological analysis.

■ *Fruitfulness of findings* Assessing the fruitfulness of any research is not easy. There are so many ways in which research may be fruitful and little research is fruitful in every respect. Most research, however, can only be judged in the short term, and longer term matters such as impact on the public or other researchers may simply be inappropriate. Fruitfulness is probably best judged in terms of the immediate pay-off from the research in terms of the number of new ideas and insights it generates. Now it is very difficult to catalogue just what are new ideas and insights but rather easier to recognise work which lacks these qualities.

■ *Relevance to social issues/political events* Qualitative research in psychology often claims an interest in social issues and politics. There are a number of well known studies which deal with social and political issues. The question needs to be asked, however, just how social and political issues need to be addressed in psychology, and from what perspective? Mainstream psychology has a long tradition of interest in much the same issue. Institutionally, the Society for the Study of Social Issues in the USA has actively related psychology to social problems (Howitt, 1992a), for example, for most of psychology's modern history. There is a distinct tradition of socially relevant quantitative research. Given the insistence of many qualitative researchers that their data is grounded in the mundane texts of the social world, one might expect that qualitative research is firmly socially grounded. One criticism of qualitative research though is that it has a tendency to regard the political and social as more text that can be subjected to textual analysis. As such the social and political text has no special status other than as an interesting topic for textual analysis. Some qualitative researchers have been very critical of the failure of much qualitative research to deal effectively with the social and political – concepts such as power, for instance (Parker, 1989). Since power is exercised through social institutions then one can question the extent to which analysis of text in isolation is sufficient analysis.

■ *Usefulness and applicability* The relevance of psychological research of any sort is a vexed question. Part of the difficulty is that many researchers regard their work as part of an attempt to understand its subject matter for its own sake without the constraints of application. Indeed, applied research in psychology has often been seen as a separate entity from academic research and often somewhat derided as ordinary or pedestrian. Nevertheless, this point of view seems to have reduced in recent years and it is increasingly acceptable to consider the application of research findings as an indication of the value of some research. It is fairly easy to point to examples from mainstream psychology of the direct application of psychological research – clinical, forensic and educational psychology all demonstrate this in abundance. Part of the success of psychology in these areas is in finding ways of dealing with the practical problems of institutions such as prisons, schools and the mental health system. Success in the application of psychology stems partly from the power of research findings to support practical activities. Qualitative researchers have begun to overlap some of these traditional fields of the application of psychology. Unfortunately the claim that qualitative research is subjective tends to undermine its impact. Nevertheless, topics such as counselling/psychotherapy sessions and medical interview are to be found in the qualitative psychology literature. As yet, it is difficult to give examples of the direct application of the findings of such research.

The above criteria are in some ways similar to those which we might apply to quantitative research. They are important in the present context since it clarifies their importance in qualitative research too. They sometimes take a slightly different form in the two types of research.

21.2 Validity

The concept of validity is difficult to apply to qualitative research. Traditionally validity in psychology refers to an assessment of whether a measure actually measures what it is intended to measure. This implies there is something fixed which can be measured. The emphasis is really on the validity of the measures employed as indicators of corresponding variables in the actual world. So the validity of a measure of schizophrenia is the extent to which it corresponds with schizophrenia in the actual world beyond that measure This is not usually an assumption of qualitative research. In qualitative research, the emphasis of validity assessment is in terms of the question of how well the analysis fits the data. A good analysis fits the data very well. In quantitative research, often a very modest fit of the hypothesis to the data is acceptable – so long as the minimum criterion of statistical significance is met.

As we saw in Chapter 13, there are a number of ways of assessing validity in quantitative research. They all imply that there is something in actuality that can be measured by our techniques. This is unlikely to be the case with qualitative research for a number of reasons. One is the insistence by some qualitative researchers that text has a multiplicity of readings and that extends to the readings by researchers. In other words, given the post-modernist emphasis on the impossibility of observing 'reality' other than through a looking glass of subjectivity, validity cannot truly be assessed as a general aspect of measurement.

Discussions of validity by qualitative researchers take two forms:

■ It is very common to question the validity of quantitative research. That is, to encourage the view that qualitative research is the better means to obtaining understanding of the social and psychological world.

■ The tendency among qualitative researchers to treat any text (written or spoken) as worthwhile data means that the validity of the data is not questioned. The validity of the transcription is sometimes considered, but emphasis is placed on ways in which the fidelity of the transcription, say to the original audiotape, may be maximised. The greatest emphasis is placed on ways in which the validity of the qualitative analysis as a qualitative analysis may be maximised. This really is the primary meaning of validity in qualitative research. So many of the criteria listed by qualitative researchers are ones which only are meaningful if we understand the epistemological origins of qualitative research. That is, there are some considerations about the worth of qualitative data which do not normally apply to quantitative research.

Potter (1998) uses the phrase 'justification of analytic claims' alongside using the word validity. The phrase 'justification of analytic claims' emphasises the value of the analysis rather than the nature of the data. He suggests four considerations which form the 'repertoire' with which to judge qualitative research. Different researchers may emphasise different combinations of these:

■ *Participant's own understandings* When the qualitative material is conversation or similar text, we need to remember that speakers actually interpret the previous contributions by previous speakers. So the new speaker's understanding of what went before is often built into what they say in their turn. For example, a long pause and a change of subject may indicate that the speaker disagrees with what went before but does not wish to express that disagreement directly. Potter argues that by very carefully paying attention to such details in the analysis, the analyst can more precisely analyse the conversation in ways which are relevant to the participant's understandings. It is a way of checking the researcher's analysis.

■ *Openness to evaluation* Sometimes it is argued that the readers of a qualitative analysis are more in contact with the data than typically is the case in quantitative research in which tables and descriptive statistics are presented but none of the original data directly. Qualitative analyses often incorporate substantial amounts of textual material in support of the analytic interpretation. Because of this, the qualitative analysis may be more open to challenge and questioning by the reader than other forms of research. But actually relatively little qualitative research is open in this way. Potter suggests that for much reported grounded theory and ethnographic research, very little is presented in a challengeable form and a great deal has to be taken on trust just as with quantitative research. Even where detailed transcripts are provided, however, Potter's ideal may not be met. For example, what checking can be done if the researcher does not report the full transcript rather than selected highlights? Furthermore, what avenues are open to the reader who disagrees with an analysis to challenge the analysis?

■ *Deviant instances* In quantitative research, deviant cases are largely treated as irrelevant. The participant who bucks the trend of the data is largely ignored – as 'noise' or randomness. Sometimes this is known as 'experimental error'. But it is really an indicator of how much of the data is actually being ignored in terms of explanation. Often no attempt is made to explain why some participants are not representative of the trend. In qualitative research, partly because of the insistence on detailed analysis of sequences, the deviant case may be much more evident. Consequently the analysis needs to be modified to include what is truly deviant about it. It may be discovered that the seemingly deviant case is not really deviant – or it may become apparent why it 'breaks the rules'. It may also prove a decisive reason for abandoning a cherished analytic interpretation.

■ *Coherence with previous discourse studies*   Basically the idea here is that qualitative studies which cohere with previous studies are more convincing than ones which are in some way at odds with previous research. There is a sense in which this is a replicability issue since not only does coherence add conviction to the new study but it also adds conviction to the older studies. This is also the case with quantitative studies. But there are difficulties with this form of validity indicator. Qualitative research varies in terms of its fidelity to previous research when a replication is carried out. Some research will be close to the original, some research may be substantially different. So in this context, if a qualitative study is merely designed to apply the theoretical concepts derived from an earlier study then the findings are more likely to cohere with the earlier studies. Studies not conceived in this way will be a more effective challenge to what has gone before – and provide greater support if they confirm what went before.

Additional criteria for the evaluation of qualitative research are available (Taylor, 2001). These are not matters of validity, but do offer means of evaluating the relative worth of different qualitative studies:

■ *Richness of detail in the data and analysis*   The whole point of qualitative analysis is to develop descriptive categories which fit the data well. So one criterion of the quality of a study is the amount of detail in the treatment of the data and its analysis. Qualitative research requires endless processing of the material to meet its aims. Consequently, if the researcher just presents a few broad categories and a few broad indications of what sorts of material fits that category, then one will be less convinced of the quality of the analysis. Of course, richness of detail is not a concept which is readily tallied so it begs the question of how much detail is a richness. Should it be assessed in terms of numbers of words, the range of different sources of text, the verbal complexity of the data, or how? Similar questions may be applied to the issue of the richness of detail in the analysis. Just what does this mean? Is this a matter of the complexity of the analysis and why should a complex analysis be regarded as a virtue in its own right? In quantitative research, in contrast, the simplicity of the analysis is regarded as a virtue if it accounts for the detail of the data well. It is the easiest thing in the world to produce coding categories which fit the data well – if one has a lot of coding categories then all data are easily fitted. The fact that each of these categories fits only a very small part of the data means that the categories may not be very useful.

■ *Explication of the process of analysis*   If judged by the claims of qualitative analysts alone, the process of producing an adequate qualitative analysis is time consuming, meticulous and demanding. As a consequence of all of this effort, the product is both subtle and true to the data. The only way that the reader can fully appreciate the quality of the effort is if the researcher gives details of the stages of the analysis process. This does not amount to evidence of validity in the traditional sense, but is a quality assurance indicator of the processes that went into developing the analysis.

■ *Using selected quantitative techniques*   Some qualitative researchers are not against using some of the techniques of quantitative analysis. There is no reason in their view why qualitative research should use systematic sampling to ensure that the data are representative. Others would stress the role of the deviant or inconsistent case in that it presents the greatest challenge to the categorisation process. The failure of more traditional quantitative methods to deal with deviant cases other than as 'noise', error or simply irrelevant should be stressed again in this context.

■ *Respondent validation* Given the origins of much qualitative research in ethnomethodology, the congruence of the interpretations of the researcher with those of the members of the group being studied may be seen as a form of validity check. This is almost a matter of definition – the meanings arrived at through research are intended to be close to those of the people being studied in ethnomethodology. Sometimes it is suggested that there is a premium in the researcher having 'insider status'. That is, a researcher who is actually a member of the group being studied is at an advantage. This is another reflection of the tenets of ethnomethodology. There is always the counterargument to this that such closeness actually stands in the way of insightful research. However, there is no way of deciding which is correct. Owusu-Bempah and Howitt (2000) give examples from cross-cultural research of such insider perspectives. Of course, the importance of these criteria is largely the consequence of allegiance to a particular theoretical stance. It is difficult to argue for universality of this criterion.

■ *Triangulation* This concerns the validity of findings. When researchers use very different methods of collecting data yet reach the same findings on a group of participants, this is evidence of the validity of the findings. Or, in other words, their robustness across different methods of data collection or analysis. The replication of the findings occurs within settings and not across settings. This is then very different from triangulation when it is applied to quantitative data. In that case, the replication is carried out in widely different studies from those of the original study. The underlying assumption is that of positivist universality, an anathema to qualitative researchers.

21.3 Criteria for novices

There is probably no qualitative study that effectively embraces all of the criteria of quality that we have discussed. The criteria are not normally discussed within a qualitative report and are more often referred to in theoretical discussions of qualitative methodology. Hence, it is difficult to provide researchers new to qualitative research with a well established set of procedures which serve as routine quality assurance checks. In this way, quantitative research is very different. Things like significance testing, reliability estimates and validity coefficients are minimum quality indicators. Similarly, the literature review is part of the process of assessing the worth of the new findings. Of course, many other indicators of quality are neglected in quantitative reports, just as they are often in qualitative ones.

While these criteria of the worth of a qualitative study can be seen to be intrinsically of value (once the intellectual roots of qualitative research are understood), it is likely that the complexity of the criteria will defeat some novice researchers in the field. They certainly do not gel as a set of principles to help launch good quality qualitative research by newcomers. So in this section we will suggest some of the criteria which beginners might wish to adopt as a more pragmatic pathway to successful qualitative research:

■ Have you immersed yourself in the qualitative research literature or undergone training in qualitative research? Analytic success is a long journey and you need to understand where you are heading.

■ Why are you not doing a quantitative analysis? Have you really done a quantitative analysis badly and called it qualitative research?

■ Can you identify the specific qualitative method that you are using and why? Qualitative research is not an amorphous mass but a set of sometimes interlinking approaches.

■ What resources are you devoting to your data collection and analysis? Qualitative data analysis probably requires more personal research skills than much quantitative data analysis. It requires a good interviewing technique, for example, to obtain the richness of data required. Qualitative data require transcription (or quantitative coding), which is time consuming and exacting. If you do not understand the point of this then your research is almost certainly of dubious quality.

■ Have you coded or categorised *all* of your data? If not why not? How do you know that your categories work unless you have tested them thoroughly against the entirety of what you want to understand? If you can only point to instances of categories you wish to use then how do you know that you have a satisfactory fit of your categories with the data?

■ Has there been a process of refining your categories? Or have you merely used categories from other research or thought of a few categories without these being worked up through revisions of the data?

■ Can you say precisely what parts of your data fit your categories? Phrases such as 'Many participants . . .', 'Frequently . . .' and 'Some . . .' should not be used to cover up woolliness about how your data are coded.

■ How deeply engaged were you in the analysis? Did it come easily? If so, have you taken advantage of the special gains which may result from qualitative research?

21.4 Conclusion

Very few of the traditional criteria which we apply to quantitative research apply to qualitative research directly. They simply do not have the same intellectual roots and, to some extent, they are in conflict. There are a number of criteria for evaluating qualitative research, but these largely concentrate on evaluating the quality of the coding or categorisation process (the qualitative analysis). These criteria can be applied but, as yet, there is no way of deciding whether the study is of sufficient quality. They are merely indicators. This contrasts markedly with quantitative and statistical research where there are rules of thumb which may be applied to decide on the worth of the research. Significance testing is one obvious example of this when we apply a test of whether the data are likely to have been obtained simply by sampling fluctuations. Internal consistency measures of reliability such as alpha also have such cut-off rules. This leaves it a little uncertain how inexperienced qualitative researchers can evaluate their research. It is clearly the case that qualitative researchers need to reflect on the value of their analysis as much as any other researcher.

Key points

- Since qualitative research is a reaction to positivism and its influence on research, qualitative research needs to be evaluated in part in its own terms.

- Some criteria apply to both quantitative and qualitative research. There criteria include how the research is located in relation to previously published research, the coherence and persuasive of the argument, the strength of the analysis to impose structure on the data, the potential of the research to stimulate further research or the originality and quantity of new insights arising from the research, and the usefulness of applicability of the research.

- Yet other criteria which may be applied are much more specific to qualitative research. These include the correspondence of the analysis with the participant's own under-standings, the openness of the report to evaluation, the ability of the analysis to deal with otherwise deviant instances in the data, the richness of detail in the analysis, which is dependent on the richness of the data in part, and how clearly the process of developing the analysis is presented.

- The criteria that novice researchers use to evaluate their own research may be a little more routine. Considerations include factors related to the amount of effort devoted to developing the analysis, the degree to which the analysis embraces the totality of the data, and even questioning whether a quantitative study would have been more appropriate anyway.

Activities

1. Could a qualitative researcher simply make up their analysis and get away with it? List the factors that stop this happening.

2. Develop a set of principles by which *all* research could be evaluated.

PART 5
Research for projects, dissertations and theses

22 Developing ideas for research

Overview

- If you are planning a research project, ideally this will be firmly based on your knowledge of psychology in general and the pertinent research literature in particular. Rarely is it satisfactory simply to replicate what other researchers have done. It is better to use their work creatively and intelligently to create a valuable variation or extension of what has already been achieved. Sometimes, student researchers hit upon ideas which have not been effectively researched previously.

- Typically, one only has a rudimentary research idea for a project. This idea will be knocked into shape by a process of reading, discussion with a supervisor or peer, and exploring the possibilities in a disciplined fashion.

- Initially, it may be helpful to draw up a list of different ideas which may be honed down into a list of manageable and feasible research ideas which are practical within the limits of time and other resources. Although psychology is a fascinating subject, be careful to concentrate on just a few ideas since the time involved in reading pertinent material, for example, is quite considerable and should not be spread too thinly over too many possibilities.

- The research you ultimately decide to carry out should be satisfying to you in a range of different ways. It should be of interest to you, it should be capable of making a contribution to the research field in question, and it should be feasible within the limits of time and resources available to you. Student research has to be completed in its entirety within a fixed time schedule and the most brilliant research design in the world is a waste if deadlines are missed.

- Sometimes student researchers find it difficult to come up with ideas for research. Don't worry too much if you are one of these since like all intellectual activity, we all have to learn to generate ideas for research and there are a number of worthwhile techniques and approaches which may help you over this difficult stage.

- After a number of years at university and having lived for a while, there will be some topics that you have studied or some experiences that you have had which have interested you. You probably have a clearer idea of the things which bore you and generate no interest at all for you so these be quickly eliminated. At some stage, and the sooner the better, every researcher has to start reading the recently published literature on the topics which interest them the most. This is not easy and takes time – one has to try to understand what others have done, how they have done it, and why they have done it. Having done this, it remains necessary to try to appreciate just what they have found out as a consequence.

■ You should also bear in mind just what you are trying to emulate. Think of what you believe a professor of psychology should be. They are expected to adopt a curious, questioning and critical attitude to whatever they read. Furthermore, they are very cautious people unwilling to take things for granted and demand evidence for everything – even things which seem self-evident. Reading like a professor should help you come up with a number of ideas about what needs to be done further. The more one reads, the more ideas come to one. It is a bit like writing a tune. Most of us would struggle to write a tune, whereas a skilled musician who has listened to and studied innumerable melodies would do so easily. Having heard and played thousands of tunes makes it easier not harder to write a tune.

■ Substantial student research projects are largely modelled on the style of academic publications. Consequently, some of the better student projects may be worthy of publication although this is not their prime purpose. Although there is no guarantee that the results of your study will turn out so that they are publishable, it is a goal worth aiming for.

The research conducted by students has as its primary purpose demonstrating that the student has achieved the necessary skills involved in planning, designing, analysing and reporting psychological research. That is the overriding requirement. To this is then added a layer of extra finesse that relates to the quality of the research ideas involved. Most psychology students have to carry out a research project as part of their training. Often this is at the undergraduate level but it may be also be involved in postgraduate work.

There is considerable variation in the extent to which a student's work is based on their own ideas. Departments of psychology will vary in this regard as will members of staff within a department. Sometimes a student is required to select a project already outlined by members of staff. Sometimes, students may be offered the choice of doing such a project or one of their own. Sometimes students are encouraged to come up with their own ideas. All of these are quite reasonable alternatives and it is very like academic research in general – for example, many junior research staff are employed simply to carry out the research plans of more senior staff. In a sense, if you take on someone else's research plan then you are acting more or less like a research assistant whereby you implement some previously determined procedure. In other situations you may be offered a rough idea of what to do, which you need to develop yourself into a project. However, in many instances, you will be left to or encouraged to come up with your own ideas as to what to do. In every case, remember that the quality of the outcome may have an important bearing on your future and so you should satisfy yourself that what you choose to do is worthwhile.

There are three main broad considerations that student researchers need to assess when planning to carry out a research project:

■ *Motivation* We all differ to some extent in terms of what motivates us best. Some students work best in fields which are especially pertinent to their experiences. For example, many students draw on their personal experiences as a basis for planning research. Research into the experience of cancer, alcoholism, dyslexia and relationships may be firmly wedded to one's earlier experiences. While it is often argued that academic researchers should be dispassionate, it would seem to us inappropriate not to be interested in topics emerging out of one's life experiences. Other students may be attracted to topics which are solely of intellectual interest to them and may not require the grounding in real life that others find helpful. Given that a research project is a long term investment of time and energy, it is a mistake to adopt a topic for research that cannot sustain one over a period of months. Many students find research projects a major trial of stamina and character.

■ *Practicality* There is little point in risking failure with a student research project. That is, be very cautious about planning research which is dependent on unknown contingencies for completion. For example, it might be a wonderful idea to study cognitive processes in a group of serial killers and, if properly done, the research might make a major contribution and even save a few lives. Fortunately, most of us do not know any serial killers and probably would need to resort to getting the cooperation of the prison service in order to obtain a sample. The likelihood of the prison service cooperating ought to be assessed seriously alongside the seriousness of the consequences if the prison service says no. Be very cautious of vague promises of cooperation – we have had cases of students finding the cooperation has been withdrawn at a late stage and the student having to completely revamp their plans.

■ *Academic value* Student research is most likely to be judged using conventional academic criteria. Research can be valuable for many other reasons but its academic weight may not be sufficiently strong. For example, it may be very important for practitioners to know young people's attitudes to safe sex and AIDS. The information gathered in a survey of young people may be highly valued by such practitioners. On the other hand, in terms of academic weight such a survey may meet few of the requirements of academics. The research might be seen as being atheoretical and merely a simple data-gathering task. Many academics would prefer research which helps develop new theories, validate theories, or is simply very clever. One should try to ensure that one's research is playing in the right playing field.

22.1 Why not a replication study?

Although research projects such as final year projects and dissertations are in part judged in terms of their technical competence, they are also judged in the same terms as any other research work. For example, that is, on the extent to which the research may be expected to make a useful or interesting contribution to a topic. One must be realistic about what any single research study can contribute. Many published papers make only a small contribution though, it should be stressed, there may be a disagreement as to the actual worth of any particular study since excellence is often in the eye of the beholder. Certainly, as we have seen, there may be disagreement as to whether a particular paper is of publishable quality (Cicchetti, 1991). Major theoretical or conceptual breakthroughs are *not* expected from student research or the run of the mill professional research paper for that matter. However, it is not unknown for student projects, if they are of top quality, to be published in academic journals. For example, the projects of a number of our students have been published (e.g. Cramer & Buckland, 1995; Cramer & Fong, 1991; Murphy *et al.*, 1984; Medway and Howitt, 2003).

Not all research projects stand an even chance of being regarded of good or high quality. Some projects are likely to find less favour than others simply because they reflect a low level of aspiration and fail to appreciate the qualities of good research. Here are a few examples and comments:

- A study which examines the relationship between a commercial (ready-made) test of creativity and another commercially available test measuring intelligence. This study, even if it could be related to the theoretical literature on creativity and intelligence, does not allow the student to demonstrate any special skill in terms of method or analysis. It has also probably been carried out many times before. The value of the study might be improved if the variables measured were assessed using newly developed measuring instruments created by the researcher.

- A study which looks at, say, gender differences on a variable or age differences. Some research questions are mundane. Gender differences or age differences may well be important but it is difficult to establish their importance without an elaborate context which demonstrates why they are important. Sometimes the technicalities of demonstrating the gender difference are challenging and would compensate for the lack of complexity of the research question. Simply showing a gender difference for an easily measured variable has probably little going for it in terms of demonstrating a student's ability.

Replication studies are an interesting case in point. It is important to understand why some replication studies would be highly valuable whereas others would be regarded as rather mundane. A replication study that simply repeats what already has been done will probably be regarded as demonstrating technical and organisational proficiency at best. It is unlikely to be regarded as demonstrating evidence of conceptual ability, creativity and originality. Now it is important to appreciate that direct replications do have their part to play in research – they are very important. For example, if it were found that eating lettuce was associated with reductions in the risk of cancer then one priority would be to replicate this finding. Unfortunately, no matter how important replication is in research work, it is not particularly effective at demonstrating the full range of a researcher's skills. This does not mean that a straightforward replication is easy – the information in a journal article, for example, may well be insufficient and the researcher doing the replication may have to contribute a great many ideas. Furthermore, if you carried out what may be called a simple or straight replication it is unlikely that you would be able to use the same participants as the original study.

Relatively few straight or direct replication studies are to be found in the research literature. This is the case despite the great emphasis placed on replicability in the scientific literature. It would seem to be a good rule of thumb to suggest that direct replication is only valued to the extent that the original study was especially important or controversial. There are only a limited number of possible outcomes of a simple replication. The results will be either the same as those of the original study or different from them – or the same in parts and different in other parts. A straight or direct replication has to be built on the assumption that the original findings will be replicated. If that were not the assumption then one must have a reason for believing that the findings of the replication would be different. In effect this implies that you could specify one of the conditions under which the original results would hold and one of them in which they would not hold. If this were the case, your study would include both the original conditions under which the results were found and the new conditions under which they were not expected to be found.

However, as soon as one begins to think of a replication study in this way then the replication becomes something very different from a simple, direct or straight replication since one is including conditions which were not part of the original study. This amounts to a part or partial replication. Part or partial replications may contribute to a better understanding of a topic. They are worthwhile because they provide information about the conditions under which a finding holds in addition to whether the finding is replicable.

Examples of straight replication and partial replication may help:

■ *Straight replication* Suppose a study found that women were more accurate at recognising emotions than men. We need not be concerned with the exact details of how this study was done. One approach would be to video people acting various emotions, play these videos to women and men, and ask them to report what emotions were expressed. Simply repeating what had previously been done would be a straight replication and would not provide any additional information other than whether this finding was replicable.

■ *Partial replication* What if we noticed that the people asked to act out the emotions were all, or predominantly, women? We may then be inclined to think that the results simply showed that women were more accurate than men at judging the emotions of women; we would not assume that women were generally more accurate at judging emotion than men. In order to extend our understanding we may want to know whether women are also more accurate than men at recognising the emotions of men. This could be achieved simply by ensuring that the video material included both women acting out emotions (as in the original study) as well as men acting out the emotions (unlike the original study). Obviously it would be important to ensure that the emotions acted by the men and women were the same ones. This new research design is a partial replication since it actually accurately reproduces the original study when using videos of women acting emotionally but extends it to cover men acting emotionally. Why is this more worthwhile? Simply because it allows us to answer more questions such as:

  – Are women better at recognising emotions in general?
  – Are women only better at recognising emotions exhibited by members of their own gender?

If the results of a straight replication are sufficiently similar to those of the original study, then we can say that the original findings are replicable. However, although this increases our confidence in the original findings, it does nothing to further our understanding of the topic. If the new findings do not reflect the original findings, then this is of interest but it does nothing in itself to explain why the original findings and the replication differ. We could think of reasons for the difference, but in itself this is merely speculative and evidence of nothing. The only new information that a straight replication provides is whether the findings are replicable. Always there is more to be gained from investigating the new questions generated by the original study than merely replicating it.

22.2 Choosing a research topic

Most researchers are, at times, stuck for ideas for their future research. They may be extremely well known and expert in their fields, yet research ideas do not flow simply because of this. It can be hard work to come up with good ideas for research no matter one's level of expertise. Furthermore, even when the ideas come they usually take a great deal of effort before they are sufficiently refined that they generate a detailed plan for research. Consequently, do not expect to wake up one morning with a fully formed research question and plan in your mind. Usually all that there is at first is a vague idea that one would like to do research on a particular topic. This is then worked on by thinking about some of the research possibilities, discussing one's tentative ideas with anyone willing to listen and chip in thoughts, reading a lot around the topic and discarding what does not seem to be working well. Virtually at the same time, one has to hone up any thoughts or ideas which seem to have potential.

It is a good idea to think about the styles of research which appeal to you. These can have an impact on what is possible in terms of research. For example, if you have been particularly interested in in-depth interviewing as a means of data collection, you might ask yourself what can be done on the topic using this method. On the other hand, if you think that a well designed laboratory experiment is your preferred mode of data collection then you can ask yourself what limitations this puts on the sorts of research questions you can ask.

Hopefully towards the end of a degree course you will have come across a range of topics which interest you. Perhaps you will be spoilt for choice since there seems to be too many different things which intrigue you. There are several ways in which you may try to narrow down this choice:

■   Try focusing on the topic that first aroused your interest in psychology. Does it still interest you? Have you been unable to satisfy your interest in the topic perhaps because it was not covered in any of the courses you took. Topics which are not covered on degree programmes may nevertheless be of importance. A research project not only gives you the opportunity to research a topic but also the chance of studying it in much greater depth than is usually possible.

■   Try choosing a topic that may be relevant to the kind of work you intend to go into after graduating from university. For example, if you intend to go into teaching it may be useful to look at some aspect of teaching such as what makes for effective teaching.

■   Choose a topic that interests you, which is part of a course that you will be taking at the same time as doing the research project. In this way, the research and your studies will complement each other.

■   If your attempts to focus on a topic are not fruitful, try thinking of a variety of topics that attract you. Read around these topics and see if one of these topics will emerge as the frontrunner. In reading around a number of topics, you may find that the way one of your topics has been fruitfully investigated can be applied to another topic.

■   If all else fails, try spending a couple of hours on a computer terminal simply skimming through the latest research abstracts irrespective of topic. Out of what you read does anything stand out as especially interesting? This is a quick way of getting an idea of the range of topics psychologists have studied and how they study them.

Regardless of how you approach selecting a topic, it is best to start thinking about the research possibilities a topic offers as soon as possible. Make a note of any ideas that come to you as you listen to lectures or read the literature. Although ideas may spring up from your own experience and your observation of what happens around you, the greatest source of ideas is likely to come from reading and thinking about the ideas of others. Without studying the work of others, it is very difficult to develop your own ideas. The work of others describes how they have conceived the topic of interest. It would be undesirable to ignore all of this past work since it amounts to a repository of hard thinking, good analysis and ways of conceptualising the important issues. Authors may propose in the *Discussion* section of their paper one or more specific suggestions about further work that may be worth carrying out on the topic that they have been investigating.

Sometimes students get disconcerted when they come across research which is similar to that which they are planning or doing. Of course there is always the chance that someone else publishes work similar to yours before your project is completed. This seems to occur very infrequently, however. Perhaps this is because the way we think about a topic is usually very different from the way that other people think about it. Whatever the reason, it is unlikely that someone will be about to publish the study that you are currently thinking of doing. However, if this does occur, simply acknowledge it in your report and remember to evaluate the two studies and describe their similarities and differences.

22.3 Sources of research ideas

There seems to be little or no research into where researchers get their ideas. So we cannot categorise these sources. Nevertheless, there are a number of different types of ways of generating research ideas. McGuire (1997) has come up with 49 different ways or heuristics of generating hypotheses! Our list is more modest. The ways listed may not be mutually exclusive in that a researcher may have adopted several of these approaches in the development of their particular study. It is also not an exhaustive list. There will be other ways in which ideas have arisen. We will illustrate these potential sources with a brief example or more of the kind of idea they may have generated wherever feasible.

■ *Detailed description of a phenomenon* It is often important to try to obtain a thorough and accurate description of what occurs before trying to understand why it occurs. It is possible that previous studies may have done this to some extent but their descriptions may omit what appears to you to be certain critical aspects of the phenomenon. For example, we do not know why psychotherapy works. One way of trying to understand what makes it effective is to ask patients in detail how it has helped them to cope with or to overcome their problem.

■ *Theory* No matter what your chosen field of research, attention to the major pertinent theories is valuable. Remember that the purpose of research is *not* primarily to get more data but to extend our conceptual understanding of our chosen subject matter. An absence of theory means that the conceptualisation of the relevant issues is much harder. After all, the purpose of theory is to present a conceptual scheme to describe and understand a phenomenon. Researchers are well advised to emphasise the relevant theory in their chosen field as a consequence. If there is an absence of theory in the published writings in the field then are there theories which can be brought into the

BOX 22.1   TOP OF THE CITATIONS

It is intriguing to find that many of the most cited psychologists in psychology journals are very familiar names to most psychology students. Many of the most cited psychologists include those who have made highly influential theoretical contributions. Freud, for example, was a major theorist but a minor contributor of research. Remember that the theories referred to in journals are those which are influential on research. Haggbloom and his colleagues (2002) generated a list which ranks the 25 psychologists most frequently cited in journals according to how often they have been cited. This list is shown in Table 22.1. (Beside the name of each psychologist we have given one major contribution that this person is known for although we do not know whether this contribution is the reason why they have been cited.) Not all the people on this list have put forward a major theory. For example, Ben Winer who is ranked fourth is most probably cited for his writings on statistical analysis. There are, of course, many other theories which are not listed which may be of greater interest to you.

Table 22.1   The 25 psychologists cited most often in journals

Rank	Psychologist	Citations	Contribution
1	Freud, Sigmund	13 890	psychoanalytic theory
2	Piaget, Jean	8 821	developmental theory
3	Eysenck, Hans J.	6 212	personality theory; behaviour therapy
4	Winer, Ben J.	6 206	statistics
5	Bandura, Albert	5 831	social learning theory
6	Siegel, Sidney	4 861	statistics
7	Cattell, Raymond B.	4 828	personality theory
8	Skinner, Burrhus F.	4 339	operant conditioning theory
9	Osgood, Charles E.	4 061	semantic differential scale
10	Guilford, Joy P.	4 006	intelligence
11	Campbell, Donald T.	3 969	methodology
12	Festinger, Leon	3 536	cognitive dissonance theory
13	Miller, George A.	3 394	memory
14	Bruner, Jerome S.	3 279	cognitive theory
15	Cronbach, Lee J.	3 253	reliability and validity
16	Erikson, Erik H.	3 060	psychosocial developmental theory
17	Edwards, Allen L.	3 007	social desirability
18	Rotter, Julian B.	3 001	social learning theory
19	Byrne, Donn	2 904	reinforcement-affect theory
20	Kagan, Jerome	2 901	children's temperaments
21	Wolpe, Joseph	2 879	behaviour therapy
22	Rosenthal, Robert	2 739	experimenter expectancy effect
23	Underwood, Benton J.	2 686	verbal learning
24	Paivio, Allan	2 678	verbal learning
25	Rokeach, Milton	2 676	values

field from elsewhere? These may help illuminate the field better than any amount of purely empirical research. It is best to integrate theory with the empirical work, of course. There is no necessary reason why a theory should merely be tested by your empirical work. Many theories are too imprecise for such a test. Nevertheless, the theory may usefully integrate the different aspects of your report. A useful minimum requirement is that you introduce the relevant theory into your writings. If it is possible to go beyond this minimum then you are doing very well. For example, if your research can explore the application of theory to a particular topic then this may have a powerful effect on the quality of your report. The big limitation is that theory in psychology tends to deal with a modest level of generalisation which can make it unsuitable for application in new contexts. Deductions from theories are discussed later.

- *Everyday issues* Frequently there are a number of different ways in which something can be done in our everyday lives. There may be no research to help choose which is the most effective procedure to adopt or what the consequences might generally be of using a particular approach. We could carry out some research to help answer these questions. For example, in terms of carrying out research, are potential participants less likely to agree to complete a longer than a shorter questionnaire? If they do fill in the longer questionnaire, are their answers likely to be less reliable or accurate than if they complete a shorter questionnaire? Does the order of the questions affect how accurate they are when disclosing more sensitive or personal information about themselves?

- *New or potential social, technological or biological developments* We live in a time when new, or the possibility of new, biological, technological and social developments are being introduced, the significance of which we are not sure. Their effects or what people perceive as being their potential effects may be investigated. What is the influence of the Internet or text messaging on our social behaviour? Has the development and spread of AIDS (auto immune deficiency syndrome) affected our sexual behaviour in any way? Do student fees influence the occupational aspirations of students?

- *A-B-C model* It may be useful to remember that any behaviour (B) that we are interested in often has both antecedents (A) and consequences (C). For example, the antecedents of the behaviour of depression may include unsatisfactory childhood relationships and negative experiences. The consequences may comprise unsatisfactory personal relationships and poor school or work attendance. Deciding whether we are more interested in the antecedents than the consequences of a particular behaviour may also help us focus. Once this decision has been made, we might try to investigate neglected antecedents of depression.

- *Predicting or changing behaviour* How could you go about changing a particular behaviour? Do you think that you could predict when that behaviour is likely to occur? Addressing these questions would require you to think about the variables which are most likely to be, or have been found to be, most strongly associated with the behaviour in question. These variables would form part of an explanation for this behaviour. You could investigate whether these variables are in reality related to the behaviour in question. This approach may encourage you to think of how your knowledge of psychology could be applied to practical problems.

- *Elaborating relationships* There may be considerable research which shows that a relationship exists between two variables. For example, there may be substantial research which demonstrates a sex or gender difference such as females being less aggressive than males. The next step once this has been established would be to try to understand why this sex difference exists – what the factors are which are responsible for this difference. If you believe that the factors are likely to be biological, you look for biological differences which may explain the differences in aggression. If you think that the factors are probably psychological or social, you investigate these kinds of factors. If you are interested in simply finding out whether there are sex differences in some behaviour, then it is more useful and interesting to include one or more factors which you think may explain this difference. In other words, it is important to test for explanations of differences or relationships rather than merely establish empirically that a relationship exists.

■ *Developing and validating measures*   Where there is no measure for assessing a variable that you are interested in studying, then it is worthwhile developing one yourself. This will almost certainly involve collecting evidence of the measure's reliability and validity. For some variables there may be a number of different measures that already exist for assessing them, but it may be unclear which one is the most appropriate to use. Consequently, you may wish to establish which one is the most suitable for a particular purpose. Alternatively, is it possible to develop a more satisfactory measure than the ones which are currently available? Your new measure may include more relevant aspects of the variable that you want to assess. Would a shorter or more convenient measure be as good a measure as a longer or less convenient one? Do measures which seem to assess different variables actually assess the same variable? For example, is a measure of loneliness distinguishable from a measure of depression in practice?

■ *Deductions from theories*   Much of psychology is concerned with developing theories to explain behaviour. Theories which attempt to explain a wider variety of behaviours are generally more useful than those which have a narrower focus because they are more general theories. While some aspects of these theories may have been extensively tested, other aspects of them may have received little or no empirical attention but may be worth investigating.

■ *Competing theoretical explanations*   In the classic view of scientific progress, there is an idea that competing theories used to describe a phenomenon may be put to a critical and decisive test. While many psychologists would believe that few psychological theories are so precise that such a critical test is possible, nevertheless attempts to do so are well regarded. For example, there are a number of theories for explaining the occurrence of depression. It may be an intellectually satisfying challenge to take the main theories of depression and examine how they might be put to some sort of crucial test. So why not consider evaluating competing theoretical explanations of your chosen topic as the basis of your research project? While it is unlikely that a death blow will be struck against one of the competing theories, your contribution would be part of the longer-term process of evaluating which theory was the most tenable.

■ *Alternative explanations of findings*   A researcher may favour a particular explanation for their findings but there may be others which have not been considered or tested. Have you come across a research publication which has intrigued you but you are not absolutely convinced that the researcher has come up with the best explanation? Do you have alternative ideas which would account for the findings? If so, why not try to plan research which might be decisive in helping you choose between the original researcher's explanation and yours? This is not quite as easy as it sounds.

One of the reasons is that you need to read journal articles in a questioning way rather than as being information which should be accepted and digested. For much of your education, you have probably read uncritically merely to gain information. To be a researcher, you need a rather different mindset which says 'convince me' to the author of a research paper rather than 'you're the expert so I accept what you say'.

- *Methodological limitations* Any study, including important ones, may suffer from a variety of methodological limitations. An obvious one for much research is the issue of high internal validity but low external validity. Basically this is a consequence of using contrived laboratory experiments to investigate psychological processes. These experiments may be extremely well designed in their own terms, but have little relevance to what happens in the real world. For example, there are numerous laboratory studies of jury decision making but would one be willing to accept their findings as relevant in the world beyond the psychology laboratory? A study which explores in naturalistic settings phenomena which have been well studied in the psychology laboratory would be a welcome addition in many fields of research. Any variable may be operationalised in a number of different ways. How sound are the measures used in the research? For example there are numerous studies of aggression which rely on the (apparent) delivery of a noxious electrical shock as a measure of aggressiveness. As you probably know from the famous Stanley Milgram studies of obedience, this same measure would be used by some researchers as an indicator of obedience rather than a measure of aggressiveness. Yet these are identical measures but are claimed to measure different things. Clearly there is the opportunity to question many measures including those used in classic research studies.

- *Temporal precedence or order of variables* Studies that involve a dynamic component of change over a period of time are relatively uncommon in psychology despite many researchers advocating their use. They are also uncommon in student research. Obviously time constraints apply, which may account partially for them being uncommon. Longitudinal or panel designs, such as those outlined in Chapter 10 that measure the same variables on the same individuals at two or more points in time, enable the temporal relationships between variables to be examined and compared. Often this sort of research takes place in a less contrived setting than is possible using an experimental design. Consider the possibility of using a longitudinal design since not only is it more challenging than other types of research but may also generate new possibilities for research in fields which are perhaps otherwise heavily researched.

- *Causality* Student researchers can often benefit from concentrating on the possibility of carrying out an experimental study in their chosen field. Despite there being limitations to the experimental method for some purposes, it remains the quintessential research method in psychology. Consequently, an experimental design will garner favour. The clarity imposed by employing a research method capable of identifying causal relationships can benefit student research enormously. Remember that the main purpose of student research is for the student to demonstrate that they have mastered the crucial skills of research. Experimental designs are a good way of doing this.

- *More realistic settings* One of the common criticisms of psychology, especially that which is taught at university, is that it dwells on the laboratory experiment too much and neglects research carried out in more naturalistic settings. Is it possible to take one of these somewhat contrived laboratory experiments and recast it in a more naturalistic and less contrived fashion? Often the way in which we study a phenomenon may be contrived in order to control for variables which may affect our findings. But this is not the only reason. For example, take the example of Stanley Milgram's famous study of obedience in which participants ostensibly gave massive electric shocks to another person in the context of a study of learning. One might ask about obedience in real-life settings, for example. Just what are the determinants of obedience to authority in real-life settings such as a sports team? What determines whether the captain's instructions are adhered to? Sometimes it can be useful to see if similar results can be obtained in less contrived circumstances than the original study in order to assess just how robust the original findings are.

■ *Generalising to other contexts*   Theories or findings in one area may be applicable to those in other areas. For example, theories which have been developed to explain personal relationships may also apply to work relationships and may be tested in these contexts.

■ *Conflicting or inconsistent findings*   It is a common comment that psychological research on a given topic has some studies finding one outcome and other studies finding the reverse outcome. That is, the findings of studies on a particular topic are less than consistent with each other. For example, some studies may find no difference between females and males for a particular characteristic, others may find females show more of this characteristic, while others may find females show less of this characteristic. Why might this be the case? If the majority of studies obtain a similar kind of finding, the findings of the inconsistent remaining studies may be due to sampling error and many psychologists will ignore the inconsistent studies as a consequence. However, it is often better to regard the inconsistency as something to be explained and taken into account. It could be that there are differences between the consistent and inconsistent studies which have not been taken into account. Is it possible to speculate about what the differences between the studies were which might account for the difference in outcomes? In this situation it is not very fruitful to repeat the study to see what the results will be because we already know what the possible outcomes are. While it may not be easy to do this, it is better to think of variables which may explain these inconsistent findings and to see whether or not this is the case. One could perhaps consider carrying out a meta-analysis of the studies in order to explore an number of differences which might account for the variation in the outcomes of the studies. Meta-analysis can be carried out using quite simple procedures. The technique is described in detail in the companion statistics text, *Introduction to Statistics in Psychology* (Howitt and Cramer, 2005*a*) at a level which is within the capabilities of most students.

22.4   Conclusion

Research projects are intended to be major tests of a student's intellectual development. While most psychology students do some research at each stage of their development, early on it is likely that they carry out a study according to a plan more or less given to them in finished form by academic staff. Individual research projects come at the end of a degree programme simply because a student needs to have mastered many skills before they can do a good job of planning research of their own. The better that you have mastered everything that has gone before, the more likely you are to make a good job of independent research.

For example, unless you have read a number of examples of how researchers formulate and justify their research ideas, you will not know how to formulate psychological research questions. At its root, this process is one of reading and study. Even then, students can find it difficult to come up with a good idea for a research project. It is something that cannot be done in a hurry and adequate time needs to be laid aside in order to develop ideas.

It is never too early to start thinking about research projects. While it may be exceptional to find a student who thinks a whole year ahead, the sooner that you can find time to think about research ideas the better. If you have given yourself enough time, you may find it helpful to keep a range of possible research topics on the table for consideration. This will minimise the damage if it should happen that the topic that you set your heart on does not turn into a workable idea. One learns to think psychologically about things through a fairly lengthy process of reading and actively studying.

You can get to understand how psychologists actually do research by reading a variety of research papers in any field that interests you. When you are planning research however, you need to focus on and familiarise yourself with the established research literature on the topic – especially recent research. By reading in this way you will learn something about what are sensible research questions to pose. You will gain insight into how people interested in the same issue as yourself have construed the topic and planned the research. You will know about what sorts of measures are typically taken and what procedures for doing research seem to work well in this field.

However, do not prevent yourself from asking what might seem to be obvious questions about the topic that do not seem to have been addressed. These obvious questions may have escaped the attention of researchers and may form the basis of your own research. Think also of situations in which the findings may not apply. We may have a tendency to seek instances which confirm what we know rather than instances which disconfirm our preconceptions. Thinking of situations in which the findings may not apply will make us aware of the extent to which we cannot generalise these findings to all contexts.

Practicalities may prevent you doing what you really want to do. Always try to anticipate these and consider more modest possibilities. For example, it is unlikely that you would be able to evaluate the effectiveness of, say, a substantial therapeutic intervention, but you may be able to investigate people's preference for or attitude to that intervention. Doing one's own research provides one of the few in-depth opportunities to learn about a topic and to make a contribution, however modest, to understanding that topic. It allows you to show and to see just what you are capable of intellectually. For many students, it will be the most fulfilling and possibly the most frustrating part of their studies. Hopefully what you have learnt from this will provide you with a sound understanding of research methods and with resources to help you develop further. Nevertheless you cannot learn to be a researcher just from a book. Conducting research is a skill which requires practice. We would be delighted to know that this book has stimulated your appetite for research.

Alternatively, there is always Plan B!

Key points

■ Developing good research ideas is not easy. Even once you have the necessary academic skills, it takes time to choose a topic and to familiarise yourself with the research on that topic. The sooner you start thinking about your research ideas the better.

■ Be realistic about what you can achieve with the limited resources that are available to you. Much of the research that you read about has probably taken a great deal more time to conceive and to carry out than you have available. Nonetheless, students at all levels can and have carried out research of value – some of which has been published.

■ Simply replicating research that has already been done is unlikely to advance our understanding of that topic. It is also unlikely to impress those assessing your work. While replication is important to determine how reliable a finding is, it is sensible to do more than just replicate the original study. At the same time as doing the replication, it is often possible to address new questions which emerge from the original research report. It is better to distinguish this kind of replication by calling it part or partial replication. Much research is partial replication.

■ Choose a topic that interests you or that may be relevant to what you want to do in your future career or further studies. Think of a few topics that interest you and start reading around your favourite. If necessary go on to the next topic once you understand why your first choice has not been productive.

■ There is no single, foolproof way of generating a good idea for research. However, ideas are most likely to be generated as one reads and ponders over the research that other people have reported. Often what you do will involve a variation of what has been previously done and may clear up an unresolved issue. It is also likely to raise a number of other issues that in turn need to be answered.

■ Carrying out a piece of original research is your opportunity to make a contribution to the topic that interests you. Make the most of this opportunity.

Activity

Think of three topics that you would like to do research on. Decide which of these three is the most promising for you and start thinking what you would like to know about it or what you think should be known about it. Do a literature search preferably using an electronic database such as Web of Science or PsycINFO. Try to locate the most recent research on the topic and read it. When reading the research adopt a critical and questioning attitude to what has been written. Try to read some of the references cited to see whether they have been accurately cited and are relevant to the point being made in the paper you are currently reading. Are the views in these references generally consistent with those in the paper? If they are not consistent, what seem to be the reasons for this? Which view do you generally support? In terms of the study, how were the main variables operationalised? Are there better ways of operationalising them? What suggestions were made for further research and do these seem worth pursuing? What questions remain to be answered? How would you design a study to test these?

References

Allen, R. E. (1992) (ed.). *The Oxford English Dictionary*, 2nd edn, CD-ROM (Oxford: Oxford University Press).

American Psychological Association (2002). 'Summary report of journal operations, 2001', *American Psychologist*, 57, 659–60.

Austin, J. L. (1975). *How To Do Things with Words* (Cambridge, MA: Harvard University Press).

Barber, T. X. (1973). 'Pitfalls in research: Nine investigator and experimenter effects', in R. M. W. Travers (ed.), *Second Handbook of Research on Teaching* (Chicago: Rand McNally), 382–404.

Barber, T. X. (1976). *Pitfalls in Human Research: Ten Pivotal Points* (New York: Pergamon Press).

Barlow, D. H., and Hersen, M. (1984). *Single Case Experimental Designs: Strategies for Studying Behavior Change*, 2nd edn (New York: Pergamon Press).

Baron, R. M., and Kenny, D. A. (1986). 'The moderator-mediator variable distinction in social psychological research: Conceptual, strategic, and statistical considerations', *Journal of Personality and Social Psychology*, 51, 1173–82.

Beaugrande, R. D. (1996). 'The story of discourse analysis', in T. van Dijk (ed.), *Introduction to Discourse Analysis* (London: Sage), 35–62.

Beecher, H. K. (1955). 'The powerful placebo', *Journal of the American Medical Association*, 159, 1602–6.

Benneworth, K. (2004). 'A discursive analysis of police interviews with suspected paedophiles', Doctoral dissertation (Loughborough University, England).

Berenson, M. L., and Levine, D. M. (1999). *Basic Business Statistics: Concepts and Applications*, 7th edn (Upper Saddle River, NJ: Prentice-Hall).

Berkowitz, L. (1962). *Aggression: A Social Psychological Analysis* (New York: McGraw-Hill).

Billig, M., and Cramer, D. (1990). 'Authoritarianism and demographic variables as predictors of racial attitudes in Britain', *New Community: A Journal of Research and Policy on Ethnic Relations*, 16, 199–211.

Binet, A. (1905). 'New methods for the diagnosis of the intellectual level of subnormals'. First published in *L'Année Psychologique*, 12, 191–244. This translation by Elizabeth S. Kite first appeared in 1916 in *The Development of Intelligence in Children* (Vineland, NJ: Publications of the Training School at Vineland). <http://psychclassics.yorku.ca/Binet/binet1.htm.

Bridgman, P. W. (1927). *The Logic of Modern Physics* (New York: Macmillan).

Bryman, A. (2001). *Social Research Methods* (Oxford: Oxford University Press).

Bryman, A., and Bell, E. (2003). *Business Research Methods* (Oxford: Oxford University Press).

Buss, A. R., and McDermot, J. R. (1976). 'Ratings of psychology journals compared to objective measures of journal impact', *American Psychologist*, 31, 675–8 (Comment).

Campbell, D. T. (1969). 'Prospective: Artifact and control', in R. Rosenthal and R. L. Rosnow (eds), *Artifact in Behavioural Research* (New York: Academic Press), 351–82.

Campbell, D. T., and Fiske, D. W. (1959). 'Convergent and divergent validation by the multitrait-multimethod matrix', *Psychological Bulletin*, 56, 81–105.

Campbell, D. T., and Stanley, J. C. (1963). *Experimental and Quasi-Experimental Designs for Research* (Boston: Houghton Mifflin).

Chan, L. M. (1999). *A Guide to the Library of Congress Classification*, 5th edn (Englewood, CO: Libraries Unlimited).

Chan, L. M., and Mitchell, J. S. (2003). *Dewey Decimal Classification: A Practical Guide* (Dublin, OH: OCLC).

Charmaz, K. (1995). 'Grounded theory', in J. A. Smith, R. Harre and L. V. Langenhove (eds), *Rethinking Methods in Psychology* (London: Sage), 27–49.

Charmaz, K. (2000). 'Grounded theory: Objectivist and constructivist methods', in N. K. Denzin and Y. S. E. Lincoln (eds), *Handbook of Qualitative Research*, 2nd edn (Thousand Oaks, CA: Sage), 503–35.

Cicchetti, D. V. (1991). 'The reliability of peer review for manuscript and grant submissions: A cross-disciplinary investigation', *Behavioural and Brain Sciences*, 14, 119–86.

Cohen, J. (1988). *Statistical Power Analysis for the Behavioural Sciences*, 2nd edn (Hillsdale, NJ: Lawrence Erlbaum Associates).

Cohen, J., and Cohen, P. (1983). *Applied Multiple Regression/Correlation Analysis for the Behavioral Sciences*, 2nd edn (Hillsdale, NJ: Lawrence Erlbaum Associates).

Cook, T. D., and Campbell, D. T. (1979). *Quasi-Experimentation: Design and Analysis Issues for Field Settings* (Chicago: Rand McNally).

Coolican, H. (2004). *Research Methods and Statistics in Psychology*, 4th edn (London: Hodder Arnold).

Cox, B. D., Blaxter, M., Buckle, A. L. J., Fenner, N. P., Golding, J. F., Gore, M., Huppert, F. A., Nickson, J., Roth, M., Stark, J., Wadsworth, M. E. J., and Whichelow, M. (1987). *The Health and Lifestyle Survey* (London: Health Promotion Research Trust).

Cramer, D. (1991). 'Type A behaviour pattern, extraversion, neuroticism and psychological distress', *British Journal of Medical Psychology*, 64, 73–83.

Cramer, D. (1998). *Fundamental Statistics for Social Research: Step-by-Step Calculations and Computer Techniques Using SPSS for Windows* (London: Routledge).

Cramer, D. (2003a). *Advanced Quantitative Data Analysis* (Buckingham: Open University Press).

Cramer, D. (2003b). 'A cautionary tale of two statistics: Partial correlation and standardised partial regression', *Journal of Psychology*, 137, 507–11.

Cramer, D., and Buckland, N. (1995). 'Effect of rational and irrational statements and demand characteristics on task anxiety', *Journal of Psychology*, 129, 269–75.

Cramer, D., and Fong, J. (1991). 'Effect of rational and irrational beliefs on intensity and "inappropriateness" of feelings: A test of rational-emotive theory', *Cognitive Therapy and Research*, 15, 319–29.

Cramer, D., Henderson, S., and Scott, R. (1996). 'Mental health and adequacy of social support: A four-wave panel study'. *British Journal of Social Psychology*, 35, 285–95.

Cronbach, L. J. (1951). 'Coefficient alpha and the internal structure of tests', *Psychometrika*, 16, 297–334.

Cronbach, L. J., and Meehl, P. E. (1955). 'Construct validity in psychological tests', *Psychological Bulletin*, 52, 281–302.

Danziger, K. (1985). 'The origins of the psychological experiment as a social institution', *American Psychologist*, 40 (2), 133–40.

Denscombe, M. (2002). *Ground Rules for Good Research: A 10 Point Guide for Social Researchers* (Buckingham: Open University Press).

Denzin, N. K., and Lincoln, Y. S. E. (2000). 'Introduction: The discipline and practice of qualitative research', in N. K. Denzin and Y. S. E. Lincoln (eds), *Handbook of Qualitative Research*, 2nd edn (Thousand Oaks, CA: Sage), 1–28.

Dereshiwsky. M. (1999) 'The five dimensions of participant observation', <http://jan.ucc.nau.edu/~mid/edr725/class/observation/fivedimensions/reading3-2-1.html>.

Dewey Services (n.d.). Retrieved 3 February 2004 from <http://www.oclc.org/dewey/>.

Drew, P. (1995). 'Conversation analysis', in J. A. Smith, R. Harre and L. V. Langenhove (eds), *Rethinking Methods in Psychology* (London: Sage), 64–79.

Ebbinghaus, H. (1913). *Memory: A Contribution to Experimental Psychology* (New York: Teacher's College, Columbia University; Reprint edition, New York: Dover, 1964).

Edley, N. (2001). 'Analysing masculinity: Interpretative repertoires, ideological dilemmas and subject positions', in M. Wetherell, S. Taylor and S. J. E. Yates (eds), *Discourse as Data: A Guide for Analysis* (London: Sage), 189–228.

Edwards, D., and Potter, J. (1993). 'Language and causation: A discursive action model of description and attribution', *Psychological Review*, 100 (1), 23–41.

Engstrom, L., Geijerstam, G., Holmberg, N. G., and Uhrus, K. (1963). 'A prospective study of the relationship between psycho-social factors and course of pregnancy and delivery', *Journal of Psychosomatic Research*, 8, 151–5.

Epley, N., and Huff, C. (1998). 'Suspicion, affective response, and educational benefit as a result of deception in psychology research', *Personality and Social Psychology Bulletin*, 24, 759–68.

Eysenck, H. J. (1980). *The Causes and Effects of Smoking* (London: Sage).

Farrington, D. P. (1996). 'Psychosocial influences on the development of antisocial personality', in G. Davies, S. Lloyd-Bostock, M. McMurran and C. Wilson (eds.), *Psychology, Law and Criminal Justice: International Developments in Research and Practice* (Berlin: Walter de Gruyter), 424–44.

Ferri, E. (1993) (ed.). *Life at 33: The fifth follow-up of the National Child Development Study* (London: National Children's Bureau).

Fincham, F. D., Beach, S. R. H., Harold, G. T., and Osborne, L. N. (1997). 'Marital satisfaction and depression: Different casual relationships for men and women?', *Psychological Science*, 8, 351–7.

Forsyth, J. P., Kollins, S., Palav, A., Duff, K., and Maher, S. (1999). 'Has behavior therapy drifted from its experimental roots? A survey of publication trends in mainstream behavioral journals', *Journal of Behavior Therapy and Experimental Psychiatry*, 30, 205–20.

Garfinkel, H. (1967). *Studies in Ethnomethodology* (Englewood Cliffs, NJ: Prentice-Hall).

Gibbs, A. (1997). 'Focus groups. Social research update', 19, <http://www.soc.surr.ac.uk/sru/SRU19.html>.

Glaser, B. G., and Strauss, A. L. (1967). *Discovery of Grounded Theory: Strategies for Qualitative Research* (New York: Aldine de Gruyter).

Goffman, E. (1959). *The Presentation of Self in Everyday Life* (Garden City, New York: Doubleday).

Goldthorpe, J. H. (1987). *Social Mobility and Class Structure in Modern Britain*, 2nd edn (Oxford: Clarendon Press).

Gottfredson, S. D. (1978). 'Evaluating psychological research reports: Dimensions, reliability, and correlates of quality judgments', *American Psychologist*, 33, 920–34.

Great Britain Office for National Statistics (2000). *Standard Occupational Classification 2000: Vol. 1, Structure and descriptions of unit groups and Vol. 2, The coding index* (London: Stationery Office). Also available at <http://www.statistics.gov.uk/nsbase/methods_quality/ns_sec/soc2000.asp#vol1>.

Greene, E. (1990). 'Media effects on jurors', *Law and Human Behavior*, 14 (5), 439–50.

Grice, H. P. (1975). 'Logic and conversation', in P. Cole and J. Morgan (eds), *Syntax and Semantics 3: Speech Acts* (New York: Academic Press), 41–58.

Haggbloom, S. J., Warnick, R., Warnick, J. E., Jones, V. K., Yarbrough, G. L., Russell, T. M. *et al.* (2002). The 100 most eminent psychologists of the 20th century. *Review of General Psychology*, 6, 139–52.

Hare, R. D. (1991). *The Hare Psychopathy Checklist – Revised* (Toronto: Multi-Health Systems).

Hepburn, A. (2003). *An Introduction to Critical Social Psychology* (London: Sage).

Hergenhahn, B. R. (2001). *An Introduction to the History of Psychology*, 4th edn (Belmont, CA: Wadsworth Thomson Learning).

Hoinville, G., and Jowell, R. (1978). *Survey Research Practice* (London: Heinemann Educational Books).

Horton-Salway, M. (2001). 'The construction of ME: The discursive action model', in M. Wetherell, S. Taylor and S. J. E. Yates (eds), *Discourse as Data: A Guide for Analysis* (London: Sage), 147–88.

Howell, D. C. (2002). *Statistical Methods for Psychology*, 5th edn (Belmont, CA: Duxbury Press).

Howitt, D. (1992*a*). *Concerning Psychology: Psychology Applied to Social Issues* (Milton Keynes: Open University Press).

Howitt, D. (1992*b*). *Child Abuse Errors* (London: Harvester Wheatsheaf).

Howitt, D. (1995). *Paedophiles and Sexual Offences Against Children* (Chichester: Wiley).

Howitt, D. (2002). *Forensic and Criminal Psychology* (Harlow: Prentice Hall).

Howitt, D., and Cramer, D. (2005*a*). *Introduction to Statistics in Psychology*, 3rd edn (Harlow: Prentice Hall).

Howitt, D., and Cramer, D. (2005*b*). *Introduction to SPSS in Psychology*, 3rd edn (Harlow: Prentice Hall).

Howitt, D., and Owusu-Bempah, J. (1990). 'Racism in a British journal?', *The Psychologist: Bulletin of the British Psychological Society*, 3 (9), 396–400.

Howitt, D., and Owusu-Bempah, J. (1994). *The Racism of Psychology* (London: Harvester Wheatsheaf).

Hutchby, I., and Wooffit, R. (1998) *Conversation Analysis: Principles, Practices and Applications* (Cambridge: Polity Press). <http://www.lsadc.org/fields/index.php?aaa=discourse.htm>.

Institute for Scientific Information (1994). 'The impact factor', *Current Contents*, 20 June. Retrieved 9 February 2004 from <http://www.isinet.com/essays/journalcitationreports/7.html/>.

Institute for Scientific Information (2002). 'The ISI® database: The journal selection process'. Retrieved 9 February 2004 from <http://www.isinet.com/essays/selectionofmaterialforcoverage/199701.html/>.

Jefferson, G. (1984). 'On stepwise transition from talk about a trouble to inappropriately next positioned matters', in J. M. Atkinson and J. Heritage (eds), *Structures of Social Action: Studies in Conversation Analysis* (Cambridge: Cambridge University Press), 191–222.

Jones, H. (1981). *Bad Blood: The Tuskegee Syphilis Experiment* (New York: Free Press).

Jones, M. C., Bayley, N., MacFarlane, J. W., and Honzik, M. P. (1971). *The Course of Human Development* (Waltham, MA: Xerox Publishing Company).

Keith-Spiegel, P., and Koocher, G. P. (1985). *Ethics in Psychology: Professional Standards and Cases* (Hillsdale, NJ: Lawrence Erlbaum Associates).

Kelly, G. A. (1955). *The Psychology of Personal Constructs. Volume 1: A Theory of Personality* (New York: Norton).

Keppel, G., and Wickens, T. D. (2004). *Design and Analysis: A Researcher's Handbook*, 4th edn (Upper Saddle River, NJ: Pearson Education).

Kirk, R. C. (1995). *Experimental Design*, 3rd edn (Pacific Grove, CA: Brooks/Cole).

Kitzinger, C., and H. Frith (2001). 'Just say no? The use of conversation analysis in developing a feminist perspective on sexual refusal', in M. Wetherell, S. Taylor and S. J. E. Yates (eds), *Discourse Theory and Practice: A Reader* (London, Sage), 167–85.

Korn, J. H. (1997). *Illusions of Reality: A History of Deception in Social Psychology* (New York: State University of New York Press).

Krause, N., Liang, J., and Yatomi, N. (1989). 'Satisfaction with social support and depressive symptoms: A panel analysis', *Psychology and Aging*, 4, 88–97.

Lana, R. E. (1969). 'Pretest sensitisation', in R. Rosenthal and R. L. Rosnow (eds), *Artifact in Behavioural Research* (New York: Academic Press), 119–41.

Latane, B., and Darley, J. M. (1970). *The Unresponsive Bystander: Why Doesn't He Help?* (New York: Appleton-Century-Crofts).

Lazarsfeld, P. F. (1948). 'The use of panels in social research', *Proceedings of the American Philosophical Society*, 92, 405–10.

Leahy, T. H. (2004). *A History of Psychology: Main Currents in Psychological Thought*, 6th edn (Upper Saddle, NJ: Prentice Hall).

Leyens, J. P., Camino, L., Parke, R. D., and Berkowitz, L. (1975). 'The effect of movie violence on aggression in a field setting as a function of group dominance and cohesion', *Journal of Personality and Social Psychology*, 32, 346–60.

Library of Congress Classification Outline (n.d.). Retrieved 3 February 2004 from <http://www.loc.gov/catdir/cpso/lcco/lcco.html>.

Lovering, K. M. (1995). 'The bleeding body: Adolescents talk about menstruation', in S. Wilkinson and C. Kitzinger (eds), *Feminism and Discourse: Psychological Perspectives* (London: Sage), 10–31.

Mace, K. C., and Warner, H. D. (1973). 'Ratings of psychology journals', *American Psychologist*, 28, 184–6 (Comment).

McArthur, T. (1992). *The Oxford Companion to the English Language* (Oxford: Oxford University Press).

McGuire, W. J. (1997). 'Creative hypothesis generating in psychology: Some useful heuristics', *Annual Review of Psychology*, 48, 1–30.

McHugh, P. (1968). *Defining the Situation: The Organization of Meaning* (Evanston, IL.: Bobbs-Merrill).

Mead, M. (1944). *Coming of Age in Samoa* (Harmondsworth: Pelican).

Medway, C., and Howitt, D. (2003). 'The role of animal cruelty in the prediction of dangerousness', in M. Vanderhallen, G. Vervaeke, P. Van Koppen and J. Goethals (eds), *Much Ado About Crime: Chapters in Psychology and Law* (Politeia: Brussels), 245–50.

Merton, R., and Kendall, P. (1946). 'The focused interview', *American Journal of Sociology*, 51, 541–7.

Milgram, S. (1974). *Obedience to Authority* (New York: Harper & Row).

Moser, C. A., and Kalton, G. (1971). *Survey Methods in Social Investigation*, 2nd edn (London: Gower).

Murphy, P. M., Cramer, D., and Lillie, F. J. (1984). 'The relationship between curative factors perceived by patients in their psychotherapy and treatment outcome', *British Journal of Medical Psychology*, 57, 187–92.

O'Connell, D. C., and Kowal, S. (1995). 'Basic principles of transcription', in J. A. Smith, R. Harré, and L. Van Langenhove (eds), *Rethinking Methods in Psychology* (London: Sage), 93–105.

OPCS (1991). *Standard Occupational Classification; Volume 3* (London: HMSO).

Orne, M. T. (1959). 'The nature of hypnosis: Artifact and essence', *Journal of Abnormal and Social Psychology*, 58, 277–99.

Orne, M. T. (1962). 'On the social psychology of the psychological experiment: With particular reference to demand characteristics and their implications', *American Psychologist*, 17, 776–83.

Orne, M. T. (1969). 'Demand characteristics and the concept of quasi-controls', in R. Rosenthal and R. L. Rosnow (eds), *Artifact in Behavioural Research* (New York: Academic Press), 143–79.

Orne, M. T., and Scheibe, K. E. (1964). 'The contribution of nondeprivation factors in the production of sensory deprivation effects: The psychology of the "panic button"', *Journal of Abnormal and Social Psychology*, 68, 3–12.

Owusu-Bempah, J., and Howitt, D. (1995). 'How Eurocentric psychology damages Africa', *The Psychologist: Bulletin of the British Psychological Society*, 8, 462–5.

Owusu-Bempah, J., and Howitt, D. (2000). *Psychology Beyond Western Perspectives* (Leicester: BPS Books).

Page, M., and Scheidt, R. J. (1971). 'The elusive weapons effect', *Journal of Personality and Social Psychology*, 20, 304–9.

Park, A., Curtice, J., Thomson, K., Jarvis, L., and Bromley, C. (2003) (eds). *British Social Attitudes: The 19th Report* (London: Sage).

Parker, I. (1989). *The Crisis in Modern Social Psychology* (London: Routledge).

Patton, M. Q. (1986). *How To Use Qualitative Methods in Evaluation* (London: Sage).

Pavlov, I. P. (1927). *Conditioned Reflexes: An Investigation of the Physiological Activity of the Cerebral Cortex*, trans. G. V. Anrep (London: Oxford University Press).

Pedhazur, E. J., and Schmelkin, L. P. (1991). *Measurement, Design and Analysis: An Integrated Approach* (Hillsdale, NJ: Lawrence Erlbaum Associates).

Peters, D. P., and Ceci, S. J. (1982). 'Peer-review practices of psychological journals: The fate of published articles, submitted again', *The Behavioral and Brain Sciences*, 5, 187–255.

Postal geography (n.d.). Retrieved 31 January 2004 from <http://www.statistics.gov.uk/geography/postal_geog.asp>.

Potter, J. (1997). 'Discourse analysis as a way of analysing naturally occurring talk', in D. Silverman (ed.), *Qualitative Research: Theory, Methods and Practice* (London: Sage), 144–60.

Potter, J. (1998). 'Qualitative and discourse analysis', in A. S. Bellack and M. Hersen (eds), *Comprehensive Clinical Psychology, Vol. 3* (Oxford: Pergamon), 117–44.

Potter, J. (2001). 'Wittgenstein and Austin', in M. Wetherell, S. Taylor and S. J. Yates, *Discourse Theory and Practice: A Reader* (London: Sage), 39–56.

Potter, J. A. (2004). 'Discourse analysis', in M. Hardy and A. Bryman (eds), *Handbook of Data Analysis* (London: Sage), 607–24.

Potter, J., and Wetherell, M. (1995). 'Discourse analysis', in J. A. Smith, R. Harré and L. V. Langenhove (eds), *Rethinking Methods in Psychology* (London: Sage), 80–92.

PsycINFO Database Information (n.d.). Retrieved 4 February 2004 from <http://www.apa.org/psycinfo/products/psycinfo.html>.

Reis, H. T., and Stiller, J. (1992). 'Publication trends in *JPSP*: A three-decade review', *Personality and Social Psychology Bulletin*, 18, 465–72.

Rivers, W. H. R. (1908). *The Influence of Alcohol and Other Drugs on Fatigue* (London: Arnold).

Rosenthal, R. (1963). 'On the social psychology of the psychological experiment: The experimenter's hypothesis as unintended determinant of experimental results', *American Scientist*, 51, 268–83.

Rosenthal, R. (1969). 'Interpersonal expectations: Effects of the experimenter's hypothesis', in R. Rosenthal and R. L. Rosnow (eds), *Artifact in Behavioural Research* (New York: Academic Press), 181–277.

Rosenthal, R. (1978). 'How often are our numbers wrong?', *American Psychologist*, 33, 1005–8.

Rosenthal, R. (1991). *Meta-analytic Procedures for Social Research*, rev. edn (Newbury Park, CA: Sage).

Rosenthal, R., and Rosnow, R. L. (1969). 'The volunteer subject', in R. Rosenthal and R. L. Rosnow (eds), *Artifact in Behavioural Research* (New York: Academic Press), 59–118.

Rosenthal, R., and Rubin, D. B. (1978). 'Interpersonal expectancy effects: The first 345 studies', *The Behavioral and Brain Sciences*, 3, 377–415.

Rosnow, R. L. (2002). 'The nature and role of demand characteristics in scientific enquiry', *Prevention and Treatment*, 5, <http://www.journals.apa.org/prevention/volume5/pre0050037c.htm>.

Rushton, J. P., and Roediger, H. L., III. (1978). 'An evaluation of 80 psychology journals based on the *Science Citation Index*', *American Psychologist*, 33, 520–3 (Comment).

Sacks, H. (1992). 'Lecture 1: Rules of conversational sequence', in E. Jefferson (ed.), *H. Y. Sacks Lectures on Conversation; Vol. 1*, 3rd edn (Oxford: Blackwell).

Sacks, O. (1985). *The Man Who Mistook his Wife for a Hat* (London: Picador).

Searle, J. (1969). *Speech Acts: An Essay in the Philosophy of Language* (Cambridge: Cambridge University Press).

Shadish, W. R., and Ragsdale, K. (1996). 'Random versus nonrandom assignment in controlled experiments: Do you get the same answer?', *Journal of Consulting and Clinical Psychology*, 64, 1290–305.

Shadish, W. R., Cook, T. D., and Campbell, D. T. (2002). *Experimental and Quasi-experimental Designs for Generalised Causal Inference* (New York: Houghton Mifflin).

Sheldrake, R. (1998). 'Experimenter effects in scientific research: How widely are they neglected?', *Journal of Scientific Exploration*, 12, 1–6.

Sherman, R. C., Buddie, A. M., Dragan, K. L., End, C. M., and Finney, L. J. (1999). 'Twenty years of *PSPB*: Trends in content, design, and analysis', *Personality and Social Psychology Bulletin*, 25, 177–87.

Silverman, D. (1997). 'The logics of qualitative research', in G. Miller and R. Dingwall (eds), *Context and Method in Qualitative Research* (London: Sage), 12–25.

Skinner, B. F. (1938). *The Behavior of Organisms* (New York: Appleton-Century-Crofts).

Smith, S. S., and Richardson, D. (1983). 'Amelioration of deception and harm in psychological research: The important role of debriefing', *Journal of Personality and Social Psychology*, 44, 1075–82.

Solomon, R. L. (1949). 'An extension of control group design', *Psychological Bulletin*, 46, 137–50.

Steffens, L. (1931). *Autobiography of Lincoln Steffens* (New York: Harper and Row).

Strauss, A., and Corbin, J. (1999). 'Grounded theory methodology: an overview', in A. Bryman and R. G. Burgess (eds), *Qualitative Research; Vol. 3* (Thousand Oaks, CA: Sage), 73–93.

Stubbs, M. (1983). *Discourse Analysis* (Oxford: Blackwell).

Tabachnick, B. G., and Fidell, L. S. (2001). *Using Multivariate Statistics*, 4th edn (Boston: Allyn & Bacon).

Tannen, D. (2004). 'Discourse analysis', Linguistic Society of America, <http://www.lsadc.org/fields/index.php?aaa=discourse.htm>.

Taylor, S. (2001). 'Locating and conducting discourse analytic research', in M. Wetherell, S. Taylor and S. J. E. Yates (eds), *Discourse as Data: A Guide for Analysis* (London: Sage), 5–48.

ten Have, P. (2003). 'Methodological issues in conversation analysis', <http://www.pscw.uva.nl/emca/mica.htm>.

Tomer, C. (1986). 'A statistical assessment of two measures of citation: The impact factor and the immediacy index', *Information Processing and Management*, 22, 251–8.

Trochim, W. M. K. (2002). 'Positivism and post-positivism', <http://trochim.human.cornell.edu/kb/positvsm.htm>.

UK Data Archive (n.d.). Retrieved 22 January 2004, from <http://www.data-archive.ac.uk/>.

van Dijk, T. (2001). 'Principles of critical discourse analysis', in M. Wetherell, S. Taylor and S. J. E. Yates (eds), *Discourse Theory and Practice: A Reader* (London: Sage), 300–17.

Velten, E., Jr. (1968). 'A laboratory task for induction of mood states', *Behaviour Research and Therapy*, 6, 473–82.

Watson, J. B., and Rayner, R. (1920). 'Conditioned emotional reactions', *Journal of Experimental Psychology*, 3, 1–14.

West, S. G., Newsom, J. T., and Fenaughty, A. M. (1992). 'Publication trends in *JPSP*: Stability and change in topics, methods, and theories across two decades', *Personality and Social Psychology Bulletin*, 18, 473–84.

Westermann, R., Spies, K., Stahl, G., and Hesse, F. W. (1996). 'Relative effectiveness and validity of mood induction procedures: A meta-analysis', *European Journal of Social Psychology*, 26, 557–80.

Wetherell, M. S., and Taylor, S. (2001) (eds). *Discourse as Data: A Guide for Analysis* (London: Sage).

Wilson, V. L., and Putnam, R. R. (1982). 'A meta-analysis of pretest sensitization effects in experimental design', *American Educational Research Journal*, 19, 249–58.

Woolfit, R. (2001). 'Researching psychic practitioners: Conversation analysis', in M. Wetherell, S. Taylor and S. J. E. Yates (eds), *Discourse as Data: A Guide for Analysis* (London: Sage), 49–92.

Index